Graeme Mercer Adam

The History and Troubles of Canadian North-West

From the Early Days of the Fur-Trade to the Era of the Railway and the Settler

Graeme Mercer Adam

The History and Troubles of Canadian North-West
From the Early Days of the Fur-Trade to the Era of the Railway and the Settler

ISBN/EAN: 9783744726665

Printed in Europe, USA, Canada, Australia, Japan

Cover: Foto ©ninafisch / pixelio.de

More available books at **www.hansebooks.com**

MAJOR-GENERAL F. D. MIDDLETON, C.B.,
Commander of the Canadian Militia.

FROM SAVAGERY TO CIVILIZATION.

THE
CANADIAN NORTH-WEST:

ITS

HISTORY AND ITS TROUBLES,

FROM THE EARLY DAYS OF THE FUR-TRADE TO THE ERA
OF THE RAILWAY AND THE SETTLER;

WITH

INCIDENTS OF TRAVEL IN THE REGION,

AND

The Narrative of Three Insurrections

BY
G. MERCER ADAM,
Ex-Capt. Queen's Own Rifles,
Late Editor of "The Canadian Monthly," etc., etc.

———▶•●•◀———

Toronto:
ROSE PUBLISHING COMPANY.

WHITBY:
J. S. ROBERTSON & BROS.
1885.

Entered according to the Act of the Parliament of Canada, in the year one-thousand eight hundred and eighty-five, by HUNTER, ROSE & Co., in the office of the Minister of Agriculture.

In Reverent Memory

OF

THEIR CANADIAN MOTHER,

IN WHOM I FOUND

The Noblest Qualities of a True Woman,

——" *No true life is long.*"——

I DEDICATE THIS VOLUME,

WITH GREAT AFFECTION, TO

MY SONS AND DAUGHTERS.

"No fabled land of joy and song is this
That lieth in the glow of eventide;
Not sung by bards of old in minstrel strain,
Yet he who reads its history shall learn
Of doughty deeds well worth all knightly fame.
It is a land of rivers flowing free,
Lake-mirrored mountains, rising proud and stern,—
A land of spreading prairies ocean wide,
Where harsh sounds slumber in the hush of gloom,
And peace hath brooded with outstretched wings.

* * * * * *

And here a mighty people shall arise,
A peopled nurtured in full liberty;
Yet, not forgetful of the mother land,
Who scans with kindly eye her child's career,
Wafting a blessing o'er the mighty sea.

* * * * *

Such be thy future; O, thou land of hope,
Where, in the fear of God and love of home,
Thy people shall increase—O, may thy soil
Bear many a thinker, many a man of might,
Many a statesman fitted to control,
Many a hero, fitted to command.
Such may thy future be—not great alone,
In never-sated commerce,—rather great
In all that welds a people heart to heart;
Among thy sons may many a leader spring,
By whom the ship of State well piloted,
Thy haven of wide Empire thou may'st reach,
An empire stretching from the western wave
To where the rosy dawn enflames the seas."

—J. H. Bowes, in *The 'Varsity.*

PREFACE.

IN adding to the already numerous works on the Canadian North-West, I have sought to make a contribution of more than passing interest. With this end in view, I have not confined the narrative to recent events; but have told the story from the beginning. It may fairly be claimed that there is some advantage in this. It will enable the reader to follow the successive steps in the development of the country, and to trace in the past history some of the remote causes of the present rebellion. These revolts, in some degree at least, are the legacy of the days of monopoly and privilege. Neither the Hudson Bay Company nor the North-West Fur Company, of Montreal was a colonising institution. Both were opposed to the settler, and both desired to keep the territory wild and uncultivated. Only thus could it be useful to a great fur-trading corporation. Though the rule of these trading corporations has passed away, jealousy of the intruding settler remains, and the aggressive spirit of monopoly which marked the dominion of the companies still manifests itself. The Indian shares the one; the half-breed inherits the other. Both, it may be said, must be exorcised ere the North-West can become a desirable possession of the Dominion, and a safe home for the settler.

In dealing with the later revolt, I have in the main confined myself to the narrative of the spirited and successful effort of he volunteers and other Canadian troops to suppress it.

However inadequately treated, the story has been told, I would fain believe, without partiality or exaggeration. Of the insurgents I have striven to write without prejudice. The immediate causes of the outbreak, and the question of responsibility for its occurrence, I have but lightly touched on, as the time has not yet come to speak or to write with full knowledge of the subject. The facts upon which dispassionateness could rely were, in truth, not before me. In whatever criticism of the Administration I have ventured upon, I hope I have not forgotten what is due by a subject to the Government of the country of which I am a citizen and have been a soldier. In what afterwards has to be said, when the nation's inquest on the insurrection has developed the facts, I would ask that the voice of patriotism be heard, rather than that of party objurgation.

In preparing the volume, I have been under repeated obligations, which I desire here to acknowledge, to Messrs. Hunter, Rose & Co., Publishers, and to my friend, Mr. Wm. Williamson, Bookseller, Toronto. I am also indebted to Mr. Wm. Houston, M.A., and to Mr. John Watson, his assistant; to Mr. W. H. Van der Smissen, M.A.; and to Mr. James Bain, jr.; the Librarians, respectively, of the Library of the Legislative Assembly of Ontario, the Library of Toronto University, and the Toronto Public Library. To Mr. Bain I am chiefly beholden for facilities in getting access to works on the early history of Canada and the North-West, with which the Toronto Public Library has been enriched by the generosity of Mr. John Hallam. Mr. Bain's intimate acquaintance with Canadian literature enhances the benefit to be derived from consultation in this valuable department of the City Library.

To Mr. R. Lovell Gibson, of Montreal, to Mr. Fulford Arnoldi, and to my son, Mr. Græme Gibson Adam, of Toronto, my thanks are also due for ready aid in placing material at my hand in the preparation of the book.

THE AUTHOR.

Toronto, July 15th, 1885.

CONTENTS.

	PAGE
DEDICATION	iii
PREFACE	v
CHAPTER I.—The Hudson Bay Company	9
II.—The North-West Fur Co., of Montreal	25
III.—Early Discoverers of the North-West:	
(a) The English Trader, Alexander Henry	38
IV.— (b) Joseph La France, and Samuel Hearne	59
V.— (c) Sir Alexander Mackenzie	79
VI.—The Selkirk Settlement and its Fate	96
VII.—The Massacre at Red River, and after	119
VIII.—The Nor'-Westers on the Pacific Coast, and the Amalgamation of the Rival Fur Companies	131
IX.—Indian Tribes of the Older Provinces and the North-West	150
X.—Fifty Years' Interval—1820 to 1870	165
XI.—Transfer of the Hudson Bay Territories to the Dominion	188
XII.—The Riel Red River Rebellion	197
XIII.—The Province of Manitoba and the Era of Settlement	209
XIV.—Riel's Second Insurrection: Causes of the Outbreak	223
XV.—The First Overt Act: Duck Lake, and the Mounted Police	236
XVI.—Calling out the Volunteers	249
XVII.—Over "The Gaps" to Qu'Appelle	264

		PAGE
XVIII.—Middleton's March to Clarke's Crossing	-	273
XIX.—Otter's Flying Column—The Dash to Battleford	-	287
XX.—The Frog Lake Massacre	-	301
XXI.—Otter Attacks Poundmaker: The Fight at Cut Knife Hill	-	317
XXII.—The Campaign on the South Saskatchewan: With Middleton at Fish Creek	-	328
XXIII.—The Crisis at Hand	-	336
XXIV.—The Lines before Batoche	-	343
XXV.—Charging the Rifle Pits—Rout of the Rebels	-	353
XXVI.—After Batoche—The "Big Bear" Hunt	-	364
XXVII.—The Nation's Heroes—Counting the Cost	-	372
XXVIII.—Remedial Measures—The Country's Future	-	381

APPENDIX.

Supplemental List of Staff and Company Officers of corps serving in the North-West - - - - - - 389

THE NORTH-WEST:

ITS HISTORY AND ITS TROUBLES.

CHAPTER I.

THE HUDSON BAY COMPANY.

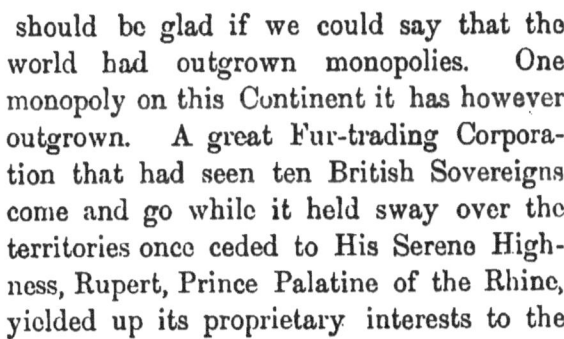

E should be glad if we could say that the world had outgrown monopolies. One monopoly on this Continent it has however outgrown. A great Fur-trading Corporation that had seen ten British Sovereigns come and go while it held sway over the territories once ceded to His Serene Highness, Rupert, Prince Palatine of the Rhine, yielded up its proprietary interests to the government of a young and lusty nation. In 1869, the rule over the "Great Lone Land" of the Honourable Company of Merchant Adventurers trading to Hudson Bay ceased, and the Dominion of Canada took over almost its entire interests. With the relinquishment of its rights and privileges, though it stipulated for the retention of some of its trading posts and a certain portion of land, the Company parted with not a few of the factors, trappers, *voyageurs*, and labourers, that had grown grey in its service. It parted with its millions of acres of territory, some of its isolated posts, and their treasuries of foxskin, marten, mink, musk-rat, and otter. It parted with the traditions and associations of centuries of traffic, and all the pretensions that adhere to absolute power in the hands of an old and wealthy corporation and a long-established monopoly. So scattered and distant were the possessions of the Company that many moons rose and waned ere the news reached the secluded inmates of its lonely stockaded posts that the great trading Company had transferred its interests to the British Government, and from it to the Canadian people. The price of the transfer was a million and a half of dollars.

The cession of the interests of the Hudson Bay Company, in the vast tract of country known as Rupert's Land, set at rest the long vexed question of the right of that corporation to the lordship of the region known as the Hudson Bay Territories. It set at rest, also, not only the validity of the Company's title to the territory, but the equally delicate question of the area over which the Company was supposed to rule. Both questions often disturbed the councils of the Company, and at successive periods were the subjects of contemplated parliamentary enquiry. Not only was it held that the Company, in the course of time, had extended its territorial claims much further than the charter, or any sound construction of it, would warrant, but the charter itself was repeatedly called in question. In the year 1670, when the Company was founded, it seems clear that the English Sovereign, Charles II, had no legal right to the country, for it was then and for long after the possession of France. By the treaty of St. Germain-en-Laye (1632) the English had resigned to the French Crown all interest in *Nouvelle France*. The Treaty of Ryswick, (1697) moreover, confirmed French right to the country. Hence Charles's gift to his cousin, Prince Rupert, and to those associated with him in the organisation of the Hudson Bay Company, was gratuitous if not illegal. The subsequent re-transfer of the country to Britain, by the Treaty of Utrecht (1713), may be said, however, to have given the Company a right to its possessions, a right which was practically confirmed by the Conquest, and by the Treaty of Paris, in 1763. But conceding this, there arose the other question, namely, to what extent of territory, by the terms of the original charter, was the Company entitled. The text of the charter conveys only those lands whose waters drain into Hudson Bay, or, more specifically, " all the lands and territories upon the countries, coasts, and confines of the seas, etc., that lie within Hudson Straits." This very materially limited the area of the Company's sway in the North-West, and nullified its claim over the country which drains into the St. Lawrence, into the Atlantic, the Pacific, and the Arctic Oceans. The Company, of course, never acknowledged this view of the matter; but had its title been tested in a court of law, its territorial assumptions would have been greatly abridged.

But, as we have said, all these disturbing questions, as to the title and the area of the possessions of the Hudson Bay Company, were settled by the sale and transfer of the territory to the Canadian Dominion. That territory, which included at first only the land bordering on Hudson Bay and Strait, by process, partly of territorial aggrandisement and partly of later trading-license, came to include : (1.) Labrador; (2.) Prince Rupert Land; (3.) The districts of the Red River, Swan River, and the Saskatchewan; (4.) The North-West Territories; and (5.) Mackenzie river, British Columbia and Vancouver. By the expiry of a special charter, the two latter districts, in 1858, reverted to the Crown, and, in 1863, were erected into a British colony. All the other districts, with the reservation of the trading-posts, and one-twentieth of the land, passed in 1869, as we have stated, to the Imperial Government, and, for the compensation named, from it to the Dominion of Canada.

To what national and commercial purposes this great acquisition has been put by the Dominion Government will be seen from later chapters in the present work. Meantime let us review briefly the more prominent incidents in the history of this great trading corporation, which so long held sway over the country. In 1610, the Bay that bears his name, or, as the French called it, "the great North Sea," was discovered by the ill-fated Henry Hudson, who found himself within its waters in quest of that will-o'-the-wisp of the period, a north-west passage to India. The winter of 1610 Hudson spent at the foot of the inland sea now known as James' Bay. The rigours of the season, and want of food, led his men to mutiny, and to leave him with his son and a small following to the tender mercies of the region, when they betook themselves with a lie in their mouth to England. In 1612 an expedition was fitted out for the relief of Hudson, under the command of Captain, afterwards Sir Thomas, Button; but no trace of the navigator or of his party was ever found.

The next venture westward was that of Champlain, who, in 1615, made his untoward voyage from the St. Lawrence, by way of the Ottawa and Lake Nipissing, to *la Mer Douce*, the inland sea of the Hurons, and the seat of the Jesuit missions on the Matchedash peninsula. Following upon Champlain's expedition came the organisation of the One Hundred Associates, which had been given its charter, in 1627, by Cardinal Richelieu, prime minister to Louis XIII. The operations of this Company were interrupted by the first English conquest of Canada; hence little was done in prosecuting trade in the West, if we except M. De Caen's enterprises, until the period of M. Montmagny's governorship. Under this Governor, another trading company was established, known as *La Compagnie de Montréal*, and M. Maisonneuve, a gallant and much-tried Frenchman, was appointed to the charge of its affairs. The calamitous condition of the Colony, owing to wars with the Iroquois, seriously hampered this Company's work;

and we have consequently little record of its operations during the period of its existence, viz., from 1640 to 1663. Three years afterwards, however, two French Huguenots made their way round Lake Superior, ascended the Kaministiquia river, and following the water-way, subsequently known as the Dawson route, reached Winnipeg river and lake, and probed a route for themselves down the Nelson to the sea discovered by Henry Hudson. In process of time they returned to Quebec, and proceeded to France, where they endeavoured to interest capitalists in opening up the fur-bearing regions of Hudson Bay to commerce. But French enterprise was then looking to the East rather than to the West, to the extension of trade in the rich archipelago of the East Indies, rather than to that in the frozen seas of the North. Silks and spices, and the diamonds of the Orient, were more attractive just then to the Gallic sense than the skins of wild beasts. The two French explorers we have referred to were thus foiled in the attempt to enlist French capital in their enterprise. One of the two, M. de Grosseliez, was, however, not to be baulked. He proceeded to England, and there met with the retired student-soldier, Prince Rupert, whose head was filled with many curious schemes of enterprise; and his imagination was readily fired with the story M. de Grosseliez had to tell him.

The result after a time was the formation of the English Hudson Bay Company, and the grant of Charles II. over the region in which the Company intended to operate. In the interval, Hudson Bay had been explored by mariners, who, in 1631, had set out from London and from Bristol, with the still delusive hope of reaching the Pacific and the far-distant Cathay. The London venture was commanded by Captain Fox, and the Bristol expedition by Captain James, the latter giving his name to the Southern inlet of Hudson Bay. Both expeditions were barren of result, save to impress upon the minds of their commanders the inhospitable character of the region and the terrors of a winter on its coasts.*

A New England captain connected with the Newfoundland trade was the first to sail to Hudson Bay to further the interests of the new-formed Company. Presently, a governor was dispatched to establish and take charge of a fort on the Rupert river, and one on the Nelson. By the year 1686 the Hudson Bay Company had organised five trading-posts round the shores of James and Hudson Bay. These were known as the Albany, the Moose, the Rupert, the Nelson, and the Severn factories. The right to establish these posts was actively combated by the French, who sent contingents from Quebec, by the Ottawa and by Lake Superior, to harass the English in their possession of them. For a number of years a keen conflict was maintained between the two races, and the forts successively changed hands as fortune happened to favour the one or the other. Possession was further varied by the Treaties of Ryswick and Utrecht, previously referred to.

Meanwhile the French were active in the lower waters of the continent; for in 1672 La Salle had discovered the Mississippi, Joliet and Marquette had traced the outline of the Georgian Bay and Lake Superior, and Father Hennepin had seen and made a chart of the Falls of Niagara. Later on M. du Luth and M. de la Verandrye had penetrated into all the bays of Lake Superior, and the latter, in 1732, had constructed a fort on the Lake of the Woods. At the period of the Conquest the French had done far more to discover and open up what is now our North-West than the English. Up to 1763, they had gone even as far west as the Assiniboine and the Saskatchewan. They had established Fort Maurepas on the Winnipeg, Fort Dauphin on Lake Manitoba, Fort Bourbon

---

* For an account of the earlier voyages to Hudson Bay—those of Wm. Baffin, Sir Martin Frobisher, and Master John Davis, with the voyages of Sebastian Cabot to Newfoundland — see Rundall's *Narrative of Voyages towards the North-West, 1496-1631*—one of the Hakluyt Society Publications: London, 1849.

on Cedar Lake, and Fort à la Corne below the forks of the Saskatchewan. The Hudson Bay Company, on the contrary, had done little, as yet, to invade the continent. The trade of the Company hardly extended beyond the shores of Hudson Bay, or, at most, a short distance down the Albany river and the Churchill. Inactive in their work, for a time they found their charter ineffectual to keep out interlopers from sharing the profits of the growing fur trade. Petitioning Parliament they, now and again, got a confirmation of their title, and increased powers of trade; though one of the objects for which the Company had originally secured its charter, the prosecution of discovery in the Arctic regions, had been little promoted. Hence, enemies in Parliament repeatedly tried to limit the Company's privileges and to annul its charter. Instigated by these enemies, rival traders fitted out expeditions to Hudson Bay to embarrass the Company and seize some portion of its trade. The fate of these expeditions was, however, adverse to rivalry; for no better sport was found for the employés of the privileged Company than to board the vessels, capture their crews, and wreck the crafts on the shores of the Bay.

But not thus could the Hudson Bay Company choke off competition from the interior. The French in the South were materially interfering with its trade, and the Company found that to retain it its employés had to organise corps of traders and *voyageurs*, who would ascend the rivers and establish posts in the valleys of the Red River and Saskatchewan and the region of the great lakes. This was a matter that entailed no little difficulty and risk. To the "Hudson Bays" the interior was an unknown wilderness; and as yet they had not learned the craft of the Indian woodsman or the skill of the French *coureur de bois*. But they had more to contend with than the tyranny of Nature and the perils of the way. The colony of New France by this time had grown to considerable proportions, and the French trader was to be met with all over the country. M. de Vaudreuil gives the population of *Nouvelle*

France, in 1760, as 70,000, exclusive of *voyageurs* and those engaged in trade with the Indians. The French, moreover, held the two great water-ways to the West, the St. Lawrence and the Mississippi. From these inlets their countrymen had spread far to the North-West; and in their traffic with the Indians of the Red River and Saskatchewan districts they had cut off much trade that previously had found its way to the Hudson Bay posts on the Albany, the Nelson, the Churchill, and the Severn. Presently war with the English again broke out, and from across the Atlantic came the invading forces of Britain and contingents from her colonies on the coast. To some extent this withdrew the French traders to their posts on the meadows of the Mississippi, and to those on the Ohio and the Alleghany. The time was therefore favourable to the Hudson Bay Company employés in again diverting the fur trade to the old posts by the Northern sea. More effectually to secure this trade, the Company sent its servants to establish posts in the South, and by the year 1774 Cumberland House was founded on the Saskatchewan, and at a somewhat later day an extensive circle of forts, tributary to that at York Factory, was established and equipped.

Of the character and trade of these forts we get an intelligent idea from a graphic sketch of the Hudson Bay Company, in a volume of an English periodical, published in the year 1870.[*] The writer is an old employé of the Company.

"A typical fort," he says, "of the Hudson Bay Company at best was not a very lively sort of affair. Though sometimes built on a commanding situation at the head of some beautiful river, and backed by wave after wave of dark pine forest, it was not unpicturesque in appearance. Fancy a parallelogram of greater or less extent, enclosed by a picket twenty-five or thirty feet in height, composed of upright trunks of trees, placed in a trench, and fastened along the top by a rail, and you have the enclosure. At each corner was a strong bastion,

---

[*] "The Story of a Dead Monopoly." *Cornhill Magazine*, August, 1870.

built of squared logs, and pierced for guns which could sweep every side of the fort. Inside this picket was a gallery running right round the enclosure, just high enough for a man's head to be level with the top of the fence. At intervals, all along the side of the picket, were loop-holes for musketry, and over the gateway was another bastion, from which shot could be poured on any party attempting to carry the gate. Altogether, though incapable of withstanding a ten-pounder for a couple of hours, it was strong enough to resist almost any attack the Indians could bring against it. Inside this enclosure were the store-houses, the residences of the employés, wells, and sometimes a good garden. All night long, a *voyageur* would, watch by watch, pace round this gallery, crying out at intervals, with a quid of tobacco in his cheek, the hours and the state of the weather. This was a precaution in case of fire, and the hour-calling was to prevent him falling asleep for any length of time. Some of the less important and more distant outposts were only rough little log-cabins among the snow, without picket or other enclosure, where a 'postmaster' resided to superintend the affairs of the Company.

"The mode of trading was peculiar. It was an entire system of barter, a 'made' or 'typical' beaver-skin being the standard of trade. It was, in fact, the currency of the country. Thus an Indian arriving at one of the Company's establishments with a bundle of furs which he intends to sell, proceeds, in the first instance, to the trading-room: there the trader separates the furs into lots, and, after adding up the amount delivers to the Indian a number of little pieces of wood, indicating the number of 'made beavers' to which his 'hunt' amounts. He is next taken to the store-room, where he finds himself surrounded by bales of blankets, slop-coats, guns, scalping-knives, tomahawks (all made in Birmingham), powder-horns, flints, axes, etc. Each article has a recognised value in 'made-beavers;' a slop-coat, for example, may be worth five 'made-beavers,' for which the Indian delivers up twelve of his pieces of wood; for a gun he gives twenty; for a knife two; and so on, until his stock of wooden cash is expended. * * * After finishing he is presented with some trifle in addition to the payment of his furs, and makes room for someone else."

Of these trading establishments of the Hudson Bay Company, the writer adds: "There were in 1860 over 150, in charge of twenty-five chief factors and twenty-eight chief traders, with 150 clerks and 1200 other servants." "The trading districts of the Company," he states, " were thirty-eight in number, divided into five departments, and extending over a country nearly as big as Europe, though thinly peopled by some 100,000 natives, Esquimaux, Indians, and half-breeds."

We make no excuse for taking up space with this extended quotation, for we deem a description of a Hudson Bay Company post, and an account of the mode of barter with the Indian, to be as novel and interesting to the untravelled Canadian as they must be to the average Englishman. The picturesque features of life in the North-West in the palmy days of the Hudson Bay Company, or of the North-West Fur Company, of Montreal, are many and full of interest,—not only to the historian, but to the narrator of adventure and the descriptive writer. How fascinating and prolific a theme the subject has been to such story-tellers as Cooper, Ballantyne, Mayne-Reid, and others, the voracious youthful reader of their books must well know. Life in the North-West in the olden time, of course, had its drawbacks, in isolation from one's kith and kin; in the utter desolation and dreariness of its long and severe winters; in the fatigues and hardships of the voyages from post to post, or those entailed in getting in and out of the territory; and in the risks run, from both white men and Indians, at a time of war between the two races that long and bitterly strove for possession of the country. On the other hand, there were many countervailing pleasures and advantages, known only to those who have realised the charm of living in Nature's solitudes, away from the worries and conventionalities of civilisation, amidst surroundings that contributed to the building up of a healthy physical frame, and, in the case of a successful factor or trader, that enabled him in time to retire with a more than average share of this world's goods. The writer from whom we have already quoted may be trusted to say what present pleasure and store of future memories were to be extracted from life in the North-West, and from employment in the Hudson Bay Company's service when that corporation was in its prime. Here is an extract from the article we have already referred to:

"We, who knew the Company in its palmy days, who drank its good wine and ate of its salt; who hobnobbed in its picketed forts with the sturdy factors, at great oaken tables laden with beaver-tails, buffalo-tongues, and huge roasts of moose, of elk, and of caribou; dishes of juicy antelope and luscious salmon from the rivers of its empire of territory; ptarmigan from Hudson Bay; oulachan, most delicious of fish, from Vancouver Island; and snowy hares from the Eskimo along the shores of the Arctic sea: We, who shared its stirring enterprises, and floated down far western rivers in its birch bark canoes, who have been honoured by seeing our names carved on tamarack 'lob-sticks' on the Albany river, and on cedar ones on the Columbia, in return for *régales* of tea, tobacco, and rum largessed unto its *voyageurs*: We, who were in a word, *of it*, have precious memories in relation to the great corporation, and may be excused for lingering fondly over its history, even at a time when the world is most disposed to hold its achievements cheaply, and to dwell severely upon its misdoings and shortcomings."

We have no wish to become one of those to whom the writer alludes in this passage, who refuse the meed of admiration for the Company's achievments, or who desire to arraign its administration in respect of its many "misdoings and shortcomings." While the Company pursued its operations, its government was paternal, and its sway, in the main, just. But it was only and wholly a trading corporation: its motive was to make money and to pay large dividends. It had no other *raison d'être*. Unlike the East India Company, its administration was not utterly unscrupulous or wholly devoid of conscience. If it was arrogant in its claims to territory, it did not disturb the natives in their rights, or dispossess them of their inheritance. Against rival trading companies it waged a long and bitter war; but its rival was in the territory with no higher motives than those that actuated the Company they desire to oust. It was the interest of neither Company to promote colonisation, though the Montreal institution, to make a point against the English traders, made a show of encouraging settlement. The influence of both upon the Indian must be conceded to be bad; though their common half-breed descendants may be said to be more useful in the country than the aboriginal inhabitant, and more likely to cultivate and civilise it. But the latter has his rights in the country, as its first possessor; and so long as the tribes exist these rights should be respected and their interests conserved. Not only should they be respected, they should be freely recognised and generously dealt with. The same may be said for their descendants, the Métis.

The exclusive privileges of the Hudson Bay Company, being opposed to the best interests of Canada, and antagonistic to the progress as well as to the spirit of the age, could not, of course, be suffered to run on *in perpetua*. Its shareholders saw this in 1838, when the last renewal of its charter was granted. They saw this more clearly in 1859, when its charter had run out. At both of these periods there was much agitation over what was termed the usurpation of the Company. While its operations were confined to the shores of Hudson Bay, there were few to call in question its charter, or quarrel with its license to trade. But when its employés ascended the rivers to the plains of the South, they came into collision with the French joint-stock Company, whose traders had long roamed over the valleys of the Assiniboine and the Saskatchewan, and excited prejudice by the claim of privilege and the assumption of power. For many years hostility to the Hudson Bay Company was actively fostered in Canada. Not only was it natural that the Colony should favour its own Company; it was peculiarly its interest to do so. The trade of the North-West Company specially enriched it. It did more: it kept open a home route to the West, and made Montreal the centre of a large and lucrative trade. After the embroilment of this Company with the Selkirk colony on the Red River, it coalesced with the older English Company, and much of the trade returned to its former outlet on Hudson Bay. This amalgamation did not a little to revive Canadian antipathy to the parent institution. The aggressions in Oregon, and the later extension of its trade to the Pacific, increased public distrust of the Company and fanned the flame of hostility. The Company, moreover, in asserting its power to enact tariffs, to levy taxes, and collect customs dues, made itself more obnoxious, and intensified public feeling against it, when it approached the Imperial authorities for a renewal of its charter.

Its policy towards settlers added to the counts of the indictment which confronted its paid advocates in parliament. Complaints were frequently made that immigrants, after fulfilling the hard conditions imposed upon the settler, failed to get from the Company's officers the title-deeds to their lands. In this respect, it is to be feared, history has repeated itself. Settlers also complained that an embargo was placed upon any little trade with the Indians, which they, on occasion, might effect. Their houses were entered in search of furs, which, when discovered, were confiscated; and the settlers' possessions not infrequently were destroyed and themselves taken captive. The Company's rule in the West was often arbitrary and oppressive. Little was done to ameliorate the condition of the settler's life, but much often to annoy and impoverish him. Water communication was nowhere facilitated, nor were roads opened up. The character and resources of the region were belied, and everything was done to dissuade or retard immigration. It may be doubted whether the country has ever fully recovered from the effects of the circulation of these falsehoods.

Such a policy as we have referred to was sure to react upon the Company. In 1857, the Imperial Parliament empowered a Committee to take evidence in regard to the administration of the Hudson Bay Company, and to consider the state of the British Possessions in North America under its rule. The report of this Committee exhausts the arguments for and against the Company : the report itself is a model of statesmanlike excellence. It is one of the most valuable State papers in connection with Canadian affairs it has been our privilege to inspect. The eminence and high character of the Committee, its adequate powers, the fulness of the evidence it elicited, and the dispassionateness and impartiality with which it discharged its functions, give a value to the Report unusual among political documents. The finding of the Committee was adverse to the continuance of Hudson Bay Company rule in such portions of the country as were fit for settlement, with which Canada was willing to open and maintain communication, and for which she would provide the means of local administration. In this finding, the Committee not only paid regard to the reasonable desires of the settlers themselves, but had in view the extension of the territory of an important and growing colony, and the interest and policy of the British Crown. The opinion was also expressed, that it would be proper to terminate the Company's connection with Vancouver's Island, as the best means of favouring the development of the great natural resources of that and other portions of the adjacent country which might afterwards become part of a British colony on the Pacific coast. In respect of the remainder of the Hudson Bay Territory, "in which, for the present at least, there can be no prospect of settlement for the purposes of colonisation," the Committee thought it desirable that the Company should continue to enjoy the privilege of exclusive trade, and to throw over it and the Indians inhabiting it whatever protection it could afford.*

---

*It is due here to say that during the sittings of this important Committee of the British Parliament the interests of Canada were most zealously watched by the late Hon. Chief Justice Draper, to whose ability and high sense of honour, the Committee made suitable acknowledgment, as well as expressed its indebtedness

The action taken by Parliament on this weighty Report, and the subsequent negotiations by the Crown for the cession of the Hudson Bay Territories, are matters of history. The immediate result of the transfer was the unhappy outbreak in 1869; though the following year saw the retreat of disloyalty and the advance of law and order. A vast continent came into the possession of the Canadian people;—boundless stretches of rich prairie, verdant slopes and navigable rivers, with, it must not be concealed, not a little of rock and reeking swamp, and, in the inhospitable north, leagues of snow and desolation. What the country has become in the fifteen years that have elapsed since it passed from the sway of the Hudson Bay Company is no slight tribute to the sagacity and foresight of those who were instrumental in negotiating its transfer to the Canadian people. As a preserve for game it has lost its value; and in this respect the native inhabitant is a keen sufferer, while the fur trader has been despoiled of his trade. But in cattle-raising and agriculture, the hunter, as well as the settler, has a more assured means of livelihood than any to be found in the fruits of the chase.

There are problems yet to be worked out in the settlement of the country, in turning the plains from a breeding-ground of buffalo to the purposes of the agriculturist and the civilised settler. But, for their solution, sagacity and prudence should be all that is necessary, coupled with patriotism and the resolution to do right, and to see that right alone is done. Whatever difficulties beset the immediate future, it is hoped that these will neither be prolonged nor insurmountable. The insurgents of the North-West must be cured of their disposition to resort to insurgency. No men, race, or class of men, whatever be their grievance, must be suffered to throw over constitutional means of seeking redress; nor should the ear of justice

---

for valuable information placed by Mr. Draper at its disposal while acting at the enquiry as the representative of the Canadian Government.

be inaccessible, or the hand of administration slow, in the application of a remedy. The resort to arms must be treated with no sentimental, still less with partisan or racial, leniency. Insurrection should meet with speedy suppression, and seditious speech sharply dealt with. There must be unfailing protection to life and property, abiding peace, and absolute security. Only on these conditions can the country be favourably settled, and a material and a moral advance made on the rule of the Hudson Bay Company.

CHAPTER II.

THE NORTH-WEST FUR COMPANY.

THE North-West Fur Company, of Montreal, was for the space of nearly forty years an active and formidable rival of the Hudson Bay Company. It was entirely a Canadian venture, a private joint-stock company, composed of French, Scottish, and, to some extent, half-breed traders, without charter, or, so far as we can make out, license from the Government. Its object was to pursue the peltry trade, and to traffic and barter with the Indians. Next to the Hudson Bay Company, it was the most powerful trading organisation that ever entered the field of commerce in the North-West. Its history is marked by chronic feuds with the employés of its great English rival, and by a sanguinary conflict with Lord Selkirk's settlement on the Red River. In its encounter with the latter, twenty-two lives were lost, including the Hudson Bay Governor. Towards the colony of the Scottish nobleman it pursued a relentless and cruel policy. In its hostility it was actuated by the same spirit of opposition as that which actuated the English Company in resisting the entrance of a rival in its own field. Neither Company loved the other; and when the colony was founded it was with glee the Hudson Bay Company officials saw the jealousy with which it was regarded by the rival institution. This jealousy it became the purpose of the Hudson Bay Company to inflame. By every art it embittered the feeling between the Nor'-Westers and the colony; and, later on, it readily lent its aid as an ally in the strife. Hard indeed was the lot of the Selkirk settlement under conditions so adverse. But it is not our purpose here to narrate the history of its career or to record its fate. This will be told in another chapter.

The feud with the Scotch immigrants of the Selkirk colony was only an incident, though a prominent one, in the history of the conflict between the two trading organisations locally known as the "Nor'-Westers" and the "Hudson Bays." The intrusion of the former into what was deemed the exclusive possessions of the latter, was the occasion of a long and bitter strife. Organised in 1783, the North-West Company was not long in building up a successful trade, for its operations were conducted with skill, vigour, and enterprise. From the period of the Conquest to that of the establishment of the Canadian Company, many private traders had penetrated into the North-West. The head of Lake Superior was their common rendezvous. From there the usual route to the west was by Rainy River, the Lake of the Woods, and the Winnipeg. Reaching the Red River they gradually extended their operations as far west as the Saskatchewan, and, ere long, to the forks of the Athabasca. There they intercepted the trade which was wont to seek the Hudson Bay posts on the Churchill. This rivalry at last woke the English Company from its lethargy, and it determined to send traders inland to recover its monopoly. By this time, however, the Montreal Company was not only in the field; it was strongly entrenched. Already it had possession of the trade of the Red River, and had established a fort at the mouth of the Souris.

But the Canadian Company was not only active; it was shrewd. The principle on which it was organised was a sort of co-operative one, which gave to its servants a share in the profits of the business. Proportionately, all were partners in the concern; hence, all had a personal interest in its success. The effect of this was to strengthen the Company, and to make it a formidable rival in the field. Every year saw its enterprising traders extend their operations further to the west. This could not go on undisturbed. The Hudson Bay Company, now fully alarmed at the encroachments of its rival, bestirred itself to oppose it. Wherever the Nor'-Westers constructed a fort there the Hudson Bays established a rival one. Brought thus into close proximity, each bidding against the other for trade, it was impossible that they could live in peace. Each, moreover, claimed a right to the territory, the one by virtue of its charter, the other by right of discovery and first occupancy. It will be seen there was no lack of matter to wrangle over.

Now began a many-years' conflict. The Hudson Bay Company was a newcomer in the territory; the French had been actively in possession for over a century. As early as 1627, forty years before the Hudson Bays had obtained their charter, a body of French traders, known as the "One Hundred Associates," was trafficing on the plains of the North-West. King Charles's deed to the Hudson Bay Company seems, indeed, to have been issued with a knowledge of this circumstance, for it cedes only those lands "*not* possessed by the subjects of any other Christian King or State." The French historian, Charlevoix, who visited Canada in 1720, and was well informed on the subject of the trade of the rival nations in Hudson Bay and the North-West, speaks scornfully of the pretensions of the English in these regions. A French Company operating in the territory, and long in possession of it, was sure to be aware of these facts, and naturally influenced by them. But the Nor'-Westers had another and a demonstrative ally in their employés, the Métis, or *Bois-brûlés*, who, of course, took the French view of the case. These "Half-breeds," who to-day form a considerable and an unsettled portion of the population of the North-West, were the progeny of the early French *voyageur* who had mated with the Indian. Later on, the Scotch trader and Company's employé was not loath to follow the example set him by his French fellow-countryman. He was of one mind with him, who, in the Laureate's poem, sighs for a barbarian's retreat, and escape from the links of habit and the ties of a conventional world:

" There the passions cramped no longer shall have scope and breathing-place,
I will take some savage woman, she shall rear my dusky race."

The writer from whom we have already quoted, * on the characteristic features of Hudson Bay rule in the North-West, speaks thus with reference to the Company's officers mating with the Indian races:

"When the young clerk," he writes, "went out to the country, a wife as a *compagnon de voyage* was out of the question; and most frequently, when he was able to marry, he was far distant from the women of his own race, or from civilisation of any sort. The same was true of the early pioneers all over the American continent, few of them caring to take wives with them, but preferring, for a time at least, to push their fortunes alone. Absence from home, and a familiarity with the race around them, soon broke the links which once bound them to their fatherland and the women of their country, and many took wives from among the daughters of the soil. This was particularly common among the servants of the great fur companies, not only because few white women cared to take up their lot with the rovers of the wide fur-countries, but that it was also a matter of policy to ingratiate themselves with the powerful Indian tribes among whom they were thrown. The Hudson Bay Company, ever the most shrewd of merchants—most cautious of Scotchmen—encouraged this mating with the Indian races among their officers and *voyageurs*, mainly in order that their employés might have ties which would retain them in the country and consolidate the foundations of the Company by bonds of relationship and friendship between all

---

* " Story of a Dead Monopoly." *Vide Cornhill*, August, 1870.

their factors, traders, and servants generally. So sons and daughters were born to the Macs and Pierres; and the blood of Indian warriors, mingling with that of "Hieland lairds" and French *bourgeois*, the traders, the trappers, and the *voyageurs* of the great Fur Company, began to flow in a steady stream all through 'His Majesty's Plantations in North America,' deepening and expanding until it reached from the Atlantic to the Pacific, from York Factory to Fort Victoria. * * * It used to be noted in the Company, in latter days, that if an officer married a "white girl" on any of his visits to Montreal or Victoria, he could give no surer guarantee of his fitness for non-advancement in the Company. 'Oor ain fish-guts to oor ain sea-maws,' used to be the motto of the Board of Management, composed of old factors who had daughters to marry. Young officers, knowing this, proceeded accordingly."

But we have digressed somewhat from the matter before us. We were speaking of the "Half-breed" as an interested party in the feud between the rival trading Companies. He was, in truth, an influential factor in the struggle. At the time of which we write the "Métis" were almost entirely of French extraction, and were exclusively in the employ of the North-West Company. At a later date, on the Hudson Bay Company beginning to trade in the south, its officers formed *liasons* with the young women of the various tribes, and an English, in contradistinction to a French half-breed race, in process of time sprung up. As yet, as we have said however, the Half-breed was of French descent and owned his allegiance to the Canadian Company. To that Company he naturally looked for employment; and he took to its service not only with alacrity but with ancestral pride. For his duties he was admirably fitted; for the Half-breed possesses, in addition to the Frenchman's versatility and ready resource, the Indian's skill as a canoeist and his intuitive knowledge of the woods. The pride and stately dignity of the old French noblesse, and the magnificence of the Highland laird, who had now become an opulent fur-trader and possessor of large interests in the vast domain of the West, attracted the eye and won the heart of the simple child of the woods. This was true, indeed, not only of the Half-breed, but of the full-blooded Indian. To the French, both were drawn by characteristics of race, which found no counterpart in the English. The French race was quick to merge into the Indian, and to pick up the habits, and not infrequently the vices, of the dusky children of the woods. Parkman, the historian, remarks that the French colonists of Canada held, from the beginning, a peculiar intimacy of relation with the Indian tribes. Here are some passages from this graphic writer,* which shew how French influence diffused itself throughout Canada, and infected both the Indian and the Half-breed. He is speaking specially of the period of French military domination in the colony:

"France laboured," he says, "with eager diligence to conciliate the Indians and win them to espouse her cause. Her agents were busy in every village, studying the language of the inmates, complying with their usages, flattering their prejudices, caressing them, cajoling them, and whispering friendly warnings in their ears against the wicked designs of the English. When a party of Indian chiefs visited a French fort, they were greeted with the firing of cannon and rolling of drums; they were regaled at the tables of the officers, and bribed with medals and decorations, scarlet uniforms, and French flags. Far wiser than their rivals, the French never ruffled the self-complacent dignity of their guests, never insulted their religious notions, nor ridiculed their ancient customs. They met the savage half way, and showed an abundant readiness to mould their own features after his likeness. Count Frontenac himself, plumed and painted like an Indian chief, danced the war-dance and yelled the war-song at the camp-fires of his delighted allies. In its efforts to win the friendship and alliance of the Indian tribes, the French Government found every advantage in the peculiar character of its subjects—that pliant and plastic temper which forms so marked a contrast to the stubborn spirit of the Englishman. At first, great hopes were entertained that, by the mingling of French and Indians, the latter would be won

---

*"The Conspiracy of Pontiac." Vol. I.

over to civilisation and the Church; but the effect was precisely the reverse; for, as Charlevoix observes, the savages did not become French, but the French became savages. Hundreds betook themselves to the forest never to return. These overflowings of French civilisation were merged in the waste of barbarism, as a river is lost in the sands of the desert. The wandering Frenchman chose a wife or a concubine among his Indian friends; and, in a few generations, scarcely a tribe of the west was free from an infusion of Celtic blood. The French Empire in America could exhibit among its subjects every shade of colour from white to red, every gradation of culture, from the highest civilisation of Paris to the rudest barbarism of the wigwam."

"The fur-trade engendered a peculiar class of men, known by the appropriate name of bush-rangers, or *coureurs de bois*, half-civilised vagrants, whose chief vocation was conducting the canoes of the traders along the lakes and rivers of the interior; many of them, however, shaking loose every tie of blood and kindred, identified themselves with the Indians, and sank into utter barbarism. In many a squalid camp among the plains and forests of the west, the traveller would have encountered men owning the blood and speaking the language of France, yet, in their swarthy visages and barbarous costume, seeming more akin to those with whom they had cast their lot. The renegade of civilisation caught the habits and imbibed the prejudices of his chosen associates. He loved to decorate his long hair with eagle feathers, to make his face hideous with vermilion, ochre, and soot, and to adorn his greasy hunting frock with horse-hair fringes. His dwelling, if he had one, was a wigwam. He lounged on a bear-skin while his squaw boiled his venison and lighted his pipe. In hunting, in dancing, in singing, in taking a scalp, he rivalled the genuine Indian. His mind was tinctured with the superstitions of the forest. He had faith in the magic drum of the conjuror; he was not sure that a thunder-cloud could not be frightened away by whistling at it through the wing-bone of an eagle; he carried the tail of a rattle-snake in his bullet pouch by way of amulet; and he placed implicit trust in his dreams. This class of men is not yet extinct. In the cheerless wilds beyond the northern lakes, or among the mountain solitudes of the distant west, they may still be found, unchanged in life and character since the day when Louis the Great claimed sovereignty over this desert empire."

In a fine passage, in the work from which we have made this extract, Mr. Parkman draws a characteristic picture of the Canadian woodsman, in contrast with the sturdy English colonist, whose political and religious life developed a type quite different from the easy-going French-Canadian, the product of feudalism and Mother-Church. Says this interesting writer:

"In every quality of efficiency and strength, the Canadian fell miserably below his rival; but in all that pleases the eye and interests the imagination, he far surpassed him. Buoyant and gay, like his ancestry of France, he made the frozen wilderness ring with merriment, answered the surly howling of the pine forest with peals of laughter, and warmed with revelry the groaning ice of the St. Lawrence. Careless and thoughtless, he lived happy in the midst of poverty, content if he could but gain the means to fill his tobacco-pouch, and decorate the cap of his mistress with a ribbon. The example of a beggared nobility, who, proud and penniless, could only assert their rank by idleness and ostentation, was not lost upon him. A rightful heir to French bravery and French restlessness, he had an eager love of wandering and adventure; and this propensity found ample scope in the service of the fur-trade, the engrossing occupation and chief source of income to the colony. When the priest of St. Anne's had shrived him of his sins; when, after the parting carousal, he embarked with his comrades in the deep-laden canoe; when their oars kept time to the measured cadence of their song, and the blue, sunny bosom of the Ottawa opened before them; when their frail bark quivered among the milky foam and black rocks of the rapid; and when, around their camp-fire, they wasted half the night with jests and laughter,—then the Canadian was in his element. His footsteps explored the farthest hiding-places of the wilderness. In the evening dance, his red cap mingled with the scalp-locks and feathers of the Indian braves; or, stretched on a bear-skin by the side of his dusky mistress, he watched the gambols of his hybrid offspring, in happy oblivion of the partner whom he left unnumbered leagues behind. The fur-trade engendered a peculiar class of restless bush-rangers, more akin to Indians than to white men. Those who had once felt the fascinations of the forest were unfitted ever after for a life of quiet labour; and with this spirit the whole colony of Canada was infected."

Such were the characteristics of the French Canadian and the half-breed who eagerly entered the employment of the North-West Fur Company, and worked long and unweariedly in its interests. For a time no other race or class of men could have been more serviceable to the Company. They were inured to hardships; they were at home in the woods; their relations with the Indians were of the happiest; and they were never home-sick, or out of humour with their surroundings. Furthermore, they were always loyal to the Company. With zest did they enter into the feuds between it and its rival, and with equal zest did they take up their masters' unfortunate quarrel with Lord Selkirk and his colony. This nobleman's settlement on the Red River was, naturally enough, considered an usurpation, for he had acquired his rights by purchase from the Hudson Bay Company, who had neither discovered the region nor had been in occupancy. On the other hand, the North-West traders were the discoverers, and for many years had been in possession. In a dispassionate review of the facts, it is important that this should be borne in mind. The Conquest may be said to have given the English a right to the territory; but in the absence of any confirmation of its charter, subsequent to that occurrence, it can hardly be said to have transferred that right to the Hudson Bay Company.

It is important also to note that the discoverers were not unauthorised adventurers. French trading operations were always coupled with the motive of discovery. It was the invariable policy of the French Government, through its representatives at Quebec, to encourage geographical research and advance the possessions of the Crown. As early as the year 1717, M. de la Noüe, a young French lieutenant, was commissioned by M. de Vaudreuil, the Governor, to proceed to the west on a mission of trade and discovery. By this and the enterprises which immediately followed it, the whole vast interior, as far west as the Rocky Mountains, became known to the French; and in the region they speedily established their forts. In 1731, they erected Fort St. Pierre, at the discharge of the *Lac la Pluie* (Rainy Lake), and in the following year founded Fort St. Charles on the Lake of the Woods, and Fort Maurepas on the Winnipeg. In 1738, all the district of the Assiniboine was within the area of their operations, and Fort La Reine, on the St. Charles, and Fort Bourbon, on the Rivière des Biches, were established. Five years later, the Verandryes took possession of the Upper Mississippi and ascended the Saskatchewan in the interest of French trade. In 1766, the famous post of Michillimackinac, at the entrance of the *Lac des Illinois* (Michigan), was established. Other parts of the continent were also covered by the operations of the French traders and discoverers. Hudson Bay had early been reached by way of the Saguenay and Lake St. John, by the Ottawa, and by Lakes Nipigon and Winnipeg. The Kaministiquia, at the head of Lake Superior, as we have seen, was the base of supplies for operations in the west, and the great rallying-place of the French trader and *voyageur*. In short, the whole country was probed and made known to the outer world by the enterprise of the French and the French Canadians. As a consequence, any maps of the interior that were at all trustworthy were those of the French: the charts of the English, until long after the Conquest, were ludicrously inaccurate. Hence the opposition to the assumptions of the Hudson Bay Company, and the hostile rivalry which it engendered. After the Conquest, it is true, the French for a time abandoned their western possessions; but the old trading habit returned, stimulated, as we have seen, by the sturdy Scotch and the organization of the Canadian "Nor'-Westers." The success of this Company was remarkable. It had, however, its periods of trade depression and its years of disaster. A scourge of small-pox would break out among the Indians and for the season destroy its trade. Another year, there would be great floods in the west, and trade would be impeded if not wholly lost. Then there came the era of strife with the Red River colony and collision with the "Hudson Bays." In these engagements forts were fired and fur-depots destroyed. For a time hostilities were keen and continuous, and on both sides ruinous. Finally, the Hudson Bays and the Nor'-Westers coalesced; and from 1821 the amalgamated corporations traded under the old English title and charter of the Hudson Bay Company. This coalition of the Nor'-Westers with its English rival gave great strength to the united Company. It brought it an accession of capable traders and intelligent *voyageurs* and discoverers. In the service of the North-West Company were men—Alexander Mackenzie and David Thompson among the number—whose names will be forever identified with discovery in the North-West. The writer from whom we have more than once quoted, an old employé of the Hudson Bay Company, thus writes of the character and social status of the men it took over with the North-West Company:

"The sleepy old Hudson Bay Company were astounded at the magnificence of the newcomers, and old traders yet talk of the lordly Nor'-Wester. It was in those days that young Washington Irving was their guest, when he made his memorable journey to Montreal. The agents who presided over the affairs of the Company at headquarters were very important personages indeed, as might be expected. They were veterans that had grown grey in the wilds, and were full of all the traditions of the fur trade; and around them circled the laurels gained in the North. They were, in fact, a sort of commercial aristocracy in Quebec and Montreal, in days when nearly everybody was more or less directly interested in the fur trade."

In Washington Irving's "Astoria," the record of John Jacob Astor's Fur-trading Expedition on the waters of the Columbia River, occurs a graphic description of the North-West Company in the days of its prime. As the passage admirably describes a gathering at the annual conference of the Company at Fort William, we make no excuse for its insertion here, and with it shall conclude the present chapter.

"To behold the North-West Company in all its state and grandeur it was necessary to witness the annual gathering at Fort William, near what is now called the Grand Portage, on Lake Superior. Here two or three of the leading partners from Montreal proceeded once a year to meet the partners from the various trading-places in the wilderness, to discuss the affairs of the Company during the preceding year, and to arrange plans for the future. On these occasions might be seen the change since the unceremonious times of the old French traders, with their roystering *coureurs de bois*. Now the aristocratic character of the Briton, or rather the feudal spirit of the Highlander, shone out magnificently; every partner who had charge of an interior post, and had a score of retainers at his command, felt like the chieftain of a Highland clan, and was almost as important in the eyes of his dependants as of himself. To him a visit to the grand conference at Fort William was a most important event, and he repaired thither as to a meeting of Parliament. The partners from Montreal, however, were the lords of the ascendant. Coming from the midst of a luxurious and ostentatious life, they quite eclipsed their compeers from the woods, whose forms and faces had been battered by hard living and rough service, and whose garments and equipments were all the worse for wear. Indeed the partners from below considered the whole dignity of the Company as represented in their own persons, and conducted themselves in suitable style. They ascended the rivers in great state, like sovereigns making a progress, or rather like Highland chieftains navigating their subject lakes. They were wrapped in rich furs, their huge canoes freighted with every convenience and luxury, and manned by Canadian *voyageurs* as obedient as clansmen. They carried with them cooks and bakers, together with delicacies of every kind, and abundance of choice wines for the banquets which attended this great convocation. Happy were they, too, if they could meet with any distinguished stranger—above all, with some titled member of the British nobility—to accompany them on this stately occasion, and grace their high solemnities. Fort William, the scene of this important meeting, was a considerable village on the banks of Lake Superior. Here, in an immense wooden building, was the great council-chamber, and also the banqueting-hall, decorated with Indian arms and accoutrements, and the trophies of the fur trade. The house swarmed at this time with traders and *voyageurs* from Montreal bound to the interior posts, and some from the interior posts bound to Montreal. The councils were held in great state, for every member felt as if sitting in Parliament, and every retainer and dependant looked up to the assemblage with awe, as to the House of Lords. There was a vast deal of solemn deliberation and hard Scottish reasoning, with an occasional swell of pompous declamation. These grave and weighty councils were alternated with huge feasts and revels. The tables in the great banqueting-room groaned under the weight of game of all kinds,—of venison from the woods, and fish from the lakes; with hunters' delicacies, such as buffaloes' tongues and beavers' tails; and various luxuries from Montreal. There was no stint of generous wine, for it was a hard-drinking period, a time of loyal toasts and Bacchanalian songs and brimming bumpers. While the chiefs thus revelled in the hall, and made the rafters resound with bursts of loyalty and old Scottish song, chanted in voices cracked and sharpened by the Northern blast, their merriment was echoed and prolonged by a mongrel legion of retainers, Canadian *voyageurs*, half-breeds, Indian hunters, and vagabond hangers-on, who feasted sumptuously without, on the crumbs from their table, and made the welkin ring with old French ditties, mingled with Indian yelps and yellings."

CHAPTER III.

EARLY DISCOVERERS OF THE NORTH-WEST.

The English Trader, Alexander Henry.

ONE of the conditions on which the Hudson Bay Company received its original charter was that it should interest itself in geographical research. To a trading corporation this was a foolish proviso. We have seen that the Company took no thought to colonise its possessions: on the contrary, it did all it could to prevent settlement. The aid it gave to discovery, if we except some little assistance to the expeditions to the Arctic Seas in search of Franklin, was very slight. It sought solely its own interests. If it opened up regions in the North-West, it was to establish a trading-post, not to set up a meteorological station or erect an observatory. We doubt if its administrative officers could give, even approximately, the latitude and longitude of any one of its stations. Many of its traders and *voyageurs* doubtless, in time, became very familiar with the North-West, but only a few of them caught the adventurous spirit of the old navigators and travellers, and forgot their trading operations in their eagerness to explore the country.

From the earliest period of colonial settlement at Quebec, the French led the van in all exploratory effort. The great water-ways of the country gave facilities in probing the continent. Quebec was but the gateway to the Far West. From its portal the Jesuit was the first to lead off in the adventurous mission of carrying the Cross into the Canadian wilderness. Closely following the Black Robes, Champlain pursued his toilsome journey, by the Ottawa and Lake Nipissing, to the inland sea of the Hurons.* From the home of the Wyandot, detachments of the French missionaries threaded their way through the maze of islands in the Georgian Bay to the St. Mary's river and Lake Superior. Later on, Marquette tracked the mighty waters of Superior, and penetrated to the Mississippi. Down this great artery La Salle carried the *fleur de lis* to the Gulf of Mexico, and finally found an unknown grave in Texas. From the beginning of the seventeenth century the adventurous spirits of old France were to be found on all the great waters of the continent; and the footsteps of French traders, guided, it may be, by an Algonquin Indian, might be traced on the crisp snow of even the western prairie. Over the latter, in 1738, the Verandryes, father and son, braved their course to the far Rockies, through untold dangers and over almost insurmountable obstacles.

War was not long in following on the trail of the explorer. Over the route taken by Joliet and Marquette to the west might be seen the armed column of Rogers' Rangers, on its way to the fort at Detroit. English garrisons were also to be found at Sault Ste. Marie, and at Green Bay, on Lake Michigan. Ere long the woods at Mackinaw resounded with the shrieks of Pontiac's victims in the treacherously captured garrison of Michillimackinac; while a storm of blood and fire was passing over the region between Lake Erie and the Alleghanies. English and French blood also flowed freely on the shores of Lakes St. George and Champlain, and the woods of the neigh-

---

* For an account of this ill-starred expedition, and the subsequent Iroquois massacre of the Hurons and Jesuit Missionaries, see the Author's article on "The Georgian Bay and Muskoka Lakes," in *Picturesque Canada*.

bourhood rang nightly with the hideous shouts of the war-dance. For a time exploration held its breath while the continent was thrilled with the shock of battle at Quebec.

We have mentioned the tragedy enacted at Michillimackinac, the result of the "conspiracy of Pontiac," whom Parkman terms the "Satan of the forest paradise." As it happened, the pioneer of the English fur trade in the west, Alexander Henry, had come to the Fort shortly after the Conquest to pursue his trade, and was one of its inmates at the time of the massacre. Some extracts from this trader's narrative of the occurrence, Mr. Parkman weaves into his own history of the Indian war after the Conquest. Henry's narrative is replete with interest, not only for the thrilling personal account he gives of the Ojibway surprise and massacre of the English garrison, but for its record of trading operations in Western Canada, and in the Indian territories beyond the Red River. His work, [*] which is dated from Montreal, in 1809, is well written, and covers a period of trade and adventure from the years 1760 to 1776. In August, 1761, while as yet there had been no treaty of peace between the English and the Indians who had taken part with the French against the conquerors of the country, Henry decided to set out on a trading expedition from Montreal to Mackinaw, at the entrance to Lake Michigan. Receiving permission from General Gage, who was then Commander-in-Chief in Canada, and providing himself with a passport from the town major, he left Montreal on the 2nd of August, and Lachine on the following day. His party followed the usual route to the west, by the Ottawa and Lake Nipissing. By the end of the month, Henry had entered the Georgian Bay, and early in September, he reached the island of Michillimackinac, sometimes called the "Great Turtle." Here our traveller was cautioned not to remain, as the Indians of the region were

---

[*] "Travels and Adventures in Canada and the Indian Territories." By Alexander Henry, Esq. New York, 1809.

LORD MELGUND

hostile to his countrymen, and the few French-Canadians at the Fort were far from friendly. But Henry disregarded this advice, for the place was important to him in preparing his outfit for trade in the North-West; though he took the precaution to cross the straits of Mackinaw and enter the Fort. The Fort at this time was garrisoned by a small number of militia who, having families, as Henry tells us, became less soldiers than settlers. Not a few of them had served in the French army; at the Conquest they entered the service and accepted the pay of Britain.

At the Fort, Henry was informed that the whole band of Chippeways from the neighbouring island of Michillimackinac intended to pay him a visit, a piece of information which was far from agreeable to the adventurous trader. The report was true. Here is Henry's account of the unwelcome visit:

"At two o'clock in the afternoon, the Chippeways came to my house, about sixty in number, headed by Minavavana, their chief. They walked in single file, each with his tomahawk in one hand and scalping-knife in the other. Their bodies were naked from the waist upward, except in a few instances, where blankets were thrown loosely over the shoulders. Their faces were painted with charcoal, worked up with grease; their bodies with white clay, in patterns of curious fancies. Some had feathers thrust through their noses, and their heads decorated with the same. It is unnecessary to dwell on the sensations with which I beheld the approach of this uncouth, if not frightful, assemblage."

In the colloquy that ensued, Henry was far from being assured; for, after an interval of pipe-smoking, during which the English trader endured the tortures of suspense, the chief addressed him in these words:

"Englishman, it is to you that I speak, and I demand your attention! Englishman, it is your people that have made war with our father, the French king. You are his enemy; and how, then, could you have the boldness to venture among us his children? You know that his enemies are ours. Englishman, although you have conquered the French, you have not yet conquered us! We are not your slaves. These lakes these woods and mountains, were left to us by our ancestors. They are our inheritance; and we will part with them to none.

"Englishman, our father, the King of France, employed our young men to make war upon your nation. In this warfare many of them have been killed; and it is our custom to retaliate, until such time as the spirits of the slain are satisfied. But the spirits of the slain are to be satisfied in either of two ways: the first, by the spilling of the blood of the nation by which they fell; the other, by covering the bodies of the dead, and thus allaying the resentment of their relations. This is done by making presents."

Here Henry, we can imagine, breathed freely. It was his trading outfit, not his life, that was most in danger.

"Englishman, your king has never sent us any presents, nor entered into any treaty with us, wherefore he and we are still at war; and, until he does these things, we must consider that we have no other father or friend among the white men than the King of France; but, for you, we have taken into consideration that you have ventured your life among us, in the expectation that we should not molest you. You do not come armed, with an intention to make war; you come in peace, to trade with us, and supply us with necessaries, of which we are much in want. We shall regard you, therefore, as a brother; and you may sleep tranquilly without fear of the Chippeways. As a token of our friendship, we present you with this pipe to smoke."

The natural apprehension with which Henry regarded the visit of the Chippeways, as will be seen, was relieved by the turn things had taken. It was not his life, but his goods, they wanted. There is a delightful *naiveté* about the chief's speech, in his remarks about the giving of presents, a hint which Henry was slow to take, though he reluctantly acceded to a later request that the delegation should be allowed to taste his English "milk," *i. e.* rum. There is an amusing delicacy about the request for the rum, as Henry states it, which the Indians wanted to drink, so as to know "whether or not there was any difference between the English and the French milk," adding, "that it was long since they had tasted any." Deeming it prudent that the rum should not be "drunk on the premises," he hastened to get some few presents, which he gave them, as he observes, with the utmost good will, and was glad to see them take their departure.

Henry's relief from this visitation was but the prelude, however, to another. No sooner were the Chippeways gone than two hundred of the neighbouring tribe of the Ottawas, from L'Arbre Croche, came out of Lake Michigan and drew their canoes up on the beach. They had heard of the arrival of the Englishman, Henry, and his trading expedition. The Ottawas, unlike the Ojibways, manifested no nice sense of delicacy in their overtures to the trader ; nor in their demands did they beat about the bush. They summoned Henry to appear before them, and without any preliminary palaver informed him of their object in coming to the Fort. Their demand was that Henry and the other traders who had come to Michillimackinac should distribute, *on credit*, to each of the tribes merchandise and ammunition to the amount of fifty beaver-skins, the value of the goods to be repaid the traders on the return next summer of the Indians from their winter hunts. The demand was refused, as the Ottawas were known to be "bad pay;" but it was threateningly renewed, and the traders were given twenty-four hours for reflection. The next day there was a Council ; but Henry and his party thought it safest not to be present, though a message was sent asking that the amount of the credit demanded might be reduced. This was not entertained ; and threats of death were returned by the messenger should their demands not be complied with. That night news fortunately reached the small garrison of the near approach of some 300 men of the 60th Regiment, who had been sent from Detroit on detachment duty at Michillimackinac and the other posts in the west. Henry and the traders spent a night of terror in their barricaded cabins, but on the morrow were relieved beyond measure to find that the Ottawas had fled with the dawn as the detachment of English troops reached the landing-place.

Free now to pursue his mission of trade, Henry got his party under way and despatched it to Sault Ste. Marie. For the next two years he seems to have spent the time alternately at the "Soo" and at Mackinaw. At the close of the year 1762, the post at the "Soo" was accidentally burned, and Henry informs us, that to obtain suitable shelter, and save themselves from famine, the garrison and the traders withdrew to Mackinaw. During the winter, rumours were rife of hostile designs against the English soldiery at Michillimackinac. The garrison at this time, according to Henry, consisted of ninety privates, two subalterns, and the Commandant. There seems to be doubt, however, of the accuracy of this statement. Parkman, who quotes from the letters of Captain Etherington, the Commandant of the Fort, gives the number of rank and file as thirty-five, exclusive of officers, traders, and non-combatants. The trader, Henry, was again an inmate of the Fort. Spring passed without incident, save an increasing restlessness among the Chippeways (Ojibways) of the district. To this little heed was paid by the deluded garrison. The Indians, indeed, were allowed to come to the Fort to buy from the traders knives and tomahawks. Henry, alone, seems to have been apprehensive. An Indian, named Wawatam, had taken a great liking to him, and imparted to him his fears for the safety of Henry and the garrison. This Henry communicated to Etherington, the Commandant, but the latter only laughed at the trader's uneasiness. The Indians, he affirmed, were friendly, and to emphasise this, he added, that the Chippeways were on the morrow to play a game of baggattaway (lacrosse) with a band of the Sac Indians from Wisconsin. Unfortunate delusion! The morrow was the 4th of June, the birthday of King George. Here is Parkman's account of what happened on that anniversary:

"The discipline of the garrison (on account of its being the King's birthday) was relaxed, and some license allowed to the soldiers.... Women and children were moving about the doors; knots of Canadian *voyageurs* reclined on the ground, smoking and conversing; soldiers were lounging listlessly at the doors and windows of the barracks, or strolling in careless undress about the area.

"Without the fort the scene was of a very different character. The gates were wide open, and soldiers were collected in groups under the shadow of the palisades, watching the Indian ball-play. Most of them were without arms, and mingled among them were a great number of Canadians, while a multitude of Indian squaws, wrapped in blankets, were conspicuous in the crowd.

"Captain Etherington and Lieutenant Leslie stood near the gate, the former indulging his inveterate English propensity; for, as Henry informs us, he had promised the Ojibways that he would bet on their side against the Sacs. Indian chiefs and warriors were also among the spectators, intent, apparently, on watching the game, but with thoughts, in fact, far otherwise employed.

"The plain in front was covered by the ball-players. The game in which they were engaged, called *baggattaway* by the Ojibways, is still, as it always has been, a favourite with many Indian tribes. At either extremity of the ground, a tall post was planted, marking the stations of the rival parties. The object of each was to defend its own post, and drive the ball to that of its adversary. Hundreds of lithe and agile figures were leaping and bounding upon the plain. Each was nearly naked, his loose black hair flying in the wind, and each bore in his hand a bat of a form peculiar to this game. At one moment the whole were crowded together, a dense throng of combatants, all struggling for the ball; at the next, they were scattered again, and running over the ground like hounds in full cry. Each, in his excitement, yelled and shouted at the top of his voice. Rushing and striking, tripping their adversaries, or hurling them to the ground, they pursued the animating contest amid the laughter and applause of the spectators. Suddenly, from the midst of the multitude, the ball soared into the air, and, descending in a wide curve, fell near the pickets of the fort. This was no chance stroke. It was part of a preconcerted stratagem to ensure the surprise and destruction of the garrison. As if in pursuit of the ball, the players turned and came rushing, a maddened and tumultuous throng, towards the gate. In a moment they had reached it. The amazed English had no time to think or act. The shrill cries of the ball-players were changed to the ferocious war-whoop. The warriors snatched from the squaws the hatchets, which the latter, with this design, had concealed beneath their blankets. Some of the Indians assailed the spectators without, while others rushed into the fort, and all was carnage and confusion, At the outset, several strong hands had fastened their gripe upon Etherington and Leslie, and led them away from the scene of the massacre towards the woods. Within the area of the fort, the men were slaughtered without mercy!"

While this butchery was going on, the traveller, Henry, tells us that he was in the Fort, employed in writing letters to be forwarded to his friends in Montreal. Presently the Indian war-cry reached his ears, and going to the window, he says:

"I saw a crowd of Indians within the fort furiously cutting down every Englishman they found. I had in the room in which I was a fowling-piece, loaded with swan-shot. This I immediately seized, and held it for a few minutes, waiting to hear the drum beat to arms. In this dreadful interval, I saw several of my countrymen fall, and more than one struggling between the knees of an Indian, who, holding him in this manner, scalped him while yet living. At length, disappointed in the hope of seeing resistance made to the enemy, and sensible, of course, that no effort of my own unassisted arm could avail against four hundred Indians, I thought only of seeking shelter."

This shelter, Henry sought at the house of his neighbour, a French-Canadian, who, with his countrymen, allies of the Indians, was exempt from attack. But its owner, a M. Langlade, refused to succour Henry, being unfriendly to the English, and disliking Henry as a rival in trade. Fortunately, a Pawnee slave of the Frenchman showed our trader the humanity which her master had withheld, and conducted him to a place of hiding. Here he was subsequently discovered, but though his life was spared, he was subjected to every horror, and taken from one place of confinement to another. The thrilling dangers through which he passed, during the next few weeks, fill many pages in his narrative. For some time, he tells us, his only covering was an old shirt; his bed was the bare ground; and for days he was left without food. In one passage he says: "I confess that in the canoe with the Chippeways I was offered bread—but bread, with what accompaniment! They had a loaf which they cut with the same knives they had used in the massacre—knives still covered with blood. The blood they moistened with spittle, and, rubbing it on the bread, offered this for food to their prisoners, telling them to eat the blood of their countrymen."

We need not further follow the fortunes of Alexander Henry, except to see what became of him and his fellow-prisoners taken at Michillimackinac, and to glance briefly at his subsequent travels in the North-West. To the friendship of the Indian, Wawatam, who interceded with the chief of the Ojibways for his life and personal safety, Henry owed his release from his savage captors. Painted and attired as an Indian, he spent the following winter with his rescuer on the north shore of Lake Huron. The remainder of the English prisoners were rescued by the Ottawas, of Lake Michigan, a neighbouring tribe who being incensed at the Chippeways' attack on Michillimackinac without having been asked to participate in it, wished to deprive them of some of the glory of the victory, and induced their captors to give up the soldiers and traders still in their possession. These the Ottawas took to Montreal, and received a ransom for them on their arrival, in August, 1763. Henry, in the summer of the following year, had the opportunity, of which he gladly availed himself, to accompany a party of the Chippeways, of Sault Ste. Marie, who were setting out for Niagara, to which place they had been summoned by Sir William Johnson, for the purpose of entering into a treaty of peace with Great Britain. On the 18th of June, we learn from his narrative, that Henry was at Lac aux Claies (Lake Simcoe), from which he proceeded with the

Indian delegation by "the carrying-place" to Toronto,* thence across Lake Ontario to Niagara.

At Niagara, Henry joined an army, consisting of some three thousand men, under General Bradstreet, who were about to proceed to Detroit, to raise Pontiac's siege of that fort, which, for over a year, had been gallantly defended by Major Gladwyn, its commandant. In the spring of 1769, we find him again at Sault Ste. Marie, pursuing his trading operations as far west as Michipicoten, on Lake Superior. Here, for a number of years, he was engaged in mining and prospecting, while at intervals he continued his fur-trade with the Indians. His success in the latter seems to have been great, for he writes, that in June, 1775, he left the Sault on his first trading expedition to the head of Lake Superior "with goods and provisions to the value of three thousand pounds sterling, on board twelve small canoes and four large ones." From here he proceeds, by the Grand Portage, to the Lake of the Woods, and ere long to the village of the Christineaux, or Crees, on Lake Winnipeg. Like most travellers of the period, Henry never fails to omit some description of the tribes among whom for a time he sojourned, and of the social customs that prevail amongst them. Here are a few extracts from his narrative, chiefly concerning the female Cree:

"The dress and other exterior appearances of the Christineaux are very distinguishable from those of the Chippeways and the Wood Indians. The men were almost entirely naked, and their bodies painted with a red ochre, procured in the mountains. Their ears were pierced, and filled with the bones of fish and of land animals. The women wore their hair of a great length, both behind and before, dividing it on the forehead and at the back of the head, and collecting the hair of each side

---

*The following is Henry's reference at this period (1769) to the capital of Ontario: "Toranto, or Toronto, is the name of a French trading-house, on Lake Ontario, built near the site of the present town of York, the capital of the Province of Upper Canada." At the time our author's book was published (1809) York had been founded some sixteen years.

into a roll, which is fastened above the ear; and this roll, like the tuft on the heads of the men, is covered with a piece of skin. The skin is painted, or else ornamented, with beads of various colours. The rolls, with their coverings, resemble a pair of large horns.

"The ears of the women are pierced and decorated like those of the men. Their clothing is of leather, or dressed skins of the wild ox and the elk. The dress, falling from the shoulders to below the knee, is of one entire piece. Girls of an early age wear their dresses shorter than those more advanced. The same garment covers the shoulders and the bosom; and is fastened by a strap, which passes over the shoulders; it is confined about the waist by a girdle. The stockings are of leather, made in the fashion of leggings. The arms, to the shoulders, are left naked, or are provided with sleeves, which are sometimes put on, and sometimes suffered to hang vacant from the shoulders. The wrists are adorned with bracelets of copper or brass, manufactured from old kettles. In general, one person is worth but one dress; and this is worn as long as it will last, or till a new one is made, and then thrown away. The women, like the men, paint their faces with red ochre; and in addition, usually tatoo two lines, reaching from the lip to the chin, or from the corners of the mouth to the ears. They omit nothing to make themselves lovely.

"Such are the exterior beauties of the female Christineaux; and not content with the power belonging to these attractions, they condescend to beguile, with tender looks, the hearts of passing strangers. The men, too, unlike the Chippeways (who are of a jealous temper), eagerly encourage them in this design. One of the chiefs assured me that the children borne by the women to Europeans were bolder warriors and better hunters than themselves. The Christineaux have usually two wives each, and often three; and make no difficulty in lending one of them, for a length of time, to a friend. Some of my men entered into agreements with the respective husbands, in virtue of which they embarked the women in the canoes, promising to return them next year. The women so selected consider themselves as honoured; and the husband who should refuse to lend his wife would fall under the condemnation of the sex in general."

Such was the far from uncommon morality of this Indian

tribe, and such the morality which Henry seems to have been obliged to countenance on the part of those who had entered his service. From the village of the Christineaux Henry and his party continued their voyage westward to Lac de Bourbon (Cedar Lake), where the elder Verandrye had established a fort about the year 1736. On the way he met the two brothers, Frobisher, who had been actively intercepting the trade of the Indians with the Hudson Bay Company, and had met with much success. He also fell in with Peter Pond, a Boston trader, of unenviable repute, who, in later years, was tried in the Quebec Courts for the murder, in the North-West, of a Mr. Wadin, a fur trader. Pond had the luck to be released, on the ground that the jurisdiction of the Court did not extend to the distant territories of the North-West. Mr. Charles Lindsey, whose knowledge of early Canadian history is both extensive and accurate, states that this Peter Pond was at the elbow of the American Commissioners in settling boundary matters after the peace of 1793. "Pond," he observes, "is said to have designated to the American Commissioners a boundary line through the middle of the upper St. Lawrence and the Lakes, and through the interior countries to the north-west corner of the Lake of the Woods, thence west to the Mississippi; a line that was accepted by the British Commissioners." *

Joining their forces, for greater safety, the traders hurried forward, as there were signs of an early winter overtaking them, for which they were as yet unprepared. Moreover, the combined party was short of provisions: one hundred and thirty men, it was found, made large demands on the commissariat. The exigencies of the situation are thus described by our traveller:

"On the twenty-first of September, it blew hard and snow began to fall. The storm continued till the twenty-fifth, by

---

* "An Investigation of the Unsettled Boundaries of Ontario." By Charles Lindsey. Toronto: Hunter, Rose & Co., 1873.

which time the small lakes were frozen over, and two feet of snow lay on level ground in the woods. This early severity of the season filled us with serious alarm, for the country was uninhabited for two hundred miles on every side of us, and, if detained by winter, our destruction was certain. In this state of peril we continued our voyage day and night. The fears of our men were a sufficient motive for their exertions."

But the party was beset by other perils besides those of the advancing season. At the mouth of the Saskatchewan, which was reached early in October, the traders were enabled to eke out their provisions with a supply of sturgeon from the river and of wild fowl from the reeds on its banks. Ascending the stream some leagues, they arrived at the village of a chief, locally known as the "Pelican," who with a large armed following barred all progress until black-mail was levied on the party. To this exaction, which was a heavy one, they had to submit rather than lose their lives, and with them, of course, all their effects. Finally, on the 26th of the month, they reached Cumberland House, a factory on Sturgeon Lake, which had been erected the previous year by Samuel Hearne, an explorer in the employ of the Hudson Bay Company. Of this notable traveller we shall have something to say in our next chapter. The post on Sturgeon Lake, which Henry informs us was then garrisoned by Orkney Highlanders, was established by the Hudson Bay Company to restore the trade which for sometime had been intercepted by Canadian merchants in its passage to the Churchill. Though the rival traders were unwelcome guests at Cumberland House, they were treated, nevertheless, with forbearance and civility. Here the expedition broke up; some portion of it going in one direction, some in another.

Henry and the brothers Frobisher resolved on joining their stock-in-trade, and on wintering together, in some favourable location, in the direction of the Churchill river. Crossing Sturgeon Lake, they ascended the Malign river, so called by the Canadians, we are told, from the vexatious delays occasioned by its numerous and strong rapids. The traders and their party of forty men at length reached Beaver Lake, where they determined to encamp for the winter. The camp-larder was kept well filled by the Indians. The supplies consisted of moose and beaver; of pike, pickerel and sturgeon; but chiefly of trout "from ten to fifty pounds weight," caught through holes in the ice, as our historian narrates, in twenty and thirty fathoms of water.

Fortunately, there was no lack of food, for the winter was long and severe; the thermometer frequently registering 32° below zero. Notwithstanding the inclemency of the season Henry, early in the year 1776, determined to see something of the western prairies, and, if possible, to reach the country of the Assiniboines. In the expedition, he was to be accompanied by Joseph Frobisher as far as Cumberland House, 120 miles distant from Beaver Lake. Attended by three men, and provided with supplies of pemmican (dried meat), frozen fish, and roasted maize, the party set out on snow-shoes, well wrapped in buffalo robes, and made Cumberland House after a four days' tramp. The snow, says the narrator, was on an average four feet deep. From Cumberland House, our trader and his party pursued a westerly course on the ice, by way of Sturgeon Lake, to the Saskatchewan. The depth of the snow greatly impeded their progress; and by the time they reached Fort des Prairies, almost a month's journey from their last stopping-place, our travellers had exhausted their provisions, and, for the time being, their strength. But for chance putting in their way a deer that had broken through the ice, and, unable to extricate itself, had been frozen to death, the expedition would have been in great straits for food.

Resting for a few days at Fort des Prairies, Henry and his attendants set out now for the plains, which they followed for many days' tramp towards the south-west. On the plains they suffered much from cold and exposure, for, in the absence of wood, they were unable to make a fire when they encamped.

They also suffered greatly from blinding snow storms and piercing cold winds. Much to their relief, they at last reached the village of the Osinipoilles, or Assiniboines, where they were received with marked hospitality and ostentatious kindness. On their arrival, there was the usual " pow-wow," with the declamation of the chief, and the " ughs" of approving warriors; a lengthened period of pipe-smoking and mental stock-taking; ending with a great feast, and its scenes of gormandising and post-prandial Indian characteristics.

The stay of our leader and his party among the Assiniboines was both pleasant and profitable. The tribal village was a considerable one, for Henry informs us that there were at least two hundred wigwams, each containing from two to four families. Here, for the first time, he saw a herd of hardy Indian ponies feeding on the skirts of the plain, and getting at the succulent grass by scraping the deep snow with their feet. Here, also, he had his first experience of a buffalo hunt, or, more properly, a *battue*. Accepting the chief's invitation, Henry tells us, that he set out with a party of forty Indians and a number of women, for an island on the plain, some five miles from the village, where the buffalo were to be entrapped. Here is his account of the incidents of the hunt.

" Arrived at the island, the women pitched a few tents, while the chief led his hunters to the southern end, where there was a pound or enclosure. The fence was about four feet high, formed of strong stakes of birch wood, wattled with smaller branches of the same. The day was spent in making repairs; and by the evening, all was ready for the hunt.

" At daylight, several of the more expert hunters were sent to decoy the animals into the pound. They were dressed in ox-skins, with the hair and horns. Their faces were covered, and their walk and gestures so closely resembled those of the animals themselves, that had I not been in the secret, I should have been as much deceived as the oxen.

"At ten o'clock, one of the hunters returned, bringing information of the herd. Immediately, all the dogs were muzzled ; and this done, the whole crowd of men and women surrounded the outside of the pound. The herd, of which the extent was so great that I cannot pretend to estimate the number, was distant half a mile, advancing slowly, and frequently stopping to feed. The part played by the decoyers was that of approaching them within hearing, and then bellowing like themselves. On hearing the noise, the oxen did not fail to give it attention; and, whether from curiosity or sympathy, advanced to meet those from whom it proceeded. These, in the meantime, fell back deliberately towards the pound, always repeating the call whenever the oxen stopped. This was reiterated until the leaders of the herd had followed the decoyers into the jaws of the pound, which, though wide asunder toward the plain, terminated like a funnel in a small aperture or gateway; and within this was the pound itself. The Indians remark, that in all herds of animals there are chiefs or leaders, by whom the motions of the rest are determined.

"The decoyers now retired within the pound, and were followed by the oxen. But the former retired still further, withdrawing themselves at certain movable parts of the fence, while the latter were fallen upon by all the hunters, and presently wounded and killed by showers of arrows. Amid the uproar which ensued, the oxen made several attempts to force the fence; but the Indians stopped them, and drove them back by shaking skins before their eyes. Skins were also made use of to stop the entrance, being let down by strings as soon as the buffalo were inside. The slaughter was prolonged till the evening, when the hunters returned to their tents. Next morning all the tongues of the butchered oxen were presented to the chief, *to the number of seventy-two.* The women brought the meat to the village on sledges drawn by dogs. The lumps on the shoulders, and the hearts, as well as the tongues, were set apart for feasts; while the rest was consumed as ordinary food, or dried, for sale at the fort."

It was the wish of our adventurous traveller to proceed further to the west, until he should reach the mountains, of which he had often heard, and the ocean that lay beyond. Like other travellers in the region, he imagined that the Rocky Mountains and the Pacific were less distant than was the fact. Even the cartographers of the period had hazy notions of the vast solitudes of the west, for they placed the coast-line of the

Pacific only a little beyond Lake Athabasca. Few as yet knew the wide extent of the prairies. In some degree, the chief of the Assiniboines undeceived our traveller, and informed him that the mountains he desired to reach were far distant. Moreover, he told him, that between the village and the snow-capped "Rockies," there lay the country of the Snake-Indians and the Blackfeet, over which it was perilous to travel. Henry reluctantly concluded to wend his way homewards.

From the interesting narrative of this trader, we shall make one more extract, describing the people among whom he had pleasantly sojourned:

"The men among the Assiniboines are well made, but their colour is much deeper than that of the more northern Indians. Some of the women are tolerably handsome, considering how they live, exposed to the extremes of heat and cold, and enveloped by an atmosphere of smoke for at least one half of the year. Their dress is of the same material, and of the same form, as that of the female Christineaux. The married women suffer their hair to grow at random, and even hang over their eyes. [The fashion we should nowadays describe as "banged."] All the sex is fond of garnishing the lower edge of the dress with small bells, deer-hoofs, pieces of metal, or anything capable of making a noise. When they move, the sounds keep time and make a fantastic harmony.

"The Assiniboines treat their slaves with great cruelty. As an example, one of the principal chiefs, whose tent was near that which we occupied, had a female slave, of about twenty years of age. I saw her always on the outside of the door of the tent, exposed to the severest cold; and having asked the reason, I was told that *she was a slave*. The information induced me to speak to her master, in the hope of procuring some mitigation of the hardships she underwent; but he gave me for answer, that he had taken her on the other side of the western mountains; that at the same time he had lost a brother and a son in battle; and that the enterprise had taken place in order to release one of his own nation, who had been a slave in her's, and who had been used with much greater severity than that which she experienced. The reality of the last of these facts appeared to me to be impossible. The wretched woman fed and slept with the dogs, scrambled with them for the bones which were thrown out of the tent. When her master was within, she was never permitted to enter; at all seasons the children amused themselves with impunity in tormenting her, thrusting lighted sticks into her face; and if she succeeded in warding off these outrages, she was violently beaten. I was not successful in procuring any diminution of her sufferings; but I drew some relief from the idea that their duration could not be long. They were too heavy to be sustained."

Contact with Europeans has had some influence, since the period of Henry's narrative, in rendering the Indian heart less inhuman. That it has not wholly civilised the tribes of the region, or taken from them their lust of blood, present day events, which have turned the strained eyes and anxious hearts of the people of the Dominion to the still desolate plains of the North-West, only too sadly indicate. But cruel as the Osinipoilles were to their enemies, our travellers found them friendly to the white man, and to those who treated them fairly, they were kind and hospitable. As yet, they had had little acquaintance with Europeans, at least not sufficient, as Henry observes, to affect their simple, pristine habits. Unlike their neighbours, the Christineaux, of whom they lived in fear, they were a harmless people, " with a large share of simplicity of manners and plain dealing."

The Assiniboines, on being apprised of Henry's decision to proceed eastward, concluded to accompany him as far as Fort des Prairies, where the chief wished to barter peltry for necessaries and the inevitable trinket. So nomadic are the Indians in their habits, that it was with little surprise Henry learned that on the morrow the whole camp would be in motion. At daybreak the lodges were struck; the poles and their bark covering were transferred to dog sleighs; and at sunrise, amid the yelps and howlings of the dogs, the village denizens filed out over the plain. The line of march, we are told, exceeded three miles in length. On the way they fell in with another tribe (numbering a hundred tents), who were also proceeding to the Fort for the purposes of trade. Nearing their destination, both tribes encamped in a wood; their principal men only coming on to the trading-post with the products of the chase.

At the Fort, after a brief rest, Henry parted with his Indian friends, and continued his way from the Saskatchewan to Cumberland House, thence to his old camp on Beaver Lake. Here he found his men all in good health, but anxious for a change of scene. As spring was returning, and the waterfowl beginning to reappear, Henry and his friend, Frobisher, thought it would be safe to undertake a journey northward to Athabasca, which they had previously agreed upon. Ere long, our indefatigable travellers were again on the way, and Henry had additional matter furnished him for his narrative. On the fifth day they reached the Churchill, from which they turned westward, towards the high latitudes of Lake Athabasca. Having gone about three hundred miles, they found the lakes and streams still frozen, and their progress consequently impeded. Reaching the Rapide du Serpent, they met a large party of Athabasca Indians journeying southward, and after a brief parley, they concluded to return with the Indians to their point of departure. From the Athabascas, Henry acquired a good deal of information about their country, and of the streams that flow northward to the Arctic Ocean. Possessed of this information, he seems to have been more content to give up his expedition. By the first of July they were back again at Beaver Lake.

Here, having completed his commercial adventure, and made over the remainder of his merchandise to a brother of Frobisher's, Henry, with his friend and following, set out on their return journey to the Grand Portage, near Lake Superior, and from there to Montreal. We need not follow our trader further, save to relate his safe deliverance from the accidents and perils of the way, and his grateful arrival at the commercial metropolis of Eastern Canada. On an island in the Lake of the Woods, Henry observes, that he hailed a party of Indians, whom he saw encamped near by, in the hope of purchasing provisions, of which he and his men were much in need. He tells us, that "he found them full of a story that some strange nation had entered Montreal, taken Quebec, killed all the English, and would certainly be at the Grand Portage before we arrived there." From this disquieting, but distorted rumour, our trader was to get his first inkling of what had been going on in the outer world while he was figuratively entombed in the wilds of the Far West. Continuing his journey, he was not long in learning of the outbreak of the American Revolution, and of Montgomery's abortive expedition to Quebec. Arriving, finally, at Montreal, the last words of Henry's narrative inform us, that "he found the province delivered from the irruption of the colonists, and protected by the forces of General Burgoyne."

CHAPTER IV.

EARLY DISCOVERERS OF THE NORTH-WEST

Joseph La France, and Samuel Hearne.

THE interest that centres in these old narratives of traders and discoverers in the Canadian North-West, few are aware of. Their unwieldy quartos, it is to be feared, are seldom looked into; the notion prevails that their writers are either egotistical or garrulous, perhaps both. In some instances, the charge is true; but allowance may well be made for this, when one considers to what danger they committed themselves, and what unrewarded toil was theirs, in venturing upon the journeys they undertook, through countries that were wholly unknown, and among tribes that were hostile and barbarous. Courageous as they were, there was need for courage; for seldom a day would pass without their being confronted by peril in some shape or other, to which the most daring would have to pay the tribute of fear. Known as the country now is, and the terrors of the way, consequently, in large measure, discounted, there are few who would care to trust themselves to even a holiday excursion in the sombre woods of the region, or on the awesome solitudes of the plains. Only a comfortable Pullman on the Canadian Pacific, well filled with friends, would give assurance to the nervous traveller in passing over a thousand miles of solitude, allay the spectre of his disturbing thoughts, and dispel the traditional memory of the stealthy Indian, his scalping-knife and tomahawk.

Of the narratives of early English discoverers in the North-West, that of Alexander Henry, of which we made free use in our last chapter, is perhaps the most attractive. With the exception of his work, we know of none, save the records of a few French travellers, that treats of the region and period with so much intelligence, and personal and literary interest. Many years afterwards, we come to later travellers, and to descriptions of the country and its people under altered circumstances. The chief English narratives of the time deal with more northern regions. We have thus little account of early travels in the districts that have since been brought within civilisation, and in some measure opened for settlement. Most writers treat of the territory round Hudson Bay, and of the waters that drain into the Arctic seas. This, of course, we naturally expect; first, because the English approach to the region was *via* Hudson Straits, and, secondly, because the main object of discovery at the period was not to explore the interior of the continent, but to find a water highway to the Pacific. Of those who did explore the interior of the Continent, as it happens, they have not, to any extent, written about it. This is notably the case with both Hearne and Mackenzie, the former of whom discovered and wrote of the Copper Mine River, and the latter of the river that bears his name—both waters falling into the Arctic Ocean. The same is true of other and less known writers. The literature that deals with the Arctic seas, in connection with a waterway to the west, far exceeds that which deals with the inland possessions of the Hudson Bay Company or the overland route to the Pacific.

From an early period the great Trading Company was importuned to extend its operations into the interior, and to do something to open up the country southward. Too long, it may be said, it refrained from adventuring in what was known to be a rough and wild country. But it was more than this; it was a dangerous one. It was a country that was in possession of a people with whom the English were almost incessantly at war, and who were not only hostile themselves, but who had infected the native with the same bitter hostility. As far as trade was concerned, the Fur Company, unless forced to do so, had no cause to take up national quarrels. So long as the Indians brought peltry to the forts, the Company's employés had neither the motive nor the desire to undergo the toil and the risk of long journeys in search of it. Were we the most partisan of the Company's apologists, this is all that can be said for its failure to open up the country.

That the Hudson Bay Company wished to conceal all knowledge of the country, and that it resorted to untruth, as well as concealment, may be taken for granted. Both are now well ascertained facts. But when a great corporation has the monopoly of a valuable trade, it need occasion little surprise if it be jealous of interference with its right and privilege. Both its right and its privilege, we know, were long called in question; and its jealousy of rivals in the field, at successive intervals, became a matter of grave public interest. One of the earliest writers to arraign the Company on its shortcomings is Arthur Dobbs, whose "Account of the Countries adjoining Hudson Bay" was published in the year 1744. Considering the early period in which he wrote, and the fact that his account of the country is written out from the oral report of a half-breed French trader, his work is of fair interest and accuracy. It has the serious drawback, however, of being without index, contents, or division into chapters. The chief source of his information was a native, named Joseph La France, whom he describes as a "French Canadese Indian." This half-breed, we learn, was born at Michillimackinac early in the eighteenth century, and on the death of his mother, when he was but five years old, he was taken by his father to Quebec to learn French. When he had grown up, he took to the fur-trade; and for over twenty years travelled through the whole of the French Colony, and into many portions of the North-West. He seems to have been an intelligent observer of the country, and to be more than usually familiar with what was going on in it.

From Mr Dobbs's narrative of La France's story, we learn that he was a French outlaw, or, at least, an unlicensed, runaway trader; and that he came to the English, at Hudson Bay, owing to a falling out with the French Governor. Here is an extract from the narrator's account of this incident: "About six years ago he (La France) went to Montreal with two Indians and a considerable cargo of furs, where he found the Governor of Canada, who wintered there. He made him a present of marten-skins, and also 1000 crowns for a *congé*, or license to trade in the following year. But in spring he would neither give him his *congé* nor his money, under pretence that he had sold brandy to the Indians, which is prohibited, and threatened him with imprisonment for demanding his money. So he was obliged to steal away with his two Indians, three canoes, and what goods he had got in exchange for his furs."

La France, the narrator states later on, was met on Lake Nipissing by a brother-in-law of the Governor, who was crossing the lake with thirty soldiers and a number of Indian guides and carriers, conveyed in a fleet of nine canoes. Here our trader was seized, as a runaway without a passport, and his goods were confiscated. During the night he managed, however, to make his escape, " with only his gun and five charges of powder and ball." After many hardships, he reached Sault Ste Marie, and here determined to go to the English post on Hudson Bay. He left the Sault in the beginning of the winter of 1739, and, as we are told, lived and hunted for a while on the north shore of Lake Superior, with the Saulteaux, among whom he had previously traded. Through the country of this tribe, and through the territories inhabited by the Sturgeon Indians, the Sioux, the Crees, and Assiniboines, he successively passed, feeding himself on the way by the aid of his rod and gun, and sheltering himself at night under brushwood, or whatever cover was available. The spring of 1742 had arrived by the time he reached the Nelson River. Here he met with a party of Indians, 100 canoes in number, on their way to York Factory, with their product of the winter's hunt. Setting out with these Indians, La France spent the next few weeks on the river, and arrived at the Factory on the 24th of June. Mr. Dobbs, quoting from our trader, gives some facts, which are here worth recording, of the trade of the period at York Factory, and the small sums allowed the Indians in exchange for the peltry.

" The natives," he says, " are so discouraged in their trade with the Hudson Bay Company that no peltry is worth the carriage, and the finest furs are sold for very little. When La France's party arrived at the Factory, in June, 1742, the prices asked for European goods were much higher than the settled prices fixed by the Company, which the Governors fix so, to shew the Company how zealous they are to improve their trade, and sell their goods to advantage. They give but a pound of gunpowder for four beavers ; a fathom (sic) of tobacco for 7 beavers ; a pound of shot for 1 ; an ell of coarse cloth for

15; a blanket for 12; 2 fish-hooks or three flints for 1; a gun for 25; a pistol for 10; a common hat, with white lace (!) 7; an axe, 4; a bill-hook, 1; a gallon of brandy, 4; a checked shirt, 7;—all of which are sold at a monstrous profit, even to 2000 per cent. Notwithstanding this discouragement, the two fleets which accompanied La France carried down 200 packs of 100 each—20,000 beavers; and the other Indians who arrived that year, he computed, carried down 300 packs of 200 each—, 30,000—in all 50,000 beavers, and above 9000 martens.*

As we have previously recorded, the half-breed, Joseph La France, an extract from whose narrative is here given by us, found his way to England in one of the trading-ships of the season. Here he seems to have met with the writer who becomes the historian of his travels. This writer appears to have been a person of influence, for he is styled, in a letter occurring in the text, the Honourable Arthur Dobbs. Mr. Dobbs has a mission, in which he takes evident delight, namely, to censure the Hudson Bay Company, and, in true John Bull fashion, to excite the feelings of his countrymen against the French, and their monopoly of the inland fur-trade in the Canadian colony. This is the burden of his work; though in his pages there is much information that, at the period, must have been new and important with regard to the colony, its characteristic features, its trade and people. From La France's knowledge of the country, supplemented by considerable reading, his historian is enabled to describe, with tolerable accuracy, the situation, extent, and physical aspects of the rivers, lakes, and plains of the interior. He is also able to give a familiar account of the Indian tribes, their habits and pursuits, and some detail of the animal life of the regions traversed.

In some parts, Mr. Dobbs's narrative reads as if he were describing a terrestrial paradise. So far as his lumbering sen-

---

* "An Account of the Countries adjoining Hudson Bay." By Arthur Dobbs. London, 1744.

tences permit, he grows eloquent over the great lakes and wide stretches of fair territory in various portions of the country. At the same time, he bemoans the melancholy fact that this great possession is cursed by the *laissez-faire* administration of a gigantic monopoly. He has a great deal to say of a Captain Middleton, a navigator in the employ of the Hudson Bay Company, whom he accuses of studied concealment of his discoveries, and wicked aspersion of the country and its Northern approaches. With Middleton he enters into a long correspondence over a presumed waterway from Hudson Bay to Japan, a waterway which Middleton, for sinister purposes, he thinks, conceals. In this delusion he his encouraged by the receipt of letters from some of the crew and subordinate officers who made voyages with Middleton. Of the practicability of the Hudson Bay route to the North-West, and its advantage in giving speedy access to the heart of the continent, Mr. Dobbs held strong opinions, and, in the main, his views were correct. We are to-day only finding this out. The Canadian Hudson Bay Expedition of 1884, for which the Dominion Parliament voted $100,000, but reiterates what Mr. Dobbs had to say of the route one hundred and fifty years ago. The commercial importance of the Expedition, and the results obtained through the labours of Lieut. Gordon and his staff, are nevertheless great. The information gleaned respecting the route establishes not only its feasibility, but its great advantage in materially shortening the passage between Europe and Asia. To those in search of facts on this subject, we commend a perusal of the Report of the Expedition, also a valuable compilation from the pen of Mr. Tuttle.*

In connection with this region, the period of which we write supplies us with one other work of more than average note in

---

* "Our North Land: a Narrative of the Hudson Bay Expedition of 1884." By Charles R. Tuttle. Toronto, 1885.

the records of discovery in the North-West. We refer to the account of the expedition, during the years 1770-72, to the Copper Mine River, undertaken at the request of the Hudson Bay authorities by Samuel Hearne, an old employé of the Company. A further object of that expedition was to discover, if possible, a practicable passage-way to the Northern Ocean. Mr. Hearne's name, it will be remembered, we have already mentioned in connection with the founding of the Company's post at Cumberland House. He was a trusted servant of the Company. Though his name appears in the literature of Arctic travel, in connection with his famous journey to the country of the Copper Mine Indians, he is well known as an early traveller and veteran explorer in the Canadian North-West. So intelligent an observer, and so capable a writer, as he is, it is a matter of regret that he left no work recording his travels in the latter region. His only published work is his " Journey to the Copper Mine River," which was issued in London, in 1795.

In the introduction to that work, Mr. Hearne pays some attention to the writers who preceded him in describing the country, and refers by name to Arthur Dobbs, whose book we have just epitomised. His object in noticing these early writers is to relieve his employers, the Hudson Bay Company, from what he terms " the aspersions of interested parties," who accuse the Company of being adverse to discovery. In the advocacy of his patrons, he points with evident pride to their encouragement of his own expedition, though he is frank enough to admit that the Company's past actions in Hudson Bay, and the secrecy which characterised investigation in the region, may have justly prejudiced public opinion against the Company. In regard to his expedition to the Copper Mine River, there is no doubt that the Company was both liberal in the treatment of its employé, and generous in providing him with repeated outfits for the journey. We say repeated, for Hearne had to return twice before making a successful start, owing to the break down of expeditions after they had been some weeks on the way. The failure of the first expedition was due to his having attached to his party two white men—favourites of the Governor of Prince of Wales's Fort, from which Hearne started,— men whom he could make nothing of, and whose idleness encouraged mutiny and desertion in the ranks. The second expedition was unsuccessful from a rather amusing cause. This cause is explained by an Indian chief, named Matonabbee, whom Hearne meets in his distress, and who, on the return of the expedition, agrees to go with it on its third venture. Here is Hearne's account of Matonabbee's explanation of the failure of the second expedition: "He attributed all our misfortunes," writes Hearne, " to the misconduct of my guides, and to the plan we pursued, by the desire of the Governor, *of not taking any women with us on this journey.* ' This,' he said, ' was the principal thing that occasioned all our wants, for,' said he, ' when all the men are heavy laden they can neither hunt nor travel to any considerable distance; and in case they meet with success in hunting, who is to carry the produce of their labour ? Women,' added he, ' were made for labour; one of them can carry, or haul, as much as two men can. They also pitch our tents, make and mend our clothing, keep us warm at night; and, in fact, there is no such thing as travelling any considerable distance, or any length of time, in this country, without their assistance. Women,' said he, again, ' though they do everything, are maintained at a trifling expense; for as they always act as cooks, the very licking of their fingers, in scarce times, is sufficient for their subsistence.' This, however odd it may appear," remarks Hearne, " is but too true a description of the situation of women in this country; it is at least so in appearance; for the women always carry the provisions, and it is more than probable they help themselves when the men are not present."

Could argument go further in support of the theory of the indispensableness of women in such expeditions as that to which Hearne had committed himself! "Revolt of women," do we hear? Why, the cry is monstrous, when they possess the priceless privilege of "licking their fingers," while their lords' share was but the crumbs of the feast, not to speak of "sly snacks" which the women might have by the way, or hoarded store, to be partaken of without fear "when the men are not present!" But the injustice to the sisterhood, among these Northern Indians, has not yet been fully told. Reading on in Hearne's narrative, we make a discovery, which we will ask our readers if it does not throw light on the Governor's despatch of the second expedition womenless. We find that our author, in a footnote, gives a sketch of the person and habits of the Governor of the Fort, which, though no doubt true, is too indelicate to transfer to our pages; and we wonder at Hearne's indiscretion in giving it publicity when he had just been making a case for his employers and their administration in the district. But for our discovery. The Governor, it seems, was an Indian, a native of the Fort, who had been educated in England. On his appointment to the Hudson Bay post, we learn that though an able and competent official, he lapsed into the practices of his ancestry. He had many wives. Of these he was jealous; and of other men's he was covetous. Need we make the deduction? Hearne's second expedition was sent off without women. After Metonabbee's explanation of its failure, not so was the third.

On the 7th of December, 1770, Hearne left Prince of Wales's Fort, at the mouth of the Churchill, on his third essay to reach the Copper Mines. The direction his party took was northwest by west, through thick scrubby woods, consisting chiefly of stunted pine, with dwarf juniper intermixed here and there, particularly round the margins of ponds and swamps, and dark willow bushes. Among the rocks and sides of the hills there were also clumps of poplar. So barren of animal life was the region that the party was frequently in great straits for food. Passing through this desolation, they found the country improve, and that deer was to be met with. By the end of the year they reached Island Lake, 102° west longitude from Greenwich, a march of 7° westward, and 2° to the north from the Fort.

At Island Lake, which is a rendezvous of the Northern Indians who trade with the Hudson Bay post on the Churchill, the party rested for a while, and took the opportunity to repair their snowshoes and sledges, in preparation for their long journey. The game of the region enabled them also to provide a bountiful stock of provisions. By the 21st of February, they reached Snowbird Lake, where they found plenty of deer, among which the Indians, with their usual improvidence, made great havoc and indulged in inordinate feasts. Feasting, however, was excusable, as the cold was intense. Several of the Indians, our author relates, were much frozen; but none of them more so than one of Matonabbee's wives, "whose thighs and buttocks were in a manner incrusted with frost; and when thawed, several blisters arose, nearly as large as a sheep's bladder." Hearne adds, that "the pain the poor woman suffered on this occasion was greatly aggravated by the laughter and jeering of her companions, who said that she was rightly served for belting her clothes so high. I must acknowledge that I was not of the number of those who pitied her, as I thought she took too much pains to show her garters, which, though by no means considered here as bordering on indecency, is by far too airy to withstand the rigorous cold of a severe winter in a high Northern latitude."

The attractions of the sex in the cold regions of the North are not many. The women, as a rule, are very masculine, and even when young are perfect 'antidotes to love and gallantry.' Their much out-door life, exposure to long and severe winters, hard labour in hauling heavy loads, and their nomadic habits, make early havoc of their beauty. In what their beauty consists, Hearne tells us; namely, "A broad, flat face; small eyes; high cheek-bones; three or four black lines across each cheek; a low forehead; a large, broad chin; a clumsy hook nose; and a tawny hide." These beauties, he adds, are greatly heightened, or at least rendered more valuable, when the possessor "is a good cook, is capable of dressing all kinds of skins, converting them into the different parts of their clothing, and able to carry eight or ten stone in summer, or haul a much greater weight in winter." Their wants are few, as are those of the tribe in general. Their whole aim is to secure a comfortable subsistence. Even in obtaining this they show little ambition. Were they to do so, they would only be unhappy; for those who exert themselves in gaining a more comfortable living, the more readily fall a prey to the strongest among the men, who afterwards make slaves of them. Among the men of this tribe it is the custom to wrestle for the women to whom they are attached, and, as a matter of course, the best athlete carries off the prize. Hearne tells us that:

"A weak man, unless he be a good hunter and well-beloved, is seldom permitted to keep a wife that a stronger man thinks worth his notice. . . . It was often unpleasant to me," he adds, "to see the object of the contest sitting in pensive silence watching her fate, while her husband and his rival were contending for the prize. I have indeed, not only felt pity for those poor wretched victims, but the utmost indignation when I have seen them won perhaps by a man whom they mortally hated. On those occasions their grief and reluctance to follow their new lord has been so great that the business has ended in the greatest brutality; for in this struggle, I have seen the poor girl stripped quite naked, and carried by main force to her new lodgings. At other times it was pleasant enough to see a fine girl led off the field from a husband she disliked, with a tear in one eye and a finger on the other: for custom, or delicacy if you please, has taught them to think it necessary to whimper a little, let the change be ever so much to their inclination."

In May, 1771, the expedition reached Lake Clowey, five degrees east of Lake Athabasca. From here, the route lay due North. While at Clowey, the party was joined by a number of neighbouring Indians, who accompanied Hearne on his expedition. Their reason for doing so transpired only on the way. It seems they had an old quarrel with the Esquimaux at the mouth of the Copper Mine River, and, without Hearne's knowledge, they had secured promise of assistance from the Indians belonging to the expedition, in avenging themselves on their enemies. Hearne's protests against this proceeding were unavailing; his entreaties were received with derision; and he was personally accused of cowardice. As his personal safety depended on the favourable opinion his followers entertained of him, he was reluctantly obliged to conceal his humanity, if not to manifest a bellicose tone and manner. As he tells us, he made no further attempt to turn the current of national prejudice.

On the first of June, the party rid itself of the women, children, dogs, heavy baggage, and other encumbrances, and with speed pursued the journey northward. By the end of the month, the lakes and rivers were free of ice, and they now made use of their canoes. Before the month was out, they reached the country of the Copper Indians; and here, by means of an interpreter, Hearne informed the natives of the objects of the expedition. The calumet was smoked with their chiefs, who declared themselves pleased with the visit and the prospect of trade with the white man. The pow-wow ended with the usual exchange of presents. Hearne remarks that though the Copper Indians "have some European commodities among them, which they purchase from the Northern Indians, the same articles from the hands of an Englishman were more prized. As I was the first whom they had ever seen, and in all probability might be the last, it was curious to see how they flocked about me, and expressed as much desire to examine me from top to toe as a European naturalist would a nondescript animal. They, however, found and pronounced me to be a perfect human being, except in the colour of my hair and eyes; the former, they said, was like the stained hair of a buffalo's tail, and the latter, being light, was like those of a gull. The whiteness of my skin also was, in their opinion, no ornament, as they said it resembled meat which had been sodden in water till all the blood was extracted. On the whole I was viewed as a great curiosity in this part of the world."

The month of July brought Hearne and his party to the upper portion of the Copper Mine River. Here, on its banks, they found the musk-ox, or moose, feeding; they also met with the ground squirrel, and got on the track of bears. Hearne proceeded with his survey. He had not gone far down the river before he was startled by the intelligence that the scouts of his party had come across a camp of Esquimaux. Instantly, the whole of his followers put on the war-paint. But we must leave Hearne to tell the story of what followed:—

"By the time the Indians had made themselves thus completely frightful," he writes, "it was near one o'clock in the morning of the seventeenth; when finding all the Esquimaux, whom they had now reached, quiet in their huts, they rushed

LOUIS RIEL,
From a Portrait of five years ago

from their ambuscade and fell on the poor unsuspecting creatures, unperceived, till close to the very eaves of their huts, when they soon began the bloody massacre, while I stood neuter in the rear.

"In a few seconds the horrible scene commenced; it was shocking beyond description; the poor, unhappy victims were surprised in the midst of their sleep, and had neither time nor power to make any resistance. Men, women, and children—in all upwards of twenty—ran out of their huts naked, and endeavoured to make their escape; but the Indians having possession of all the land side, to no place could they fly for shelter. One alternative only remained, that of jumping into the river; but, as none of them attempted it, they all fell a sacrifice to Indian barbarity.

"The shrieks and groans of the poor expiring wretches were dreadful; and my horror was much increased at seeing a young girl, seemingly about eighteen years of age, killed so near me, that when the first spear was stuck into her side she fell down at my feet and twisted round my legs, so that it was with difficulty I could disengage myself from her dying grasp. As two Indians pursued this unfortunate victim, I begged very hard for her life. The murderers made no reply till they had stuck both their spears through her body, and transfixed her to the ground. They then looked at me sternly in the face, and began to ridicule me, by asking if I wanted an Esquimaux wife; and paid not the smallest regard to the shrieks and agony of the poor wretch who was twisting round their spears like an eel. . . . My situation and the terror of my mind at beholding this butchery cannot easily be conceived, much less described. Even to this hour I never reflect on the transactions of that horrid day without shedding tears."

After this scene of wanton atrocity, Hearne's task in completing the survey of the river, and making an examination of the region, as may readily be imagined, was not a pleasant one. A neighbouring camp of Esquimaux, whose inmates had escaped, though they had heard of the massacre, kept Hearne's party on the *qui vive* for reprisals. None, however, was offered; and our traveller was enabled to reach the Arctic Sea and the mouth of the Copper Mine River in safety. Here, he tells us, he erected a mark, and took possession of the coast on behalf of the Hudson Bay Company. The appearance of the coast was desolate in the extreme. Landward, nothing was seen, save a few cranberry bushes, and a range of barren hills and marshes. Seaward, broken ice was still visible. In a ravine were a few miserable hovels, mostly underground, which had been deserted by some wandering family of Esquimaux. Strewn about was the *debris* of bones and scraps of skins; in some of the huts were stone kettles, horn dishes and spoons, and several hatchets, rudely headed with copper.

The animal life of the region consisted of mice, Alpine hares, wolverines, and ground-squirrels. Musk-oxen, bears, and deer, and a beautiful breed of dogs, with sharp, erect ears, pointed noses, and bushy tails, were also met with. About the shores were flocks of sea-fowl, comprising loons, geese, and Arctic gulls. On drifting hummocks of ice, seals were visible. Of the richness of the copper mines, Hearne, evidently, was not convinced. One piece of the ore, weighing over four pounds, he found tolerably pure and of good quality; but his search for the metal was on the whole indifferently rewarded. He appears to have contented himself, however, with a surface survey; and, probably from want of tools, made no excavations. Seemingly to justify his unsuccess in finding copper, Hearne, with no little simplicity, tells the following story, which he gathered from the Indians of the region:

"There is a strange tradition among those people, that the first person who discovered those mines was a woman, and that she conducted parties to the place for several years. On one occasion some of the men were rude to her, and she made a vow to be revenged on them. She is said to have been a great conjuror. Accordingly, when the men had loaded themselves with copper and were going to return, she refused to accompany them, saying that she would sit on the mine till she sunk into the ground, and that the copper would sink with her. The next year, when the men went for more copper, they found her sunk up to the waist, though still alive, and the quantity of copper much decreased. On their repeating their visit the following year, she had quite disappeared, and all the principal part of the mine with her; so that after a period nothing remained on the surface but a few small pieces, and these were scattered at a considerable distance from each other. Before that period, they say the copper lay on the surface in such large heaps that the Indians had nothing to do but turn it over and pick such pieces as would best suit the different uses for which they intended it."

Hearne, by this time, made all haste out of the country inhabited by the Copper and the Dog-rib Indians. With his followers, the Northern Indians, he set out for the south, hoping to be able to make a detour westward, to Lake Athabasca, before returning to the shores of Hudson Bay. He had no motive for lingering in the scenes of his discovery. The country he found disappointing: it was poorly settled; and any trade to be done with the native tribes he was willing should be done through the medium of the Northern Indians. This tribe, after Hearne's visit, he tells us, fell a prey to smallpox, contracted through contact with the Athabascas of the south; while the once powerful race of the Dog-rib Indians sank back into barbarism.

By the end of July, Hearne's party rejoined the women of the tribe, whom they had left behind when on their way down the Copper Mine River. It was January of the following year before they arrived at Lake Athabasca, and the end of June (1772), ere Hearne reached Prince of Wales's Fort. The incidents of the return journey are few, and need not detain us. It was a long and toilsome undertaking; how long and toilsome one fails to realize by the mere reading of Hearne's narrative. To gain any adequate conception of the extent of this journey, one should have at hand a large English chart or

Survey map, when the distance will begin to dawn upon one as the numerous meridional lines, in tracking the route of our adventurous explorer, are crossed. The time consumed in the expeditions was two years, seven months, and twenty-four days. On his march southward, Hearne seems not to have heard anything of Great Slave Lake, the eastern flank of which he must have passed close by on his way to the Athabasca. Of the latter lake and surrounding country, not very much is yet known, for the district is beyond hope of any likely settlement from the North-West. On Hearne's visit to the Lake, now over a hundred years ago, he found it stocked with quantities of fish, and numerous herds of deer were grazing on its banks. The lake was full of islands, most of which our author found clothed with fine tall poplars, birch, and pines. The pictorial representation of the lake, which appears in his book, except for the absence of life, would indicate the presence of the landscape gardener. Nature's solitudes are not so tidy and prim as his engraving represents them.

Only one other incident in this remarkable journey must we take up space to recount. About the middle of January, the author relates, as some of his companions were hunting, they saw the track of a strange snow-shoe, which they followed; and at a considerable distance came to a little hut, where they discovered a young woman sitting alone. As they found that she understood their language, they brought her with them to the tents. On examination, she proved to be one of the Western Dog-rib Indians, who had been taken prisoner by the Athabasca Indians two summers before. In the following summer, when the Indians who took her prisoner were near this region, she had eloped from them, with the intent of returning to her own country. The distance, however, was great; and, having come there by a tortuous canoe voyage, she could not discover the track, and despaired of ever finding her way out. So she built the hut in which she was found, and here she had resided since the first setting in of the Fall.

"From her account of the moons past since her elopement," Hearne states, "it appeared that she had been nearly seven months without seeing a human face; during all which time, she had supported herself by snaring partridges, rabbits, and squirrels. She had also killed two or three beaver and some porcupine. That she did not seem to be in want, is evident, as she had a small stock of provisions by her when she was discovered; she was in good health and condition, and I think one of the finest women, of a real Indian, that I have seen in any part of North America.

"The methods practised by this poor creature to procure a livelihood were truly astonishing, and are great proofs that necessity is the real mother of invention. When the few deer-sinews that she had an opportunity of taking with her were expended in making snares, and in making her clothing, she had nothing to supply their place but the sinews of the rabbits' legs and feet; these she twisted together for that purpose with great dexterity and success. What she caught in these snares not only furnished her with a comfortable subsistence, but, with their skins, she was enabled to make herself suits of neat and warm clothing for the winter. It is scarcely possible to conceive that a person in her forlorn situation could be so composed as to be capable of contriving, or executing, anything that was not absolutely necessary to her existence. But there was sufficient proof that she had extended her care much further, as all her clothing, besides being calculated for real service, showed great taste, and exhibited no little variety of ornament. The materials, though rude, were very curiously wrought, and so judiciously placed as to make the whole of her garb have a very pleasing, though rather romantic, appearance.

"Her leisure hours from hunting had been employed in twisting the inner rind, or bark of willows, into small lines, like net-wire, of which she had some hundred fathoms by her; with this she intended to make a fishing-net, as soon as the spring advanced. Five or six inches of an iron hoop, made into a knife, and the shank of an arrow-head of iron, which served her as an awl, were all the metals this poor woman had with her when she eloped; and, with these implements, she had made herself complete snowshoes, and several other useful articles. Her method of making a fire was equally singular and curious: having no other materials for that purpose than two hard sulphurous stones, these, by long friction and hard knocking, produced a few sparks, which at length communicated to some touchwood; but as this method was attended with great trouble, and not always with success, she did not suffer the fire to go out all winter. The singularity of the circumstance, and the comeliness of her person, and her approved accomplishment, occasioned a strong contest between several of the Indians of my party, who should have her for wife; and the poor girl was actually won and lost at wrestling by near half a score of different men the same evening."

Let us hope that the wilderness joust furnished this exemplary maiden with a chivalrous knight for husband. On the 16th of January, Hearne's party crossed the Athabasca River, which flowed into the southern side of the lake; and from this point they headed for the east, taking advantage, as much as possible, of the ice in the lakes to facilitate travel. Soon they left the level country of the Athabasca region, and approached the Stoney Mountains, which bound the northern Indian country. With May, the annual thaw set in, and travelling became bad. But with Spring came the water-fowl and a change of diet; and the party made continuous and sometimes merry progress. The remainder of Hearne's narrative is taken up with extended discussions on natural history, and with accounts of the Indian tribes. Into these we shall not follow him, but dismiss his interesting work with the announcement of his safe arrival at the Hudson Bay Factory, at the end of June, 1772.

CHAPTER V.

EARLY DISCOVERERS OF THE NORTH-WEST.

Sir Alexander Mackenzie.

E now come to the other important publication of the period, Alexander Mackenzie's Journal of his Voyage through the North-West Continent of America. This interesting work, which appeared in London, in 1801, contains the record of two journeys undertaken by this able and enterprising representative of the North-West Fur Company, in the years 1789 and 1793. The first of these journeys deals with the river which bears his name, and which was traced from its source, in Great Slave Lake, to the Arctic Sea. The second consists of his diary while exploring the Peace River, from the Lake of the Hills, through the Rocky Mountains to the waters of the Pacific. Prefixed to these narratives is a description of the route and the characteristics of the Canadian Fur Trade, from Montreal, via the Ottawa and the upper shores of Lake Superior, across the Continent, to the Canading trading-post, Fort Chipewyan, on the Lake of the Hills. The situation of the latter, which for some years was Mackenzie's headquarters, may be roughly located, as in latitude 58° North, and longitude 110° West (of Greenwich). It lies immediately south of Great Slave Lake, with which it is connected by the Slave River. The Elk, or Athabasca, River flows into it on the south; and, at its eastern end, the Peace River joins its waters.

Almost the whole of the route, from Montreal to this distant post on the Lake of the Hills, can be followed by water, though it is broken by innumerable and toilsome portages. Mackenzie's introductory chapter will still be found a lucid and accurate guide over this great stretch of country, a valuable record of the Indian tribes met with *en route*, and an instructive history of the growth and development of the Canadian fur-trade. At its outset, Mackenzie has something to say of the native forester, the *coureur des bois*, and the habits which the European acquired from him, of a free, but far from correct manner of living in the woods. The influence of the early French missionaries, if it was ever practically operative on the Indian tribes, in Mackenzie's day had long lost its savour. Any restraint upon lawlessness, in his time, was exercised, not through the missions, which had languished or by stake and torch had been hastened to a close, but through the military and trading-posts that had taken their place. The initial work of the missionaries, however, was done: they were the *avant-couriers* of civilisation in Canada; and however few the converts they made to their faith, they glorified it through weariful years of toil and bloodshed, and to-day the Canadian people reap the priceless benefit. Nor must it be forgotten in speaking, as Mackenzie does, of the merely transient influence of the Church in the Wilderness, that this is due less to the failure of the work of the missionaries than to the pernicious example set before the Indians by the lay European. It may be true, what Mackenzie says, that greater results would have followed evangelisation, had the missionaries first taught the Indians how to surround themselves with the comforts of civilisation; but perhaps a more important truth lies back of that, in the step which should have preceded it, namely, to have kept their countrymen out of the wilderness until they themselves were Christianised. Having made these strictures upon this portion of Mackenzie's narrative, it is only justice to let our author himself be heard. Here is the passage which arrested us:

'As for the missionaries, if sufferings and hardships in the prosecution of the great work which they had undertaken deserve applause and admiration, they had an undoubted claim to be admired and applauded; they spared no labour, and avoided no danger, in the execution of their important office; and it is to be seriously lamented that their pious endeavours did not meet with the success which they deserved; for there is hardly a trace to be found, beyond the cultivated parts, of their meritorious functions.

"The cause of this failure must be attributed to a want of due consideration in the mode employed by the missionaries to propagate the religion of which they were the zealous ministers. They habituated themselves to the savage life, and naturalised themselves to the savage manners, and, by thus becoming dependent, as it were, on the natives, they acquired their contempt rather than their veneration. If they had been as well acquainted with human nature as they were with the articles of faith, they would have known that the uncultivated mind of an Indian must be disposed by much preparatory method and instruction to receive the revealed truths of Christianity, to act under its sanctions, and be impelled to good by the hope of its reward, or turned from evil by the fear of its punishment. They should have begun their work by teaching some of those useful arts which are the inlets of knowledge and lead the mind by degrees to objects of higher comprehension. Agriculture, so formed to fix and combine society, and so preparatory to objects of superior consideration, should have been the first thing introduced among a savage people; it attaches the wandering tribe to that spot where it adds so much to their comforts; while it gives them a sense of property and of lasting possession, instead of the uncertain hopes of the chase and the fugitive produce of uncultivated wilds."

Our author, before delivering himself of this judgment, had better have enlarged his reading on the subject of French missionary enterprise in the wilds of Canada. Had he considered what had been the experience of the Church previous to his own day, or could he have known what has been the experience of Government farm instructors since, he would have been slow to hazard an opinion on so knotty a problem as the civilisation of the Indian. He forgets, moreover, that a common necessity, and often a common peril, herded missionaries and Indians together, in constant fear from the hereditary foes of each, with few opportunities to sow fields, and fewer still to reap them. Querulousness is free to say, of course, that "the missionary habituated himself to the savage life;" but querulousness does not say how else he could have subsisted. It may have been a mistake to have sent the missionary first, and the squatter and politician land-agent afterwards; but had the process been reversed, we fear, there would have been little, if any, need to send the missionary.

On his own field, Mackenzie is strong. He knows the fur-trade; and he had exceptional opportunities of becoming acquainted with the country. We have previously observed that, after the Conquest, many Canadians withdrew their trading operations from the West. The war unsettled the whole land. It brought together, in mortal combat, the two great European nations that had long striven for dominion on the continent of the New World. To the north of the lakes, war threw the Indians into the French camp, and infected them, far and wide, with a bitter hostility to the English. The loss of Canada to France did little to soften the feeling of antipathy. Despite this feeling, the great English Fur Company on the shores of Hudson Bay thought the time favourable to extend its trade to the south. It did so; but for a time it was at great disadvantage. In coming inland, it had a difficult road to get over, and a long and toilsome transport. The risks were many; for the country was unknown and trade unsettled. Moreover, its agents knew little of the people, and less of their language. With Canada, the case was different. In resuming her commerce in the woods, she walked in her old paths. After the war the people took heart, and the pulse of trade again began to beat. Once more Lachine was gay with the throng of departing *voyageurs*. The little chapel at Ste Anne's heard again the *Pater Nosters* of the kneeling boatmen, or the heart-flutterings of his deserted sweetheart. The rugged *coureur des bois* toiled once more across the portages of the dark Ottawa, lightly skimmed his canoe over the gleaming water-sketches of Lake Nipissing, and stoutly stemmed the rapids of the Sault and the Kaministiquia. Camp fires were lit, as of yore, on the banks of the Lake of the Woods; and sturgeon were speared through the ice of the distant Saskatchewan. Canadian trade was again in full blast.

Just before Mackenzie's advent, a number of traders had gone to the Far West. Among the number was the Englishman, Henry, and the brothers, Frobisher. Pond, from Boston, and his victim, the Swiss Wadin, were also in the territories. About this time the North-West Fur Company was founded, with the Frobishers' and Simon M'Tavish at its head. Mackenzie tell us, that at this period he had spent five years in the counting-house of a Mr. Gregory, a Montreal merchant. In 1784, he left that employment, with a small adventure of his own in trade, and set out for Detroit. Here he was followed by one of his late principals, who proposed to him a journey to the Indian country, to be undertaken next summer. This he agreed to; and proceeding to the fair meadows of the Grand Portage, he formally entered the service of the North-West Fur Company. From its post on the Rainy River, Mackenzie set out for Fort Chipewyan, on the "Lake of the Hills," or as it is now known, Lake Athabasca. Two months afterwards he arrived at the post. Here, for eight years, was his headquarters; and from here he started on his two celebrated voyages. The post received its name from the Chipewyans, a tribe of Indians, whose principal lodges lay in the district, and who, in Mackenzie's day, were a numerous people. Their territories extended from the Churchill, in the east, to the Columbia River, in the west. The origin of the tribe, like that of the aborigines of the whole country, can only be conjectured. Like other members of the Algonquin family, they are very superstitious. Mackenzie tells us that they have a tradition amongst them, that:

"They originally came from another country, inhabited by a wicked people, and had traversed a great lake, which was narrow, shallow, and full of islands, where they suffered great misery, it being always winter, with ice and deep snow. They believe, also, that in ancient times their ancestors lived till their feet were worn out with walking, and their throats with eating. They describe a deluge, when the waters spread over the whole earth, except the highest mountains, on the tops of which they preserved themselves.

"They believe that immediately after death they pass into another world, where they arrive at a large river, on which they embark on a stone canoe, and that a gentle current bears them on to an extensive lake, in the centre of which is a beautiful island; and that, in the view of this delightful abode, they receive that judgment for their conduct during life which determinates their final state and unalterable allotment. If their good actions are declared to predominate, they are landed upon the island, where there is to be no end to their happiness; which, however, according to their notions, consists in an eternal enjoyment of sensual pleasure and gratification. But if their bad actions weigh down the balance, the stone canoe sinks at once, and leaves them up to their chins in the water, to behold and regret the reward enjoyed by the good, and eternally struggling, but with unavailing endeavours, to reach the blissful island, from which they are excluded for ever."

While an inmate of Fort Chipewyan, Mackenzie was ever haunted by projects of discovery. He was a born traveller, capable in command, full of resource, able to withstand the toil of arduous undertakings, and anxious, as we learn from his work, to extend the boundaries of geographical science, and add new countries to the realms of commerce. Such a task as he proposed to himself, to trace the water-ways from Lake Athabasca to the Frozen Ocean, was both laborious and hazardous. Never before had the waters of the region borne any other craft than the canoe of the savage; nor had the report of a firelock ever disturbed its solitudes or rang through its wastes. It was known that from Great Slave Lake a great water flowed out towards the mountains that hem in the vast plains; but whither, and through what devious paths it led, no man knew. Mackenzie set himself to solve the problem. In solving it he gave his name to the river.

On the 3rd of June, 1789, Mackenzie set out on his voyage of discovery. His party consisted of four Canadians, two of whom were attended by their wives, and a German. For guide and interpreter, he took with him an Indian, who had accompanied Hearne in his journey to the Copper Mine River. Two wives of the guide, and two young Indians, were also of the party. A convoy from the Fort accompanied the expedition until it was well under way. At the outset there occurred the usual defection from the ranks, owing to some of the party losing heart in presence of the difficulties of the undertaking. This defection was soon, however, though only in part, made good. After our travellers had been out some ten days, they came to rapids and other obstructions to navigation on the river, which entailed considerable and toilsome portaging. At the end of the portage, the expedition made a lengthened halt to recruit strength, overhaul the supplies for the voyage, and repair their canoes. While in camp, a section of the party added to the stores the product of a good day's hunt. This consisted of moose, buffalo, and beaver, with a basketful of carp, trout, and *poisson inconnu.*

Proceeding on the journey, the party passed by the lodges of some of the Red-Knife Indians, one of whom they took for a guide, but who was not long in losing his course on the lake portions of the river. It turned out that he had travelled no great distance down its waters. As they were now in sight of the Rocky Mountains, they speedily recovered their course; and, being favoured with a good wind, to catch which they rigged a light sail, they got well again on the way. About the middle of July they reached the encampment of some families of the Slave and the Dog-rib Indians. So novel a sight to them were Europeans that they fled at their appearing. Recovering from their alarm, and being attracted by trinkets held out for their acceptance, they suffered themselves to be approached. On seeking information from them respecting the river, Mackenzie could only extract from them the fabulous. They earnestly dissuaded him from pursuing his voyage, saying, that it would require several winters to get to the sea, that the party would encounter monsters of horrid shape and destructive power on their way, and that old age would certainly come upon ere they could possibly return. The effect of these fables was to discompose for a time the minds of

Mackenzie's Indian employés, who had already tired of the voyage. They had themselves gathered more exaggerated stories than had come to their leader's ears; and it was with difficulty he could persuade them of their absurdity, and reasure them that no mishap would befall them. Their greatest dread was that they would find few animals in the country beyond them, and that, as they proceeded, the scarcity would increase, and all would perish from want. By dint of bribery, and the exercise of some little tact, Mackenzie was fortunate, however, to induce one of the Indians of the region to join the party, and this allayed the fears of his nervous following. The Indians of this encampment were fancifully dressed. "Their ornaments," our traveller relates, "consists of gorgets; bracelets for the arms and wrists, made of wood, horn, or bone; garters; and a kind of band to go round the head, composed of strips of leather, embroidered with porcupine quills, stuck round with the claws of bears or wildfowl inverted, to which are suspended a few short thongs of the skin of an animal that resembles the ermine, in the form of a tassel. Their cinctures and garters are formed of porcupine quills woven with sinews, in a style of peculiar skill and neatness."

As the expedition proceeded down the river its current quickened, and, though it was only the middle of July, the temperature rapidly fell. Camping on its banks one night, Mackenzie noticed the water rise and flow visibly towards his tent. In the morning it had receded. This was a clear indication of approach to the sea. There were also solar indications of a high latitude. Some pages later on in the narrative we find the following:

"I sat up all night to observe the sun. At half-past twelve I called up one of the men to view a spectacle which he had never before seen. On seeing the sun so high, he thought it was a signal to embark, and began to call the rest of his companions, who would scarcely be persuaded by me that the sun had not descended nearer to the horizon, and that it was now but a short time past midnight."

A few voyages further on, the river perceptibly widened, now expanding into an estuary, with numerous islands within its embrace, and anon, contracting its banks. The cold became more intense; and the animal life changed. Presently, a wandering family of Esquimaux was sighted; and with difficulty the interpreter made out that our *voyageurs* had reached the sea, and that a few more camps would close it against them. Continuing their passage a day or two further, they found the river full of broken ice, with whales disporting in the clear water, and traces visible of the Polar bear and the Arctic fox. Seaward, a heavy fog rested on the waters and concealed the view. Setting sail in the larger canoe, Mackenzie visited many of the islands of the region, in the hope of meeting other parties of Esquimaux, from whom he might learn something of the unknown beyond. His search was unrewarded, and the party prepared to return.

Retracing their course, a few camps back, the expedition came upon a lodge of Northern Indians. From them they learned that a strong party of Esquimaux occasionally ascended the river in large canoes in search of flint stones, which they make use of to point their spears and arrows. They told Mackenzie that the Esquimaux were now at a lake due east from the spot where he was now encamped, and that they were there killing reindeer, and would soon begin "to catch big fish for the winter stock." They also informed our traveller that the Esquimaux had reported their seeing, some winters ago, a number of large canoes full of white men far to the westward, in a lake which they called "White Man's Lake." It was difficult, they said however, to reach the lake, for when the ice breaks up, it soon freezes again. This was the extent of the information Mackenzie could glean with reference to an open sea and a North-West passage to the Pacific. He pursued his return journey. Nothing of note happened on the homeward voyage, save a repetition of the incidents that marked the passage of the expedition outwards—the consternation of Indian tribes that had never seen a white man. With one consent they fled at his approach. In August, our travellers had returned to a region where it was sufficiently dark at night to render the stars visible. By the middle of September they had completed their journey.

Three years after Mackenzie returned from his thousand-mile voyage on the great river that was henceforth to bear his name, he undertook a second voyage, with a view to trace the course of the Peace River and its affluents, and to endeavour, if possible, to find a passage by its waters to the Pacific Ocean. This new voyage was a much more serious undertaking than the former one. In the Mackenzie River he had a noble stream that drained a vast territory, a stream that presented few obstacles to the *voyageur*, its early course being facilitated by a succession of almost unbroken lacustrian pathways. In his new journey, though the region presented a like terraqeous aspect, the difficulties of navigation were tenfold what he had experienced on his first voyage. The Peace River, which drains into Lake Athabasca, has its source in the Rocky Mountains, the brooding cliffs and gigantic firs of which frown all along its course, and frequently throw themselves into its waters to fret and obstruct their passage.

In October, 1792, Mackenzie journeyed to a western post of the Company, some distance from Fort Chipewyan, there to spend the winter and make preparations for the outfit of his expedition in the following spring. In May, 1793, he and his party left the post and launched their canoes on the river. Passing the confluence of the Bear River, the course of the Peace River for a time took our travellers south-west; but they had not gone far until a succession of rapids and cascades compelled them to leave its course and portage for a considerable distance. Returning to the river, Mackenzie relates that: "We now continued our toilsome and perilous progress west by north; and as we proceeded the rapidity of the current increased, so that in the distance of two miles we were obliged to unload four times, and carry everything but the canoe; indeed, in many places, it was with the utmost difficulty that we could prevent her being dashed to pieces against the rocks by the violence of the eddies. At five o'clock we had proceeded to where the river was one continuous rapid. Here we again took everything out of the canoe, in order to tow her up with the line, though the rocks were so shelving as greatly to increase the toil and hazard of that operation. At length, however, the agitation of the water was so great, that a wave striking the bow of the canoe broke the line, and filled us with incredible dismay, as it appeared impossible that the vessel could escape from being dashed to pieces, and those who were in her from perishing. Another wave, however, more propitious than the former, drove her out of the tumbling water, so that the men were able to bring her ashore, and though she had been carried over rocks by the swells which left them a moment naked after, the canoe had received no material injury. The men were, however, in such a state from their late alarm that it would not only have been unavailing but imprudent to have proposed any further progress at present, particularly as the river above us, as far as we could see, was one white sheet of foaming water."

Proceeding on foot some distance through the woods, Mackenzie could see no end to the rapids, and he returned from his reconnoitring excursion tired out in body and in spirit. Next day he despatched several of the Indians to the summit of the hills in the neighbourhood, with instructions to force a way northward, keeping the river in sight, and to advise him when they saw smooth water. After a time they returned with a favourable report. Another party of Indians was now instructed to cut a path through the woods, for the transfer of the canoes and the baggage. This toilsome work accomplished, they proceeded on the voyage, at every new turn of the river great hills and defiles revealing their menacing fronts as they passed by. Each day's journey added new terrors to the way. Huge precipices rose sheer up from the water, and lofty snow-capped peaks gleamed down the ravine upon them as they poled their fatiguing course up the torrent. Suddenly the river would utterly change its appearance, the waters breaking away from the beetling crags that frowned upon it, and for a time, quietly meandering over brief stretches of placid meadow. As suddenly would it dash in again on the flanks of the mountain, and burrow hiding-places in gloomy caverns, or impetuously cleave a channel for itself under clammy over-hanging cliffs. On the banks of the river Nature presented itself in like varying moods. Towards the bottom of the heights, which were clear of snow, the trees might be seen putting forth their leaves, while those in the middle and upper parts still retained all the characteristics of winter. Another day's advance was made, but only to meet with new discouragements and more formidable difficulties.

Presently, the expedition was forced to face a new problem From the melting of the snow, the river became too swollen to enable the canoes to live in the current. It also overflowed its banks; and it was found impossible to keep in the channel. For some weeks the party made what advance they could, proceeding alternately along its banks and in the stream. The prospect finally became too discouraging. Now, however, they fell in with some natives of the district, who for a time conducted them on another branch of the river; until it, too, became unnavigable. The Indians here suggested an ascent of the mountains, and a tramp through its defiles to the sea. This bold project Mackenzie was ready to carry out. "In the present state of my information," he narrates, "to proceed further up the river was considered a fruitless waste of toilsome exertion; and to return unsuccessful, after all our labour, sufferings, and hunger, was an idea too painful to indulge." After mature consideration, he determined to be the first white man to cross the Rockies to the Pacific.

Coming to this conclusion, the party proceeded to "cache" the larger canoe, and the stores they were not likely to want until their return. Making their burdens as light as possible, they began the ascent of the mountains, and by relays of guides, they were able to make satisfactory though wearisome progress.

"We carried on our backs," writes Mackenzie, "four bags and a half of pemmican, weighing about eighty-five pounds each; a case with my instruments, a parcel of goods for presents, weighing ninety pounds, and a parcel containing ammunition of the same weight. Each of the Canadians had a burden of ninety pounds, with a gun and some ammunition. The Indians had about forty-five pound weight of pemmican to carry, beside their guns, &c., with which they were very much dissatisfied, and if they had dared would have instantly left us. . . . In this state of equipment we began our journey, the commencement of which was a steep ascent of about a mile; it lay along a well-beaten path, but the country through which it led was rugged and ridgy and full of wood. When we were in a state of extreme heat, from the toil of our journey, the rain came on and continued till the evening, and even when it ceased the underwood continued its drippings upon us."

It would weary the reader to record even a tithe of the details of this painful journey. Day followed day, with the same tale of weariful plodding, through deep canyons, over mammoth fallen timber, and across shoulders of the mountains—one hope sustaining the party, that the furthest ridge would be reached and the curtains roll up and disclose the sea. At length this cheer was theirs. "They came to a hill," writes Mackenzie, "the descent of which was more steep than its ascent, and was succeeded by another, whose top, though not so elevated as the last, afforded a view of the range of mountains, covered with snow, which, according to the intelligence of our guide, terminates in the ocean." As they neared this range, the mountains seemed to recede, as if in mockery of their anxious longings. Finally the goal is reached. By a rapid descent, they get down to a lower elevation, and reach a stream on which they were able to launch their canoes and transfer their burdens to the river. Through further vicissitude and many days' toil, the expedition is at last rewarded by a sight of the coast. It is reached at a meridian which Mackenzie registers as 52° 21' 33", a little to the north of Queen Charlotte Sound.* Here, as our traveller relates he mixes some vermilion in melted grease, and with it inscribes on a rock on the coast this legend: "*Alexander Mackenzie, from Canada, by land, the twenty-second of July, one thousand seven hundred and ninety-three!*"

This feat of Mackenzie and his party, in crossing the Rocky Mountains at that early period, deserves high praise. It may be that the route which he took from the Peace River, across the "Mountains of the Sea," and what is now known as British Columbia, does not present the obstacles to be met with in the passes in the higher elevations to the south. But that it was a toilsome and daring venture, no one can prudently deny. The route he followed, we judge, must been either the

---

* Later research has enabled the writer to state more definitely the region where Mackenzie reached the waters of the Pacific. It appears he approached the coast by the Bella Coola River and North Bentinck arm, thence down Burke Channel to the Sea. Turning North-Westward, he subsequently entered Dean Channel, and ascended Cascade Inlet, to the rock on which he painted his inscription and where he took his observations.

Pine River or the Peace River Pass; and the great river he speaks of sailing down after crossing the mountains, no doubt, was the Fraser. Leaving that stream about the region of Lake Quesnel, and following westward the course of the Salmon River, he would reach the sea in the neighbourhood of Dean Channel, in an alignment with the southern point of Queen Charlotte Islands, or about the latitude indicated in the text. At the coast, Mackenzie met with Indians who had previously seen and traded with the white man. The previous year, Captain Vancouver, a Dutch navigator of the Royal Navy, had cruised round the Island, surveyed its deeply fissured coasts, and claimed it for the British Crown. Fourteen years earlier, Captain Cook had coasted all along the Northern Pacific; while in the interval a British colony had planted itself on the shores of Nootka Sound, which was the occasion of historic trouble with the Court of Spain.

Mackenzie's return voyage was exceedingly tedious. The party was short of provisions; the guide decamped, taking the canoe with him; and many of the natives were hostile. As the season was now the end of July, the weather was warm and genial; and this in some degree ameliorated the condition of the party. In the sad plight they were in, Mackenzie had time to note the beauty of the natural surroundings. Here is a description of a scene on his return journey:

"It was now one in the afternoon, and we had to ascend the summit of the first mountain before night came on, in order to look for water. The fatigue of ascending these precipices I shall not attempt to describe. It was past five when we arrived at a spot where we could get water, and in such an extremity of weariness, that it was with great pain any of us could crawl about to gather wood for the necessary purpose of making a fire. But it was not possible to be in this situation without contemplating the wonders of it. Such was the depth of the precipices below, and the height of the mountains above, with the rude and wild magnificence of the scenery around, that I shall not attempt to describe such an astonishing and awful combination of objects, of which, indeed, no description can convey an adequate idea. Even at this place, which is only, as it were, the first step towards gaining the summit of the mountains, the climate was very sensibly changed. The air that fanned the village, which we left at noon, was mild and cheering; the grass was verdant; and the wild fruits ripe around it. But here the snow was not yet dissolved, the ground was still bound by the frost, the herbage had scarce begun to spring, and the berry bushes were just beginning to blossom."

Mackenzie followed the path by which he had come to the sea. In time the expedition got over the mountains, and, recovering the canoe and the provisions they had concealed on the Peace River, they made rapid progress homeward. The water of the river was much lower than on the upward voyage, though the portaging was still frequent and wearisome. Salmon were plentiful and the whortleberries ripe. But for heavy rains the condition of the returning *voyageurs* would have been pleasant and happy. On leaving the mountains, the rains however ceased; and for the rest of the voyage they had the rich valleys of the Peace River, which lie within the Fertile Belt to journey through, and to invigorate both mind and body. " Each day," says our traveller, " we were on the water before daylight; and when the sun rose a beautiful country appeared around us, enriched and animated by large herds of wild cattle. . . . . As we approached Fort Chipewyan, the country increased in beauty, though the cattle appeared proportionately to diminish. At length, as we rounded the point and came in view of the Fort, we threw out our flag, and accompanied it with a general discharge of our firearms; while the men were in such spirits and made such an active use of their paddles, that we arrived before the two men whom we left here in the spring, could recover their senses to answer us. Here, on the 24th of August, 1793, my voyages of discovery terminate. Their toils and their dangers, their solicitudes and sufferings, have not been exaggerated in my description. On the contrary, in many instances, language has failed me in the attempt to describe them. I received, however, the reward of my labours, for they were crowned with success."

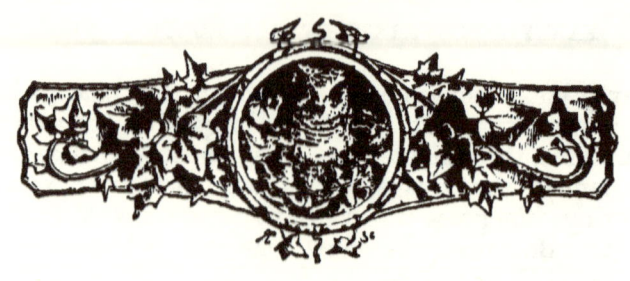

CHAPTER VI.

THE SELKIRK SETTLEMENT AND ITS FATE.

FEW records of colonial settlement are more sad than those of the community that strove to root itself, early in the century, in the soil of the Red River. Sorely tried as the Scot has ever been, seldom has it been his lot to suffer so keenly. In the year 1811, a small band of Scottish Highlanders, with a sprinkling of Celts from the west of Ireland, landed at York Factory, and after a winter spent on the Nelson River, proceeded to settle on the virgin prairies of the Canadian North-West. Cheerless as was their surroundings on the bleak moorlands of the Old World they had left, more cheerless still was their introduction to the wild wastes of the New. When they came inland from the forbidding shores of Hudson Bay, to the banks of the Red River, they found that the heart of the continent did not warm to them. It gave them no welcome. Tear-dimmed eyes had watched their departing forms, as the vessel bore them from the home of their fathers; but knit brows scowled upon them as they set down their household gods to domicile themselves in a land which they now looked upon as the heritage of their children. What a step-mother the country was to be to them and theirs, it was not long ere they unhappily found out.

We have already seen that the North-West Fur Company was in occupancy of the region to which the colony had emigrated, and that the title to possession of its rival, the Hudson Bay Company, was held in light esteem by it and its employés. But the Nor'-Westers themselves had acquired no proprietary interests in the soil : they were merely traders, doing business in the territory, and had no pretext to dispossess even the wandering Indian of his hereditary claim to the land. The Selkirk settlers were there not only by right of purchase from the Hudson Bay Company, whose title to possession, however imperfect it was, was certainly better than that of the Nor'-Westers; but they were there after the Indian title had been quieted for a consideration paid them by the founder of the colony. The claim of the colony to possession was thus doubly valid. But however valid it might be, it did not suit the Nor'-Westers to have their hunting-grounds encroached upon by a people whose pursuits would prove disastrous to the interests which, as a trading corporation, they wished to conserve. It still less suited this Canadian Company to have a settlement grow up in the midst of its trade, by right of purchase from an organisation whose claims to possession it ignored, and which had been founded under the direct auspices of a powerful, and now likely to be actively aggressive, rival. In this latter circumstance is the gravamen of the matter. It was unfortunate that the colony came upon the scene at the time and in the manner it did. It was unfortunate even in the route by which it came to the country. All the circumstances attending its arrival at Red River were construed as a menace to the rival traders. First of all, the colony was unwelcome because it was an undesirable intrusion upon lands which both Companies were interested in preserving for the purposes of the fur-trade. Secondly, it was unwelcome, because it had come to the country directly from the headquarters, the trading-posts, of its rivals. And, thirdly, it was unwelcome, because it had acquired the right to its location from a Company whose territorial claims were strenuously opposed by an organisation that had long been in occupancy. For these several reasons, the North-West Fur Company and its people, from the first, manifested hostility to the intruders, and looked sullenly upon the arrival of each instalment of the colonists. How this aversion afterwards found expression in overt acts of hostile intent, and finally, ended in foul murder and ruthless expatriation, we shall soon discover. Meantime, let us see who were these people that had taken up their abode in the solitudes of the Far West, and who was the promoter of the scheme under which the colony came to settle.

After the Rebellion of 1745, a change came over the national and social condition of the Scottish Highlands. The heavy hand of power that then fell upon romantic Caledonia broke up the clans and severed many of the links that bound the Gael to his chieftain. With the snapping of these links were also severed the patriarchal relations the head of the clan held with his following. England's foreign wars, no less than the suppression of Jacobinism, broke up the feudal system, and drew the Highlander from his glens and straths to dye Continental battle-grounds with his life-blood. This break-up of the old order of things entailed great suffering upon the faithful clansmen of stern Caledonia. They were now as sheep without a shepherd. From being sturdy, well-fed retainers, and liegemen of the chiefs of their ancestral houses, they became cottars and crofters, holders of small farms, from which they strove to wrest a poor and often precarious subsistence. Later on, the well-to-do, and moneyed, lowland farmer came in among them and outbid them for their holdings, while the southern magnate began to buy up their ancestral acres, to turn them into game-preserves and mammoth sheep pastures. For long it went hard with the poor Highlander. There was a time when

> " — the fish of the lake, and the deer of the vale,
> Were less free to Lord Dacre than Allan-a-dale ; "

but that time was not now. In this period of transition the noble endurance and many sterling qualities of the Scottish Celt were manifested in full and heroic force. The drain of absenteeism went on, and the poor Highlander, in his struggle with the hard conditions of his lot, daily became poorer. But, unlike the Irish Celt, upon whom governments ever lavished their consideration and bounty, the Scottish Celt never shewed the world that he had a grievance. Nor did he manifest his distress in petulance and crime.

It has been remarked, that the Scot rarely complains that the world he has been brought into is too stern for his temper. The little world of Celtic Scotland, at the beginning of the century, was, however, a hard foster-father to the poor cottar, who was struggling for existence by the firths and estuaries of Northern Britain. Self-reliant as he was by nature, if he could not extract a living in the scenes of his birth, he was determined that he would not stay there to disgrace himself and his country by becoming a pauper. In other climes he would find that subsistence which his own had denied him. Deeply attached to the land of his fathers, the spirit of his fathers was in his breast, and in other lands he would achieve success and make a fairer home for his children. Emigration was the stern but accepted remedy.

Just at this time, there comes upon the scene a philanthropic Scottish nobleman, some thirty years of age, " full six feet high," with a kindly heart and pleasant countenance. His name is Thomas Douglas, and his title, fifth Earl of Selkirk, Baron Daer and Shortcleugh. He it was who was to become the Moses of the Scottish Exodus. On the family escutcheon were the arms of the Douglasses of Marr, and in the traditions of the house the record of their noble deeds. But knightly service was to take a new form: this scion of the twin-houses of Douglas and Angus was now to lead, not a cavalcade to battle, but the quieter pageant of a ship-load of simple, trusting hearts bound to a new Land of Promise. Early had the attention of this compassionate nobleman been drawn to the condition of the expatriated cottars in the north of Scotland. He had appealed to Government for their relief, and had frequently addressed the public, through pamphlets and articles in the press, on the subject of emigration to the British Colonies. In this he saw a remedy for the poverty and distress that were prevalent in the less fruitful regions of his country. In emigration, moreover, he saw the bettering of the lot of those who would take advantage of it. In 1803, at his own expense, and under his personal supervision, he transferred a band of 800 Highlanders from their native moors to comfortable homes on Prince Edward Island, in the Gulf of St. Lawrence. The descendants of those Highland colonists, now grown a numerous people, form the substantial yeomanry of one of the most prosperous provinces of our Young Dominion.

From the New Canaan of these cottars of Skye and Inverness, Lord Selkirk came to Canada, to cast about him for other desirable sites for colonial settlement. We find him interested in the western portion of what is now the Province of Ontario; and, in 1804, we learn that he was in correspondence with the

Provincial Executive, with a view to giving aid to schemes of colonisation in Upper Canada. For some reason, however, his proposals were not taken advantage of, and, for a time, he returned to Scotland. There, his earnest desire to benefit the peasantry of his native country, led him to urge emigration in the most hearty manner, and, ere long, to formulate a scheme for planting a colony somewhere in the interior of the Hudson Bay Territory. To extend to the incipient colony every advantage it could have, in material as well as in moral support, the Earl and other members of his family acquired a large monetary interest in the Hudson Bay Company. The amount of this interest is said to have been £35,000, or about a fourth of its entire capital. A meeting of the general Court of Proprietors of the Company was then called, and the Selkirk proposal submitted to it. A grant of land was asked on which to settle a colony, to be located in the Assiniboine district,—the expense of transport, the purchase of necessaries for the voyage, and the support of the colony for a time after settlement, the cost of agricultural and house-building implements, and the outlay for quieting the Indian title,—were all to be borne by the noble applicant. The proposal, owing to alarm being taken at the scheme by some members of the Court, who were stockholders in the rival Canadian Company, met with active opposition. The grant was, however, carried by a large majority vote. The prospectus of the scheme was now launched, and emigrants were invited to join the colony. In the summer of 1811, a party of some seventy Highland cottars from Sutherlandshire, with a small contingent from the west of Ireland, set sail for Hudson Bay. Mr. Miles Macdonell, formerly a Captain in the Queen's Rangers, a corps that had done duty in Canada during Simcoe's administration, was appointed Governor by the Hudson Bay Company, and by Lord Selkirk, was given charge of the colony. The emigrants spent the winter at the Company's post on the Nelson, and the next season arrived at Red River.

We have referred to the opposition to the colony, manifested at the meeting of shareholders in London, which was convened to consider Lord Selkirk's application for a grant of land for the purposes of settlement. It is worth while particularly to notice from whom this opposition came, and what were the apparent motives that prompted it. We have already said that objection was taken to the founding of the colony by men who held stock, not only in the Hudson Bay Company, but in the rival Canadian institution. From the literature of the period we learn that these objectors had acquired shares in the Hudson Bay Company only a short time before the call for a general meeting. The disingenuousness of their protest against the grant of land to the colony may therefore be judged from this fact. But not only were they largely interested in the North-West Fur Company, they were known to be its active London agents, and notoriously hostile to all settlement in the fur-trading territory. After this statement, little argument we think is needed to support the opinion, that the enmity of these gentlemen was incited by questionable motives, and that they had acquired their interest in one commercial company to work out purposes of their own in the administration of another. Such a proceeding, unhappily, is not unknown in the world of commerce: its effects in this instance, as we shall see, were to bring on the ill-fated colony a pall of disaster.

So far as Lord Selkirk is concerned, he is to be relieved of any reflection in regard to the arrangements he made for the weal of the colony. His care and forethought were in a thousand ways manifested; and everything he could reasonably do he did to make smooth the path of settlement. The situation chosen for the Colony was the banks of the Red River, near the confluence of the Assiniboine,—now the site of the Prairie capital, the city of Winnipeg. The title given to it was the Kildonan Settlement, from the name of the parish in Sutherlandshire from which the bulk of the settlers had emigrated. Here, in the autumn of 1812, when other sections of Canada were in the turmoil of invasion, a peaceful colony sought to found homes for themselves in the wilderness. "The spot which had been selected,"—so writes a chronicler of the period, —"had been ascertained to be of the highest fertility and the most easy of cultivation. Houses were built; a mill was erected; sheep and cattle were sent up to the settlement; and all practicable means were taken to forward the agricultural purposes of the colony." Two years afterwards, it received some additions to its number, and in September, 1814, we learn, that the whole colony comprised two hundred settlers. The first two winters were spent at the wooded region of Pembina, close to the international boundary line, where Fort Daer had been erected by Governor Macdonell's orders, so as to afford better shelter and protection through the severe winter months. In the spring the settlers returned to their summer operations in the neighbourhood of the Colony's location, close by the Forks of the Assiniboine. Here Fort Douglas was erected as a refuge in emergency, and as a storehouse of supplies. As yet the colony had not become self-supporting; some root-crops had been raised, but, so far, little had been done in growing grain. There was want of horses and oxen. Abundant supplies of fish were to be had; but buffalo and even smaller game were scarce. For the latter they had to depend upon the Indians, who though at first friendly, were now being alienated by the malice of the hostile Nor'-Westers. While there was likelihood of the colony suffering from the malevolence of these traders, it was in no apprehension as to its future. For contingencies, in the event of trouble, the settlers were in some measure prepared. Fort Douglas was capable of defence, for, thanks to the prevision of Lord Selkirk, some light brass field-pieces had been sent into the country, to be mounted on its ramparts; and the settlers had been furnished with arms and ammunition. But, as we have said, the settlement felt quite secure in its peaceful mission to the country, and had no dread of serious molestation. An authority of the period * emphasises this fact:

"In short, the settlers appeared confident of their security, contented with their situation, and happy in their prospects; nor did there exist any reasonable ground to doubt that, if left undisturbed, the colony in a few years would have been completely and firmly established. This, indeed, must have been the decided opinion at the time, even of those who proved to be its most inveterate opponents, otherwise they never would have thought it necessary to take violent means to destroy it. Had the settlement been likely to fail from causes inherent in its nature, or arising from the remoteness of its situation, or other local circumstances, its enemies (and none were better judges than they) would doubtless have left it to its fate; and, remaining passive spectators of its destruction, would gladly have permitted the colony to die a natural death, instead of incurring anxiety, expense, and the risk of the vengeance of the law, by adopting those active measures to which they resorted for the purpose of strangling it in its infancy."

But had the situation of the colony been more serious than it was, Scottish resoluteness and tenacity of purpose in the face of danger, would have acquiesced in the dispensation and contentedly accepted it. The Highland heart, though it had its tender spots, and was keenly sensitive to kindness, partic-

---

* "Statement respecting the Earl of Selkirk's Settlement of Kildonan, on the Red River, its destruction in the years 1815 and 1816, and the massacre of Governor Semple and his Party." London, 1817.

LIEUT.-COL. VAN STRAUBENZIE.

THE SELKIRK SETTLEMENT AND ITS FATE.

ularly in amelioration of an exile's lot, was "dour" when opposition thwarted, and hard as flint when it had to fight. Unkindly as was his lot in the land of his fathers, there is no doubt, for a time at least, that the Scottish settler pined for its shores again. Years hence, did all go well, there was prospect of he and his being better off in the wilderness to which he had come. But as yet he had not got over his home-sickness, and the memory of the old land was heavy on his heart. We can imagine him wistfully recalling the loved scenes of his former life; and, as he looks on the rough surroundings of his inland home, longing for a sight of his native hills, and sighing for the sound of the sea.

> "O! gie me a sough o' the auld saut sea,
> A scent o' his brine again,
> To stiffen the wilt that this wilderness
> Has brought on this breast and brain.
>
> Let me hear his roar on the rocky shore,
> His thud on the shelly sand;
> For my spirit's bowed, and my heart is dowed,
> Wi' the gloom o' this forest land."

In the year 1814, the smouldering fires of the Nor'-Wester's enmity emitted puffs of flame. In January, Miles Macdonell, the Governor of the colony, had found it necessary to issue a proclamation forbidding the export from the territory of the food-supplies that were required for the support of those who had come to the colony and of those who were about to arrive in it. The proclamation was construed by the North-West Fur Company as a menace to its traders, and likely to deprive them of a source, hitherto relied upon, of their support. There would appear little ground of justification for this view of the matter. The truth is, the Company was not so much apprehensive for the safety and comfort of its employés, as it was anxious for a pretext to quarrel with the colony. However this may be, the proclamation was considered a *casus belli*. Before proceeding further, it may be well to give an extract from the offending document. Here is the essential part of it. Says the Governor:

"And whereas the welfare of the families at present forming settlements on the Red River, with those on the way to it, passing the winter at York or Churchill Forts in Hudson Bay, as also those who are expected to arrive next autumn, renders it a necessary and indispensable part of my duty to provide for their support. In the yet uncultivated state of the country, the ordinary resources derived from the buffalo and other wild animals hunted within the territory are not deemed more than adequate for the requisite supply; wherefore, it is hereby ordered, that no persons trading in furs or provisions within the territory, for the Honourable the Hudson Bay Company, the North-West Company, or any individual or unconnected traders or persons whatever, shall take out any provisions, either of flesh, grain, or vegetables, procured or raised within the said territory, by water or land-carriage, for one twelve-month from the date hereof; save and except what may be judged necessary for the trading-parties at this present time within the territory, to carry them to their respective destinations, and who may, on due application to me, obtain license for the same. The provisions procured and raised as above shall be taken for the use of the colony; and that no losses may accrue to the parties concerned, they will be paid for by British bills at the customary rates.

"And be it hereby further made known, that whosoever shall be detected in attempting to convey out any provisions prohibited as above, either by land or water, shall be taken into custody and prosecuted as the laws in such cases direct; and the provisions so taken, as well as any goods or chattels of what nature soever which may be taken along with them, and also the craft, cattle, and carriages, instrumental in conveying away the same, to any part but the settlement on Red River, shall be forfeited. Given under my hand, at Fort Daer, Pembina, the 8th of January, 1814. By order of the Governor."

This proclamation, however essential its issue to the preservation and comfort of the colony, was a brusque assertion of rights in the territory ill for the Nor'-Wester to brook. In its effect on his own comfort, in placing an embargo on supplies, he was naturally eager to resent its publication and defy its authority. But the proclamation was the result of causes which the Nor'-Westers themselves had set in motion. From the time of the colony's first appearing, they had maliciously taken care to keep the territory clear of game Nor was this all: to prevent the settlers from obtaining provisions they systematically bought up any surplus food to be had; and, through the active agency of the unfriendly half-breeds, they had dissuaded the Indians from selling them the produce of the chase. For the Governor's edict there may not have been immediate and pressing necessity; but as a precautionary measure, in view of additions to the colony, its issue was justifiable. That its promulgation gave offence to the Nor'-Westers, we can readily believe; but we are far from sympathising with them in the use they made of it as a brand of strife.

The issue of this document, if it was not the beginning, was the active fomenter, of lengthened hostility to the Selkirk Settlement. The partners of the North-West Fur Company who met at Fort William, in 1814, for their summer parliament, were loud in their protest against the Governor's proclamation, and fixed in their determination to suppress the colony. They spoke excitedly of their rights in the interior and bitterly of their dislike of the Hudson Bay Governor. Scotch, as was the Kildonan Settlement, its active suppressors were of the same nationality. It was the old story, their foes were of their own household. The partners who were entrusted with the grim work of breaking up the colony were' the twin-worthies, Duncan Cameron, and Alexander McDonell. They were instructed to proceed to Fort Gibraltar, a trading-post of the Company, at the Forks of the Assiniboine, within half a mile of the Red River Settlement. From this station, which had not heretofore been honoured by the presence of a resident-partner of the Company, they were to do what they could to harass the settlers. At first the Company was wary in showing its animus to the colonists. The initial step was to coax the settlers to leave the territory, and, failing in that, to intimidate them by threats of Indian massacre. In the art of coaxing, Cameron displayed much talent: he was moreover assisted in his overtures by a knowledge of Gaelic, by a cunning tongue, and a plausible address. With these gifts he was enabled, first, to disarm suspicion of the intentions of the Company; secondly, to ingratiate himself with the heads of influential families in the Settlement; and, finally, to make them discontented with their surroundings, dissatisfied with their superiors, and doubtful of their prospects in the territory. This was the first assault on the integrity of the colony.

The next undermining act was to excite the fears of the settlers by disseminating reports of Indian treachery and threatened massacre. These reports, so far as the Indians were concerned, were wholly and cruelly untrue. Their dusky brethren had always shown themselves friendly; and in supplying the colony with game from the plains, they had found it to their advantage to continue in amity. They were, however, insidiously approached by the Nor'-Westers, with the view of exciting them to rise against the colony. Both the Salteaux and the Crees were repeatedly urged to destroy it. It is on record, that a Chippewa chief was offered rum and tobacco for his tribe, if he would even intercept the bearer of despatches to and from the Governor. From these malignant acts the intriguers of Fort Gibraltar resorted to more violent measures. But the measures were not only violent, they were base and pitiful. They comprised acts of daily harassment, and weariful attacks upon a peaceable and dependent colony. The horses and cattle of the settlers were shot by stealth in their enclosures; and, as was threatened, the downfall of the colony was decided upon by fair means or foul. The next step was to starve the settlers out of the country. A Hudson Bay party, with 600 bags of pemmican, was captured on the Qu' Appelle river, on the way to Fort Douglas. To reduce the Settlement to a more tractable and dependent mood, a raid was also made upon the arms and ammunition. From Fort Douglas a howitzer and other field-pieces were boldly abstracted; and drunken Indians were sent in among the women and children to frighten them out of their wits. Cameron, the Company's agent, now gave out that he had been armed with official authority to protect the peace of the territory, and that he was in receipt of His Majesty's commission to enforce obedience to his orders. To give colour to this imposture, he issued sundry intimidating proclamations, and ostentatiously paraded himself in the uniform of what turned out to be a disbanded Canadian regiment. Under this pretended authority, he employed his half-breeds to enter the houses of the settlers, to serve them with injunctions, to abstract their weapons of defence, and, in some instances, to take their inmates prisoners. By bribery, and such harassing acts as we have mentioned, a few of the colonists were induced to abandon their homes, and received money and supplies to quit the country. But most of the colony were true to one another, and loyal to their common interest. No arts could allure or threats intimidate them to give up possession of their territory. Opposition only the more firmly rooted them to the soil.

It would be tedious to dwell longer upon the means adopted by Cameron and his colleagues to seduce the settlers from their allegiance and to weaken their hold upon the Settlement. The Nor'-Westers quickly saw that half measures would have little effect in putting a stop to colonisation, and that recourse must needs be had to harsher procedure. We have already said that Cameron had made the settlers liberal offers to leave the country. These overtures were renewed; and large bribes of money and land in Canada were held out as an inducement to desertion. This lure of the Company, and the discouragement of the situation, at last had effect upon a few of the indentured servants of the colony. These were prevailed upon to desert before the expiration of their contracts, and to carry away with them their working tools and many of the implements of husbandry. Their defection had its influence upon others; for during the winter of 1815 more of them deserted their employments, and others secretly engaged to abandon the settlement in the spring. After the raid upon the Fort, and the loss of their means of defence, many of the settlers began to despair; and this feeling was intensified by still further acts of hostility and aggression.

About this time Miles Macdonell, the Governor of the district, had been served with a warrant of arrest, issued by a magistrate of the Indian territory, on a charge of having feloniously taken a quantity of provisions belonging to the North-West Company. This warrant, Macdonell, at first, paid no heed to; but the colony being threatened with dire mishap unless he surrendered himself, he thought it prudent to do so, and proceeded to Canada for trial. The Governor was taken to Montreal, where he was long and vexatiously detained. Meanwhile the poor colony was subjected to further and more wanton outrage. The settlers were frequently fired upon by the half-breeds; their houses were broken up and pillaged; many of the labourers, quietly employed in tillage, were forcibly seized and detained as prisoners; horses were stolen and cattle driven away; and, finally, the whole colony was ordered to leave the Red River. Things had now come to such a pass that nothing but abandonment could save the lives of the colonists. In June, 1815, about sixty of the settlers fled for safety to a Hudson Bay post on Jack Fish River, at the northern end of Lake Winnipeg. To mark the triumph of this serious defection, a number of clerks and servants of the North-West Company proceeded to the Settlement, and " setting fire to the houses, the mill, and other buildings, burnt them to the ground." On this happening, the remainder of the settlers— 134 in number—abandoned the place, and accompanied the North-West traders to the annual rendezvous at Fort William. From this post on Lake Superior they proceeded to Upper Canada.

Before we come to a new era of disaster, in connection with the history of this ill-fated colony, let us see what report was given to the outer world of these inhuman proceedings of the agents of the North-West Fur Company. In a volume issued at the period, from which we have already quoted, we have the means of ascertaining what colour was given to the foul acts of the Canadian Fur-traders. The Honourable Wm. M'Gillivray, the founder and chief partner of the North-West Company, and a member of the Lower Canada Legislature and Executive Council, had been written to for information respecting the Red River colonists by Sir Frederick Robinson, at the time in command of His Majesty's forces in Upper Canada. From the report of this chief of the Canadian traders we learn of the infamy of the Company's gloss upon their years of hostility to the colony. His language is that of humane concern for the settlers, and of artfully simulated compassion for their fate. We are unwilling even to seem to do a wrong to this gentleman's memory, or unfairly to hold his Company responsible for acts which they no doubt disowned. But the evidence is both clear and strong against this corporation; and it is impossible to think that McGillivray was ignorant of the true facts of the case. Here are a few extracts from his report. In accounting for the failure of the colony he first arraigns the Governor, Miles Macdonell, for his indiscretions, and goes on to say that "the disorder excited in the country by those (Macdonell's) acts of violence, the disgust given to the settlers by the extensive disadvantages of the country, as well as the violence and tyranny of their leader, and the dread of the native Indians and mixed breed, all contributed to break up the colony. Some few of the settlers," he adds, "have returned to Hudson Bay, and the remainder threw themselves upon the compassion of the North-West Company to obtain means of conveyance to Canada. . . . Under these circumstances," the writer continues, "partly from compassion towards these poor people, and partly from a dread of the consequences of their remaining in the interior (because, in the event of the Indians attacking them, it was feared that the Hatchet, once raised, would not discriminate between a trader and a settler, but that all the white men in the country might become its victims), the North-West Company has offered these settlers a conveyance to this province, and the means of subsistence since they left the Red River." McGillivray concludes by begging Sir Frederick Robinson's "protection and favour for the poor settlers."

Of course, no reasonable man will nowadays grow very indignant over the cant, not to speak of the deceit, of this letter. History is likely to docket it at its true worth. From the testimony taken in the Courts at the period, and particularly from the sworn evidence of credible agents of Lord Selkirk, and of honest people connected with his Settlement, there can be no question of the criminality of the traders of the North-West Company in the outrages committed upon the Red River colony, or of the responsibility of the administration of that trading corporation for the acts of its servants. The writer of the above letter knew but too well, not only what was the attitude of his company towards the colony, but he also knew the declared and avowed policy of the Trading Partners, of whom he was one, towards Lord Selkirk and the rival English Company with which he was associated. Occupying the position he did, as the ear and mouthpiece of all the doings of his Company, it was impossible that he could be ignorant of the instructions that had been issued from his Board to harass the colony, to make life a burden to the settlers, and if need be, to resort to violent measures to ruin the Settlement and root it, stem and branch, from the country. The abundant evidence, existing in contemporary affidavits, to criminate this trading corporation in its policy of extermination, renders it unnecessary to dwell upon the matter further. We shall quote but a sentence or two from a letter of one of the partners, written to a friend in Montreal, just after the general conference of the traders at Fort William, in the summer of 1814. The writer is Alexander McDonell, the colleague of Duncan Cameron, who was in command of Fort Gibraltar. A contemporary critic says, "the letter speaks a language that cannot be misunderstood:"

"You see myself and our mutual friend, Mr. Cameron, so far on our way to commence open hostilities against the enemy in Red River. Much is expected from us, if we believe some —perhaps too much. One thing is certain, we will do our best to defend what we consider our rights in the interior. Something serious will undoubtedly take place. Nothing but the complete downfall of the colony will satisfy some, by fair or foul means—a most desirable object if it can be accomplished. So here is at them with all my heart and energy!"

The writer of this letter is Alexander McDonell, one of the most zealous instigators of strife in the North-West Fur

Company's employ, a frequent leader of raids upon the colony, and an inciter to acts of wanton aggression. It is told of him that on one occasion he brought from the plains into the Settlement a number of Cree Indians, whom he thought that by filling with liquor he could inflame to attack the colony and murder the settlers. As it mercifully happened, however, an Indian drunk was more humane than a white man sober. In the history of European intercourse with Indians, this is not the first time the world has known them to possess, not only a high ideal of morality, but a realisation of it that would put to shame many of those who conceive themselves to rank higher in the scale of humanity. They returned to their wigwams on the Qu'Appelle without doing the behests of McDonell, but, instead, sent the pipe of peace to the colony as an assurance of friendship. Nor were the acts of this man, and of his fellow-conspirator, Cameron, unauthorised, or at least unapproved of, by the North-West Company. The contrary is on record: they were not only rewarded but honoured by the Company; while there is also evidence that considerable sums were paid, on their report of partisan service being rendered by the deserters of the colony, to these and other disaffected settlers who had been incited to revolt by Cameron's treachery. Here are some extracts from this worthy's report to headquarters of the men who rendered, and the value put upon, these services. Of one man McDonell speaks thus:

" A smart fellow. Left the H. B. Company in April last—a true partisan, steady and brave. Took a most active part in the campaign of this spring, and deserves from fifteen to twenty pounds. He has lost about £20 by leaving the Hudson Bay Co. a month before the expiration of his contract." Of another the same writer affirms that: "This man left the H. B. Co. in the month of April, owing to which he lost three years' wages. His behaviour towards us has been that of a true partisan, steady, brave, and resolute; was something of a leading character among his countrymen, and deserves at least about £20." But these were minor Judases: here we have a traitor whom thirty pieces of silver would not satisfy. Cameron thus writes of George Campbell: "This (Geo. Campbell) is a very decent man, and a great partisan, who often exposed his life for the N. W. Co. He has been of very essential service in the transactions of the Red River, and deserves at least £100, Halifax, and every other service that can be rendered to him by the North-West Company. Rather than his merits and services should go unrewarded, I would give him a £100 myself, although I have already been a good deal out of pocket by my campaign to Red River."

But we must get back to the larger theatre of events. During these trying times for the Selkirk settlers the founder of the colony had not been idle. We may be sure he was not callous to the ruin of his colony, or indifferent when he heard of its dispersion. For more than a year he had been in correspondence with the Canadian authorities, with a view to obtaining military protection for the Settlement. In this, however, he had failed. The North-West Company was a powerful institution in the provinces, and its coils of interest and partisan favour were even wound about the Executive. Lord Selkirk came to Canada to see what could be done. Here he heard with dismay of the fate of his colony. There was but one ray of hope. The detachment of settlers that had gone north to Lake Winnipeg might not have left the country. This was the case: they had even now returned to the smoking ruins of their homesteads, and, figuratively, had sat down by the waters of Babylon and wept. To clear the *debris* from the ground, re-erect devastated homes, and plant something for the wants of the coming winter, was the determined resolution, as it was soon the accomplished work, of the returned settlers. The resurrected colony had had by this time an important addition of new settlers, who had come to Hudson Bay in the summer of 1815. In spite of the past, and the far from pacific present outlook, there were those who fondly thought the colony might yet live.

Lord Selkirk was still detained in Canada endeavouring to induce the Government to extend its authority, with the symbol of its power, to the North-West. In this task he found himself seriously handicapped by the overshadowing influence of the Canadian traders. They had possession of all the avenues to Government favour, and had effectually prejudiced public opinion against him and his colony. It was hard to do battle against such odds. His representative, Governor Miles Macdonell, was still under arrest in Montreal, and others of his agents were in trouble. To add to the difficulties of his position, detachments of refugees from his colony came dribbling into Canada, and they naturally turned to him for support. This was not denied them. But his chief effort was at present directed towards obtaining evidence, to enable him to fasten responsibility for the troubles upon those who had occasioned them. This was important, not only to put another face upon things in Canada, and meet the lies of the North-West Company, but to enable him to set himself right in Britain. The undertaking was no light one; but Lord Selkirk shirked no difficulties, and was too much in earnest to spare himself labour. His correspondence at the period indicates a man of great ability, of untiring energy, and of self-sacrificing enthusiasm. His most striking characteristics are his manifest fairness, control of temper under great provocation, and conscientious desire to get at the truth. No one dipping into the history of the time can fail to gain this impression of the man, or remain insensible to the honourableness of his actions and the high impelling motive of his work.

Leaving Lord Selkirk for a while at Montreal, let us see how it fared with the partially restored colony. With the return of the contingent that had gone to Jack Fish River, there had come from Scotland an infusion of new blood. With the recruits to the colony and the returned emigrants was a Mr. Colin Robertson, a Hudson Bay Company officer, who was able to render great service in re-establishing the Settlement. Encouraged by this official, it fast regained its old spirit and strength. Once again, however, in this western paradise, was seen the trail of the serpent. Our quondam friends, Duncan Cameron and Alexander McDonell, were back in the region. The former re-occupied Fort Gibraltar; while the latter proceeded to his late post on the Qu'Appelle River. Neither of these worthies expected to see aught again in Kildonan of Lord Selkirk's settlers; but Lord Selkirk's settlers were not only there, they were there in force. If a bold front augured anything, they were there also to stay.

Cameron was not long in resuming his old tactics. But this time he counted without his host. Robertson, who had assumed charge of the colony, determined to act not alone on the defensive. On the first occasion of trouble emanating from Fort Gibraltar, out he and his force sallied from Fort Douglas. Quickly traversing the distance between the two Forts, the Selkirk banners gained speedy access to the rival post. Robertson's following took the garrison by surprise, captured Cameron, and recovered the field-pieces and stands of arms that had been previously carried from the Settlement. This was a new turn for things to take. Fortunately, no blood was shed. Cameron was released on promise of good behaviour and reinstated in his command of the Fort. The winter passed without incident, save rumours of some ominous movement in the west. There McDonell, who had been indignant at the capture of the Fort and the humiliation of his partner, was actively preparing a campaign for the Spring. When that season arrived, Cameron was again caught plotting against the colony, and was once more laid by the heels and taken to Hudson Bay. This precipitated events, and brings us to a crisis in the history of the Settlement. It also brings on the scene an ill-fated Hudson Bay Governor.

This officer was Governor Robert Semple, who had been appointed to the chief control of all the factories in the territory. On his tour of inspection of the posts he came to Red River in the Spring of 1816. At the moment the prospects of the colony seemed brighter. The new Governor brought fresh courage, and the prestige and authority that belonged to his position. Colin Robertson, who was a host in himself, had also stayed the heart of the colony; while its old head, Miles Macdonell, had by this time returned. It really seemed possible for the Settlement to survive: the Scotch thistles were hard to eradicate.

CHAPTER VII.

THE MASSACRE AT RED RIVER, AND AFTER.

HERE is a story told of a child whose eyes had been operated upon for cataract. One stormy night while the thunder roared and the lightning flashed, the child is reported to have become frightened, and to have torn the bandages from her eyes. As she did so a flash of lightning illuminated the darkened room. The bright light she saw for an instant; but the glare was too much for her weak eyes, and she relapsed into the gloom of the sightless and became permanently blind. The story recalls the situation of the Red River colony and its momentary streak of hope. For an instant there was a flash of bright anticipation and a gleam of promise. The next moment it was gone, and darkness once more enveloped the Settlement.

Just after Governor Semple's arrival, the storm clouds gathered fast over the doomed colony. The news of its reconstruction had reached distant Canada, and there was a pressing forward of partners to strangle the new birth. As the weeks passed, a cordon of fate converged upon this cradle of western civilisation. In the east, an expedition was fitting out at Fort

William: in the west, Alexander McDonell was marshalling the half-breeds. Northward, on the Qu'Appelle, a French Canadian banditti were engaging in all sorts of lawlessness; and all around there was ferment and trouble. On the 12th of May, as a Hudson Bay party was coming down the Qu'Appelle river, it was set upon by a number of Canadians and Half-breeds, in the employ of the North-West Company. In command of the attacking party was a man named Cuthbert Grant, who was now to earn his title to infamy for his share in the coming events. The Hudson Bay employés were taken prisoners; their furs and food-supplies were confiscated; and another post of the Company was captured and wrecked. A junction of Cuthbert Grant's rabble was now formed with the Nor'-Westers under Alexander McDonell, and all proceeded to Portage des Prairies. From here, on the 18th of June, McDonell despatched Grant, with seventy Ishmaels of the plains, to attack the colony on the Red River. On the 20th a messenger brought report of an affray which had occurred at Seven Oaks, or as it is otherwise known, Frog Plain, in front of Fort Douglas. Here is the language in which McDonell announces the result of the engagement to his ruffian crew: " *Sacré nom de Dieu! Bonnes nouvelles! Vingt-deux Anglais de tués!*"

An account of this atrocity will have more interest if we quote the deposition of an eye-witness, taken down immediately after the massacre. The narrator is John Pritchard, an Englishman, who had been in the employ of the North-West Company, but who had left its service to become a settler at Red River. Pritchard's account of the affray substantially agrees with that of other credible witnesses. They all testify to the fact that the Indians had no hand in the massacre; on the contrary, they were the first to apprise the colonists of danger, and were anxious, if not to avert their fate, to share it with them. The attacking party, composed of *Bois-Brûlés*, in the service of the North-West Company, was commanded by the unscrupulous Cuthbert Grant. Here is Pritchard's narrative:

"On the afternoon of the 19th of June (1816) a man in the watch-house called out, that the half-breeds were coming. The Governor (Mr. Semple), some other gentleman, and myself, looked through spy-glasses, and distinctly saw some armed people on horseback passing along the plains. A man then called out, they, (meaning the half-breeds) are making for the settlers; on which the Governor said, 'we must go out and meet these people; let twenty men follow me. We proceeded by the old road leading down the settlement. As we were going along we met many of the settlers running to the fort, crying, "the half-breeds! the half-breeds!" When we were advanced about three-quarters of a mile along the settlement, we saw some people on horseback behind a point of woods. On our nearer approach the party seemed more numerous; on which the Governor made a halt and sent for a field-piece, which, delaying to arrive, he ordered us to advance. We had not proceeded far before the half-breeds on horseback, their faces painted in the most hideous manner, and in the dresses of Indian warriors, came forward and surrounded us in the form of a half moon. We then extended our line, and moved more into the open plain; as they advanced we retreated a few steps backwards, and then saw a Canadian, named Boucher, ride up to us waving his hand and calling out 'What do you want?'

"The Governor replied, 'What do *you* want?' To which Boucher answered, 'We want our fort.' The Governor said, 'Go to your fort.' They were, by this time, near each other, and consequently spoke too low for me to hear. Being at some little distance to the right of the Governor, I saw him take hold of Boucher's gun, and almost immediately a general discharge of fire-arms took place; but whether it began on our side, or that of the enemy it was impossible to distinguish: my attention was then directed towards my personal defence. In a few minutes almost all our people were either killed or wounded. Captain Rogers having fallen, rose again and came towards me, when, not seeing one of our party who was not either killed or disabled, I called out to him, 'for God's sake give yourself up.' He ran towards the enemy for that purpose, myself following him; he raised up his hands, and in English and broken French called out for mercy. A half-breed shot him through the head, and another cut open his belly with a knife, with the most horrid imprecations. Fortunately for me, a Canadian, joining his entreaties to mine, saved me, though with the greatest difficulty, from sharing the fate of my friend at that moment. After this, I was rescued from death, in the most providential manner, no less than six different times on my road to and at the Frog Plain, the headquarters of the murderers. I there saw Alexander Murray and his wife, two of Wm. Bannerman's children, and Alexander Sutherland, settlers likewise, Anthony McDonell, a servant, all prisoners, having been taken before the action occurred. With the exception of myself, no quarter was given to any of us. The knife, axe, or ball put a period to the existence of the wounded; and on the bodies of the dead were practised all those horrible barbarities which characterise the inhuman heart of the savage.

" The mild and amiable Mr. Semple, lying upon his side (his thigh having been broken), and supporting his head upon his hand, addressed the chief commander of our enemies, by inquiring if he was Mr. Grant, and, being answered in the affirmative, said, 'I am not mortally wounded, and if you could get me conveyed to the fort, I think I should live.' Grant promised he would do so, and immediately left him in the care of a Canadian, who afterwards related that an Indian of their party came up and shot Mr. Semple in the breast. I entreated Grant to procure me the watch, or even the seals of Mr. Semple, for the purpose of transmitting them to his friends, but I did not succeed. Our force amounted to twenty-eight persons, of whom twenty-one were killed, and one wounded. The Governor; Captain Rogers; Mr. J. White, surgeon; Mr. A. McLean, settler; Mr. Wilkinson, private secretary to the Governor; and Lieutenant Holt of the Swedish navy; and fifteen servants were killed. Mr. J. P. Bourke, store-keeper, was wounded, but saved himself by flight. The enemy, I am told, numbered sixty-two persons, the greater part of them were the contracted servants and clerks of the

North-West Company. They had one man killed and one wounded."*

Such are the incidents of this calamitous story. The colony had no chance of making a fight for itself, for before it could sally out to support its chiefs, the scuffle had ended in wholesale murder. Inflamed with passion, and intoxicated with success, the half-breeds demanded the instant surrender of Fort Douglas, prefacing their demand by threats of indiscriminate slaughter if it was not complied with. Each male inmate of the Fort now nerved himself for the crisis. The desire was to defend the stockade, and to trust to relief arriving from some heaven-directed quarter. But relief there could be none. On the contrary, other besiegers were pressing forward, under McDonell from Portage des Prairie, and under McLeod from Fort William. Meanwhile a message arrived from Grant, stating that "an attack would that night be made upon the Fort, and that if a single shot was fired in defence of the place, a general massacre would ensue." Pritchard, who had been taken prisoner, endeavoured to make terms with Grant for the safety of the colony; but no terms would satisfy him, save unconditional surrender. "You see," observed Grant, "the little quarter we have shown you, and now, if any further resistance is made, no man, woman, or child shall be spared." "Being fully convinced," remarks Pritchard, "of the inevitable destruction of these poor souls, I asked Grant if there was any means by which the lives of the women and children could be

---

* Those who find a grim satisfaction in tracing judgments in this world for wrongs committed against our fellow-creatures, will be interested in a record, which appears in Ross's "Red River Settlement," of the fate that befell half of the ruffians who were concerned in the murder of Governor Semple and the settlers. Ross traces to a violent or sudden death no less than twenty-six out of the sixty-five who composed the attacking party. The list, if to be relied upon, is significant of the Nemesis that pursues ill-deeds.

saved. I entreated him, in the name of his deceased father, whose countrywomen they were, to take pity and spare them." His answer, at last, was, "that if all public property were given up, the settlers should be allowed to depart in peace, and that he would give a safe escort until they had passed the North-West Company's track near Lake Winnipeg." Extorting these terms from Grant, Pritchard begged to be allowed to go on parole to the Fort to state them to his countrymen. This was agreed to, and he had thus an opportunity of dissuading those in the Fort from resorting to a fruitless defence, and of bringing death, and worse than death, upon those who would otherwise become the half-breeds' victims.

On his arrival at the Fort, Pritchard observes, "what a scene of distress presented itself! The widows, children, and relations of the slain, in the horrors of despair, were lamenting the dead, and trembling for the safety of the survivors." After a long and anxious parley, a surrender was decided upon; and the settlers once more accepted the inevitable—banishment from the homes they had endeavoured to rear in the wilderness. On his way back to Frog Plain, "the shades of night," relates the intermediary, "hid from my view what the dawn of the following day too clearly exposed—the mangled and disfigured bodies of the dead. From what I saw, and what I have been told, I do not suppose that more than one-fourth of our party were mortally wounded when they fell, but were most inhumanly butchered afterwards." Two days later saw the embarkment of the Red River colony for Hudson Bay, and the razing, from the desolate wastes of Rupert's Land, of the foundations of its first civilised community. On the way to Lake Winnipeg, the colony met the incoming bands of the North-West traders, under Norman McLeod, the Fort William partner, accompanied by other influential agents and shareholders of that powerful company. To this partner, high in authority, the poor persecuted colonists might naturally have looked for succour and sympathy in this the hour of their dire distress. It would not have been too much to hope that, being a magistrate, he would have taken their depositions with the view of visiting upon lawlessness the righteous punishment of outraged law. As a fellow-creature, he might at least have spared them indignity, while their kindred lay yet unburied on the lands from which they had just been driven

This was not their fate. The first accost of McLeod was "whether that rascal and scoundrel, Robertson, was in the boats ?" and if Governor Semple was with them, if not, what was his fate ? The whole party was disembarked, and for days was subjected to the closest and most insulting examination. Every trunk, box, and chest was pryed into, and the books and diaries of the late Governor were abstracted. The private papers and family records of a number of the settlers were also overhauled, and many of them retained, particularly those that preserved the history of the misdoings of the North-West traders. Not a few of the colonists were deprived of their liberty, and prevented from going off with their departing kinsmen. Not only were they deprived of their liberty, however, but, as a contemporary historian grimly relates, " they were all imprisoned together, in order that they might become better accquainted, " with a guard set over them, composed of those very ruffians by whom their friends had been butchered, and from whom they themselves had almost miraculously escaped at the time of the massacre. " In the whole of these proceedings," the same authority writes, " there appears such a horrible mixture of mock judicial solemnity and real cruelty,—such a medley of folly and atrocity ; of the semblance of law and the substance of injustice, as might, indeed, stagger the belief of any one who has not had an opportunity of perusing the documents which have been collected."

While the remainder of the again exiled settlers were being permitted to make good their escape to the bleak shores of Hudson Bay, let us see what Lord Selkirk was about in Canada. Enmity between the North-West Company and his people, he might well think, could not last forever: surely there would come a time when the colony would be suffered to exist. The territory was vast; only a fringe of it was really known. For generations, a settlement on the Red River, compared with the extent of the whole territory, could be no more than a barnacle on the side of a vessel, or a handful of seaweed flung upon the shore. To resent the intrusion of settlers seemed to Lord Selkirk the most fatuous policy, as it was the most cruel attitude for a body of wealthy Scotchmen to assume towards their poor, but deserving, countrymen. Moreover, in the coming time, as Lord Selkirk no doubt saw, to encourage the half-breeds in their opposition to the colony was sure, as it has done, to bring a harvest of trouble. To-day Canada is paying for that time of devilment.

But back of the half-breeds was ever the implacable enmity of the Nor'-Westers. Against this enmity Lord Selkirk could make no headway, either with the chiefs of the Company or with the leaders of the Government. The administration of a country was never more thoroughly identified with the concerns of a private enterprise, and never more careful not to interfere with its interests or offend its officers, than was the Canadian Executive of the period in its relations with the North-West Fur-traders. To discover this must have been an occasion of grief to the high-minded nobleman, through whose instrumentality the poor cottars of the Orkneys had been relieved from dormant poverty only to meet wandering wretchedness. But Canada was just then in its most unlovely and immature political condition. It was ruled by an oligarchy whose motto, as has been remarked, was expressed by the French proverb: *Nous avons l'avantage, profitons nous.* An official class had grown up, composed of social aristocrats, who were not over scrupulous, at times, of the means by which they attained power, or conscientious in the use they made of it. Liberalism, at a later day, changed all that; but though the necessity for reform was even then urgent, the means by which it could be brought about were not yet available.

Failing in all attempts to procure from the Government an armed force for the protection of the colony, or even to get an official representative, with the requisite authority and essential impartiality, to go to the Settlement as its resident guardian, Lord Selkirk looked in other quarters for the aid he was in need of. Though at heavy cost to himself, he was fortunate in being able to obtain this. The close of the struggle with France, and the termination of the War of 1812-14, had released from active service two Swiss regiments, then in Canada, that had borne a good reputation for efficiency and discipline. A number of the men of these disbanded corps Lord Selkirk was able to engage for the defence of his colony and to take a share in its settlement. They were just the material he was in need of, capable from their military training to withstand attack upon the colony, and being men of respectable character likely to make good settlers. He made a bargain with about a hundred of them, or more precisely, with eighty of the De Mueron, and twenty of the Watteville, regiments. These he clothed and armed at his own expense, and with thirty canoemen started off to Red River. All that the Government furnished him was a personal body-guard of one sergeant and six soldiers.

Before leaving Canada Lord Selkirk had taken care to get himself officially appointed and sworn in as a magistrate. On his way westward, looking to the contingency of having to take civil proceedings against those who had been, or were likely yet to be, troublesome to the colony, he endeavoured at Sault Ste Marie to induce two magistrates of the place to accompany him. In this, however, he was not successful, a circumstance which he thus regrets: "I am therefore reduced to the alternative," writes his Lordship," "of acting alone, or of allowing audacious crimes to pass unpunished. In these circumstances I cannot doubt that it is my duty to act, though I am not without apprehension that the law may be openly resisted by a set of people who have been accustomed to consider force as the only true criterion of right." Crossing Lake Superior, his party fell in with Miles Macdonell, who having again been driven from Red River, was on his way to Canada with the news of the further destruction of the colony. From the Governor Lord Selkirk heard with dismay of the butchery on Frog Plain, and the murder of Semple and his party. With aid so near, how bitter was the news of this second overthrow of his colony, and the wrecking of the hopes he had cherished for its future, the reader may imagine.

On the 12th of August Selkirk and his armed contingent arrived at Fort William. Here, as the reader will be aware, was the western headquarters of the North-West traders, and here were imprisoned some of the prominent men of the Selkirk Settlement. Their release was instantly called for, an order which the partners, in presence of such a force as accompanied Lord Selkirk, were not slow to obey. Selkirk now took the depositions of the released prisoners, and found out the enormity of the crimes either perpetrated or instigated by the servants of the North-West Company. So clearly was their guilt established, and so incensed was his Lordship at the outrages that had been committed, that, by authority invested in him as a magistrate, he arrested a number of the leading partners of the Company, and sent them under escort to York for trial. The military expedition spent the winter at Fort William, and in the Spring proceeded to Red River.

It was the end of June before Lord Selkirk himself reached the colony, and for the first time set eyes upon the scene of its troubles. The settlers who had sought refuge at Norway House, on Lake Winnipeg, were again recalled, and the despoiled homesteads once more put in habitable condition. A general muster of the resurrected colony being now made, the Settlement was formally inaugurated and received its designation, of Kildonan. The land, the title of which had been further secured by treaty with the Indians, was now ordered to be fully surveyed, and roads and bridges were commissioned to be built. Under these favourable conditions, the colony took now a new start, and though, in later chapters we shall hear of its chequered career, the future was more auspicious to it than had been the past. Passing southward to the Mississippi, thence eastward to Washington, its founder made a wide detour on his return to Canada. There he was wanted to confound the machinations of his inveterate enemies, the fur-traders, and there he desired to bring them to justice.

From chronicling the incidents of this portion of the Selkirk career, the historian may well wish to escape. It is a part of the drama upon which he and any lover of Canada may be excused for dropping the curtain. Justice, at the period, had either departed from the country, or had become afflicted with a serious moral and physical squint. Not in Lower, not in Upper

Canada, could Selkirk receive fair hearing or decent treatment. With subservient juries, a besmirched judiciary, and a partisan government, honour and good faith hid their heads. Men of good standing and large stake in the country, men otherwise humane and reputable, vied with each other to defeat justice and to shield crime. Nor did the clerical office hasten to extend its comfort, or even refrain from persecution. A certain redoubtable Rector of York, whom we otherwise love to recall as one of the sturdy founders of the Province, and whose soul, in later days, we believe was right before God, was among the most noisy of Selkirk's defamers, and the most influential withholder from him of justice. Never was man more persecuted than was Lord Selkirk, during the year of the state trials in Canada, and never in the history of the older provinces has there been so flagrant and prolonged a violation of law. In sadness of spirit the would-be founder of the Selkirk Settlement betook himself from the country, and in broken health returned to the Old World to die.

CHAPTER VIII.

THE NOR'-WESTERS ON THE PACIFIC COAST, AND THE AMALGAMATION OF THE RIVAL FUR COMPANIES.

BEFORE dealing, in historic order, with the amalgamation of the rival Fur Companies, let us look a little more closely at the events that preceded it, in connection with the chief commerce of the country, the Fur trade of the continent, and at the explorations that followed upon its enterprising pursuit. To this pursuit we chiefly owe the opening up of the vast region embraced in the Dominion of Canada, from the slender thread of settlement on the banks of the St Lawrence westward to the Pacific, and from the shores of Hudson Bay to the 49th parallel, which in 1846 became the international boundary. South of this line, the principal voyages of exploration across the continent, at the beginning of the century, were the American expeditions in 1804-6 of Lewis and Clarke, up the Missouri and down the Columbia rivers, and the later trading operations of John Jacob Astor, who established Astoria, the great western emporium of the Fur-trade. In this trade Astor laid the foundations of his colossal fortune. Closely following on these enterprises, and growing out of them, came the prolonged international controversy on the Oregon question, which from the year 1818 down to the year 1846 formed a bone of contention between Great Britain and the United States. The treaty of 1846 between the two countries established the Canadian boundary line and settled the vexed question of the national ownership of the northern California coast.

Lewis and Clarke accomplished for the United States what Sir Alexander Mackenzie had accomplished for Canada. They opened up an overland route to the Pacific, and divested the region of much of its terror to the heart of incoming civilisation. Over much of the territory opened up by these explorers, French enterprise had already traversed. Indeed, to the French and the Scotch belong the honors of discovery over most of the continent. The whole country west of the Great Lakes was early made known by Frenchmen. In 1679 La Salle erected Fort Michillimackinac, at the entrance of Lake Michigan, and penetrated by the waters of the Mississippi to the Gulf of Mexico. In the same year Du Luth reached the western extremity of Lake Superior, and took possession of the sources of the Mississippi. About the same period Perrot and Le Sueur journeyed over the region and established forts at suitable points by order of the French Governor. In 1742, Verandrye reached the country of the Mandans, in what is now the territory of Dakota, and tracked the upper waters of the Missouri. Later on we find him roaming over the vast plains of the Saskatchewan, and probing the continent as far west as the Rocky Mountains. In the track of the French traders, a series of posts was established, extending from Sault Ste Marie and the Kaministiquia to the distant Saskatchewan and the hyperborean Athabasca. Later still we have the chain of trading establishments of the North-

West Company, that linked the country from New Brunswick Post, at the source of the Moose River, to the distant Fraser, the Thompson, the Peace, and the Mackenzie rivers. Then came the cluster of Hudson Bay posts that figure so prominently in connection with the fur-trade in the North-West—Cumberland House, Norway House, Hudson House, Carlton House, Manchester House, and the inumerable trading stations of that great Corporation.

But in this enumeration we by no means exhaust the enterprise, or tell the whole story, of Franco-Canadian and Scottish-Canadian trade. Even American historians give the palm to Canada for her labours in opening the continent to commerce. We know how enthusiastically Parkman speaks of French achievement in conducting enterprises of territorial conquest, and in heroically bringing the recesses of the wilderness to the knowledge of the outer world. Now comes a later historian, Mr Hubert Bancroft, who, in one of his many rich historical volumes, gives us this further testimony to the zeal and enterprise of Canadians in prosecuting discovery on the continent. Says Mr. Bancroft, speaking of Lewis and Clarke's expedition up the Missouri:

"In the course of our narrative we shall see that army captains and soldiers were no match for Scotch fur-traders and Canadian *voyageurs* in forest travel. When Lewis and Clarke set out on their expedition the great Unknown Region, as it was called, equivalent to one thousand miles square and more, between the headwaters of the Missouri and the Pacific Ocean, was, if we except the interior of Alaska and the Stikeen country, further removed from civilisation than any other part of North America. The Hudson Bay Company had explored its borders north. English ships had sailed through many channels in search of Anian Strait and a northern passage, and Hearne had pursued his grumbling way from Fort Churchill to the mouth of the Copper Mine. The Canadian merchants had taken possession of the Canadian North-West, and had planted their forts from Lake Superior to Athabasca, while the determined Mackenzie had followed the river which bears his name to the Arctic Ocean, and had crossed from Peace River to the Pacific."*

In addition to Mackenzie's work on the west of the Rocky Mountains, we must not omit to note the labours of James Finlay, another Scotchman, who ascended the Peace River some four years after Mackenzie, and explored the branch of that river to which he gave his name. In this region the name of another Scot is associated with the waters of the Fraser; while the other great river of British Columbia bears the name of yet another Scotchman, David Thompson. All three were employés of the North-West Company, of Montreal; Fraser indeed was one of Cuthbert Grant's followers in the Company's raids on the Selkirk settlement, and was present at the massacre of Governor Semple and his party. Of David Thompson we get a portrait in Mr. Bancroft's volume, which we take the liberty to quote:

"David Thompson was an entirely different order of man from the orthodox fur-trader. Tall and fine looking, of sandy complexion, with large features, deep-set studious eyes, high forehead and broad shoulders, the intellectual was set upon the physical. His deeds have never been trumpeted as have those of some of the others; but in the westward explorations of the North-West Company no man performed more valuable service or estimated his achievements more modestly. Unhappily his last days were not as pleasant as fell to the lot of some of the worn-out members of the Company. He retired almost blind to Lachine House, once the headquarters of the Company, where he was met with in 1831 in a very decrepid condition,"†

---

*"History of the North-West Coast." Vol. ii. 1800-46. By Hubert Howe Bancroft. (Vol. 28 of Works.) San Francisco, 1884.

†A manuscript volume of Voyages in the North-West, undertaken by David Thompson, is in the possession of Mr. Charles Lindsey, City Registrar, Toronto, which we should be glad to see published.

With Simon Fraser was intimately associated a brother Scot, named John Stuart, whose memory is perpetuated in Stuart's Lake and River, in British Columbia. In their way, these Scotchmen were odd characters, though of great service to the North-West Company, in establishing trading posts on the hither side of the Rockies. Fraser, we learn, was " an illiterate, ill-bred, fault-finding man, of jealous disposition, but ambitious and energetic, with considerable conscience, and in the main holding to honest convictions." Of Stuart, who accompanied Fraser in his journeyings in British Columbia, in the years 1806-8, and who was with him in his tracking the Fraser River, Bancroft quotes a description from an M.S. journal of a navigator, named Anderson, who had made a voyage along the Pacific Coast. The sketch is as follows :

" In comparing these two persons I should call Stuart the nobler, the more dignified man, but one whose broad, calm intellect had received no more culture than Fraser's. Stuart's courage and powers of endurance were equal in every respect to those of his colleague, and while in temper, tongue, ideas, and bodily motion he was less hasty, within a given time he would accomplish as much or more than Fraser, and do it better. Both were exceedingly eccentric, one quietly so, the other in a more demonstrative way; but it happened that the angularities of one so dovetailed into those of the other that co-operation, harmony, and good-fellowship characterised all their intercourse. Stuart was one of the senior partners in the North-West Company, and for a time was in charge of the Athabasca department. As his territory in the west was boundless, he deemed it his duty to extend the limits of his operations. Twice he traversed the continent, besides undertaking many minor excursions. In fact, he was always on the move. On retiring from the service he settled at Torres, Scotland, where he died in 1846."

On the Walla-Walla and the Columbia rivers, the North-West Company had in its service a whole colony of Scotchmen, of whom some mention should be made, in connection with the Canadian Fur-trade in the region the fervid Scot loved to call New Caledonia. The area of the Company's trading operations was by no means confined to the district of the Red River, the doings in which engrossed our attention in the last chapter. The Nor'-Westers did a thriving trade on the Columbia River, in Oregon, where they had an important and lucrative post. Their business on the coast was also extensive, reaching from California in the south to New Archangel in the north. On the Pacific slope, in the year 1817, the Company had over three hundred Canadians in its employ. From its ports three or four ships were annually despatched to London, by way of Cape Horn, freighted with furs. The ships on the return passage brought supplies for the various establishments on the coast. The North-West Company had here no Hudson Bay rival; its chief competitor was John Jacob Astor, the wealthy fur-monopolist of the United States. In 1810, this young German trader founded Fort Astoria, the great Fur mart on the Columbia River, familiar to readers of Washington Irving's narrative of the western fur-trade. Astor, it seems, was very anxious to attach to his service some of the more prominent Scotchmen among the Nor'-Westers. He even made overtures to the Company to join him in partnership. The advantage of an alliance, he pointed out, was his ability to ship furs in American vessels to India and China, which the North-West Company was unable to do, in consequence of the East India Company's monopoly of trade.

The resident agents took the matter into consideration, but after an exchange of views with the wintering partners in the interior the proposition was declined. But not only was the proposition declined; it was decided to give Mr. Astor and his Pacific Fur Company a lively opposition in Oregon territory. This, of course, occurred long before international boundaries

THE LATE LIEUT.-COL. A. T. H. WILLIAMS,
Commanding the Midland Battalion

were determined; indeed, it happened within two years of the breaking out of the War of 1812. But if Astor could not form an alliance with the Canadian Company, he could seduce from its employment the men he sought to aid him in his enterprise. By dint of offers of partnership and rapid promotion, he enticed some twenty Canadians to enter his service. Placing these men at the head of two expeditions, Astor despatched one overland, and the other he sent round Cape Horn to the mouth of the Columbia. The breaking out of the war, and the active competition of the North-West Company, made havoc, however, of Astor's plans, and ere long broke up the arrangement between him and his Montreal Scotchmen. On the Pacific, Britannia's "wooden walls" were cruising about, and made trading operations too hazardous to be profitably engaged in. Fort Astoria, in the fortunes of war, and through the ceaseless rivalry of the Nor'-Westers, changed hands and became Fort George, though, by the Treaty of Ghent, in December, 1814, the post was restored.

With the collapse of Astor's project, his Scotch partners returned to their former allegiance, and again entered the service of the North-West Company. Of these Scotchmen, and their countrymen who had remained in the service of the Canadian Company, now gathered in the Oregon district, we find representatives of almost all the clans whose patronymic have the prefix of *Mac*. There were McTavishes, McGillivrays, Mackenzies, McGillises, McKays, McLellans, McDougalls, MacMillans, and McDonalds. Besides these, there were Rosses, Frasers, Keiths, Stuarts, and Bethunes, Highland and Lowland—a terrible array of Scots. Is there a Scotchman who will forgive us if, in conjunction with the names of these sturdy sons of Caledonia, we place an extract from a local

I

history* of the doings of a once national day of revelry, at that distant period of time, and amid savage surroundings, uncheered by the restraining and refining influences of Scottish gentlewomen? We quote from a writer who has not failed to give a picture of the nobler side of the Scottish character.

"As these were days of intoxication, before absolute monopoly regulated the morals of the region, New Year's day was the signal among the Canadians for a grand debauch, which the sober savage begged leave to witness. Drinking set in, and quarrelling soon followed, whereat the natives hid themselves, saying the white men had run mad. When they saw those who had raved the loudest in the morning becoming quiet in the afternoon, they said the white man's senses had returned to him. Then they went their way, wondering how such superior beings should voluntarily lay aside their reason for a time and become beasts."

But these bacchanalian indulgences were necessarily of rare occurrence; and fortunately they were so, for the employés of the North-West Company were naturally mettlesome, and if too much "fool's-water" flowed, they would have made a nice bear-garden of the country. On the Pacific coast, and particularly in the disputed Oregon territory, at the time we speak of, alcohol, however, flowed freely. Bancroft relates that, at a somewhat later period, the entire property of a village would sometimes be swept into the pockets of a trader during one debauch. Through drink, the outrages committed by settlers and desperadoes of the border on the poor Indian, equal any in the annals of crime. But drink, alas! was not always the excuse for inhumanity to the Indian. It is said that five hundred millions of dollars have been spent by the Government of the United States on Indian wars. The bloodshed is incalculable. "All our Indian wars," writes Bancroft, "may be traced imme-

---

*Hubert Bancroft's "History of the North-West Coast." Vol. 2, p. 281.

diately to one of three causes, namely, outrages by border men, failure of Government in fulfilling its promises, and frauds perpetrated by agents."

"Nowhere," writes the same authority, "does the Hudson Bay system claim our admiration to greater extent than in its treatment of offenders. The object was in all cases even and exact justice, not indiscriminate retaliation. Unlike the people of the United States, the British North Americans did not seek to revenge themselves upon savage wrong-doers after the fashion of savages. When an offence was committed they did not go out and shoot down the first Indian they met; they did not butcher innocent women and children; they did not scalp or offer a reward for scalps. Professing Christianity and civilisation, the argument that as brutes or savages treat us, so we must treat brutes and savages, had no force. A stolen article must be restored, and the tribe harbouring a thief was cut off from commercial intercourse. The fort gates were closed to them; they could neither sell nor buy until the thief was brought to punishment.

"If an Indian murdered a white man, or any person in the employ of the Company, the tribe to which he belonged were assured that they had nothing to fear, that King George men were single-hearted and just; that unlike the Indians themselves, they did not deem it fair to punish the innocent for the deeds of the guilty; but the murderer must be delivered to them. This demand was enforced with inexorable persistency; and herein was the secret of their strength. In all that vast realm which they ruled there was not mountain distant enough, nor forest deep enough, nor icy cave dark enough, to hide the felon from their justice, though none but he did have aught to fear. This certainty of punishment acted upon the savage mind with all the power of a superstition. Felons trembled before the white man's justice as in the presence of the Almighty,"

It is a common failing to call every nation but one's own a hard name, and to some it is extremely agreeable to find that other nation's escutcheons are stained by crimes from which their own is free. We have no sympathy with this national self-righteousness. Being conscious of our own national shortcomings, we think it better befits us to bemoan these than to point the finger at another's misfortunes or another's mistakes. Were we inclined to indulge the boasting propensity, we should content ourselves with setting against this tribute to the humanity and justice of the Hudson Bay Company but one extract from the unhappy history of the dealings of our neighbours to the south of us with the aborigines. It occurs in the legislative journals of the State of Idaho:

"*Resolved:* That three men be appointed to select twenty-five men to go Indian-hunting, and all those who can fit themselves out shall receive a nominal sum for all scalps they may bring in; and all who cannot fit themselves out shall be fitted out by the committee, and when they bring in scalps it shall be deducted out. That for every buck scalp be paid $100; for every squaw, $50; and $25 for everything in the shape of an Indian under ten years of age. That each scalp shall have the curl of the head, and each man shall make oath that the said scalp was taken by the company."

To the care of such men was committed the wards of the American nation!

But we have allowed our finding ourselves on American territory, where the North-West Company had established trade relations, to take us into subjects somewhat foreign to the immediate purpose of this chapter. We were referring to the Scotch in the Columbia district, and to the palmy days of the Nor'-Wester supremacy in Oregon, under James Keith, Angus Bethune, and Donald Mackenzie. The story of these times, just after the close of the War of 1812-14, reads like a romance. Innumerable books have been written on the fur trade of the Columbia, perhaps the best of which are Washington Irving's "Astoria;" Ross Cox's "Adventures on the Columbia River;" Alexander Ross's "The Fur Hunters of the Far West," and his

"Adventures of the First Settlers on the Oregon." Ross was among the first to join the Astor enterprise, which he fully and graphically describes in the latter mentioned work. After spending some fifteen years in the Columbia district, he went to settle at Red River, and there wrote one of the best accounts we have of the Selkirk Settlement and its subsequent history, a work which appeared in London, in 1856. Irving's "Astoria" contains some severe strictures upon the Scotchmen who had joined Astor in his enterprises in Oregon. Its author rates them soundly for being the cause of the failure, as he thinks, of the wealthy trader's schemes. But Bancroft, in his "History of the North-West Coast," comes chivalrously to their rescue, and shows that it was the war and the shrewd competition of the rival Canadian Company that occasioned his discomfiture.* Another interesting work, dealing with the region we are referring to, is Harmon's "Journal of Voyages and Travels in the Interior of North America," which was published in Andover in 1820. Daniel Harmon was also a partner in the North-West Company, though, by nationality, neither a Scot nor a Canadian, but, we believe, a Vermonter. It is said of this "Green Mountain Boy" that he was one of the few among the fur traders who carried his religion into the wilderness; but while stationed at Fort McLeod near the Fraser River, a daughter by an Indian mother was born to him, whom he called Polly Harmon; so that this good man's piety did not prevent his propagating his kind in the wilderness. It is added, however, that Harmon

---

*" That these Scotchmen were bad men, disloyal to Astor by reason of their nationality and former associations, as certain writers would have us believe, is in view of the circumstances absurd. In their agreement with Astor they reserved the right to close the business should their interests seem so to dictate. Whatever loss might arise from the failure of the enterprise fell on them in proportion to their share."— *Hubert Howe Bancroft.*

was most affectionately attached to his dusky offspring, and that he always endeavoured to do his duty by them. In his journal occurs an earnest passage anent Sabbath desecration among the servants of the Company in their lonely stockaded posts. "Our men," he writes, "play at cards on the Sabbath the same as on any other day. For such improper conduct I once reproved them; but their reply was, there is no Sabbath in this country, and, they added, no God or devil; and their behaviour but too plainly shows that they spoke as they think." But however much was unrobust in Harmon's Christianity, and is didactically nauseous in his narrative, he did one noble act on his emerging from the wilderness, which, as Bancroft remarks, "partners with more gentlemanly pretensions might well have followed. His uncouth progeny by their Indian mother he did not desert, but took them all with him to his old home, made the woman his lawful wife, and educated his children in all his own high and holy principles." For the credit of the Scottish and the Canadian name, it is to be said, that this act of justice and humanity found many a parallel in the careers of servants of both the Hudson Bay and the North-West companies.

But events recall us to the Canadian side of the boundary line. In 1818, when Fort Astoria again changed its flag, after its restitution to the Americans, under the Treaty of Ghent, most of the Canadian traders returned to Fort William, to Red River, and to Montreal. Donald Mackenzie was the only one of the influential partners to remain. For a number of years he continued to trade on the Williamette and Snake rivers and in the country of the Nez Percés, having Fort Walla-Walla as his headquarters. In 1822 he, however, crossed the mountains to York Factory, and three years later succeeded Robert Pelly in the Governorship of the Red River colony. The departure of the Canadians from Oregon is thus graphically sketched by Bancroft:

"It was a grand affair, this journey of the North-West brigade from the mouth of the Columbia to Fort William and Montreal; it was at once a triumph and a dead-march. Ten canoes, five of bark and five of cedar, each carrying a crew of seven and two passengers, ninety in all, and all well armed, embarked at Fort George (Astoria.) Of the party were McTavish, McDonald, John Stuart, David Stuart, Clarke, Mackenzie, Pillot, Wallace, McGillis, Franchère, and others, some of whom were destined for the upper stations. Short was the leave-taking for so large a company, for now there were not many left at the fort to say farewell. The *voyageurs* donned their broadest bonnets; arms were glittering, flags flying, the guns sounded their adieu, and midst ringing cheers, in gayest mood the party rounded Tongue Point, and placed their breast under the current.

"On the 17th of April they arrived at Rocky Mountain House on their way to the Athabasca river. This post was more a provision depot for the supplying of the North-West Company's people in their passage of the mountains, than a fur-hunting establishment. The glittering crystal eminences on which was perched the curved-horn mountain-goat, beyond the reach even of hungry wolves; the deep dense forests, snow-whited and sepulchral; the resting streams, laughing or raging according as their progress was impeded; the roystering torrent which no cold, dead, calm breath of nature could hush; these and like superlative beauties met the eye of the foot-sore travellers at every turn."

From the Company's supply-house in the mountain pass, the Scotch traders pushed forward to the Athabasca river, down whose waters the gay flotilla proceeded at a rapid pace. From the Athabasca they portaged across to Beaver River, descending which they entered Moore River, and traversed Moore Lake. From here the route lay across the plains to Fort Vermilion, on the Saskatchewan, thence to Cumberland House and on to English Lake. Crossing this they proceeded to lakes Bourbon and Winnipeg, thence by the Winnipeg River to the Lake of the Woods, and over the portage to Fort William, where they arrived about the middle of July.

At Fort William the Nor'-Westers were greatly exercised over the discussion in the English Parliament of the affairs of the rival trading companies. Both companies had considerable influence in English politics. Each was eager to have its own version of the Selkirk affair laid before the House and the country. Neither hesitated to resort to sharp dealing to accomplish its purpose. Associated as was Lord Selkirk with the Hudson Bay Company, it does not seem that the latter very warmly espoused his interests. Its concern was more about its charter and its rights in the territory, which the North-West Company was continually assailing. There is truth, we fear, in what the Canadian traders affirmed, that their rivals cared little for Selkirk's philanthropy, and only used it as a lever against the Nor'-Westers to drive them from the field and secure a monopoly of trade. With Selkirk, the case was different. He was no trader, but a lover of his kind. Stock in the Hudson Bays he purchased only to give influence to his name in the territory, to secure facilities in the transport of his people to Red River, and, as he hoped, protection when they got there. We have seen how his expectations failed him. On his return to England, in 1818, it was to hear still ringing in his ears the notes of conflict on the distant continent he had left. The whole matter of his colony's troubles was brought up in the House of Commons, and a Blue Book was the result of the call for papers and correspondence. Little else, however, was done. From London the broken-spirited nobleman retired for rest to the continent; but the most untroubled rest he could find he found in the grave. Surrounded by his wife and daughters, this true patriot and baffled philanthropist died at Pau, in the south of France, on the 8th of April, 1820.* So ended a sorely-troubled, but not wholly wasted, life.

With the death of Lord Selkirk the occasion for further dissension between the rival Fur Companies in some measure ceased. The English Government, though it did not see its way to effect anything by legislative enactments, endeavoured to do something by mediation. With its aid, and the interposition of the Hon. Edward Ellice, one of the most influential of the resident English partners of the North-West Company, a basis of agreement between the companies was arrived at. This basis of agreement developed into a joint-stock partnership, which was entered into on the 26th of March, 1821. Each company was to furnish a like amount of capital, and the profits were to be equally divided. The name of the older chartered institution was to be retained. The stock of the united company was to be divided into one hundred shares, forty of which were to go to the chief factors and traders in the territory, and the remaining sixty were to be appropriated by the resident partners of both companies in England.† The terms of the partnership required the appointment of the chief factors and chief traders to be made equally ‘from the old servants of the companies. Thus in every respect the two companies came together upon an equal footing. An Act of

---

* It is both a duty and a pleasure here to call attention to an interesting memorial of this unselfish nobleman and his life-work—the substance of a book issued in London, in 1882, on "Manitoba: its Infancy, Growth, and Present Condition," by the Rev. Prof. Bryce, M.A., of Manitoba College.

† "Each contributed either in money or in stock £200,000. The capital stock of the Hudson Bay Company at this time was but £100,000 ; and it was obliged to call in a like amount to make its contribution equivalent to that of the North-West Company. After the union, profits were added to the principal after paying ten per cent. dividends annually, until the capital stock was £500,000.—*Vide* House of Commons Report, quoted by Bancroft."

Parliament was passed uniting the two corporations, and renewing the license to trade in the Hudson Bay territories. The license was for a period of twenty-one years. Provision was made in the Act for commissioning the Company's servants as justices of the peace; while the jurisdiction of the Upper Canada Courts was extended to the Pacific. Thus was the union consummated between these long hostile Fur Companies.

With the union of the companies, fur stock again rose to a premium. Dividends that for years had fallen to 4 per cent., and even to nothing, now mounted to 10 and to even 20 per cent., with a handsome rest and an occasional large bonus. Posts that had fallen into decay were re-established, and trade was extended in all directions. Nor was amalgamation without its benefit on both human and brute life in the territories. The demoralisation of the Indians, occasioned by the introduction of intoxicating liquors during the period of strife, ceased; while hunting "out of season," which was now strictly forbidden, had its effect upon the peltries and tended to conserve trade. But the country, in the years of even the poorest yield, was drained to an enormous extent of game. There are records extant of the "take" of one year, that of 1800, by the traders of the North-West Company. We give the figures in a footnote, that the reader may realise the extent and value of the trade.* The gross returns of this one company for the year 1790, amounted to £40,000 sterling. Some fifteen years later, when the Nor'-Westers had absorbed the X.Y. Company, a rival Canadian institution, the gross value of its trade was £120,000. To affiliate with so enterprising a company of traders might well wake the Hudson Bay Company from its frozen sleep.

---

* The fur yield for 1800, of the N.-W. Co. was as follows: 106,000 beaver, 2,100 bear, 5,500 fox, 4,600 otter, 17,000 musquash, 320 marten, 1,800 mink, 600 lynx, 600 wolverine, 1,650 fisher, 100 raccoon, 3,800 wolf, 700 elk, 1,950 deer, and 500 buffalo! British America, it might well be said, was the fur-hunter's paradise.

The competition, though deadly between the heads of the rival companies, was not always carried on by the employés at swords-point. Tricks were sometimes in order to get the advantage of a rival. In close proximity as were many of the forts of the companies, there was sometimes a good deal of manœuvring to get hold of Indians known to be approaching the posts after a hunting expedition. The question often presented itself to the inmates of one or other of the forts, how to inveigle the returned hunters to their special trading-post and secure the furs without the interference of their rivals. Bancroft tells the story how this question was on one occasion answered.

"There were too many," he writes, "to coerce, therefore courtesy should do it (*i.e.*, defeat the vigilance of the rival traders). Childish rivalry for the moment should give place to friendship's hallowed communion. A grand ball should be given to the honourable North-West Company, and on the spot. When drink was not wanting, a ball in fur-hunting circles was a matter quickly arranged. Invitations were answered by the dancers presenting themselves in the evening at the hour named in grandest apparel, with clean capotes, bright hat-cords, and new embroidered moccasins. The native fiddler struck up a Scotch reel, and while from the huge fire came fitful gusts from savoury roasts, the guests were invited to manifest their appreciation of the entertainment by the measure of their potations. Would they not drink? Would they not dance? Would they not take another drink? and another, and another?

"This within the palisades; while down in the hollow behind the fort muffled men with packs and snow-shoes were hurrying to and fro, hitching dogs to sledges, patting the creatures to keep them quiet, and directing their eager movements only by signs and whispers. Finally, the sledges being well loaded with goods and the bells all removed from the dogs' necks, the party started at a round pace for the Indian camp. Long after the noiseless train had departed, the sound of revelry was borne upon the frosty air, until finally stillness reigned. Next day the North-West look-out reported the returned hunters. With bells ringing merrily a party set out in pursuit, only after a long day's journey to find the hunters all dead-drunk, with not so much as a musquash left to sell.

"Yes, it was a brilliant ball, but the Nor'-Westers swore there should be dancing to another tune ere long. Soon opportunity offered. Rival trains in search of the same hunters meeting one cold day, it was proposed to build a rousing fire, and eat and drink together. Soon a huge pile of logs was crackling furiously, and spirits were flowing freely. This time the Nor'-Westers by spilling their liquor upon the snow were at length enabled to put their competitors into a state of intoxication; then, tying them to their sledges, they sent the dogs homeward, while they went forward to the Indian camp and secured the furs."

But all occasion for these rivalries, with the enmities they gave rise to, had now happily passed. Even hostility to colonisation, by the conditions of the new license, was specifically forbidden, and was now also a thing of the past. Under the régime of toleration, the much trampled on colony of the Red River shewed germs of new life. Since the troubles of 1816, it had, however, a new and peculiar visitation, from which it was now happily recovering. But we must leave one of its settlers, the historian, Alexander Ross, to tell the story of this new misfortune:

"Every step," writes Ross, "was now a progressive one: agricultural labour advanced, the crops looked healthy and vigorous, and promised a rich harvest. In short, hope once more revived, and everything put on a thriving and prosperous appearance: when, lo! in the midst of all these pleasing anticipations, just as the corn was in ear, and the barley almost ripe, a cloud of grasshoppers from the west darkened the air, and fell like a heavy shower of snow on the devoted colony. This stern visitation happened in the last week of July, and late one afternoon. Next morning, when the people arose, it was not to gladness, but to sorrow; all their hopes were in a moment blighted! Crops, gardens, and every green herb in the settlement had perished, with the exception of a few ears of the barley, half ripe, gleaned in the women's aprons. This sudden and unexpected disaster was more than they could bear. The unfortunate immigrants looked up towards heaven and wept."*

Not figuratively, but in sad truth, there was left to the colony neither "seed to the sower nor bread to the eater!" Is it a wonder that many a Scottish immigrant turned heart-broken from the settlement? And turning from the settlement he might be excused for saying that it was "no abode for civilised men!"

---

* While this chapter was passing through the press, the author had the pleasure to receive a courteous invitation to visit the library of Wm. J. Macdonell, Esq., a worthy Scottish gentleman, well known in Toronto for his literary tastes, for his unostentatious charity, and for his many years zealous representation of France as local Consul. In the course of a pleasant chat, among his books, the writer discovered that his venerable entertainer was a nephew of Miles Macdonell, first Governor of the Selkirk Colony, and was shown, appended to the Selkirk "Memorial" to the Duke of Richmond, the Canadian Governor-General, in 1819, a manuscript letter of Lord Selkirk to Mr. Macdonell's father, brother of Governor Miles Macdonell, with a number of letters from the latter, referring to the affairs of the colony.

The purport of the Selkirk letter, which is dated Montreal, Dec. 1, 1815, is to interest his correspondent, then in Boston, to secure for him a few chosen men of good character, to go with him to Red River, and to whom he would give a free passage and good wages for a time while in his service. To those accepting the proposal, and accompanying his Lordship, a grant of land would be given at the close of the engagement, should the person settle in the colony, or if not, a free passage back to Canada. A free passage is also offered to any young woman who may agree, at the invitation of the person entering his employ, to come to the colony as his wife. The interesting letter thus concludes: "I propose, early next spring," says Lord Selkirk, "to go up with these people myself, which may serve as an answer to anyone who apprehends danger from the Indians. I think these men will be satisfied when they know that they will be exposed to no danger but such as I must share with them. I have the most unquestionable evidence that the people who committed such unjustifiable outrages against your brother Miles, were not Indians, but British subjects, whom I am determined to bring to justice, and I trust that the example of their punishment will prevent any similar attempt from being made in future."

The existence of these letters, and their value in throwing light on the early history of the country, call urgently for the founding, in our midst, of an Historical Society, in the archives of which they may be preserved, and where they may be accessible to students of our local annals.

CHAPTER IX.

THE INDIAN TRIBES OF THE OLDER PROVINCES AND THE NORTH-WEST.

SAVAGERY, it has been said, is civilisation's childhood. We should like to think so. Despite past experience of the Indian in his savage state, we should like to think, that in his brutalised condition there were the makings of something better. We should like to think, that as it has been the fate of some portions of the race to lapse into barbarism, that out of barbarism they will yet emerge. We should like to think, that, in the philanthropies of a coming day, forces will yet be moved to restore the Indian to civilisation, and to eradicate from his nature those dispositions and tendencies that drag him backward in the path of progress, or, while imitating bad examples set before him, that civilise him out of existence. We are told that a race that cannot itself contribute its redeemers will never be redeemed. But this is too pessimistic a view to be willingly entertained. We admit it would be encouraging to find, that, when some advance has been made by the savage towards civilisation, reversionary tendencies did not persistently crop out, and undo the work that had been done. But have the conditions been favourable to the experiment?

Has the reclamation of the Indian been tried under conditions so auspicious that one might look for anything but failure; and has it been tried with earnestness and persistence? People who speak hopelessly of the civilisation of the aborigines have spoken with like hopelessness of the "lapsed masses" of their own kind. There is one feature, at least, of encouragement in the Indian's case, namely, that we have never enslaved him, though, unfortunately, he has enslaved himself. But for the latter we are more responsible, perhaps, than he. Too often we have made of the noble savage an ignoble brute.

The problem of Indian civilisation is a profoundly interesting one. To the people of this continent, it is more however than this. On three specific grounds it is of momentous import: first, as a duty incumbent upon governments, in the management of those wards of a nation whose hunting-grounds the country has appropriated; secondly, as a Christian people, responsible for the care and wellbeing of their less favoured brethren; and thirdly, in the relation of all towards subject tribes whose good-will it is desirable to propitiate, for the sake of the poor settler who makes his habitation among them. The Indian Question, long ago, became one peculiarly appropriate for the white race to discuss. As has been said of it, it is a question entirely of the white man's making. We came to the Indian, not the Indian to us. We were the aggressors. We invaded his territory, and we made of it an aceldama of blood. With one hand we held before him the Cross; with the other we cut him down with the sword. While we taught him that Christ's kingdom was peace, we showed him that man's mission was war. So far from bringing him the olive branch, we have brought him fire-arms and fire-water, and what was worse, the diseases of lust, and an example in morals he has not been slow to copy. We speak of the failure of efforts to civilise, but we do not boast of the failure to exterminate. In the face of our relations with him, it ill becomes our humanity to say, that "the only good Indian is a dead one!"

Before passing any hasty judgment upon what civilisation is pleased to call "the savage tribes" of this continent, it is worth while for a moment to look at the relations civilisation has had with the savages. Tribal wars, we know, are of immemorial antiquity; but had the incoming of Europeans no influence in either extending them, or in adding to their ferocity? It would be easy to prove that the contrary is the fact. What, for instance, gave increased violence to Iroquois enmity to the Hurons, but the intermeddling, in 1615, of Champlain and his French following. In the early colonial days, settlement on the Atlantic seaboard was effected only after devastating wars had been waged upon the natives. What story is more harrowing in all history than that of Spanish settlement in Florida, or more revolting than the narrative of King Philips' War in New England? Nor do we find the records of Dutch colonisation in New York State, or the contemporary history of Virginia, less full of horrors. Westward, the same tale of carnage is written over the face of the country. Let the reader recall the strife between the red man and the white in the region between the Alleghanies and the Ohio, and say on which side was displayed the greatest ferocity. But we need not go so far back in history for instances of inhumanity towards the Indian. To read the relations with the red man of recent border men in Kentucky, of Indianized white men in Texas, and of the traditional trader and cow-boy of the western plains, would curdle the blood of the most abandoned representative of modern civilisation. In all the range and license of human passion, history has no greater atrocities to chronicle.

The blood of white men, it is true, has been freely outpoured by the hand of the Indian. But this blood has, in the main, flowed at the instigation of white men, to revenge themselves on their European rivals. In shedding it the Indian ally has not scantily shed his own. A recent American writer,* on colonial relations with the Indians, bears testimony to this fact. Here are his remarks:

"During our whole colonial and provincial period it was the hard fate of the Indians to bear the brunt of every quarrel between the rival European colonists in their jealousies and struggles for dominion and the profits of the fur-trade. No sooner had one of the rivals conciliated or established friendly relations with one or more of the tribes, than the representatives of the other rival would seek to thwart any advantage of their opponents by openly or covertly forming alliances with other tribes. Tribes which might otherwise have lived in a state of suspended animosity towards each other were thus driven to take the war-path. So, too, it has happened that the whole or a portion of a tribe, or of allied tribes, in the course of a century was found in the pay and service of the French against the English; of the English against the French; of the Spaniards against the French; and of the French against the Spaniards; and then of the armies of Great Britain and our own provincial forces against the French, followed in a few years by their enlistment by Great Britain to aid her in crushing the rebellion of her own colonies."

The heat of these periods of conflict among Europeans on this continent has long passed, and we ought now to be just and humane enough to lay at our own doors responsibility for inciting the Indians to acts of savagery. There is the more reason for this, as these acts were mainly the result of our own follies and our own intrigues. It may be that, as Horace Greeley on one occasion wrote, "it needs but little familia-

* "The Red Man and the White Man in North America." By George E. Ellis, Boston, 1882. (Page 346).

J

rity with the actual, palpable aborigines to convince any one that the poetic Indian, the Indian of Cooper and Longfellow, is only visible to the poet's eye." But while we divest the child of the woods of those fictional fascinations that have made him an interesting and picturesque figure in the world of western humanity, we are not called upon to paint him in the pigments of the pit, or to endow him with the attributes of fiends. No doubt, the Indian, in mental characteristics, is alien to the European race, that his thoughts run in a different channel from our thoughts, and that he is a creature of instinct rather than of reason; but though of another mental type, it does not follow that we should visit upon him giant injustice, or that he should even forfeit his claim to considerate treatment at our hands.

The late General Custer, of the American army, has told us that while he found much to interest him in the study of the Indian character, particularly in the wonderful power and subtlety of his senses, he was compelled to admit, from his intimate association with the red man, that he was essentially a savage; and that while civilisation may and should do much for him, it can never civilise him. But this unfortunate, foolhardy officer lived among Indians who were the hunted of the earth, and whose every instinct was trained to its acutest sense, that their possessors might cunningly hold their own against men who were known to glory in the professional title of "Indian fighters." How different is the judgment of Catlin, the great delineator of Indian character. Of the North American Indian, this great painter sympathetically, though frankly writes, that in his native state, "he is an hospitable, honest, faithful, brave, warlike, cruel, revengeful, relentless, yet honourable, contemplative and religious being." He adds, "I have lived with thousands and tens of thousands of these knights of the forest, whose whole lives are lives of chivalry, and whose daily feats with their naked limbs, might vie with those of the Grecian youth in the beautiful rivalry of the Olympian games." In another passage he affirms, that " they have learned their worst vices from contamination with Europeans," but withal that they are nature's noblemen, and deserve ever to be spoken of with sympathy, " as a people who are dying of broken hearts, and who never can speak in the civilised world in their own defence."

The truth is, that on this continent, as elsewhere among tribes living in a state of nature, opinions are formed about the aboriginal inhabitants pretty much as individual experience has enabled the writer personally to judge. This experience has been more or less determined by the attitude assumed towards them of the observer of their manners and customs. The mild Livingstone, travelling unarmed in the heart of Africa, has given us a picture of the native tribes of the Dark Continent altogether different from that of the bumptious, self-asserting Stanley, with his self-cocking revolver and explosive bullets. Similarly, in the western world, we have diversities of portraiture of our native tribes, limned according to the dispositions and bearing of the writers who have made their acquaintance. As with the white man so with the red, there are two sides to the Indian shield; each represents the Indian character in the mood in which you force the savage to look at himself. Take this one other, and a dispassionate, view of the Indian character from Jonathan Carver:

" That the Indians," writes he, " are of a cruel, revengeful, inexorable disposition, that they will watch whole days unmindful of the calls of nature, and make their way through pathless, and almost unbounded woods, subsisting only on the scanty produce of them, to pursue and revenge themselves on an enemy; that they hear unmoved the piercing cries of such as unhappily fall into their hands, and receive a diabolical pleasure from the tortures they inflict on their prisoners, I readily grant; but let us look on the reverse of this terrifying picture, and we shall find them temperate both in their diet and potations (I speak of those tribes who have little communication with Europeans) that they withstand, with unexampled patience, the attacks of hunger, or the inclemency of the seasons, and esteem the gratification of their appetites but a secondary consideration. We shall likewise see them sociable and humane to those whom they consider their friends, and even to their adopted enemies; and ready to partake with them of the last morsel or to risk their lives in their defence. The honour of their tribe and the welfare of their nation is the first and predominant emotion of their hearts; and hence proceed in a great measure all their virtues and their vices. Actuated by this, they brave every danger, endure the most exquisite torments, and expire triumphing in their fortitude, not as a personal qualification, but as a national characteristic."*

Ethnically, the Indians of Canada, if not one people, have descended from a well-defined parent stock, the Huron-Iroquois tribe. Professor Huxley hypothetically represents the old Mexican and South-America races as the true American stock, and speaks of the Red Indians of North America as the product of an intermixture of the autochthonous, or indigenous, native race with the Eskimo. The affinity of the latter with the Asiatic Mongol is now pretty well established; and we may look upon our native races as remote descendants of the Asiatic continent. We shall leave to Dr. Daniel Wilson, the learned President of Toronto University, the ethnological questions that arise out of this aspect of the Indian problem, premising that the bulk of our readers are not absorbingly interested in skull formations, as indications of racial unity, or in the subtler philological questions that bear on the problem of Indian origin. Whether the dolichocephalic head-form, charac-

---

* Carver's "Travels through the Interior Parts of North America, in the years 1766-68," (page 409-12), London, 1779.

teristic of the Huron-Iroquois stock, had precedence, when it crowned the body of the savage nomad, over the brachycephalic cranial features of the southern Indian tribes, in this part of the continent, we take it, is to most readers not a theme of delirious popular excitement, though in saying this we are far from wishing to slight the valuable labours of our native antiquaries. It will suffice for the unlearned (among the hosts of which the writer sadly finds himself) to know that our precursors in the occupancy of the soil of Canada were of the great Huron-Iroquois family, and that their earliest home, as Dr. Wilson tells us,* was "within the area latterly embraced in Upper and Lower Canada."

There are some facts connected with the early movements of the primitive Indian tribes of Canada which are worthy to be noted, as they enter into the history of the country ; and these, with the assistance of the authority we have quoted, we may for a brief moment glance at. Though research has enabled our ethnologists to trace to one parent stock the Iroquois and the Huron, or Wyandot, history knows them for centuries only as cruel, bitter, and relentless foes. Let us see how this came about. When Cartier discovered the St. Lawrence, and wonderingly threaded his way up to the palisaded Indian towns of Stadacona and Hochelaga, he found these strongholds and the whole valley of the St. Lawrence populous with Indians of the Huron-Iroquois tribe. Seventy years later, when Champlain came to the country, the Huron-Iroquois warriors had vanished, and only a few Algonquins, in their birch-bark wigwams, were found in their place. Tradition furnishes but a hazy clue to this Hegira. A woman, so the story goes, was the cause of the migration.

---

* See an interesting and erudite article on " A Typical Race of American Aborigines," contributed by President Daniel Wilson, LL.D., to the Transactions of the Royal Society of Canada, for the year 1884.

When both tribes sojourned together in neighbouring villages at Hochelaga, it seems, that a Seneca maiden was wronged in her affections by a Seneca chief. To avenge herself, she plighted her troth to a young Huron warrior, on his undertaking to slay the ungallant betrayer. This accomplished, the Iroquois, taking up the dead man's quarrel, fell upon their Huron kinsmen, and, to save themselves, they fled up the Ottawa to the homes they are subsequently known to have founded. The story further goes, that the Iroquois, under a similar incentive to revenge, themselves deserted the region to visit their wrath upon the Eries, to the west of Niagara, after which they settled where we subsequently find them, in the valley of the Mohawk. Another tradition accounts for the Seneca exodus from Hochelaga, by the assertion that they were driven from the region by the Algonquins. This is not improbable, for in the subsequent many years struggle between the Hurons and the Iroquois, we find the Algonquins active allies of the Hurons. They were themselves also to suffer from the fierce onslaughts of the common foe. The story of the Huron-Iroquois conflict, during the years 1640-48, will always be sadly, though proudly, associated with the unquenchable zeal of the Jesuit missionaries and their heroic martyrdom. There is no grander page in the world's religious history than that which records the doings of their Church in the wilderness, and enshrines the names of Brebeuf, Bressani, Lallemant, Jogues, and Daniel.

The different families of the great Huron nation that once peopled New France have almost wholly disappeared. Nearly all that is left of them are the ossuaries, the bone-pits, of a race that were once the sole possessors of the land. Their few modern representatives are gathered in meagre bands on reserves in various sections of the two older Provinces. These comprise some 29,000 in all, of which about 17,000 are in the Upper, and 12,000 are in the Lower Province. In Quebec Province, of these 12,000, the bulk are Algonquins and Iroquois. The habitat of the latter is chiefly Caughnawaga and St. Regis: the Algonquins are scattered throughout the Province, though the largest portion are in Pontiac county and the Ottawa and Temiscamingue districts. Other branches of the Algonquin family, the Montagnais, the Naskapees, and the Micmacs, are mainly to be found on the Lower St. Lawrence. Only a remnant, under 300, of the Huron tribe finds a home at Lorette. About the same number of Abenakis are domiciled in St. Francis. The Indians of the Maritime Provinces, numbering some 4,000, are chiefly Micmacs and Amalicites.

Generically, the bulk of the Indians of the Province of Ontario are of the Algonquin family. They are known by their tribal names, Chipeways, Ojibways, Mississaguas, and the various branches of the Iroquois stock—the Mohawks, Oneidas, and those included in the colony of the Six Nations, on the Grand River. This latter colony furnishes, perhaps, the best example in the Province of the civilised Indian, who has left his nomadic ways and settled down to agricultural and industrial pursuits. It is composed of remnants of the Six Nation confederacy, descendants of the Mohawk chief, Brant, and his followers, who, during the revolutionary war, remained attached to Imperial interests. The Ojibways and Ottawas are principally met with on the islands and shores of the Georgian Bay, and on Lakes Huron and Superior. The demand for labour, occasioned by the extensive lumbering operations of the district, affords these Indians a good field for lucrative work. Some are successful traders, while many make a fair support by fishing. The Algonquins of the Province are almost entirely confined to the County of Renfrew: to the north of these are the Nipissings, who belong to the Chipeway tribe, and at present find remunerative employment in the construction of a local section of the Canadian Pacific railway. The Mississaguas find their home on the lakes in the County of Northumberland, and about the neighbourhood of Peterboro': the Mohawks have a fine reserve on the Bay of Quinté, and are making encouraging progress in agriculture. Portions of the lands of the latter are leased to white tenants. On the Thames, and in the Sarnia district, are the reserves of the Chipeways, the Munceys, and the Oneidas. These tribes farm considerably, and have a number of flourishing schools in their allotted districts. In the township of Gibson, in the Muskoka district, a small colony of Iroquois and Algonquins came recently from the Lake of the Two Mountains to settle; during the year 1883 they added fifty acres to the cleared land within their reserve and are prosperous and contented. Less than a hundred of enfranchised Wyandots, or Hurons, have an asylum in the township of Anderdon, in the county of Essex. These, with the three hundred of this tribe at Lorette, are the only representatives of the Hurons now in Canada.* In 1648, prior to the Iroquois extermination of their kinsmen, they numbered some thirty thousand souls, lodged in villages on the Matchedash peninsula, between Lake Simcoe and the Georgian Bay.

---

* From late official documents we find the total number of Indians in Canada to be about 132,000. They are dispersed as follows.

In Ontario and Quebec...29,000
— Maritime Provinces.. 4,000
— Labrador and Arctic Coast.. 9,000
— Manitoba and the North-West Territories...............34,000
— Athabasca District, and on the Peace and } 17,000
    the Mackenzie Rivers
— British Columbia 39,000

132,000

The Indians of the North-West may be said to represent five distinct families, viz., the Algonquins; the Assiniboines, or Stoneys, who are allied to the Sioux; the Blackfeet, including the Sarcees, Bloods, Piegans, and the Indians of the eastern slope of the Rocky Mountains; the Chippewyans, or Tinnés, a branch of the Montagnais; and the Eskimos, or Innoits, who belong to the Algonquin family, and are allied to the Kamschatkans or northern Mongols. The total number of Indians in the Province of Manitoba and the North-West Territories is in the neighbourhood of 34,000. Besides these some 17,000 inhabit the region of the Peace River, the Mackenzie River, and the watershed of the Athabasca. To the north and east of these, some 9000 are supposed to frequent the sterile shores of Labrador and the Arctic Coast. In British Columbia, the number of Indians is estimated at 39,000. Unhappily, a large proportion of the latter are degraded and dissolute; they are given to polygamy, to indulgence in a pernicious feast, known as the "Potlach," and to heathenish dances, the most disgusting of which is the "Tamanawa." The depravity of many of the women of the British Columbia tribes is great; large numbers of them frequent white centres and live a life of prostitution. There is much need of a moral regeneration on the Pacific, and particularly of legislation that will suppress the degrading spectacle of the tribal orgies.

The Manitoba Indians are mainly Algonquin. The tribe to the east of the Province is the Salteaux, or Chipeway, who roam westward from Sault Ste. Marie, round the north shore of Lake Superior, and along the margin of those "liquid battalions" that mark with a "silver streak" the country between the Kaministiquia and the Red River. "The Salteaux," remarks Archbishop Taché,* " are a high-spirited, proud, and

---

* " Sketch of the North-West of America." By Mgr. Taché, Bishop of St. Boniface. Translated by Captain D. R. Cameron, Montreal, 1870.

excessively superstitious people, and, in consequence, difficult to tame. Of all our Indians, these have had the greatest facilities for learning the truths of religion, and they, too, have least profited by their opportunities, and count fewest Christians amongst their number. . . . Nearly all have a great liking for intoxicating drink, which is one of the causes of their callousness." To the north and west of the Province are the Christineaux, or Crees : this tribe consists of two classes, the Crees of the Plains, and the Wood Crees. The former live in "loges," or leathern wigwams, while the latter, like the Salteaux, house themselves in birch-bark huts. In 1874, Government made a Treaty (No. 4) with the Cree Salteaux, in which the latter surrendered their right to a territory estimated at a hundred thousand square miles. Allied to the Crees are the Muskegons, or Swampies, so called from the swampy character of the district which they inhabit,—" the neighbourhood of the group of lakes which collect the water of the great rivers flowing into Hudson Bay." Many of the Cree tribe are leaders of the present revolt in the North-West, that notorious rascal, Big Bear, and the participants in the atrocities at Fort Pitt, being of the number. Westward, outside of the Province, are the Assiniboines of the plain and of the forest. With the Salteaux, this tribe formerly kept up lively hostilities against the Sioux, to the south ; and, with the Crees, they have long been at enmity with the Blackfeet. The latter are the Iroquois of the west, and with the Bloods, Piegans, and Sarcees, to whom they are related, are a warlike people. Treaty No. 7, effected in September, 1877, includes this tribe. The Indians of the remaining family to be enumerated in the North-West are the Chippewyans, or Montagnais ("Tinnés" they are familiarly called). The region occupied by this peaceful tribe covers the district of the English, or Churchill, the Athabasca, and the Mackenzie rivers. This tribe includes the Cariboo Eaters, the Yellow Knives, the Castors, the Slaves (which embrace the Dog-rib and the Hare-skin Indians), and the Montagnais proper.

The condition of the Treaty Indians in Manitoba and Keewatin is on the whole gratifying. Some bands lead a shiftless and vagabond life; but the majority are prosperous, and not a few are well-to-do. On some reserves, it occasionally happens, that a tribe will want Government assistance more largely in one season than in another. This may arise from a period of drought, or from a visitation from the grasshopper, or from the year's fishing being poor and the product of the chase light. The Indians of Manitoba, however, may be said to be comfortably off, and to be rapidly acquiring facility in the management of the farm. The scarcity of large game now on the plains must drive them to agriculture, as a means of subsistence, unless they betake themselves to the northern lakes for fish and fowl. Those with large families have a goodly income from the Government annuities; and the increasing number of settlers gives them opportunity, in various employments, to add to their means of livelihood. As herdsmen, they are finding increasing demand for their services, though in this, as in other light vocations, they are brought into competition with their partial kinsmen, the Half-breed.

Of the tribes in the Territories, an encouraging number have of late years taken to agriculture, and to living in substantial huts on their reserves, in place of the conventional wigwams. Many of these Indians follow agriculture with a fair measure of success, in which the Government lends its aid, by money grants for seed, oxen, and implements, and by farm instruction, and the agency of good schools. In addition to the practical encouragement given the tribes through the Government's

Indian Agencies, sustained by liberal annual grants from Parliament, the Indians have the benefit of instruction in industrial and educational institutions, which are maintained by the various religious denominations, Protestant and Roman Catholic. These missions, however, are in sad need of augmentation and extension. So vast is the territory, and so numerous are the reserves, that only a large and efficiently maintained staff can overtake the work.

The Parliamentary appropriation for 1884, we learn from a recent Government Blue Book, was, for Manitoba and the North-West Territories, over a million of dollars. Of this large sum, almost a half was disbursed for provisions for destitute Indians. This fact, while it speaks well for the liberality of Parliament, and attests the humanity of our treatment of the red man, is not creditable to the Indian's industry, or to his disposition to improve his environment. Evidently, in the North-West, savage life, if it has begun has not advanced far in the effort to raise itself in the scale of being. Looking at the events of the past few months, it would seem that whatever has been done for the Indian, that and more we must continue to do. Among some of the tribes there is a culpable amount of sloth and vagrancy. The idle Indian must be taught that if he is to be fed he must work. And while he is fed, if he is not effusively grateful, he must, at least, be passively loyal.

CHAPTER X.

FIFTY YEARS' INTERVAL—1820 TO 1870.

UPON the amalgamation of the rival Fur Companies, the Red River colony began a new era in its chequered career. Its troubles, however, were not over: its cup of bitterness was not yet full. The Iliad of its woe, besides narrating the doings of the turbulent Fur traders, and chronicling the visitation of its plague of grasshoppers, has yet to recount disaster from floods, and the continued grindings of a hard-visaged monopoly. For long there was little progress and few additions to the population, for the Hudson Bay Company had locked the door on the colony and put the key in its pocket.

Though a good deal of space has been taken up in the preceding chapters with Scottish lawlessness in the region, it is not to be supposed that this was a new and sinister development of the national character. On the contrary, these disturbances were as exceptional as, in point of time and place, they were local. They arose out of peculiar circumstances; and when the occasion passed that gave them birth, Scottish humanity and respect for law and order quickly asserted their presence and influence. Speaking of a later time, a thoughtful writer,* who has recently passed away, has left on record this testimony to the wholesome conservatism of the Scottish character, in its influence on the social fabric of the North-West. Says the writer: "The Scottish respect for constituted authority, for the ordinances of religion, and the Christian code of morality, which is instinctive with many of the old settlers as well as the more recent arrivals, has fortunately proved a strong barrier against the disintegrating and unsettling influences of a sudden influx of settlement." But the day of rapid colonisation was yet distant. There was a long period of quiescence between the restoration of peace in the settlement and the manifestation of anything like national life. The period of development to manhood, with the activities of a well-organised and progressive community, was long in coming. But this was occasioned by the circumstances of the colony; and is explained by its isolation, its remoteness from the seaboard, its small and half-savage population, and by the repressive influences of the monopoly that still hung over it. More than all, perhaps, its non-progress was due to the false reports the monopolists circulated of the poor soil of the colony and its rigorous climate. It received a character in those days that long stuck to it.

How the country was slandered by the agents of the great Fur Company was not only outrageous, it was farcical. To use an early phrase of Horace Walpole, "history never can describe it and keep its countenance." When the true facts came out, the shifts and contradictions to which its servants had to resort, were most amusing. The evidence of officers of the Hudson Bay Company, taken at the examination before a Committee of the English Parliament, was tinged with that

---

* "The Scot in British North America," Vol. 4. By Wm. J. Rattray, B.A. Toronto: 1883.

delightful bias which a writer of the period describes, as being "congenial to find old gentlemen deeply interested in fur." This, in short, is the explanation of the matter: the Company was interested in fur, and not in settlement. Meanwhile, the giant stripling was kept in small clothes.

Through the generosity of Lord Selkirk, the effects of the grasshopper blight were got over by the bringing in of seed, and of provisions for the time being, from Illinois and other regions to the south. This occasioned a draft of over a thousand pounds sterling upon the Selkirk estate. But this aid, however timely, was merely temporary. The colony was ere long thrown upon its own resources, and these unhappily were not well managed. Abortive enterprises, such as the Buffalo-Wool Company, and the experimental Hay Field Farm, long kept the colony back, and still further discouraged the settlers. The latter, however, had some relief in getting rid of the governorship of Alexander McDonell, whose stewardship was notoriously bad, and whose imposts on goods coming into the country were vexatious and fraudulent. Despite the difficulties, the colony made progress, and time brought cheer. Cattle were imported, and with better agricultural implements came improved farming. Industries, too, soon began to stir in the womb of the colony, and ere long had their auspicious birth. As they awoke to life, the stoical Indian paused for a moment in his basket-making, and Jean Baptiste thought his trapping days had come to an end.

About this time the colony was consolidated, by gathering round a common centre, known as "The Forks," formed by the junction of the Red River and the Assiniboine. The French Canadians, who had come from the border settlement, at Pembina, removed to St. Boniface, alongside the Scotch colony; while the half-breeds stationed themselves at White

Horse Plains, some little distance up the Assiniboine. In the coming together of these incongruous elements of race and religion, we see the first beginnings in the community of creed warfare and political strife. Ross, the early historian of the colony, thus writes of the event:

"We have now seen all the different classes of which this infant colony was composed brought together. The better to advance each other's interest, as well as for mutual support, all sects and creeds associated together indiscriminately, and were united like members of the same family, in peace, charity, and good-fellowship. This state of things lasted till the Churchmen began to feel uneasy, and the Catholics grew jealous; so that projects were set on foot to separate the tares from the wheat. Whatever reason might be urged for this division, in a religious point of view, it was, politically considered, an ill-judged step; yet the measure was carried, and the separation took place, inflicting a wound which has never been healed to this day. From these original causes party spirit has been gaining ground ever since. The Canadians became jealous of the Scotch, the half-breeds of both; and their separate interests, as agriculturists, *voyageurs*, or hunters, had little tendency to unite them. At length, indeed, the Canadians and the half-breeds came to a good understanding with each other; leaving them but two parties, the Scotch and the French. Between these, although there is, and always has been, a fair show of mutual good feeling, anything like cordiality in a common sentiment seemed impossible; and they remain to this day politically divided."

But for a time party strife was to give way before the grief of a common sorrow. The winter of 1826-7 brought to the colony such a disaster as it had never known. Already it had suffered from almost every plague that malignancy could dream of: it was now to complete its experience of the cycle of woe. Hardly had the autumn closed when the settlement was invaded by legions of mice, which, like the grasshoppers, devoured every bit of grain, standing or stalked, together with the straw in the barns and even the stubble on the field.

LIEUT.-COLONEL W. D. OTTER.

Before this army of rodents all game disappeared, and the plains were soon barren of life. Winter set in with unusual severity, and with it came the most continuous storms that had ever been known, which drove the buffalo beyond the hunter's reach, and buried the colony under mountains of snow. For a time there could be no communication between the colonists, and no assistance rendered to those most sorely in need. A famine, moreover, was in every home.

"Families here and there"—writes Ross—"despairing of life, huddled themselves together for warmth, and in too many cases their shelter proved their grave. At first, the heat of their bodies melted the snow; they became wet, and being without food or fuel, the cold soon penetrated, and in several instances, froze the whole into a body of solid ice. Some, again, was found in a state of wild delirium, frantic, mad; while others were picked up, one here and one there, frozen to death in their fruitless attempts to reach Pembina—some half way, some more, some less; one woman was found with an infant on her back, within a quarter of a mile of Pembina. The poor creature must have travelled at least 125 miles in three days and nights, till she sunk at last in the too unequal struggle for life."

Those who were found alive had devoured their horses, their dogs, raw hides, and even their shoes. Ross states that thirty-three lives were lost: one man, with his wife and three children, were dug out of the snow, where they had been buried for five days and nights, without food, fire, or the light of the sun. Such are the incidents of this heart-rending tale. But hardly had those of the colonists as were in a position to see the winter through escaped from its terrors ere new disaster came upon them. The cold had been intense, the thermometer often registering 45° below zero, while the snow lay on the ground to the depth of four or five feet. The ice measured five feet seven inches in thickness! With the spring

K

all this came to be melted, and the colony, with its varied experience, had added to it that of a deluge. We again resort to the narrative of an eye-witness:

"On the fourth of May, the water overflowed the banks of the Red River, and now spread so fast, that almost before the people were aware of the danger it had reached their dwellings. Terror was depicted on every countenance. So level was the country, and so rapid the rise of the waters, that on the fifth the settlers had to fly from their homes for dear life, some of them saving only the clothes they had on their backs. The shrieks of children, the lowing of cattle, and the howling of dogs, added terror to the scene. The country presented the appearance of a vast lake. The ice now drifted in a straight course from point to point, carrying destruction before it; and the trees were bent like willows by the force of the current. While the frightened inhabitants were collected in groups on any dry spot that remained visible above the waste of waters, their houses, barns, carriages, furniture, fencing, and every description of property, might be seen floating along over the wide extended plain, to be engulfed in Lake Winnipeg. Hardly a house or building of any kind was left standing in the colony. Many of the buildings drifted along whole and entire; and in some were seen dogs, howling dismally, and cats that jumped frantically from side to side of their precarious abodes. The most singular spectacle was a house in flames, drifting along in the night, its one half immersed in water, and the remainder furiously burning. This accident was caused by the hasty retreat of the occupiers. At one spot the writer fell in with a man who had two of his oxen tied together, with his wife and four children fixed on their backs, as on a floating stage. The water continued rising till the 21st, and extended far over the plains; where cattle used to graze boats were now plying under full sail."

From the perils of inundation the ill-fated settlers at last escaped. It was the middle of June ere they saw the waters abate, and the sodden site of their colony, which had been covered by a flood fifteen feet deep, show itself. The distress that followed this period of horrors was piteous. The little market of the place, as a matter of course, was sensibly affected by the famine. We are told that "wheat, which had fallen to 2s. per bushel at the commencement of the disaster, now rose to 15s.; and beef from ½d to 3d per pound." What wonder that, speaking of another misfortune which befell the settlement, its Governor, in the bitterness of his heart, should exclaim: " Red River is like a Lybian tiger; the more I try to tame it, the more savage it becomes; . . . for every step I try to bring it forward, disappointments drag it two backward!" Both man and nature seem to have conspired to crush the colony.

Courage was not lacking, however, to grapple with disaster, and to renew the effort to put the colony yet on its feet. At this time Red River received a great impetus from the exertions of a new Governor-in-chief of the Hudson Bay Company, Mr. (afterwards Sir) George Simpson, a worthy Scottish gentleman, who, for forty years, was to conduct its affairs in this country. The great public services of this distinguished officer of the Company, no less than his admirably performed official duties, well deserve to be recorded in any history of the North-West. He was the one servant of the Company who, while mindful of its trading mission, did not forget the claims of science, or the obligations that lay upon it to advance the interests of geographical discovery. As has been well said of him : " To his skilful direction and the eagerness with which he assisted Franklin, Richardson, Ross, Back, and other explorers, the most valuable results were due. It was he who sent out Dease, Thomas Simpson, Rae, Anderson, and Stewart upon the path of research; and at every fort or factory, controlled by the Governor, any explorer was sure of shelter, supplies, information, and advice." He has left behind him a most interesting record of a journey round the world,* in the early portion of which we have a graphic narrative of his trans-continental tour from Lachine, near Montreal, where he long resided, to the Pacific. Our fast contracting space prevents us from giving any notice of this journey; but the volume itself is well worthy of perusal, and we heartily commend it our readers. We content ourselves with making but one extract, a tribute to the arduous labour and high motive of Lord Selkirk in founding the colony of Red River. Says Sir George:

"To mould this secluded spot into the nucleus of a vast civilisation was the arduous and honourable task which Lord Selkirk imposed on himself. . . His was a pure spirit of colonisation. He courted not for himself the virgin secrets of some golden sierra; he needed no outlet for a starving tenantry; he sought no asylum for a persecuted faith: the object for which he longed was to make the wilderness glad and to see the desert blossom as the rose."

During Governor Simpson's long tenure of office not only were the material affairs of the colony advanced, but old wounds were healed, old jealousies removed, clashing interests reconciled, and the various elements of strife pacified and allayed. However afterwards he belied the country, in his advocacy of the trading monopoly of his employers, he was a sincere friend of the colony, and in his book wrote truthfully, though perhaps with a too exuberant colour, of the attractions of the Canadian North-West. Unfortunately, there came a time when the ever out-cropping monopoly of the Hudson Bay Company again jarred upon the colony, and as the wedge, cleaving its way inward, severed the interests of traders and

---

* "An Overland Journey round the World, during the years 1841-2. By Sir George Simpson, Governor-in-chief of the Hudson Bay Territory." London, 1843.

settlers, Sir George took up a position, if not inimical to the colony, at least hostile to its expansion.

In 1835, the Hudson Bay Company acquired from the representatives of Lord Selkirk all the family's interest in the lands and buildings embraced in the colony of the Red River. The interest was acquired by purchase, the price being the amount—£85,000—which it had cost his Lordship and his executors to found, and so far maintain, this settlement in the wilderness. The Selkirk family, it seems, had found it difficult and unsatisfactory to maintain relations with the colony while its affairs were managed by the Hudson Bay Company. Whatever the motive to sell, we can well understand the family desiring to get rid of its burden of responsibility. With this change of masters came the era of quasi-constitutional rule, and the organisation of local courts of justice, with a code of laws for the colony. That the first council was largely composed of old fur-traders, sinecurists, and other servants of the Company, need occasion little surprise; though in justice, it is to be said, that these were the men who had the most influence in the country and had the largest stake in it. This change in the management of the Settlement at first was not quietly acquiesced in by the colonists. Indeed, for some time they were kept in the dark about the transfer. The Scotch portion had always chafed under the paternal system of the Company's agency; they now feared being subject to its exclusive control. But while the ruling power was in the hands of Sir George, they had little cause to complain; and the colony made an unchecked advance in the march of progress.

Meanwhile, the Scotch, as perhaps it was well for them, though not for the colony, were not having it all their own way. The half-breeds, who were the hunters, and consequently the main feeders of the colony, were, by reason of their usefulness, pampered and spoiled. As they were much made of, crowds of them clustered round the Settlement, and they soon became a formidable party. "Time and numbers," we are told, "increased their boldness, until it became their habit to bully the Company into their views." In 1834 we meet with the first instance of their intractableness, and of the igniting of the inflammable materials of which the race is composed. The exciting cause of the trouble was the trivial circumstance of one of the Hudson Bay people chastising a half-breed, named Larocque, "who had provoked him by his insolent and over-bearing conduct." The race instantly took up the aggrieved man's quarrel, and demanded the surrender from the Governor of the person who had made the assault. The whole half-breed race of French extraction, we learn, took up the war-song, and, after the fashion of the Indians, resorted to the war-dance, while a buzz of anxiety pervaded the colony. Overtures were made to pacifiy the breeds, and a deputation was sent by the Governor to effect, if possible, a friendly settlement. Mr. Ross, the colony's historian, who was one of the deputation, thus narrates the result:

"On arriving at the place where the hostile party were assembled, we were struck with their savage appearance. They resembled more a troop of furies than human beings, all occupied in the Indian dance. As the arguments upon which we entered would only tire the reader, we shall pass them by, simply remarking, that reason is but a feeble weapon against brute force. Nevertheless, after a two hours' parley, reason triumphed, and we got the knotty point settled by making a few trifling concessions, taking no small credit to ourselves for our diplomatic success. We must confess, however, that the bearing of the half-breeds became haughtier than ever, for the spring was no sooner ushered in, than another physical demonstration took place at the gates of Fort Garry. This was the introduction of a new series of demands. . . . . Demand after demand now followed in close succession. These were all feelers set forth covertly by designing and disaffected demagogues, who made dupes of the silly half-breeds to answer their own vile purposes, by always pushing them forward in the front rank to screen themselves; yet, during all these hostile attempts and foolish demands, no act of outrage was committed. " Left to themselves," adds the historian, "the half-breeds are credulous and noisy, but are by no means a bad people."

How far this character is still true of the half-breed, many to-day have their doubts. The present writer inclines to the belief that it *is* true: that the half-breed, and even the whole breed, is not the human monster some would depict. In many of their characteristics they are mere children; and, like children, they are readily influenced by example, and are plastic in the hands of designing people. Those of French parentage have in an exaggerated degree the faults of their sires—they are volatile and unsedate. " They farm to-day, hunt to-morrow, and fish the next:" the world's cares sit lightly upon them; but in the main they are contented and happy, and if they are let alone, they are a peaceable and friendly people. They suit the country in which they find a home, and, if properly treated, can be well-behaved and useful in the community. At the time of which we write, and for some years afterwards, the great drawback to the colony was the want of a market and the precariousness of the trapper's trade. This is well brought out in Mr. Ross's volume, a further and final extract from which we here take the liberty to quote.

" Our population is made up of two classes nearly equal in number: the European or agricultural party, and the native or aboriginal party, called hunters or half-breeds, differing as much in their habits of life and daily pursuits as in the colour of their skin. In the present state of things, their interests are exactly opposed to each other, inasmuch as a market for one party shuts up all prospect against the other. The plain business is as uncertain as the wind that blows. One year may prove abundant, and the next a complete failure. When the plains fail, the farmer's produce is in demand; and when the crops fail, the hunter finds a ready market; but when both are successful, there is not a tithe of a market for either within the colony. Such a state of things as now exists cramps industry, and renders labour—the great source of wealth in other countries—utterly fruitless. Hence an idle, vagrant, and grumbling population—a population with barns full, stores teaming with plenty, and yet their wives and children half naked, insomuch that the more industrious and wealthy can scarcely command a shilling to pay the doctor's bill, or their children's education. Singular assemblage of wealth and want, of abundance and wretchedness!"

Such, up to a comparatively recent period, was the condition of things in what used to be the remote and isolated Red River Colony. But its day of small things finally came to an end. An era dawned when the new wine burst the old bottles: the scaled book was at last opened. Parental rule, contracted horizons, jealously-guarded enclosures—were all sloughed off, and the fledgeling prepared itself for a far, circuitous flight.

From the parent nest went forth other timid flutterers to colonise new sections of the country, and to form centres of life where life had hardly ever been. The question of colonisation now took a wider range than the development of a local colony. The outer world began to hear facts about the country so long defamed: whisperings of its fertile soil and wonderful crops were eagerly caught up and circulated; and many came to augment the population. These saw for themselves that the ill-conditioned fellows who had been protesting against the absolute power of a trading monopoly, so long exercised to keep the country unknown, were right, and that the region was not, as it had been represented, a sterile waste. It was found that even the name of the territory, associated in the mind with the Arctic surroundings of Hudson Bay, was itself a prejudice. Had they thought at all, they would have surmised that a region extending through twenty degrees of latitude and fifty of longitude, must vary much in climate, in soil, and in physical characteristics. But there were other facts they could not well know. They did not know, for instance, that "nature marching from east to west, showered her bounties on the land of the United States until she reached the Mississippi, but there she turned aside and went northward to favour British territory." They did not know of those fertile zones, " which curve towards the north, as they proceed westward, so that the western extremity of the belt is several degrees of latitude higher than the eastern, the curves apparently corresponding pretty closely with certain isothermal lines."* When these facts became known, there was, for a time, a rage for the literature of travel in the North-West, a rage which the present writer hopes, with a pardonable degree of interest, may not have died out ere his book appears.

Among the first of these modern books of travel in the region is one we have already referred to, which contained glowing descriptions of the country, descriptions which came to be in curious contrast to later, though far from impartial, public testimony from the same writer. Sir George Simpson was bound up body and soul, if we may so speak without irreverence or disparagement, in the Hudson Bay corporation; but before he allowed himself to look upon the country in the light of a furtrader, he spoke eulogistically of its attractions and hopefully of its future, as the happy abode of thousands of his countrymen. There may be poetry, but there is also fact, in this early, unwitting testimony of the worthy Governor to the fertility of portions of the valley of the Kaministiquia and the sylvan beauties of the Lake of the Woods:

---

* From an article, entitled, " The Last Great Monopoly," in the *Westminster Review*, for July, 1867.

"The river during the day's march," writes Sir George, "passed through forests of elm, oak, fir, and birch, being studded with hills not less fertile and lovely than its banks; and many a spot reminded us of the rich and quiet scenery of England. The paths of the different portages were spangled with violets, roses, and many other wild flowers, while the currant, the gooseberry, the raspberry, the plum, the cherry, and even the vine, were abundant. All this bounty of nature was inspired as it were with life by the cheerful notes of a variety of birds, and by the restless flutter of butterflies of the brightest hues. Compared with the adamantine deserts of Lake Superior, the Kaministiquia presented a perfect Paradise. One cannot pass through this fine valley without feeling that it is destined, sooner or later, to become the happy home of civilised men, with their bleating flocks and lowing herds and their full garners."

Equally impassioned, though perhaps more justified by facts, is his description of the luxuriant banks of the Saskatchewan, where were

"Lofty hills, and long valleys full of sylvan lakes, while the bright green of the surface, as far as the eye could reach, assumed a foreign tinge under an uninterrupted profusion of roses and blue bells. On the summit of one of these hills we commanded one of the few extensive prospects that we had of late enjoyed. One range of heights rose behind another, each becoming fainter as it receded from the eye, till the furthest was blended in almost undistinguishable confusion with the clouds, while the softest vales spread a panorama of hanging copses and glittering lakes at our feet."

From this imaginable "Land of the Lotus" came the testimony of other writers who, in quick succession, were to traverse the country. About this time the Imperial and the Canadian Governments commissioned experts to report upon the territory. Captain Palliser, in command of the British Expedition, wrote of the Fertile Belt in terms that at the time seemed extravagant. He speaks of a partially wooded country, abounding in lakes and rich natural pasturage, "in some parts rivalling the finest park scenery of England." Comment is also made on the fact that, in the region, spring commences about a month earlier than on the shores of the great lakes to the eastward; which are four or five degrees of latitude further south, and that even in the winter horses and cattle may be left for the season out of doors to obtain their own food. Professor Hind's testimony was an equal surprise to the outer world. He states that in one district only—that of the Red River and the Assiniboine—millions of acres of land which cannot be surpassed for fertility, being composed of rich prairie mould nearly two feet deep, lie free and unoccupied, awaiting settlement. Westward of this region, he brought before a wondering world the extraordinary luxuriance of the alluvial plains of the North Saskatchewan, rich in water, wood, and pasturage. Of these plains he thus writes:

"It is a physical reality of the highest importance to the interests of British North America that this continuous belt can be settled and cultivated from a few miles west of the Lake of the Woods to the passes of the Rocky Mountains; and any line of communication, whether by waggon-road or railway, passing through it, will eventually enjoy the great advantage of being fed by an agricultural population from one extremity to the other. No other part of the American continent possesses an approach even to this singularly favourable disposition of soil and climate; which last feature, notwithstanding its rigour during the winter season, confers, on account of its humidity, inestimable value on British America south of the fifty-fourth parallel."*

Following the reports of these Government expeditions came graphic records of the journeys of distinguished English and Canadian travellers, who fell under the fascination of a holiday tour through the woods and waters of the Canadian Far-West.

---

* "Narrative of the Canadian Red River Exploring Expedition of 1857, and of the Assiniboine and Saskatchewan Exploring Expedition of 1858." Undertaken by Authority of the Canadian Government. By Prof. Henry Youle Hind, M.A. 2 vols. London, 1860.

The more notable of these records are the volumes of the Earl of Southesk (1859); Lord Milton and Dr. Cheadle (1863); Captain Butler (1870), and our own Dr. Grant, the genial Principal of Queen's University (1872). Later days have brought us a whole library of books on the North-West, each with its own feature of interest, yet each freighted with the burden of commendation of the country and its wonderful resources. Before leaving this literature, let us sample the records of two of these English travellers. The first shall be from the narrative of Milton and Cheadle, with regard to the Red River and the Saskatchewan regions.

"In 1862, we found them (the Red River colonists) a very heterogeneous community of about 8,000 souls—Englishmen, Irishmen, Scotchmen, English Canadians, French Canadians, Americans, English half-breeds, Canadian half-breeds, and Indians. Nearly the whole population, with the exception of a few store-keepers and free-traders, live by the Hudson Bay Company, and the Company is King. The Company makes the laws, buys the produce of the chase and the farm, supplying in return the other necessaries and luxuries of life. The farmers of Red River are wealthy in flocks, and herds, and grain, more than sufficient for their own wants, and live in comparative comfort. The soil is so fertile that wheat is raised, year after year, fifty and sixty bushels to the acre, without any manure being required. The pasturage is of the finest quality, and unlimited in extent: the countless herds of buffalo which the land has supported is sufficient evidence of this. * * *

"We now entered a most glorious country—not indeed grandly picturesque, but rich and beautiful: a country of rolling hills and fertile valleys, of lakes and streams, groves of birch and aspen, and miniature prairies; a land of a kindly soil, and full of promise to the settlers to come in future years, when an enlightened policy shall open out the wealth now uncared for or unknown. * * The flowers in the open glade were very gay; tiger lilies, roses, the *Gallardia picta*, the blue borage, the white and purple vetch, red orchis, and the marsh violet were the most conspicuous. * * *

"Rich prairies, with from three to five feet of alluvial soil are ready for the plough, or offer the luxuriant grasses, which in the old time fattened countless bands of buffalo, to domesticated herds. Woods, lakes, and streams diversified the scene, and offer timber, fish, and myriads of wild fowl; yet this glorious country, estimated at 65,000 square miles, and 40 millions of acres of the richest soil, capable of supporting 20 millions of people, is from its isolated position, and the difficulties put in the way of settlement by the governing power, hitherto left utterly neglected and useless, except for the support of a few Indians and the employés of the Hudson Bay Company." *

Our extract from Captain Butler, for the sake of variety, shall be of another character. Let us select a passage in which that graphic writer describes the exhilarating experience of "running a rapid" on the Winnipeg River. The experience was gained while the writer was making his way to Fort Garry, with the Wolseley Red River Expedition, as an intelligence officer attached to the 69th Regiment of Foot.

"It is difficult to find in life any event which so effectually condenses nervous sensation into the shortest possible space of time, as does the work of shooting or running a rapid. There is no toil, no heart-breaking labour about it, but as much coolness, dexterity and skill, as man can throw into the work of hand, eye, and head; knowledge of when to strike and how to do it; knowledge of water and of rock, and of the one hundred combinations which rock and water can assume—for these two things, rock and water, taken in the abstract, fail as completely to convey any idea of their fierce embracings in the throes of a rapid, as the fire burning quietly in a drawing-room fire-place fails to convey the idea of a house wrapped and sheeted in flames. Above the rapid all is still and quiet, and one cannot see what is going on below the first rim of the rush, but stray shoots of spray and the deafening roar of de-

---

* "The North-West Passage by Land; a narrative of an expedition from the Atlantic to the Pacific," By Viscount Milton, M.P., and W. B. Cheadle, M.A., M.D. London, 1864.

scending water tell well enough what is about to happen. The Indian has got some rock or mark to steer by, and knows well the door by which he is to enter the slope of water. As the canoe—never appearing so frail a thing as when it is about to commence its series of wild leaps and rushes—nears the rim where the waters disappear from view, the bowsman stands up and, stretching forward his head, peers down the eddying rush; in a second he is on his knees again; without turning his head he speaks a word or two to those who are behind him; then the canoe is in the rim; she dips to it, shooting her bows clear out of the water and striking hard against the lower level. After that there is no time for thought; the eye is not quick enough to take in the rushing scene. There is a rock here and a big green cave of water there; there is a tumultuous rising and sinking of snow-tipped waves; there are places that are smooth-running for a moment, and then yawn and open up into great gurgling chasms the next; there are strange whirls and backward eddies and rocks, rough and smooth and polished— and through all this the canoe glances like an arrow, dips like a wild bird down the wing of the storm, now slanting from a rock, now edging a green cavern, now breaking through a backward rolling billow, without a word spoken, but with every now and again a quick convulsive twist and turn of the bow-paddle to edge far off some rock, to put her full through some boiling billow, to hold her steady down the slope of some thundering chute which has the power of a thousand horses: for remember, this river of rapids, this ·Winnipeg, is no mountain torrent, no brawling brook, but over every rocky ledge and wave-worn precipice there rushes twice a vaster volume than Rhine itself pours forth. The rocks which strew the torrent are frequently the most trifling of the dangers of the descent, formidable though they appear to the stranger. Sometimes a huge boulder will stand full in the midst of the channel, apparently presenting an obstacle from which escape seems impossible. The canoe is rushing full towards it, and no power can save it. There is just one power that can do it, and the rock itself provides it. Not the skill of man could run the boat *bows on* to that rock. There is a wilder sweep of water rushing off the polished sides than on to them, and the instant that we touch that sweep, we shoot away with redoubled speed. No, the rock is not as treacherous as the whirlpool and twisting billow."*

Never, it will be said, has pen better described the peril and excitement of this characteristically Canadian sport. But we must more rapidly bridge over our half century of Red River history, and speed on to events of immediate interest and later date. Let us return to the colony where, in Whittier's words,

> " Out and in the river is winding
> The links of its long, red chain,
> Through belts of dusky pine-land
> And gusty leagues of plain."

Here, in this oasis of civilisation, the primeval solitudes which once had been given up to the musquash and buffalo, were now beginning to be populous with immigrants and the descendants of the early Orkney settlers. The flowery meadow, which used to be the haunt of the prairie-bird and the blue-winged teal, was now being covered with the comfortable habitations of well-to-do traders and thriving farmers. The little settlement of Kildonan blossomed out into the town of Winnipeg. The successive incidents of note in the progress of the colony can be briefly enumerated. On the establishment, in 1835, of a Council of Assiniboia, the colony assumed a civic status and dignity which boded well for its future development. Its judicial system began, in 1839, with a Recordership; but its ecclesiastical and educational systems had an earlier start.

The Anglican Church in the Province may be said to have been founded, in 1820, by the Rev. Archdeacon Cochran; though some few years earlier, the Rev. John West, M.A., a Hudson Bay Chaplain, ministered to the Protestant commu-

---

* "The Great Lone Land : a Narrative of Travel and Adventure in the North-West of America." By Captain W. F. Butler, F.R.G.S. (pages 184-5). London, 1872.

nity. In 1849, the Church had so flourished as to have a Bishopric in the district, the Rev. David Anderson becoming first Bishop of Rupert's Land. It was not until 1852, that the Presbyterian body had a resident minister. In that year the Rev. Dr. John Black arrived in the colony, and was gladly hailed by the Scotch settlers, who had long hungered for a shepherd of their own communion. On his arrival, it is recorded, that 300 of the settlers, who had previously worshipped in the Anglican fold, rallied round Mr. Black, and formed a Church after the faith of their fathers. The Methodist denomination, at an early day, had labourers in the field, and flourishing missions, not only in Red River, but on the Saskatchewan and other districts in the West. Its permanent foothold in Winnipeg dates, however, from the arrival, in 1868, of the Rev. Mr. Young, a zealous representative of his Church. It is sad to note the fate of the predecessor of this gentleman, the Rev. George McDougall, who, as Methodist Missionary among the Indians, like St. Paul of old, was often in perils by the way, and who, as it has been said of him, "crowned a life of heroic struggle and self-sacrifice, by a martyr's death at his perilous post of duty." The incidents of the death of this fearless soldier of the Cross are thus feelingly narrated in *The Scot in British North America*:

"On the 24th of January, 1876, while hunting buffalo about thirty miles from Morleyville, to procure a supply of meat for the mission, he started to return to camp in advance of his party. It was a wild, stormy night, and a fierce wind swept the prairie laden with drifting snow. Mr. McDougall missed his way, and as a protracted search by his friends proved fruitless, the painful conclusion that he had perished from cold and exhaustion forced itself upon them. Twelve days afterwards, his body was found by a half-breed, stretched in death on the snow-covered prairie, the folded hands and placid expression of the features showing that the intrepid soul of the missionary had met death in the spirit of calm and trustful resignation—

> 'Like one who draws the drapery of his couch
> Around him, and lies down to pleasant dreams.'"

But the earliest missions in the country were those of the Roman Catholic Church, whose first representative was the Rev. Father Provencher. This worthy priest came to Red River in 1818, and was made Bishop of Juliopolis four years afterwards. On his death, in 1853, the present distinguished Archbishop Taché succeeded him in the See, the title of which was changed to St. Boniface. Convents and other educational agencies of the Romish Church were established in 1844. But much as we may wish to dwell on the Christian work of the Roman Catholic priesthood and sisterhood in the North-West, our space here does not justify our doing so. As the work was too good and self-sacrificing to be merely passingly acknowledged, we hope elsewhere to do it justice.

Recurring to the material progress of the incipient city, we may note the fact that for some time it rejoiced in the honors of a garrison town. From 1846 to 1848 a wing of the 6th Regiment of Foot was quartered at Red River; and for a number of years following the colony was protected by a corps of enrolled pensioners. Lord Selkirk's detachment of disbanded Swiss did not remain in the colony, but emigrated to more rapidly rising settlements on the Upper Mississippi. From 1857 to 1861 a company of the Royal Canadian Rifles occupied Fort Garry, during the excitement caused by the restless movements on the borders of the Sioux Indians. Their massacre of white settlers in Minnesota occurred in 1862; happily, in their visits to Red River, they were got rid of without bloodshed. In 1853 a public mail service was established,

L

which, to the delight of the settlers, took the place of the bi-annual packet-post *via* Hudson Bay. In 1859, that distinguishing mark of civilisation, a local newspaper, was founded, —the "Nor'-Wester" becoming the pioneer of the very able and enterprising modern press of Winnipeg. Three years afterwards, in the placing of a light draft steamboat on the river, facilities were afforded for communicating with the outer world; and the same season the village of Winnipeg was officially ushered into being. Could these means of communication be improved, many of its far-seeing inhabitants prophesied that the day would not be distant when it would become a great city.*

In the history of the Red River colony we now near modern times. The era of absolutism was to go, and that of freedom and progress was to usurp its place. The "Company of Adventurers" that for two centuries had been the absolute lords and proprietors of this great domain of the west, and that had adventured little in the territory save the money which had earned it royal dividends, was to abrogate its privileges and waive its long claim to monopoly. The Hudson Bay traders had not even been called upon to pay the considertion which King Charles had stipulated should bind the bargain—viz., " two elks and two black beavers, whensoever and as often as we, our heirs and successors, shall happen to enter the said countries, territories, and regions." Verily, Prince Rupert had had a cousinly gift, and the descendants of the Prince and his associates have been royally dealt with. But

---

* Ross gives the total population, in 1849, of the Red River Settlement, as 5391, housed in 745 dwellings. The area of cultivated land at the period, he states, was 6392 acres. He adds, in 1855, when his narrative went to press, that "there is no later census than the above; but the population of the colony this year is supposed to be about 6500 souls.".

the age was averse to monopolies; and when the interests of its equally favoured eastern rival had been assumed by the Crown, the great North-Western trading Company, however many and influential its advocates, could not long expect immunity from a like fate. The colony was now to yield to civilisation something more than beaver-skins and other products of the chase.

CHAPTER XII.

TRANSFER OF THE HUDSON BAY TERRITORIES TO THE DOMINION.

THE conflict between the past and the future, after these years of repression and strife, was now to be settled in favour of the coming time. The old was at last to give way to the new. In the unequal struggle with the advancing tide of civilisation, the Hudson Bay Company saw that it was finally to be worsted; and before the fate that impended was forced upon it, it discreetly endeavoured to secure terms upon which it might gracefully capitulate. While negotiations were pending, we can imagine with what feelings gouty old directors of the Company would meet at the London Board Room, in Fenchurch Street, and rail at the times being out of joint. How irately they would storm at the colonising spirit, and, in testy mood, splutter out expletives against the restless ambition of a young and progressive people! Yet, they were wise in their day and generation. They did not stand broom in hand, like Mrs. Partington, and hope successfully to sweep back the incoming tide of settlement, but allowed themselves to be borne shoreward to pick up on the beach the rich wreckage the ocean had spared them of their doomed argosy.

That the day was coming—had indeed now come—when the Company's rule was to cease, and the teeming life of the East was to be poured in upon the favoured plains of the West, the Company saw but too clearly; and seeing this, it made haste to set its house in order and make the best bargain possible. Already the voice of the colonists, petitioning the Canadian Parliament for relief from the tyranny of their situation, had been heard, and favourably heard, in England. As freemen they asked to be free. They asked for immunity from arbitrary arrest; from exorbitant imposts upon goods brought into the country; from the outrage of having their houses entered and effects confiscated at the caprice of a self-constituted authority; and relief, generally, from a rule that had become obnoxious, and a tyranny that was now galling. Here is the concluding portion of the colonists' petition, after reciting the grievances of which they complained:

" The Council (called into existence by the Hudson Bay Company) imposes taxes, creates offences, and punishes the same by fines and imprisonment,—*i.e.*, the Governor and Council make the laws, judge the laws, and execute their own sentence. We have no voice in their selection, neither have we any constitutional means of controlling their action. Under this system our energies are paralysed, and discontent is increasing to such a degree that events fatal to British interests, and particularly to the interests of Canada, and even to civilisation and humanity, may soon take place. When we contemplate the mighty tide of immigration which has flowed toward the north these six years past, and has already filled the valley of the Upper Mississippi with settlers, and which will this year flow over the height of land, and fill up the valley of Red River, is there no danger of being carried away by that flood, and that we may thereby lose our nationality? We love the British name! We are proud of that glorious fabric, the British Constitution. We have represented our grievances to the Imperial Government, but through the chicanery of the Company and its false representations, we have not been heard, much less have our grievances been redressed. We, therefore, as dutiful and loyal subjects of the British Crown, humbly pray that your Honourable House will take into immediate consideration the subject of this our petition, and that such measures may be devised and adopted as will extend to us the protection of the Canadian Government, laws, and institutions, and make us equal participators in those rights and liberties enjoyed by British subjects in whatever part of the world they reside."

This petition foreshadowed the close of the Company's anomalous rule in Rupert's Land. But the document was not alone instrumental in bringing about a change. The time had come for a new order of things. The time had come for extensive settlement in territories now known, not only to be of vast extent, but capable of great and successful colonisation—a colonisation which the Company had long resisted, and, could it have had a renewal of its Charter, it would still have exercised its power and influence to resist. From 1857, when its affairs were discussed in the British and the Canadian Parliaments, the Company showed commendable zeal in endeavouring to adapt the machinery of its organisation to the purposes of colonisation; but in this it signally failed, with all the aid it had from a syndicate of financiers, to whom it turned in a fright to save its doomed monopoly. But though its administration was doomed, there was no serious desire, on the part of either governments to do it injustice, far less a wrong. Nor, finally, was injustice or wrong done it, save, it may be, in the extravagant rhetoric of such of the colonists as had petitioned against the continuance of its rule.

We have no motive in pressing the case unduly against the Hudson Bay Company; and in proof of this, we shall not burden our pages with any of the indictments which at this period found ready, and perhaps not over temperate, voice against its administration. On the other hand, we shall not quarrel with its advocates. There were partisans on both sides; and, as usually happens, on both sides there was something for partisans to say. Objection has been taken to the statement that the settlers of Red River were in a condition of thraldom, and that the Hudson Bay Company was a monster of tyranny and oppression. We have not made either statement, though as a matter of history we record the fact that both statements were repeatedly and publicly made. It may be true, as was urged by the objectors, that unprincipled men in the colony put themselves in an attitude of culpable and unreasoning defiance towards the Company; that they filled the minds of the settlers with exaggerated notions of their being an abused people; and that the local press was made reprehensible use of to keep the colony in a ferment, and to incite a peaceable and uncomplaining community to revolt. These counter-statements may, or may not, be true; in any case, the common sense of impartial readers of the colony's annals will guide them to a conclusion that will not far outrage facts.

What these facts are the reader who has followed us so far will not require to be told. The Company had had a long term of right and unrestricted power in the territory. The right was always questioned; the power was now going to be disputed. It had exercised both to the detriment of the settlers who had long been in the country; and to those who were now coming into it the Company was not disposed to abate one jot or tittle of any right or prerogative it had hitherto possessed, and was able to maintain the possession of. A policy so obstructive, as well as anomalous, could not hope in these modern days to withstand the assaults of freemen, or be other than a bone of contention among those who saw that the country was being held, not for the good of the settler, not for the development of the territory, not for the advancement of civilisation, but for the sole enrichment of a few privileged monopolists. This view of the case may not be altogether just to the Company, the paternal rule of which was in many respects good, and suitable to the time and the people. But in the evolution of time, and in the development of the people, it was impossible that that rule could continue to be suitable; sooner or later, antagonism to it was sure to come.

Meanwhile, as the hopes of the settlers rose, in anticipation of early political connection with Canada, distrust began to be felt by the servants of the Company, of the permanency of their relations with Fenchurch Street. Should this link snap, and the traders be thrown over by the great monopoly, it was foreseen that the official class would at once lose influence, and be at the disadvantage of the settlers. This feeling served to unite in a closer bond the French and the half-breeds, whose interests were specially bound up in the fur trade, and to range them in sharper hostility to the other section of the colony composed of the farmers and the free-traders. In this attitude of class-antagonism, it cannot be disguised, that the French received encouragement from the Church; and hence arose new elements of disaffection, and new grounds for dislike of the coming change.

The change, nevertheless, was to come. The French people, jealous of their language, their religion, and their institutions, naturally found support from the Roman Catholics in their desire to uphold their racial possessions; and the Church had its own reasons for assuming this position. As the Hudson Bay Company had hitherto objected to the settler, that the Province might be kept as a preserve for game, so the Romish Priesthood wished now to exclude the English Protestant, that the country might be kept as a preserve of the Church. But the dread of interference, with their religion at least, was an unfounded one, as French Catholics, who had had experience of English toleration in the Province of Quebec, might have been assured. The only ground of apprehension, which could cause a moment's uneasiness to Frenchman or Catholic, lay in the subordination of the language of France to that of the invading Anglo-Saxon, who, in the opening up of the country, was sure to be in the ascendant. But to object to the encroachment of the English tongue was to object to the encroachment of the sea. And the sea was now fast approaching. The wave of Canadian sympathy was soon to break over the plains of Red River, and to draw into its embrace the return attachment of kin to kin. In this meeting of the waters there was to be no receding. For a time the intruding wave was to be dyked out by the antipathies of a half-alien people, but the waters were to have their way and begin to submerge the land.

The language in which these antipathies was expressed may be judged, in some respects at least, from the guarded comments of Archbishop Taché, in a work which appeared in 1868, entitled, "A Sketch of the North-West of America." Says this distinguished Prelate:

"In the Colony there is nervousness and uneasiness about the future. Some who hope to gain by any change are clamorous for one: others dwelling more upon the system of government than upon its application, would like to try a change, certain that they would never return to the primitive state from which they desired to escape; a greater number—the majority—dread that change. Many are very reasonable; the country might gain by the change, and it would obtain many advantages which it now lacks; but the existing population would certainly be losers. As we love the people more than the land in which they live, as we prefer the well-being of the former to the splendour of the latter, we now repeat that for our population we very much dread some of the promised changes."

The language of the Archbishop, under the circumstances, is very natural. There is uneasiness expressed at not knowing in what the change is to consist; and, reading between the lines, we see a strong preference for the continuance of the *status quo*. The attitude of the French half-breeds is equally plain, and to some extent reasonable. They looked coldly on any movement which was to ally them with the East without their consent, and without some assurance that what they termed their "superior rights" in the country, were to be respected. Nor was the feeling of uncertainty as to the future, and the desire first to be consulted ere any change was made, less marked in the case of many of the English. As a local writer has put it: "they wanted to escape from the incubus of the Hudson Bay Company; but they (especially those who had emigrated from Ontario), wanted to have a voice in the management of their own affairs, and they were greatly disappointed when they found that the Canadian authorities proposed sending up a government 'all ready made,' to take the place of the Company's rule. They felt as if they were getting from under one dead weight to place themselves under another."*

The Hon. William Macdougall, C.B., was to take the first step in the Canadian Parliament towards admitting into the Confederation the territorial possessions of the Hudson Bay Company. This gentleman, who was at the time Minister of Public Works, moved a series of Resolutions with the design of incorporating Rupert's Land and the North-West Territory into the new-formed Dominion. On these Resolutions† was based

---

* "History of Manitoba," By the late Hon. Donald Gunn, and C. R. Tuttle, Ottawa, 1880.

† These Resolutions were moved on the 4th, and passed on the 11th, of December, 1867, during the First Session of the First Parliament of the Dominion of Canada, —provision having been made in the British North America Act in anticipation of the admission of the territory into Confederation.

an Address to Her Majesty, praying for Imperial sanction to the union, and for authority to legislate for the future welfare and good government of the country. The answer to this overture was, that when the value set upon the territory had been determined and agreed upon between the Hudson Bay Company and the Canadian Government, Her Majesty's consent would be obtained and an Imperial Act would be passed ratifying the transfer. In the following year, to expedite matters, Mr. Macdougall, the mover of the Resolutions, and Sir Geo. E. Cartier, visited England to arrange the terms of purchase. After some delay, and not a little haggling, these were agreed to ; and late in the year 1869, a formal Deed of Surrender of the Territories was executed. The terms and conditions of that surrender were, in brief, that the Canadian Government was to pay to the Hudson Bay Company the sum of £300,000 ; that the Company was to be permitted to retain all the trading posts or stations then actually in possession or in occupation, with the blocks of land adjoining ; and that one-twentieth of all the lands in the Fertile Belt, when the same were surveyed and set out for settlement, was to be allotted to the Company. It was moreover stipulated, that all titles to land conferred by the Company, up to the 8th day of March, 1869, were to be confirmed, and that the Indian claims to portions of the territory were to be settled by the purchasing party.

Such were the terms on which the Canadian Government acquired this vast territory, a territory estimated at over 2,300,000 square miles. In the Fertile Belt alone, which covers an area exceeding three hundred million acres, it is calculated that there is agricultural lands sufficient to support a population of twenty-five millions. In acquiring this great possession, the next step was to provide it with some territorial form of government. In taking this step our Canadian authorities, unhappily, met with difficulty.

This difficulty was no inconsiderable one; but the Canadian Government, if it was premature in its action, was not half-hearted in its purpose to acquire and enter into possession of the territory. Our public men, it may at least be said, appreciated the value of the domain the country had just acquired. With spirit they determined that it should at once be opened up. During the Session of 1869, an Act was passed at Ottawa providing a provisional form of government in the territory; and in October of the same year, the Hon. Wm. Macdougall was appointed Lieutenant-Governor. Surveying parties had already been sent to the Red River Settlement to lay out townships, and to institute an extended series of surveys. Governor Macdougall was now himself to set out to assume the duties of his office, and, in conjunction with the local Hudson Bay Governor, to organise the territory, and "to be in the place of his government when, by the Queen's Proclamation, it should become a portion of the Dominion of Canada." The embarassing incidents connected with this step are so well known that we need not take up much space to chronicle them. They will be more fitly told, however, in a succeeding chapter.

CHAPTER XII.

THE RIEL RED RIVER REBELLION.

MONSIEUR W. MACDOUGALL.

Monsieur,—Le Comité national des Métis de la Rivière Rouge intime à Monsieur W. Macdougall l'ordre de ne pas entrer sur le territoire du nord-ouest, sans une permission spéciale de ce Comité.

Par ordre du Président, John Bruce,

LOUIS RIEL,

Daté à St. Norbert, Rivière Rouge,   Secrétaire.*
ce 21e jour d'octobre, 1869.

With such courtesy did the "The New Nation" greet the duly constituted Governor of the North-West Territories, on his arrival at the frontier of his kingdom, in the month of November, 1869. To give éclat to the occasion, Nature had laid a carpet of snow on the threshold of the territory, and the Half-breed had erected an arch of welcome, which closer

---

* *Translation :* To Mr W. Macdougall.

    Sir,—The National Committee of the Métis (Half-breeds) of the Red River order Mr. W. Macdougall not to enter the territory of the North-West without the special permission of this Committee. By order of the President, John Bruce,

LOUIS RIEL, Secretary.

Dated at St. Norbert, Red River,
  the 21st Oct., 1869.

observation discovered to be a combined bulletin-board and barricade. It was an ill-mannered act of the enemy to keep at the bleak outskirts of the country the whole machinery of an imported government, and to guard its portals with a structure upon which the thunder of proclamations was powerless to make an impression.

But what was the motive of this obstruction? All told, there were not over five hundred white people in the Settlement, including the Half-breeds, who, as we have seen, were of French-Canadian and English and Scotch extraction. The Half-breeds were pretty equally divided in the community, one portion being of the house of Esau, and the other of the tribe of Jacob. The former were hunters, the latter farmers. Both were full of the past, a past of isolation from the world, and of inherited possession of the territory, the latter being strongly impressed upon their minds. Under the circumstances, it was natural that the tribal instinct should rebel at intrusion. Like people who were not quite sure of their social position, or of the strength of their moral claim to generous treatment at the hands of the Government, they were ready to take any false step which jealousy or intrigue whispered into their ears.

At the period the little colony was a seething cauldron of intrigue. There were clashing interests of race and religion, each striving for dominancy, and the favoured expansion of its objects and views. There were the interests of the old Company traders, who were sullen at the recent trend of affairs, and were mentally and, in their representative, McTavish, physically sick of the situation. Then there were the Fenian filibusters, who would fain find lodgment in the territory, and whose recently awakened hopes led them to instil disaffection, and busily to distribute the apples of discord. Finally,

there was Nova Scotia, in the person of the Hon. Joseph
Howe, who, in his recent visit to the country, had spread
abroad the significance of "better terms." The combustible
material was simply waiting the application of a match. The
match somehow was found, and M. Louis Riel was the man
who lit it. Riel, though not a Half-breed, had many Half-
breed connections; and by his powers of oratory he had gained
great influence over them. He eagerly espoused their cause,
and thoroughly identified himself with their assumptions and
interests. Without physical courage, he had considerable
moral determination, and a force of character, which however
had its fits of weakness. On the threatened transfer of the
territory he assumed the role of a mimic revolutionist, and, as
we shall see, for a time posed as a successful dictator.

"To appreciate the inner history of the Red River revolt,"
says a modern writer, with a delightful sense of humour, "it is
necessary to observe the exceptional variety and intricacy of
the interests that were involved. Never was there such a mixture of elements in such a little pot before! No wonder it
came to spasmodic ebullition, and boiled over in wide-spread
confusion. When the history of Red River shall some day be
written gravely, it will be read as an extravagant burlesque.

"First must be named the difference of race, dividing the
little community with natural rivalries. Next the difference
of religion, separating the people into two antagonistic parties.
Then must be considered the separate interests of the powerful
Hudson Bay Trading Company, with its own policy to pursue,
and its great profits to make, an association surrounded, of
course, with enemies, as every monopoly is sure to be. With
all this, however, it must be remembered that the isolated condition which the people here all shared tended strongly to unite
all interests against the outside world of foreigners. But to
assist the complication we must take into account the diver-
gent interest of a number of energetic American residents, and
their sympathisers within and without the settlement, who
covertly or openly avowed a policy of annexation to the United
States. Add still the influence of a restless but imbecile Fenian

party, whose aim was to establish an Independent Republic, from which they might make wars upon Canada and Great Britain. The imbroglio is not yet complete. It is no secret that the Government at Ottawa were themselves divided as to the policy to be adopted in Manitoba. The Quebec party were naturally for increasing their own influence, perpetuating the Catholic religion, and strengthening the French interests in the new country. The Ontario party were equally determined to prevent the growth of a second Quebec in the Dominion, and set themselves in unreasoning haste to secure Protestant and English ascendancy.

"Here are the ingredients of our olla podrida: Rivalries of race and of creed; Orangeism, Ultramontanism, Red Republicanism, Monopolies, Fenianism, Spread-Eagleism, and Annexation; and, not least active, Ishmaelism, the natural sentiment of the country."*

It is of course possible unwisely to belittle the incidents connected with the Red River revolt, which we are free to admit, were, with one exception, ludicrously disproportionate to the serious aspect affairs at one time assumed and the belligerent attitude of the disaffected elements in the community. That the insurrection aimed at being something more than "a tempest in a teapot" is clear from the array of so many warring forces enumerated in the above extract. That it fell far short of its aims is due more to the good fortune of the friends of the Settlement than to the ambitious designs of its enemies. But in saying this, we are not to be understood as paying the friends of the colony a compliment. They are as little entitled to credit for what they accomplished as their foes are entitled to credit for what they did not accomplish. Luck, for once, was on the side of the blunderers. The whole history, indeed, is one huge blunder, a blunder that, had the designs of the malcontents not miscarried, would have entailed the most calamitous consequences to Canada and to the Empire.

---

* "The Canadian Dominion." By Charles Marshall. London, 1871.

LIEUT.-COL. MILLER.
Commanding Q. O. R.

The loss of the Red River, as has been remarked, would have prevented the Confederation of the North American Colonies and the consolidation of British power in the New World. It is proverbially easy to criticise after the event, and to indicate what ought to have been done, before taking possession of the country, and what ought to have been left undone. Of what ought to have been done, nothing will more readily strike the non-political reader of the history than the propriety of first consulting the wishes of the people, in regard to taking over them and the territory, and of giving them a representative voice in determining what mode of government they thought suitable for the country and their choice of the men who were to rule over it. But to do this, it may be said, was to usurp the prerogative of the politician, and the politician, then as now, was paramount. Then as now, "Ishmaelism revolted."

But let us return to Mr. Macdougall and the barred-out government on the threshold of the territory. This gentleman became the unfortunate victim of conspiring Fate. We have seen that he was stopped at Pembina by order of a so-called Committee of the Métis, who had usurped authority in the district, and refused to let him in to the Canaan of his hopes. From this awkward position he did all that man could do, in a dignified way, and with the slender means at his disposal, to relieve himself. But the dilemma continued. A provisional government had been formed by the French half-breeds, who had previously extended their politeness to the Canadian surveyors, in notifying them to desist from their work and to quit the south side of the Assiniboine. Colonel Dennis, who was at the head of the surveying staff, had interviews with the local Hudson Bay Governor, and, later, had invoked the aid of the dominant Church, to bring to terms the belligerent

M

half-breeds. The result, in both cases, was failure: Governor McTavish is reported to have said "that the Canadian Government had no right to proceed with the surveys without the consent of the half-breeds;" and Rome was sullen, the priests declining to interfere on the plea that to do so would imperil the influence of the Church.

Protests and proclamations from the Lieutenant-Governor on the confines of the country were equally unavailing. The National Committee had him at a disadvantage, and it determined to keep him in an embarassing position until "terms" could be come to with the authorities at Ottawa. Nor was there hope from within the colony. The Hudson Bay representative, if he had cared, might have nipped the insurrection in the bud; but we have seen that, by extraordinary fatuity, this official was not even advised of a change of masters. It is true, that the sale of the territory had not at this time been formally completed; the money had not been paid over; and the Queen's Proclamation had not yet issued. These facts increased the delicacy of Mr. Macdougall's position, and tied the hands of both him and his Government. Nor could force be legally resorted to, had it been prudent to use it, and had the Government been able on the spot to exercise it. Other arts failed, and time brought discomfiture.

Meanwhile, the insurgents, growing bolder, had taken possession of Fort Garry. The Half-breed Council, pluming themselves on having expelled the invaders of their rights, by Proclamation now called upon the inhabitants to send delegates to a National Convention. To the Convention the English were invited to send representatives to discuss the situation; and this, at the last moment, they agreed to do in the hope of influencing the Committee to some good purpose. They soon found, however, that they were being made use of to give a colour of unanimity to proceedings which they could not endorse. Pacific measures were not to be expected from men whose heads had been turned by the elevation of their position. At first respecting the authority of the Hudson Bay Company, the insurgents proceeded ere long to disregard it, and to erect an authority of their own. They seized the books and records of the Council of Assiniboia, and prepared to form a Provisional Government. On the 1st of December, the now famed "Bill of Rights" was passed, which sent the English delegates to their homes, and left Riel and his councillors to unmask their designs and unfurl the flag of rebellion. The first act in the drama of rebellion was to seize many of the loyal inhabitants and to incarcerate them as political prisoners. Insurgency now reigned, and the year closed on loyalty abashed and law discomfited.

On the 18th of December, the Hon. Mr. Macdougall, finding his commission as Lieutenant-Governor worthless, left Pembina and returned to Canada. His withdrawal removed one obstacle to peace in the Colony; but peace was not now the object sought by the insurgents who, through intimidation, had snatched power, and were eager to retain it. During the winter anarchy continued to reign, and the loyal inhabitants, in consequence of disunited counsels and from want of a leader, were powerless to allay it. A prominent resident of Winnipeg, Dr. John Schultz, for a time led the only organised opposition to the triumvirate who composed the Provisional Government; but he and his following were ere long made prisoners and marched into Fort Garry. Terrorism unnerved the remainder of the community. Meanwhile the Provisional Government enjoyed its easily won honours and conducted itself autocratically.

The insurgent leaders were not more than three in number. The first was Louis Riel, who had supplanted Bruce in the Presidency, and was an old protégé of Archbishop Taché; the second, was the so-styled Honourable W. B. O'Donoghue, Secretary of the Treasury, and the representative of Fenianism in the Rebel Cabinet; the third was a French-Canadian, the Hon. A. Lepine, who was dignified with the title and honours of Adjutant-General, and was subsequently to stain his hands by carrying out Riel's orders in the foul murder of a prisoner. These worthies were the chief actors in all that was done during this period of usurped authority. In the main, they were careful to pay some regard to the forms of law, and cunning enough to throw over their acts the ægis of the Provisional Government. By this course they were able to coquette with the Dominion authorities; to send and receive delegates to and from Ottawa; and to secure recognition of their representative status, and some degree of sympathy for what they termed their "Bill of Rights." They were thus also able to make use of the influence of the Church, and to keep the Hudson Bay officials, though they made free use of the Company's supplies, in an obliging state of masterly inactivity.

For the next few weeks the monotony of flushed success was broken by musterings on one side and dispersions on the other; by records of bloodless battles and hollow victories; of prisoners captured and prisoners released; and of thrilling announcements in the "rebel rag," *The New Nation.* In this official newspaper of the insurgent chiefs, the whole miserable farce of playing at Government may be read, with the pitiful gasconade of Gallic cockiness, Fenian sedition, and Half-breed insolence. How the constituted authorities of the country came to trifle and temporise with all this treason, and suffered themselves to be bullied by the presumption of vain braggarts and arrant cowards, in this wretched fiasco, will remain a humiliating reflection to the Canadian patriot. But an event was now to happen which, unchallenged and condoned, was forever afterwards to bring the blush of shame to the cheek of every Canadian who recalls it. To such depths partyism at the time consigned patriotism, that the murder of Thomas Scott, though it evoked the righteous indignation of the whole country, was ineffectual with the politicians to bring the culprit to justice. But, as the proverb expresses it, "there is good in things evil;" and there was one good to come of the atrocity now about to be perpetrated—it, for a time, rid the country of the assassins who had possessed it. In this damning act of Riel's usurpation of power—the outcome of personal malignity and lawless passion—his voluntary flight and accepted outlawry enabled the district to receive its political autonomy unembarrassed by his malign presence and influence. This, at least, was something to be thankful for.

Let us now record what has been termed " the dark crime of the rebellion." Thomas Scott, a young English-speaking Canadian, it seems had become obnoxious to Riel in the Colony by his somewhat effusive loyalty and a rather reckless disregard of his own life. As an Orangeman, the Fenian flag on Fort Garry, to this sturdy Briton, was a hated symbol of disloyalty and an irritating emblem of rebellion. Scott's blood boiled at sight of the flaunting flag, and he became a bitter and outspoken foe of the Catholic usurpers of Government. Captured once by Riel, he refused to acknowledge his authority, and, escaping, defied it. Captured a second time, Riel found him confirmed in his contumacy, and he determined to wreak his spite upon him. He ordered a court-martial, of his own choosing, to try his victim, but took care to hear no defence, to allow him no counsel, and to keep him in ignorance of the crime of which he was accused. He did not even know the language and purport of the proceedings that were taken against him. The mock trial occurred on the evening of the 3rd of March, 1870, and lasted a little over two hours. Its finding was fatal; Scott was sentenced to be shot at ten o'clock the next morning.

The sentence fell on the incredulous ears of Riel's victim, but was impressed by the grim humanity of the offer to send for a clergyman. On the fatal morning, the clergyman—the Rev. George Young—secured a two hours' respite for the condemned loyalist, so as to obtain time to summon those who would intercede for Scott's life, or, if unsuccessful, to prepare the unfortunate for death. No intercession availed: Riel's black heart was obdurate; and his victim's death was to him too sweet revenge to forego it. At noon, in the courtyard of Fort Garry, the revolting scene, the tragic horror, took place; Scott was in very truth shot down like a dog, and like a dog was buried.

The assassins called the event 'a military execution,' and spoke of it as 'a military necessity.' It was the former, after no fashion known in military circles among civilised people: it could only have been the latter to craven-hearted knaves, who wanted to play the despot in a cowed, unprotected, and isolated community. By this bloodthirsty display of power, Riel entrenched himself more firmly in the position he had usurped. The inhabitants of the district shunned him as they would a wild beast: the news of his cold-blooded murder created horror wherever it reached. Presently Archbishop Taché, who had been absent at Rome during the winter, came upon the scene, with power delegated him by the Canadian Government to negotiate for peace. This power, it may here be said, had been conferred some time before Riel's deed of darkness had been committed. It seemed to make little difference, however, to the Archbishop, for, on his arrival in the colony, he took the red hand of murder, and proceeded to confer with the *quasi*-Government with which he had been commissioned to treat. Happily, the Prelate's influence was beneficent, for turbulent passions were sensibly allayed, and reason, if not conscience, again asserted itself.

As the season advanced, the influence of pacific measures, both at Ottawa and in the colony, had its effect. To the influence, in the scene of strife, of the Hon. Donald A. Smith, Commissioner of the Dominion Government, and a director of the Hudson Bay Company, much was due, in softening the asperities of the conflict, and in securing redress of grievances when the trouble was over. The Dominion Parliament passed an Act erecting the Red River settlements into a separate Province, called Manitoba, with a representative legislature, instead of the territorial form of government at first proposed.*
The Act provided for the representation of the Province in the Federal Parliament, and the maintenance of government. It also made provision for the allotment of land to the half-breeds. A new Lieutenant-Governor was at the same time appointed.

The reign of terror now drew to a close. Word came from Canada of the despatch of troops to the mimic seat of war under Colonel (now Lord) Wolseley. Much was expected from this expedition; though whether Riel and his rabble troops would resist, or flee from, its approach, was a matter of doubt. Fortunately, the expedition was of sufficient strength to incite to discretion: moreover, it was of good stuff, and admirably commanded. Leaving Toronto on the 25th of May, 1870, Colonel Wolseley and his force proceeded by water to Fort William, thence over the 600 miles of the Dawson route, with

---

* Morgan's " The Dominion Annual Register," for 1879.

its innumerable and toilsome portages, to Fort Garry. There the first detachment arrived at 10 o'clock on the morning of the 24th of August, and at once entered the Fort. One hour before,—fitting end to the farce,—"the Little Napoleon" of the Red River revolt, in craven fear, fled. With like stealth, did the "Provisional Government" vanish, and the rebel army dissolve before the approach of the troops.*

---

* Literature has well preserved the history of this expedition of Colonel Wolseley, who, with his English and Canadian troops, made a gallant entry into Red River, over a most difficult route, from Port Arthur, *via* Lake of the Woods, to the Settlement. Its record in Capt. Huyshe's Narrative (London, 1871), is still interesting reading.

CHAPTER XIII.

THE PROVINCE OF MANITOBA, AND THE ERA OF SETTLEMENT.

THE Mission of the Red River Expedition was one of peace, and in peace it accomplished its purpose. It established, as Colonel Wolseley, its commanding officer, phrased it, "Her Majesty's Sovereign authority in the district," which lawlessness for a time had set at naught. Representing no party in religion or in politics, it afforded equal protection to all. Peace, happily, being restored, the troops were withdrawn, and the Hon. Mr. Archibald, the new Lieutenant-Governor, arrived on the scene. For a time partisan feeling ran high; one side clamouring for arrests and imprisonments, the other for conciliatory measures and an amnesty. But the new Governor was judicious, and took no hasty step. Time, he thought, would bring sobriety and returning reason, and with time the breach between parties would heal.

The immediate care of the authorities was to re-establish peace and order; and, with security to life and property, to set up some civil authority which would impress the native mind with a distinct and tangible idea of government. In January, 1871, a general election was held in the new Province, for the return of members to the Legislative Assembly: in the same month a Ministry was formed, the members of which, after re-election in the usual way, took charge of their respective portfolios. Members were also elected to represent the Province in the Federal Parliament; and gentlemen were nominated to serve on the Executive Council of the North-West. The function of the latter was to assist the Lieutenant-Governor of Manitoba, who in the meantime was to be *ex officio* Lieutenant-Governor of the region without the area of the Province, in passing laws and ordinances for the Government of the territory. Thus the first steps were taken to raise the new territorial acquisition of Canada in the political and social scale, and to supplant the Hudson Bay Company as a governing body.

In the Dominion Act calling the Province into existence, provision was made to meet the cost of Government, by an annual subsidy, and a grant of so much money per head of the population, as determined by the decennial census. To do justice to the half-breeds, and to remove their grievances, in Canada's assuming the Government of the territory, nearly a million and a-half of acres of land were reserved by the Dominion Government for allotment among those who at the time of the transfer were resident within the limits defined as the boundaries of Manitoba. By a subsequent Act, scrip, representing in land the equivalent of $160, was given to each head of a half-breed family; and, similarly, scrip was issued to the Selkirk colonists who had been in the country between the years 1813 and 1835. The claims of actual settlers to consideration were also duly acknowledged, and provision made that they should receive patents from the Crown for all lands of which they were in *bona fide* possession at the date of the transfer.*

---

* Morgan's " Dominion Annual Register," for 1879.

A system of survey was also proceeded with ; townships, thirty-six miles square, were blocked out ; roads and bridges were built; and public buildings erected. As the surveys advanced, the allotment of lands was made to the Hudson Bay Company, to the half-breeds, and to the early white settlers; while land was appropriated for school purposes. Arrangements were now made by Treaty for extinguishing the Indian title throughout the territory. From 1871 to 1876 seven treaties were concluded with various Indian tribes inhabiting the region, extending from Lake Superior to the eastern base of the Rocky Mountains. The area embraced in the surrendered territory is estimated at 450,000 square miles, and covers the whole Fertile Belt as described in the Hudson Bay Company's Deed of Surrender. Of this area, reserves, of the tribes own choosing, were set apart for the support of the Indians, each family receiving a tract equal to about 160 acres. The conditions of the relinquishment were the payment of an annuity of $5 to each member of the tribe, $25 to each chief, with a suit of clothes every third year, together with an appropriation for schools, and supplies of cattle and implements when the Indians settled down on their respective reserves to agricultural pursuits. It was furthermore stipulated, that the sale of all intoxicating liquors should be absolutely prohibited, either on or out of the reserves.

Such, in brief, were the steps taken by the Canadian authorities to organise the once Hudson Bay Territory, and to carve a section out of it that would worthily rank among the older Provinces of the Dominion. In time the boundaries of the new Province were enlarged, and a more extended area was embraced in its limits. At a later date, the North West Territory was further parcelled out and given a separate government. Manitoba now extends from the western boundary of

Ontario, long in dispute, to 101° 30′ west longitude, and from the international boundary to nearly 53° north latitude. The desolate territory of Keewatin, lies to the north of this Province, sweeping past the western shores of Hudson Bay, to the Frozen Ocean. On the west, lie the rich districts of Alberta, Saskatchewan, Athabasca, and Assiniboia, bounded by the towering Rockies and British Columbia, the Dominion Province on the Pacific. Through these districts run twenty meridian lines of longitude, and, at least, ten of latitude, that are adapted for settlement. This vast basin is channelled by great fertilising streams, and gemmed by the most beautiful prairie flowers, fringed on the north by a sheltering line of forest. For farming and grazing purposes, no land on this planet is more suitable; the soil is a black alluvium of great depth and almost inexhaustible fertility, broken by occasional groups of low hills, composed chiefly of sand and gravel. The soil of Manitoba, having originally been the bed of a lake, is mainly formed of a rich silt deposited during the eons of the past. No account of its amazing productiveness can possibly be exaggerated; and being comparatively free of timber, it is at once ready for the settler's plough. Of the beauty of the Red River prairie, under different aspects and lights, we get a charming description from the pen of an eminent native geologist, the son of an equally eminent Canadian savant.*

"But the country must be seen in its extraordinary aspects before it can be rightly valued and understood, in reference to its future occupation by an energetic and civilised race, able to improve its vast capabilities and appreciate its boundless beauties. It must be seen at sunrise, when the vast plain suddenly flashes with rose-coloured light, as the rays of the sun sparkle

---

* From the Report of Dr. George M. Dawson, Geologist and Naturalist to the British North America Boundary Commission, quoted by Prof. Macoun, in his interesting work on "Manitoba and the North West."—Guelph, 1882.

in the dew on the long rich grass, gently stirred by the unfailing morning breeze. It must be seen at noonday, when refraction swells into the forms of distant hill-ranges the ancient beaches and ridges of Lake Winnipeg, which mark its former extension; when each willow bush is magnified into a grove, each far-distant clump of aspens, not seen before, into wide forests, and the outline of wooded river banks, far beyond unassisted vision, rise into view. It must be seen at sunset, when just as the ball of fire is dipping below the horizon, he throws a flood of red light, indescribably magnificent, upon the illimitable waving green, the colours blending and separating with the gentle roll of the long grass, seemingly magnified toward the horizon into the distant heaving swell of a particoloured sea. It must be seen too by moonlight, when the summits of the low green grass waves are tipped with silver, and the stars in the west suddenly disappear as they touch the earth. Finally, it must be seen at night, when the distant prairies are in a blaze, thirty, fifty, or seventy miles away; when the fire reaches clumps of aspen, and the forked tips of the flames magnified by refraction, flash and quiver in the horizon, and the reflected light from rolling clouds of smoke above tell of the havoc which is raging below. These are some of the scenes which must be witnessed and felt before the mind forms a true conception of those prairie wastes, in the unrelieved immensity which belongs to them, in common with the ocean, but which, unlike the everchanging and unstable sea, seems to offer a bountiful recompense, in a secure, though distant home, to millions of our fellow men."

The next, and an important undertaking, in connection with the acquirement of the North-West, was to provide facilities for getting access to it. In 1871, British Columbia expressed a desire to enter Confederation, but stipulated before doing so, that it be connected with the East by a railway across the continent. The Canadian reader will not need to be reminded of the difficulties, of a party character, that beset this enterprise, or of the political crisis that came upon the country at its inception. Into these difficulties it is of course unnecessary here to enter: we simply refer to them as part of the history of the undertaking, and as forming serious obstacles in the way of carrying out the contemplated project. After many misadventures, the construction of a road fell into competent hands, and the beneficent project of a Canadian Pacific Railway was got under way. Already this mammoth enterprise nears completion; but years must elapse ere its influence can be fully felt, in ministering to the wants of a Greater Britain in the Canadian North-West, and even in determining the destiny of the country.

Not only, however, does the iron road span the continent, but that other agent and bond of civilisation, the telegraph, is fast spinning its web throughout the North-West. It seems but yesterday that we read the congratulatory messages which passed between the Governor-General at Ottawa, and the Lieutenant-Governor of Manitoba, at Winnipeg, on the completion of the telegraphic communication with the Prairie Province. Yet, since 1871, what marvellous progress has been made! In that year Winnipeg had only a weekly mail from the East, *via* the United States; though, in the following year, on the opening of the Pembina Branch Railway, postal facilities were greatly increased. Now, on the completion of the connecting links of the Canadian Pacific, in the region north of Lake Superior, a daily mail and through transport connect East and West in closest embrace; and the Canadian can travel on the road and its connections for three thousand continuous miles, without quitting British Territory.

Within the Province of Manitoba, the same tale of advancement may be told. Winnipeg, "the Bull's Eye of the Dominion," as Lord Dufferin termed it, has assumed quite a metropolitan character, and has a large and rapidly increasing population. The value of the real and personal property within its limits would astound the old Selkirk colonist; while its social and intellectual progress are no less a marvel. In some respects, one may regret the absence of the simplicity and restful aspect of the old-time colony, and its homely, primitive life; but there is room on the plains for innumerable Arcadias of thrift and comfort, and no lack of opportunity, in Nature's solitudes, for getting near to Nature's God. In recounting these prosaic facts of North-West progress, let us pause a moment to hear the poet's description of the prairies, and his vision of the coming life which is to people them:

"These are the gardens of the desert, these
The unshorn fields, boundless and beautiful,
For which the speech of England has no name—
The prairies. I behold them for the first,
And my heart swells, while the dilated sight
Takes in the encircling vastness. Lo ! they stretch,
In airy undulations, far away,
As if the Ocean, in his gentlest swell,
Stood still, with all his rounded billows fixed,
And motionless forever. *   *
Man hath no power in all this glorious work ;
The hand that built the firmament hath heaved
And smoothed these verdant swells, and sown their slopes
With herbage, planted them with island groves,
And hedged them round with forests. Fitting floor
For this magnificent temple of the sky—
With flowers whose glory and whose multitude
Rival the constellations. The great heavens
Seem to stoop down upon the scene in love—
A nearer vault, and of a tenderer blue,
Than that which bends above our eastern hills.
As o'er the verdant waste I guide my steed,
Among the high rank grass that sweeps his sides,
The hollow beating of his footsteps seems
A sacrilegious sound. I think of those
Upon whose rest he tramples. Are they here—
The dead of other days ? And did the dust
Of these fair solitudes once stir with life
And burn with passion *   *   a race

That long has passed away ?   *   *   The red man
Has left the blooming wilds he ranged so long,
And nearer to the Rocky Mountains sought
A wilder hunting-ground. The beaver builds
No longer by these streams, but far away
On waters whose blue surface ne'er gave back
The white man's face.   *   *   In these plains
The bison feeds no more. Twice twenty leagues
Beyond remotest smoke of hunter's camp
Roams the majestic brute in herds that shake
The earth with thundering steps—yet here I meet
His ancient footprints stamped beside the pool.

Still this great solitude is quick with life.
Myriads of insects, gaudy as the flowers
They flutter over, gentle quadrupeds,
And birds, that scarce have learned the fear of man,
Are here, and sliding reptiles of the ground,
Startlingly beautiful. The graceful deer
Bounds to the wood at my approach. The bee,
A more adventurous colonist than man,
With whom he came across the eastern deep,
Fills the savannas with his murmurings,
And hides his sweets, as in the golden age,
Within the hollow oak. I listen long
To his domestic hum, and think I hear
The sound of that advancing multitude
Which soon shall fill these deserts. From the ground
Comes up the laugh of children, the soft voice
Of maidens, and the sweet and solemn hymn
Of Sabbath worshippers. The low of herds
Blends with the rustling of the heavy grain
Over the dark brown furrow. All at once
A fresher wind sweeps by, and breaks my dream,
And I am in the wilderness alone."

But the solitudes were now being broken in upon by a stream of immigrants, whose condition in life was here to be bettered, and whose future, with ordinary prudence and industry, would at least be relieved from apprehension. By the possession of this vast domain, which now dignifies Canada and adds immeasurably to her resources, the Dominion was at length to place herself in line with her powerful neighbour to the South. She was also to take her rightful position as the great Northern nation of the Western Continent, the inheritor of those mental and physical endowments that distinguish the Anglo-Saxon race, and the perpetuator of the honours and traditions that shed a glory on the country from which she sprung. Important, also, in its central situation, is the possession of the Prairie Province to the Dominion, in its tendency to gather within its rich and attractive limits the best brain and muscle of other sections of Canada, and thus rivet the links that bind the whole Confederation. In this view, the Province may truly be termed the national heart of the country, or, as Lord Dufferin, with a statesman's vision, phrased it, "the future umbilicus of the Dominion." The Winnipeg speech, in 1877, of that clever and versatile nobleman, will doubtless be fresh in the memory of our readers. In praise of Manitoba, the Governor-General spoke in impassioned and felicitous terms. Let us quote but a brief paragraph :

"From its geographical position, and its peculiar characteristics, Manitoba may be regarded as the keystone of that mighty arch of sister Provinces which spans the continent. It was here that Canada, emerging from her woods and forests, first gazed upon her rolling prairies and unexplored North-West, and learnt, as by an unexpected revelation, that her historical territories of the Canadas, her Eastern seaboards of New Brunswick, Labrador, and Nova Scotia, her Laurentian lakes and valleys, corn lands and pastures, though themselves more extensive than half a dozen European kingdoms, were but the vestibules and antechambers to that, till then, undreamt-of Dominion, whose illimitable dimensions alike confound the arithmetic of the surveyor and the verification of the explorer. It was hence that counting her past achievements as but the preface and prelude to her future exertions and expanding

N

destinies, she took a fresh departure, received the afflatus of a more Imperial inspiration, and felt herself no longer a mere settler along the banks of a single river, but the owner of half a continent, and in the amplitude of her possession, in the wealth of her resources, in the sinews of her material might, the peer of any power on earth."

With like heartiness did a later Governor-General, the Marquis of Lorne, speak of the new Province and its exceptionally advantageous position; though, in some respects, his words are an echo of his eloquent predecessor. Says Lord Lorne:

"To be ignorant of the North-West is to be ignorant of the greater portion of our country. Unknown a few years ago, except for some differences which had arisen amongst its people, we see Winnipeg now with a population unanimously joining in happy concord, and rapidly lifting it to the front rank amongst the commercial centres of the continent.. We may look in vain elsewhere for a situation so favourable and so commanding, many as are the fair regions of which we can boast. There may be some among you before whose eyes the whole wonderful panorama of our Provinces has passed—the ocean garden Island of Prince Edward, the magnificent valleys of the St. John and Sussex, the marvellous country, the home of 'Evangeline,' where Blomidon looks down on the tides of Fundy, and over tracts of red soil richer than the weald of Kent. You may have seen the fortified Paradise of Quebec, and Montreal, whose prosperity and beauty are worthy of her great St. Lawrence, and you may have admired the well-wrought and splendid Province of Ontario, and rejoiced at the growth of her capital, Toronto, and yet nowhere can you find a situation whose natural advantages promise so great a future as that which seems ensured to Manitoba, and to Winnipeg, the Heart City of the Dominion."

Winnipeg's progress was naturally that of other towns within and without the Province. As if by enchantment, have sprung up villages and hamlets in favourable locations over the face of the country. The present troubles have made the names of many of these settlements familiar to Canadian ears. Maps of the line of railway, telegrams chronicling local items, and postmarks on correspondence from the region, have so prominently brought the localities of the North-West to the everyday knowledge of our people, that we can scarcely realise the fact that but a few years ago the towns were non-existent and their sites the virgin prairie. To contrast the City of Winnipeg of to-day with the Fort Garry of fifteen years ago, is relatively to contrast the modern British metropolis with the Londinium of the Romans, and to reach it from civilisation was as difficult as to reach York from London at the time of the Heptarchy. Hear an old resident of Winnipeg, as he recites his experience in reaching the colony from the Mississippi, in the year 1867.

" I remember well the difficulties experienced during my first trip to Fort Garry, the site of the present City of Winnipeg. An Indian pony attached to a rude ox-cart was the only conveyance to be had, and with that I set out to travel some 600 miles over the houseless prairie to my destination. . . . . To-day you may make the journey in less than twenty-four hours (which originally took me three weeks), seated in a comfortable Pullman car, instead of the Red River cart of former years. When I first travelled over the route, no houses were to be met with, no settlers to offer you hospitality; the cart-trail of the prairie was the only mark to guide you on your way. Now the country is studded with farms and farm-houses; cities, towns, and villages have sprung into existence, and railways are to be found running in every direction. . . Never shall I forget the scene that presented itself when I first saw Fort Garry. Hundreds of Indian lodges and tepees covered the plain, many of the aborigines and plain hunters having congregated at the spot to obtain supplies for the winter hunt. Half a mile from the Fort stood about a dozen houses, the homes and shops of the free-traders. There were not, I suppose, one hundred men, all told, living in the place where to-day is a city of over 30,000 inhabitants."*

---

* From a paper entitled "Seventeen Years in the North-West," read by Mr. Alexander Begg, before the Royal Colonial Institute. Vol. 15 of Proceedings 1883-4. London, 1884.

In the organisation and development of this great territory it was hardly to be expected that the Dominion authorities would meet with no difficulty, or wholly succeed in satisfying the wants, reasonable and unreasonable, of the North-West. The Government, naturally enough, had to feel its way in adapting the machinery of the State to the circumstances of the country and the people. While feeling its way, it was at an early day committed to a vast project which complicated its dealings with Manitoba, as well as added to its Parliamentary trials. In the Land Question it had one source of trouble; in the Railway Question it had another. Both matters have somewhat strained Federal relations with the Province, and made it difficult for the Ottawa authorities to moderate the Provincial demands upon the public chest. In the example which had been set it by Provinces to the east of Ontario, in clamouring for "better terms," this difficulty has not been lessened. The railway project was so great an undertaking that no capitalists could well be got to take hold of it without imposing conditions which the Government had to accept. None of these conditions, happily, were very onerous; and few can be said to be disadvantageous, if we except the not unreasonable granting of a monopoly. In the contract certain prohibitions were imposed upon the country by the Canadian Pacific Railway Company, which had to be respected by the young Province. Manitoba, proving restive under these conditions, passed several Acts in her Local Legislature adverse to the interests of the Pacific Railway Company, and in violation of the agreement with the Federal Government. These Acts had to be disallowed, and disallowance created ill-feeling. Looking back on the bargain, it is now to be regretted that the Government was compelled to yield a monopoly to the Syndicate; but no Company was likely to be got to construct the road without being assured that, for a time at least, it would not have to meet competition. Competing lines there must one day be; but before these become urgently necessary the Pacific Railway Syndicate is likely to find it to be its interest to meet any reasonable demand of commerce, though the monopoly clause, we believe, operates for twenty years.

Besides the Railway policy, and growing out of it, there is another cause of irritation, expressed by the "Farmer's Union," at what is spoken of as the excessive charges of the Railway Company in transporting the surplus wheat to a market. Other grievances, in the fiscal policy of the Dominion, which it is claimed is unsuited to a purely agricultural people, perpetuate soreness of feeling, and, with chronic complaints against the Land Regulations, more or less agitate and unsettle the community. These irritations the Government, however, must, in some measure, smooth over by concessions which, while not doing injustice to the other members of the Confederation, will meet the special circumstances of the Province.

Fortunately, none of these grievances have led the people of Manitoba to do more than agitate, in a legitimate and constitutional way, for their redress. There is throughout the Province a profound respect for law and order; and though, as in all communities, there are senseless brawlers, the strong common sense of the people has kept them, and is likely to keep them, loyal to the nation, and true to the men, whatever the party badge may be, who guide its destinies. It is a gratifying fact, and it speaks well for the political and social progress of the Province, that in the present trouble on the Saskatchewan, no element of disaffection finds lodgment within its borders. The scene of strife lies without the limits of the Province; and no body of men engaged in the conflict has done more than have the Winnipeg regiments to quell disaffection and restore the blessings of peace. In the chapters to follow, in dealing with the trouble in the North-West, we trust that we shall pen no word that will even seem to be unjust, still less vindictive. Whatever has given rise to the rebellion, and actuated its chiefs in their criminal course, we shall not forget that a certain sympathy is due to men who, while they have unwisely resented intrusion, are the country's pioneers, and have at least a sentimental claim to possession, and to generous treatment by the nation.

Justice, it has been wisely said, issues from two factors—sympathy and intelligence. Lacking these no one can be absolutely just. The exercise of both sympathy and intelligence seems to be a special necessity in treating of the present outbreak and the Government's dealings with the North-West. Intelligence with regard to facts must precede safe criticism: it is a necessary postulate of all discussion. Sympathy, in some degree at least, is essential to the formation of correct opinions, and a safeguard against hasty or harsh judgments. We need sympathy and intelligence in considering the acts of those who have been in revolt, and particularly in weighing the motives which prompted them in their course. A measure of both is also needed in discussing the acts of the Government of the country, no matter of what party, that assumes the responsibility of efficiently and in good faith administering its affairs. In approaching the subject of the present insurrection, and particularly in tracing its origin and the motive of its actors, both sympathy and intelligence are needed. We hope to be guided by these essential qualities.

CHAPTER XIV

RIEL'S SECOND INSURRECTION.

Causes of the Outbreak.

WHETHER it is possible, and if possible, whether it is wise for the writer of contemporary history to endeavour to divine the causes of events just happening, are questions that may well be asked by those interested. They are questions, moreover, the writer may well ask himself. As one grows older, if age would gain by experience, one learns the wisdom of keeping silence on many things. Where causes are not on the surface, and where there is a conflict of opinion as to the agencies that have provoked disturbance, silence is fitting, until a full light can be shed upon the matter at issue. If one reflects at all, there is another thought worth considering. Some one has remarked, that a deliberate inquiry into the causes of trouble is apt to raise a doubt whether the matter is worth inquiring into. And there is wisdom in the observation; for, after the event has happened, what matters it to know its producing cause, and what profit is there in getting into a wrangle as to who is responsible, or upon whose shoulders the blame should rest, where responsibility and blame can never justly, perhaps, be fixed. There is, of course, necessity in getting, if possible, at facts, for facts are the bases of experience; and it is proper for the nation, if it has gone wrong, to get that information which will set it right and afterwards guide it in the right. In the interests of justice, no less than for the purposes of punishment, it is also necessary to be informed of facts, and to get at the accurate results of inquiry. The sooner this is done, the sooner sound objects of inquiry are satisfied and a knowledge of facts made serviceable. Premature discussion of a matter has only one justification: it clears the way for more intelligent inquiry. In discussing the matter at the head of our chapter, this is the only excuse we can offer for introducing the subject.

What then are the facts of the case, and where lies responsibility for the present outbreak? The facts lie deep; deeper, in our judgment, than party hostility is inclined to look for them. With some, the disposition, at present, is to hold the Department of the Interior responsible, and to arraign the Government before the country for its defective Land Regulations and for the chicanery of its officials in the North-West. Well, nothing is easier to some people than to jump at conclusions; and, in these days, nothing is more common than for one political party to cast reproaches at the other. To make political capital out of the saddest calamity that could befall a nation, we would fain hope there is no party in the State to attempt. In this serious matter, we are not careful to defend the Government, if the Government is in default. Neither shall we raise a voice to exonerate negligent or corrupt officials, if officials have been negligent and corrupt. We are not writing a political history, still less a partisan one; nor are we even sitting on a Commission of Inquiry. What facts are before us we shall deal with impartially, knowing neither party in our conference with truth.

Reference in our last chapter has been made to grievances complained of by the people of Manitoba, which, though real and oppressive, and which some day are likely to find voice in tones that will startle the politicians at Ottawa, had little or nothing to do with the insurrection on the Saskatchewan. The rising on the Saskatchewan was not a rising of settlers, but of French half-breeds, and through the influence of the latter, to some extent of Indians. In the history of the affair, the majority of the Indian tribes have, so far, maintained their traditional loyalty to the Great Mother beyond the sea. Their historic attitude, as allies of the nation, has been little disturbed; and they have, happily, been true to the fealty pledged in the several treaties which at various times have been entered into with them. The nature of the obligations which they came under in the latter will be better understood if we quote a clause from one of the treaties. We shall select the one known as the Lake Winnipeg Treaty (or Treaty No. 5) which was negotiated in 1875 by the Hon. Alex. Morris, P.C., at the time Lieutenant-Governor of Manitoba. It is to the following effect:

"And the undersigned chiefs, on their own behalf, and on behalf of all other Indians inhabiting the tract within ceded, do hereby solemnly promise and engage to strictly observe this treaty, and also to conduct and behave themselves as good and loyal subjects of Her Majesty the Queen. They promise and engage that they will, in all respects, obey and abide by the law, and they will maintain peace and good order between each other, and also between themselves and other tribes of Indians, and between themselves and others of Her Majesty's subjects, whether Indians or whites, now inhabiting or hereafter to inhabit any part of the said ceded tracts; and that they will not molest the person or property of any inhabitant of such ceded tracts, or the property of Her Majesty the Queen, or interfere with or trouble any person passing or travelling through the said tracts or any part thereof: and that they will aid and assist the officers of Her Majesty in bringing to justice and punishment any Indian offending against the stipulations of this treaty, or infringing the laws in force in the country so ceded."*

These obligations, comprehensive as they are, most of the Indians of the North-West, as we have said, have respected, and to the letter been faithful. Even the non-treaty Indians, and those who have come into the country from the United States, have been orderly and well behaved. Though some bands of them, such as Sitting Bull and his Sioux, have been a source of anxiety to the Government, they have occasioned little trouble, and on the whole been grateful for obtaining the means of subsistence on Canadian soil. Such of them as have not been faithful to their treaties we shall deal with in another chapter. That they have broken faith with their Queen has hardly been their own fault, for they were cajoled into rebellion by the half-breeds. During a period of lawlessness among the latter, it is not to be wondered at that the Indians should become unsettled, and take a license which, in the absence of incitement, they would never dream of taking. It would be a surprise, indeed, had their attitude been other than friendly, for the Indians have never been oppressed, and they had therefore no grievances to redress. They have always been well, if not generously, treated by the Government; its agents have in the main been faithful, and not a few of them have been compassionate; while the attitude towards them of the settler has been uniformly kind and conciliatory. The influence of the

---

* "The Treaties of Canada with the Indians of Manitoba and the North-West Territories; including the negotiations on which they are based, &c." By the Hon. Alex. Morris, P. C., late Lieut.-Governor of Manitoba, &c. Toronto, 1880.

missions has also been an ameliorating factor, and has removed any root of bitterness between the white man and the red. So much of a victory, and a bloodless one, has been gained over barbarism.

Where then has been the trouble ? The trouble, as we have said, has arisen with the half-breeds ; and it is a trouble we have brought upon ourselves. It is a trouble that has seen its counterpart in civilisation, in families where illegitimate offspring have had to be dealt with, and the penalty paid for youthful indiscretion. This lies at the root of the matter : the higher civilisation in its contact with the Indians during the fur-trading period imposed little restraint upon passion; and, in cohabiting with the dusky womanhood of the plains, the trader has left us a legacy of mischief. From the early days of the Selkirk Settlement we have inherited another legacy, which to-day calls for its meed of punishment. We then taught the half-breed how to act towards the intruding settler in the North-West, and gave him lessons in lawlessness and disregard of justice, which the traditions of the *bois-brûlés* of 1816 have kept fresh in his memory.

We do not say that this explains the whole matter, for, however harmonious the relations may be between the white man and the half-breed, there is in the composition of the latter a restlessness and craving for excitement which must find vent in some direction. Hitherto this restlessness has been drawn off in the exciting life of a *voyageur*, a *coureur de bois*, or a hunter on the plains; but so soon as there is nothing for Nimrod to do, save to take up agriculture and pursue the quiet tenor of settlement duties, the temperamental characteristics are bound to show themselves, though not, as we should expect, in wholly unregenerate acts. As a class, we have no disposition to say an unkind word of the half-breed: in our pages we have already seen much of him, and generally to his advantage. Lord Dufferin was just as well as happy in the compliment he paid to them, in his notable Winnipeg speech, which is here worth recording.

"There is no doubt," said his Excellency, "that a great deal of the good feeling subsisting between the red men and ourselves is due to the influence and interposition of that invaluable class of men the half-breed settlers and pioneers of Manitoba, who, combining as they do the hardihood, the endurance, and love of enterprise generated by the strain of Indian blood within their veins, with the civilisation, the instruction, and the intellectual power derived from their fathers, have preached the gospel of peace and good will and mutual respect, with equally beneficent results, to the Indian chieftain in his lodge, and the British settler in his shanty. They have been the ambassadors between the east and the west, the interpreters of civilisation and its exigencies to the dwellers on the prairie, as well as the exponents to the white man of the consideration justly due to the susceptibilities, the sensitive self-respect, the prejudices, the innate craving for justice of the Indian race. In fact, they have done for the colony, what otherwise would have been left unaccomplished, and have introduced between the white population and the red man a traditional feeling of amity and friendship, which, but for them, it might have been impossible to establish." *

But whatever have been the relations between the Indian and the half-breed, and undoubtedly they have been happy, those between the latter and the English Protestant settler have not always been amicable. We have seen what they were in 1869, in 1849, in 1834, as well as at the Selkirk period. Throughout the course of their history, the half-breeds have shown much jealousy of English-speaking immigrants, and a disinclination to settle down peaceably to the routine occupation of an advanced civilisation. In their relations with Govern-

---

* Leggo's " History of the Administration of the Earl of Dufferin, late Governor-General of Canada." (Page 605-6.) Montreal, 1878.

ment they have thoroughly understood the art of being troublesome, and had a keen knowledge of what gains are likely to be got by a troublesome people. With a section of the half-breeds it has been especially difficult to deal. We refer to those who do not identify themselves with the Indians, live with them, and speak their language, or who have not taken to farming and a settled life, but who retain their nomadic habits, and live by and trade in the products of the chase. In the extinction of large game in the country, their existence is an increasingly precarious one, and their means of livelihood uncertain. It is with this class, though not altogether, that trouble has arisen, and continued trouble is to be feared. They do not settle on the lands Government has given them, but look upon the whole country as their own and the Indians exclusive possession. They have been known repeatedly to play the game of the "bounty jumper," receiving scrip for lands in one part of the country, which they sell to speculators, and turn up elsewhere to make further claims upon the Government.

How far the domiciled half-breeds have legitimate grievances to complain of, it would be premature to say. Of late, we know, there has been considerable friction in the relations between them and the Indian agencies of the North-West, for which there may be good reason, and the full extent of which the unofficial public may not know. It is possible that these grievances have gone long without redress, not because the authorities were ill-disposed, but because they were afar off, and, it is to be feared, were too much occupied with the party game. If this be the case, there is ground for sympathy, though not for armed rebellion.

In connection with the Saskatchewan outbreak, and as an excuse for it, we hear a good deal of "pigeon-holing" of complaints in the Department of the Interior, which, if true, is not only a gross dereliction of duty, but an inexcusable cruelty and wrong. In this matter, not only the Opposition, but Ministerialists and the whole country have a right and a duty to perform in getting at the facts. The facts, we trust, will belie current rumour, and relieve from an uncomfortable suspicion both the Department and its head. The nation's honour and good faith are concerned in this matter, and he would be no friend of the country who, in the absence of proof, would meanwhile believe the charge to be true. How far the Lieutenant-Governor of the North-West Territories and the local machinery of his administration can be relieved from blame, we shall not undertake to say. Being on the spot, and the immediate source of appeal, it is unaccountable that any pretext for insurrection should exist without the officials of the Territory being aware of it. If aware of it, how comes it that the Government was not advised, and preparations made to redress the grievances and forestall treason ?

There can be little question that the Departmental System of Government, and the remoteness of the controlling hand from the scene of operations in the North-West, have created dissatisfaction among the settlers generally. This was almost sure to be the result of a distant Government's administration, and of the withholding, from political reasons, or perhaps because it could not trust its officials, of plenary power in dealing with the settler on the spot. We do not know, of course, all the difficulties of the position; and Government in this, as we trust in other matters, may be justified in pursuing a policy which came to be obligatory. Hence, caution here becomes us. It must also be said, in regard to other causes of complaint, that the Government could not be responsible for discontent occasioned by the misdirected ambition of land speculators, still less for discontent incident to the failure of the crops. In the years 1883-4, we know that severe frosts visited the region of the North Saskatchewan, and did incalculable damage. In this region, also, the change in the route of the Pacific Railway confounded the designs of speculators, and provoked much discontent, which, as was sure to happen, was vented on the Government. However wise and prudent Government may be, and however immaculate the character of its officials, neither can hope always to escape attack from grumbling farmers or from ruined speculators. In this imperfect world, Governments, and Government officials and machinery, are sure to be railed at. With Providence, and the weather, they must take their share of abuse.

Referring to the character and actions of Government officials in the North-West, and particularly to charges against a person high in authority in the region, we here may be permitted to quote a paragraph bearing on the subject, from the correspondence of a Ministerial organ, which is manifestly unprejudiced and wisely admonitory. The matter is a delicate one, because personal; and though we do not shirk responsibility for any strictures of our own, we have no desire to do injustice to any one by uninformed comment or indiscriminate criticism, where what seems good authority can be cited for statements, the publicity of which may do good, or throw light on the causes of the insurrection. In lieu of any remarks of our own we therefore, with more confidence, quote the following from the Toronto *Mail*, of April 20th:

"Complaint," says the journal's North-West correspondent, "is also made of the character of some of the officials sent up here. One thing is certain, that Half-breeds ought to be employed, wherever practicable, to deal with the Indians. Another thing is measurably true—that it will not do to put scaly ward politicians from Eastern Canada into positions of trust, where they come in daily contact with the settler, standing, as it were, between him and the Government. Both political parties have been guilty of this sort of thing; and the sooner an end is made of it the better for the peace of the country. As for the attacks on Lieutenant-Governor Dewdney, he seems to me to have acted imprudently in some things; but nobody, except the more violent partisans and those speculators whose efforts to grab land or contracts he has foiled, deems him corrupt or incompetent. He was badly advised, however, when he became interested in town sites and bonanza farms. His connection with them at once brought him into antagonism with the proprietors of rival booms, and the dignity of the office has suffered in consequence."

What other producing causes of insurrection exist, inquiry, we trust, will elicit and time prove. An individual may from varied motives, such as ill-directed ambition, morbid vanity, or religious fanaticism, be incited to take up arms against constituted authority; but these are not the motives that prompt a whole community to rebellion, though religious and racial jealousies, we know, are frequent incentives to strife. That there is a close bond of sympathy between the Métis and the French Canadians there is plenty of evidence. How far this sympathy has acted, if not as a stimulant to insurrection, then as a more than likely condoner of it, we may judge from the *emeute* of 1869-70. The intrigues of the Church in the North-West, it is abundantly plain, have found active abettors in the Quebec Province; and both politics and religion have not lacked a channel of communication between Ottawa and Winnipeg. French dominion, losing its hold in the east, naturally enough, sought to make good its losses in the west. But if it failed also in the west, this should be the end of it; there should be no plotting of rebellion.

It is but just to say, however, that Riel seems to have had little or no countenance from the Roman Catholic priesthood

LIEUT.-COL. GRASETT.
Commanding Royal Grenadiers.

in his present insurrection. There would seem to be an entire breaking away from the Church, so far as its local representatives are concerned. Whether this is the result of a general loosening of religious bonds, in a time of relaxed faith, or of the influence of Montana godlessness upon the chief insurgents, it would be hard to say. Riel, himself, seems to be still under religious influences; though, in the motives that have inspired him, whether affected or not, he appears to be under the hallucination of some Mormon Joe Smith, rather than under the sober dictates and restraints of Mother Church. The imprisonment and murder of priests, and the disregard of their sacred calling, is undoubted proof that the clergy were opposed to the rebellion, and withstood lawlessness to the shedding of blood. Riel, moreover, is reported to have told his people not to ask for the support of the clergy in their defiance of authority, as they would not receive it. He adds, significantly, that, "this is a matter affecting our civil and political rights, and has nothing to do with the Church."

But time will bring all this out. It will also bring out how far the half-breeds have received encouragement from reckless white settlers in the Saskatchewan region. Already it is talked of that the insurgent leaders were abetted in their course by other communities than the half-breed village of Batoche. Agitators in Prince Albert are said to have invited Riel to the settlement, and to have given him hope of aid in his rising against authority. This is a matter that should be closely inquired into: if the officials of the administration in the district were worth anything, it ought long ago to be within the privity of the Government.

But the curious fact with regard to the outbreak, is Government's alleged ignorance of the circumstance that serious trouble impended. Of this we are assured by the repeated statements of the Premier, by the asseverations of various members of the Ministry, and by emphatic protests from the Department of the Interior. Accepting these statements, as we are bound to do, in reliance on the *bona fides* of honourable gentlemen, we can scarcely doubt the fact, however, that the Government was aware of discontent among the half-breeds and informed of their many unsettled claims. With the large staff of officials and representatives in the North-West, and the Government's many friends, ecclesiastical and political, it is incredible that the authorities were not made acquainted with the designs of Riel and his lieutenants. If the land-claims of the half-breeds were solely the cause of trouble, this surely was also known to Government; and, if known, why was justice withheld, and why did humanity disregard them? The promptness with which they are now being settled by Commissioners would indicate that the claims were just; and this makes the case look ugly for Government.

Our own opinion, however, is that the land-claims, though doubtless a source of irritation, were not the sole cause of trouble. Riel, at least, has no such pretext to advance in justification of his conduct. Some time ago he became an American citizen, and had therefore no rights in the country to champion. We have already referred to the historical causes which, though in the background, seem to have been operative in producing disaffection, and in widening the breach between the half-breed and the settler. The movement has an historical and scientific side. This is a side which the popular, and even the political, mind does not very closely look at. But it is a point of view which has its advantages and its instruction. The social position of the half-breed has never been much considered; and his civil status in the community, in common justice, has yet to be determined. The half-breeds have been treated neither as white men nor as Indians. The failure to recognise, and to do justice to their civil rights, has therefore had much to do with the present uprising. Again we say, that grievances do not justify rebellion, far less the atrocities of Indian warfare. But that the half-breeds had unredressed grievances goes far to mitigate their crime, and to call for clemency in settling accounts.

Like the Indians, the half-breeds have suffered heavy loss by the intrusion of the settlers. They have seen the game, which hitherto was their sole means of livelihood, driven from the plains. They have also, in great measure, lost employment by the Fur Company. With their half kin, they have looked upon the land as their exclusive and inalienable possession; but, unlike their half kin, they were not disposed to submit quietly to be dispossessed of it. Receiving no Government annuity, and scorning the charity of the Indian Department, their case has called for exceptional treatment. Exceptional treatment have they had? This is a question the nation has to put to itself; and in it lies the kernel of the matter. If they have not received this treatment, there is little difficulty in tracing the causes of the rebellion.

CHAPTER XV.

THE FIRST OVERT ACT.

Duck Lake and the Mounted Police.

FROM the cause we now come to the effect,—from the consideration of the motive of the actors to the act itself. After more than a year of agitation on the North Saskatchewan, Riel and his half-breeds had worked themselves up to action, and were now about to slip in the path of wrong. Already the leader of the movement had steeled his heart against every humane feeling that ennobles mankind, and was calling on the Spirit of Evil to

> "—— make thick (his) blood,
> Stop up the access and passage to remorse
> That no compunctious visitings of nature should
> Shake (his) fell purpose, or keep peace between
> The effect and it."

But to picture the rebel chief possessed of such nerve and resolution as Shakespeare represents Lady Macbeth as being endowed with, is to make a hero of a very unheroic figure. Whatever influence Riel exercised over the half-breed mind, it was not the influence derived from courage. To his powers of stump oratory, and his gifts as an agitator at Métis gatherings, he owed his sway. But when it came to acts, Riel's star paled before that of his able lieutenant, Gabriel Dumont, who is a born leader of men, the embodiment of physical courage, and a military tactician of no mean order. It was at Dumont's invitation that Riel returned from Montana to his mother's homestead at St. Vital, and from that slumbering French village on the Red River it was Dumont who carried him off to the half-breed settlement on the Saskatchewan. With Dumont he stumped the St. Laurent region, and re-kindled the embers of half-breed discontent and jealousy. In Dumont's company he appeared among the white settlers of Prince Albert, and there, with cunning purpose, loosened the rough tongue of misdirected speculation and noisy grumbling. At the St. Laurent meetings, in the early part of March, Riel had Dumont's active assistance in drawing up the Revolutionary Bill of Rights; * and it was Dumont who, reckless of danger, was to take the field to assert them.

---

* This Bill of Rights, or what may be termed, the Rebel Platform, makes the following among other demands :

(a) " That the half-breeds of the North-West Territories be given grants similar to those accorded to the half-breeds of Manitoba by the Act of 1870.

(b) That patents be issued to all half-breed and white settlers who have fairly earned the right of possession to their farms ; that the timber regulations be made more liberal ; and the settler be treated as having rights in the country.

(c) That the provinces of Alberta and Saskatchewan be forthwith organised with legislatures of their own, so that the people may be no longer subject to the despotism of Mr. Dewdney ; and, in the new provincial legislatures, that the Métis shall have a fair and reasonable share of representation.

(d) That the offices of trust throughout these provinces be given to residents of the country, as far as practicable, and that we denounce the appointment of disreputable outsiders and repudiate their authority.

(e) That this region be administered for the benefit of the actual settler, and not for the advantage of the alien speculator ; and that all lawful customs and usages which obtain among the Métis be respected.

(f) That better provision be made for the Indians, the Parliamentary grant to be increased, and lands set apart as an endowment for the establishment of hospitals and schools for the use of whites, half-breeds, and Indians, at such places as the provincial legislatures may determine.

In seeking to enforce the demands embodied in the "Bill of Rights," which we herewith append, the delegates to the St. Laurent meeting, after unanimously adopting the Resolutions, sanctioned the instant forming of a Provisional Government. In this action, history, with ludicrous exactitude, repeats itself. Just fifteen years before, in the Red River Rebellion, Riel guardedly prefaced his usurpation of authority by a similar, *quasi* legal act. How anxious he was to shield himself under the forms which are supposed to give sanctity to rebellion, it might be well to indicate before proceeding with the narrative of events that were now to happen. We cannot better do this than by quoting from the *Mail's* despatch the report of its intelligent correspondent. Says the writer:

"At the meeting speeches were made on behalf of the half-breeds by Riel, Maxime Lepine, and Charles Nolan; and on behalf of the white settlers by Archibald Davidson, George Fisher, and Alexander Waller (or Walter). It was determined to embody this Bill of Rights in a memorial and send it to the newspapers, to leading members of Parliament, and to the Dominion authorities. Nolan and Riel then moved that, as the Government had for fifteen years neglected to settle the half-breed claims, though it had repeatedly (and more especially by providing for their adjustment in the Dominion Land Act of 1883) confessed their justice, the meeting should assume that the Government had abdicated its functions through such neglect, and should proceed to establish a Provisional Government based upon the principles involved in the Bill of Rights. This

---

(*g*) That the Land Department of the Dominion Government be administered as far as practicable from Winnipeg, so that settlers may not be compelled, as heretofore, to go to Ottawa for the settlement of questions in dispute between them and the land commissioner."

[For the above the author is indebted to the Toronto *Mail* of the 13th of April last, in which issue the "Bill of Rights" appears as a special despatch to that journal. Its correspondent states, in sending it, that he does not pretend to give the actual language, but merely the substance, of the Resolutions. We have somewhat abridged the report, and altered the order, though not the wording, of the text.]

THE FIRST OVERT ACT. 239

was agreed to, and a Government was there and then formed with Riel as president. The latter announced that no hostile movement would be made unless word were received from Ottawa refusing to grant the demands in the Bill of Rights. If, however, the Government should appoint a Commission to deal with the half-breed claims and pledge itself to deal with the questions affecting white settlers, then the Provisional Government, on obtaining reasonable guarantees that this would be done, would disband. Bloodshed was to be avoided unless the provocation amounted to life or death for the revolted settlers. In the meantime the authority of the Dominion would be repudiated, and supplies collected to provide against the emergency of war. Immediately after the meeting, Alexander Fisher, Lavallée, and Lepine, who had charge of supplies, began to levy on the freighters and settlers. Riel, Dumont, and others turned their attention to the Indians, with whom they had had talks during the winter; and tobacco men were sent out in all directions informing the chiefs and head-men regarding what had been done."

With these acts the insurrection had its beginning. In time we shall discover how far the half-breeds had justification for thus resisting authority, and for committing the country to the horrors, not to speak of the expense, of civil war. The dispassionate reader of the proceedings we have quoted will not fail to see much of an exculpatory character in the actions, so far, of Riel and his following. If constitutional means were tried and failed them, and patience gave out in seeking the redress of their grievances, there is a strong argument for leniency, at least, in passing judgment upon the acts of rebellion. So early as 1882, the half-breeds had protested against the action of the Dominion surveyors, in disregarding the peculiar conformation of their little farms on the banks of the Saskatchewan, and in cutting up their holdings under what is known as the block system of survey. This action of the surveyors, if not purely wanton, was supremely silly and impolitic. Equally impolitic was the alleged disregard by the authorities of the protests of the Métis; though, it is said, the protests were not disregarded, but, on the contrary, that the surveyors were withdrawn. But the mischief had already been done; and the half-breeds seem to have had no assurance that the obnoxious system of surveys would not afterwards be pursued. Neither does assurance seem to have been given them that their complaint with regard to the cutting of timber on their lands, which was the cause of further discontent, would receive attention, and a more liberal policy be adopted.

There is more excuse for the Government's refusal to assign new lands in the North-West Territories to half-breeds who had already received land-grants in Manitoba. At the same time, there is reason in what they urged, that if the white settler was not debarred from taking up two free homesteads, why should the native of the soil be refused a similar privilege. To discriminate in this matter, and against the half-breed, was surely a perilous policy.

But the period of discussion was past; the time had now come for action. Riel, as we have seen, cast about him for Indian support, and the storekeepers and freighters were fallen upon for supplies to arm and feed the insurgents. Crossing the river at Batoche, the stores were pillaged, and a look-out kept for the Mounted Police, who might be expected to make a descent from Carlton. Fort Carlton is an old trading-post (dating from 1797) of the Hudson's Bay Company, on the north branch of the Saskatchewan. Here at Carlton, up the river at Edmonton, and down the river at Prince Albert, portions of the Mounted Police were stationed; and, with the main body at Forts McLeod and Calgary, in the neighbourhood of the Rockies, it performed its functions as a constabulary force. The Mounted Police were organised in 1874, and have been of great service in maintaining a wholesome check upon Indian lawlessness, in the vast and comparatively unorganised regions of the Far West. The force now consists of about 500 men, commanded by Commissioner Irvine, assisted by Adjutant Cotton. Under these officers there are six superintendents and twelve inspectors, who take charge of detachments of the force at various posts throughout the territory. Among the former, the names of superintendents N. F. Crozier, and W. M. Herchmer, and among the latter, the names of Inspector Francis Jeffrey Dickens, a son of the celebrated novelist, and S. B. Steele, will be most familiar to Canadian ears. Though the force can hardly be said to inspire the Indian and half-breed with that awe which should strike terror to the heart of conscious guilt, as a conservator of peace it has, time and again, rendered signal service to the country, and had its courage and temper often sorely tried, under circumstances that have called into exercise the highest qualities of the patriot soldier.

It was upon a portion of this force, on its way from Carlton to Duck Lake, to convey Government stores to a place of safety at Prince Albert, that Riel's first blow was to descend. To seize these stores, and probably to display their fighting qualities before the admiring eyes of Beardy's band of Indians, whose reserve was close to Duck Lake, the half-breeds mustered early in the day of the 26th of March, 1885. The rebel force was about 200 strong, under the command of Gabriel Dumont, Garnieu, and other notable plain hunters of the insurgent Métis. Many were well mounted on their hardy Indian ponies, and were armed with Winchester rifles and shot-guns.

Duck Lake lies about half-way between Batoche, on the south branch, and Carlton, on the north branch, of the Saskatchewan,—the whole distance between the rivers being not more than fourteen miles from village to Fort. About fifty miles to the north east the two branches of the river meet at a point, called " The Forks," below Prince Albert, and near to the site of the old French trading-post, erected in 1753, by M. de la Corne. The country between the rivers here partakes of the usual undulating character of the North-West, occasional bluffs and high land alternating with open rolling prairie, over which is a well-defined trail, flanked by *coulees* with a profusion of scrub, and here and there a sheet of water. Winter's unsullied mantle was still on the ground.

Posting the bulk of his force in a wood near by Duck Lake, Dumont moved forward his mounted half-breeds and Indians to reconnoitre the ground and await the approach of Crozier's unsuspecting cavalcade. The strength of the Mounted Police was under eighty, with whom were about forty volunteers and civilians, in sleighs, from Prince Albert, the whole being commanded by Superintendent Crozier. With Crozier was Captain Moore, of the Prince Albert volunteers, and a loyal half-breed interpreter, named Joseph McKay. On the forces sighting each other, there was a forward movement on both sides for a conference. Taken by surprise, the Police were especially at a disadvantage ; while the half-breeds were ready for action, and with instinctive shrewdness had well chosen their ground. The engagement which followed has many points of resemblance to the Frog Plain affray, at the Selkirk Settlement, in 1816. Both actions were between white men and half-breeds, and both began in a scuffle during a parley, and ended in a few moments in a massacre.

In the absence of accurate official reports, it is almost impossible to describe the order and details of the encounter. Nor do the accounts of eye-witnesses of the engagement at all help one, for these are confused and contradictory. The whole affair was a matter of but a few minutes' duration. The

Mounted Police on their approach, were, it seems, summoned by the half-breeds to surrender, a summons which, of course, they did not obey. Confronted by this menacing group of half-breeds, Crozier's column halted, and McKay, the interpreter, came forward to confer with the advanced party of the insurgents. The Cree chief, Beardy, was with the latter. During the brief parley, Beardy took hold of McKay's rifle; and Dumont, seeing the action, and anticipating the result of the scuffle, signalled his half-breeds to withdraw to the coulées for protection. Crozier, some paces off, at the head of his column, interpreting this movement as a hint to surround his force, with more haste than discretion, gave the order to fire. The half-breeds instantly replied; and their superior aim wrought fell havoc in the loyal ranks. Death's fleet message came to twelve of Crozier's following, and their lifeless bodies strewed the snow-white plain. Exposed as was his whole party, Crozier gave the command to retire, and until out of gunshot another dozen became the target for rebel bullets. Fortunately the retreating column was not pursued, and the one-sided slaughter ceased. The rebel casualties, according to first report, was but one wounded, though later accounts acknowledge a loss of four killed.

The losses of Crozier's escort were heavy, falling chiefly on the brave Prince Albert Volunteers and civilians who had accompanied the Mounted Police on their mission to Duck Lake. The Police, on the action opening, drew the sleighs across the trail for a breastwork, and so in great measure, protected themselves. The Prince Albert men, unfortunately, had but a slight three-rail fence for cover; and even this failed them, for their leader (Lieutenant Morton) had advanced unguardedly to within a short distance of Chief Beardy's house, from which came a galling flank fire from the Indians and half-breeds who were concealed within it. It was here they sustained their heaviest loss. Among those to fall were Lieut, Morton, a farmer from County Bruce, Ontario; A. W. R. Markley, an old resident of the Red River Colony, and formerly of Ottawa; S. C. Elliott, son of Judge Elliott, of London, Ont., and nephew of the Hon. Edward Blake; Wm. Napier, late of Edinburgh, Scotland, nephew of Sir Charles Napier, and law student in the office of McLean & Elliott, of Prince Albert; Robert Middleton and Daniel MacKenzie, natives of Prince Edward Island; Charles Hewitt, formerly of Portage La Prairie; Daniel McPhail, of McPhail Bros., Prince Albert; Alex. Fisher, a young Englishman; Wm. Baikie, of Orkney, an old Hudson Bay employé; and Joseph Anderson, a native half-breed.

The wounded Prince Albert volunteers were Captain Moore, whose leg was broken; Sergeant A. McNabb; and Alex. S. Stewart. Two of the Mounted Police were killed, viz., Constables T. G. Gibson, and George P. Arnold. The wounded Policemen were Inspector Howe, of the Gun Detachment, son of the late Hon. Joseph Howe; Corporal Gilchrist; and Constables M. K. Garrett, J. J. Wood, Sidney F. Gordon, A. M. Smith, and A. Miller. From correspondence which appears in the Battleford *Herald*, and the Winnipeg *Sun*, we learn that the bodies of the civilians who fell during the engagement had to be left on the field, as they lay so close to the house garrisoned by the rebels that it would have been foolhardy to have brought them in before the retreat. The last words of a few of the stricken brave, we transcribe from the same correspondence. The faltering messages to friends and dear ones may well be preserved in this narrative. As Arnold fell, he cheerily said, " Tell the boys I died game !" Gilchrist's request was that his comrades should not " let the black devils get his scalp." Napier's last gasp was broken by the utterance, "Write to my father, and tell him I died manfully." The gallant Elliott cried, "Fight on, boys; don't let them beat us!" Baikie's prayer was, "I am shot, God have mercy on my soul!" while Morton whispered to a volunteer who had come to his succour: "You can't do anything for me. I am mortally wounded. Take care of my wife and family, and tell them 'I died like a man on the battlefield!'"

> "Glorious it is to emulate the brave;
> And for a country, and a country's right,
> To strive, to fall, and gain a bloody grave
> Amid the foremost heroes in the fight."

In such sorrow and anger as may be imagined but not described, Crozier and his detachment reached Carlton, where he was presently joined by Commissioner Irvine with a strong contingent of the Police. Irvine's column had itself been in danger on the way to Carlton, but escaped attack by making a wide detour through the Birch Hills on the east. As it was determined not to hold the post at Carlton, it was evacuated and burnt, and the combined party proceeded to Prince Albert. Here the greatest excitement prevailed; for, learning of the uprising, the settlers and their families throughout the district flocked to the town for safety, and for weeks were in alarm of an attack upon the place.

The arrival of the Carlton garrison at Prince Albert gave a measure of security to its inhabitants, though the dread of attack, the remoteness from succour, and the interruption of telegraphic communication, kept the settlement for a long while in the agonies of suspense. Apprehension was increased by uncertainty with regard to the attitude of the large bands of Indians whose reserves extend along the North Saskatchewan. A descent of Indians might come from any quarter. White

Cap and his Sioux were close by, at Moosewood. The pagan, Beardy, was known to have been with the half-breeds at Duck Lake; while Okemasis and One Arrow were in the immediate proximity. North of Carlton were the bands of Atakakoop, Mistowasis, and Pete-qua-quay, who, it was feared, might take the war-path at any moment. Nor was the outlook more assuring in the region between Battle River and the N. Saskatchewan. There Poundmaker and Strike-him-on-the-back were known to be ugly. Westward, matters were worse; for Big Bear had left his reserve and was threatening mischief; while at Frog Lake, near Fort Pitt, immediate trouble seemed brewing. Throughout the region the aspect appalled the stoutest hearts, and gave occasion for the greatest alarm and uneasiness.

On the South Saskatchewan disquieting rumours were also rife; while apprehension was increased by the interruption of the mails and the cutting of the telegraph wires. Already the Government had taken active steps to assert its authority and save life. News of the uprising had electrified the whole country; and the volunteers of Winnipeg and the chief centres in the east were eager to offer their services to the Government. The Minister of Militia and the officials of his Department, at Ottawa, nobly rose to the occasion, and gratifyingly met the demands made upon them. In these demands assurance was given to Canada and the Empire that the heroic qualities of the race had not degenerated in the New World, and that the Colonial status had not wholly dwarfed patriotism.

The Dominion authorities were fortunate at this juncture in having in command of the militia a distinguished officer of the British army, who had seen varied service, and was known to possess, in happy combination, the essential soldierly qualities of courage and discretion. This officer, Major-General Middle-

THE FIRST OVERT ACT. 247

ton, C.B.,* after a hasty conference with the Militia authorities, in concert with the Governor-General, the Premier and the Cabinet, proceeded instantly to Winnipeg, thence to Qu'Appelle, to place and take charge of a small army in the field. On the General's staff was Lord Melgund, military secretary to the Marquis of Lansdowne.† Meanwhile, Riel and his halfbreeds were not idle. Runners speedily carried, far and wide, the "news of battle" to Indian and half-breed settlements;

---

* Major-General Frederick D. Middleton, who came to Canada in November, 1884, as successor to General Luard in the command of the Militia of the Dominion, is the third son of the late Major-General Charles Middleton of the British army. In 1842, he graduated at the Royal Military College, Sandhurst, and obtained an ensigncy in the same year. He saw his first active service in New Zealand, but won his chief laurels in India during the Sepoy Rebellion, of 1857-8. He was present at the relief of Lucknow, acting first as Orderly Officer to General Franks, and later as Aide-de-Camp to General Lugard. For gallant conduct during skirmishes with the mutineers, and in command of storming parties, he repeatedly won promotion ; while for cool daring on the field he was recommended to Lord Clyde as having deserved the honour of the Victoria Cross. Unfortunately, being at the time on the personal staff of the General, the honour, though richly deserved, was withheld. Throughout the Mutiny, General Middleton was on many occasions specially mentioned in home despatches. In 1861, he came to Canada as Major of the 29th Regiment, and remained here on the staff of General Windham, from the period of the Trent affair to the withdrawal of the British troops from the country. The gallant General is married to a Montreal lady, and so far, at least, may be claimed as a Canadian.

† Viscount Melgund, eldest son of the Earl of Minto, came to Canada as Military Secretary to His Excellency, the Governor-General. At the outbreak of the Insurrection in the North-West, he received permission to attach himself to General Middleton's staff at the front. Lord Melgund has seen military service in many quarters of the Empire, and taken part in various campaigns, at one time as a Volunteer, at another as a Regular. In 1867, he entered the Scots Fusilier Guards, but retired three years later. He was in Paris during the Commune ; served with the Carlist Army in Spain ; and was an *attaché* with the Turkish Army in 1877. In 1879, he was on the staff of Sir Frederick Roberts in Afghanistan, and accompanied the General to South Africa in 1881. In the following year he served in the Egyptian Campaign, as Captain in the Mounted Infantry, was severely wounded at Magyr, and was present at Tel-el-Kebir. Under the pseudonym of "Mr. Rolly," Lord Melgund is widely known in England as one of the most daring gentleman riders in Britain.

and an army of scouts radiated from Batoche to keep rebeldom advised of every movement outside.

While these events were happening, the pallid dead who had fallen at Duck Lake, and were yet alas! unburied, slept the sleep of the brave, and with eager and touching enthusiasm Canada's sons in the east rose to avenge them.*

---

*Since this chapter was written, the successes of the North-West Field Force have enabled the friends of one of the fallen at Duck Lake to recover the body of a hero from the battle-field. A despatch from London, Ontario (June 19th), conveys the intelligence that the body of Lieut. Skeffington C. Elliott, the esteemed son of Hon. Justice Elliott, was exhumed and brought to London for interment in the family burying vault. As befited the occasion, the brave Prince Albert volunteer was given the honors of a military funeral in his native city, representatives being present of the various metropolitan and county corps, together with the municipal officers, members of the Middlesex Law Association, the London Board of Education, and other local societies. The funeral obsequies were most impressive, the populace turning out *en masse* to do honor to the fallen officer. The Rector of the Cronyn Memorial Church officiated, and the firing party was furnished by the 7th Fusileers.

CHAPTER XVI.

CALLING OUT THE VOLUNTEERS.

IF there is one circumstance more than another that gives hope for the future of Canadian Nationality it is to be found in the alacrity and enthusiasm with which the youth of the country rally on occasion for its defence, or for the suppression of armed disturbance within its borders. The military spirit has always been strongly marked in the training and temper of the Canadian people ; though, oddly enough, in the Mother-land, credit has rarely been given them for the fact. It has been the fashion in England to speak slightingly of this spirit, and to represent Canadians as unwilling to bear their share in the defence of the Empire. For long, it was considered doubtful whether Canada, in the event of embroilment with her great neighbour to the South, would unite heartily in making an effective resistance to invasion. It was affirmed that, when danger menaced, some organic weakness would show itself, fatal to vigorous and united action. But not only were the people misrepresented; the country itself was given up. It was alleged that its peculiar conformation, and long line of frontier, made it impossible of defence; and the belief was entertained that, if invaded, the colony would become an easy conquest. To retain it was therefore long held to be an element of national weakness. Such were the calumnies which insular ignorance was wont to heap upon Canada and Canadians.

After the withdrawal of the English troops from the country, it was seen that Canada did not seriously miss them. It was then seen that, colony as she was, she aspired to be a nation, and in the aspiration, she sought to rely upon herself. If the events of the War of 1812 were not remembered to her honour, the attitude of Canada during the Trent affair, and the prompt rallying of her hardy sons to repel Fenian invasion, in 1866, must have opened the eyes of old countrymen to the loyalty and valour of her citizen soldiery. More recently, the offer of Canadian contingents, for Britain's service in Egypt, shows the spirit that animates her people, and is the most effective reply to the popular misapprehension. The number of Canadian military school cadets that annually find their way into English regiments is another proof, were proof wanted, of their aptitude for military service, and their readiness to aid the Motherland in her hour of need. The annual presence at Wimbledon of her crack rifle shots should also count for something in removing misapprehension, and in assuring old Albion that her military prestige is not likely to suffer eclipse beyond the Atlantic.

But the assurance was of most value to her own people. When the insurrection broke out in the North-West, it was with pride the country saw the eager rallying of her sons to repress it, and to restore the blessings of peace. The response to the call for troops was immediate and enthusiastic. It was a response which gave assurance that, young as the nation was, it had passed from the adolescent stage into full manhood. It was a response which showed that Canada had resources within her borders equal to any emergency, and that if she spread herself over a Continent, over a Continent she was able to throw the shield of her protection. Nor was this all, for it also showed that

> "Old England still hath heroes,
> To wear her sword and shield!
> *We knew them not while near us,*
> *We know them in the field.*"

In Toronto, the military as well as civil heart of the Province, the last days of March saw an unusual sight. News of the rising on the Saskatchewan had been telegraphed over the country, and the Ontario Capital was one of the first to be communicated with, in the call for troops for active service in the North-West. To the prompt call of the Hon. A. P. Caron, Minister of Militia, the citizen-soldiery of Toronto made prompt response. The two city battalions mustered in the drill shed in full force; while the Department at Ottawa, and the Brigade Office at Toronto, were inundated with applications from officers commanding country regiments, to be allowed to go to the front. The "Queen's Own," whose military record deservedly stood high at Ottawa, was called upon for a quota of 250 men. The summons to arms of its commanding officer brought 550 rank and file at a few hours' notice. The same quota was asked for, and with like alacrity furnished, in the case of the "Royal Grenadiers."

The scenes in the Toronto drill shed, from the 28th to the 30th of March, were long to be remembered. No such excitement had been witnessed since the closing days of May, 1866, when, for the most part, a former generation, the sires of the eager youths, who were now fitting themselves out at the call of duty, took hurried leave of those dear to them in the summons to the Niagara peninsula, to repel the Fenian invader. Again were the scenes enacted of that stirring time: the hurrying to and fro from armoury to parade ground ; the bugle summons to " fall in " ; the hasty roll call ; the " proving " the companies ; the inspection of clothing, arms and accoutrements ; and the momentary "stand at ease !" Then came the sharp calling of the brigade to " attention " ; the few words of orders ; the march off to the station ; and the final leave-taking, with the ardent hand-clasp and tender look of farewell, which spoke the words the tongue could not articulate.

> "Let them go with the cheers of the country to speed them,
>   The gallant, devoted, and flower of the land ;
> We well may be proud that young Britain could breed them,
>   And match her past heroes at Freedom's command.
> They have joined honest hands for the future of nations,
>   The grandeur of law and humanity's due :
> Belief that God's blessing through all their relations
>   Is with them, inspires our success to the True !"

From early dawn on the 27th March the headquarters (Toronto) of Military District No. 2, were astir with the exciting duties of the hour. On that day the Deputy-Adjutant General, Lt. Col. R. B. Denison, received orders from Ottawa to call out " C " Company, School of Infantry, at Toronto, Lt.-Col. W. D. Otter, Commandant. Col. Otter, with the military promptitude which characterises all his movements, was ready with his command at an hour's notice. The same day this able officer was given charge of the Toronto Expeditionary Force, and had instructions to hold himself in readiness, with " C " Company, and the contingents of the Queen's Own and the 10th Royals, for route orders, *via* the Canadian Pacific Railway, to the North-West. All Saturday and Sunday, the 28th and 29th insts., the required quota of the city Rifle and Infantry regiments paraded at the Drill Shed, and received the necessary outfit for proceeding to the front. In view of the still inclement weather, and the exposed route by which the force was to reach the North-west, this outfit was largely added to by the thoughtful provision of the Mayor and various members of Toronto municipality.

By Monday, the 30th, thanks to the efforts of the City Corporation, and the unwearied labours of the District Staff— Deputy Adj.-General Denison, Brigade-Major, Lt.-Col. Milsom, and the Sup't. of Stores, Lt.-Col. Alger—the volunteers were in readiness to leave Toronto.* Marching orders had been impatiently awaited. For forty-eight hours dark coat and red had massed together on the rallying ground, inspired with but one purpose and animated by a common feeling. With beautiful enthusiasm all were eager for the fray. During the period

---

* The composition and strength of the Toronto Expeditionary Force (Lt.-Col. W. D. Otter in command), were as follows:

(a) Infantry School Corps, "C" Company, 85 men and 4 officers (Major Henry Smith; Lieutenants J. W. Sears, and R. L. Wadmore; Surgeon, Dr. F. W. Strange).

(b) 2nd Battalion "Queen's Own Rifles" (Lt.-Col. A. A. Miller in command), 257 men and 18 officers (Major D. H. Allan; Adjutant, Capt. J. M. Delamere; Quartermaster, James Heakes; Surgeons, Drs. Jos. W. Lesslie, and W. Nattress; Capts. T. Brown, H. E. Kersteman, J. C. McGee, W. C. Macdonald; Lieutenants P. D. Hughes, W. G. Mutton, H. Brock, R. S. Cassels, E. F. Gunther; 2nd Lieuts., A. Y. Scott, A. B. Lee, J. George.)

(c) 10th Battalion "Royal Grenadiers" (Lt.-Col. H. J. Grasett [late Lieut. 100th Foot] in command) 250 men and 17 officers (Major G. D. Dawson [late Lieut 47th Foot]; Adjt., Capt. F. F. Manley; Paymaster and Acting Quartermaster, Lieut. W. S. Lowe; Surgeon, Dr. G. S. Ryerson; Capts. F. A. Caston, James Mason, O. L. Leigh-Spencer, C. Greville Harston; Lieuts. D. M. Howard, And. Irving; G. P. Eliot, Forbes Michie, W. C. Fitch; 2nd Lieuts. Jno. Morrow, J. D. Hay, A. C. Gibson).

The Expeditionary Force had attached to its staff as Supply Officer, Lt.-Col. E. Lamontagne, Deputy Adj.-General of the Ottawa Military District (No. 4.)

[For the revision of the above lists the author is indebted to Lt.-Col. C. T. Gillmor, formerly Commanding Officer "Queen's Own Rifles," and to Major A. B. Harrison, in temporary command of the 10th "Royal Grenadiers."]

the Drill Shed had been almost continuously filled with an immense concourse of townspeople, anxious to spend the parting moments with those dear to them, and with tender solicitude bent on seeing them off with a fervent "God speed!" As the morning passed, the crowd grew more dense, and by noon, not only the approaches to the Drill Shed, but the streets on the line of march to the station, were choked with a surging mass, which, heedless of the threatening rain, had gathered to give the brave lads a farewell cheer. What had been the home parting from each familiar figure in dark green and red there is no need to lift domestic veils to divine. That assuredly was tender; and now, while excitement glistened in the eye of love, the heart was filled with misgivings in taking, it might be, *the last* farewell. Nor was the solicitude confined to those who were to be left behind: in the effort to suppress emotion in many a manly breast we saw the eye averted, the muscles of the mouth quiver, and the lip bitten, that the mind might be kept from its sorrow and the rising tear be suppressed. But now came the enlivening music, with the roll of drums, and the heart recovered its composure as the eye caught sight of the compact column and the martial bearing of Toronto's chivalry.

> "Now all with life and motion swarms,
> Glistens the street with burnished arms."

It was a proud moment! a moment which Canadian verse, we doubt not, will yet enshrine in its treasures, and long keep green the memory of. As we looked on the stirring scene, we mentally observed, what an impetus to patriotism was here, and how deep must be the impress of such a sight on the national heart! Than this, what influence, we thought, could be more effective to weld Confederation, or more potent to charge the nation's veins with the tingling thrill of patriot enthusiam and the nation's brain with the fire of a common sentiment!

But while Toronto's volunteers were leaving the Union Station, and the hearts of ten thousand onlookers went out in sympathy with their ready response to the call of duty, the summons to arms was elsewhere being answered with like patriotic ardour. Manitoba's gallant sons were already in the field. The 90th "Winnipeg Rifles," under Lt.-Col. A. Mackeand; a Cavalry Troop, under Capt. Knight; and a Field Battery, under Major Jarvis, all of Winnipeg, were the first to be with General Middleton at Qu'Appelle. Besides these local corps the 91st Winnipeg Infantry, 400 strong, under Lt.-Col. Thos. Scott, M.P., was instantly organised, together with three companies of Scouts and one of Rangers, under Major Boulton, and Capts. Dennis, White, and Stewart. Capt. Dennis's Scouts were composed of Dominion Land Surveyors. The other Scouts and Rangers were drawn from the loyal yeomen of the territories.

"A" Battery, from Quebec, and "B" Battery, from Kingston, under the command of Lt.-Col. Montizambert, had gone forward from the East. The Governor-General's Foot Guards, and a company of sharpshooters, from Ottawa, under Capt. Todd, were also under way. To follow these, in rapid succession, there went forward a Battalion from York and Simcoe, commanded by Lt.-Col. Wm. E. O'Brien, M.P.; the "Midlanders," under Lt.-Col. A. T. Williams, M.P., of Port Hope; the "65th," Lt. Col. Ouimet, M.P., of Montreal; the "9th," Lt.-Col. Amyot, M. P., of Quebec; the Governor-General's Body Guard (73 men and horses), Lt.-Col. G. T. Denison, of Toronto,*

---

* The Governor-General's Body Guard for Ontario was called out on the 1st of April and left Toronto for the front five days afterwards. The following are the officers who accompanied the corps on active service: Major Commanding, (Lt.-

and the 7th Fusiliers, Lt.-Col. W. M. Williams, of London. Later in the month of April, there were also to go to the front, "A" Troop, Cavalry School Corps (45 men and horses), Lt.-Col. Turnbull, of Quebec; and a Provisional Battalion from Halifax (350 strong) under Lt.-Col. Bremner.

But this hasty mobilising of volunteers was creditable not only in the numbers that turned out at a day's call for the nation's service; its strength and effectiveness lay in the spirit that animated the men. To see the force on parade, those who usually fail to dissociate the volunteer from the tradesman and the clerk, must have found it difficult to realise the fact that it had never seen active service; that its ranks knew war only by tradition; and, for the most part, had received military training, not on the open field, but in a contracted drill shed. In the ranks were mingled the brawn and muscle of machine shops, athletes from cricket and lacrosse grounds, clerks from store and office, undergraduates from the universities, together with the delicately nurtured sons of wealth, and the blest blood and intellect of local families of influence. But, shoulder to shoulder, there was no distinction of birth, nor in the spirit of emulation that infected all ranks. All were actuated by a genuine desire to serve the country, and unconscious of the destiny that lay before them on the lonely prairies of the west, were eager to win the badge of a nation's honour and the laurel of military renown.

As an indication of the martial spirit by which young and old were actuated in the eager press to the front, the following "Incident," told in verse by J. A. Fraser, jr., a talented young Torontonian, is worthy of preservation in these pages:

Col.) G. T. Denison; Captain Orlando Dunn; Lieut. Wm. H. Merritt; 2nd. Lieuts., F. A. Fleming and T. B. Browning; Adjutant, Capt. C. A. K. Denison; Surgeon, Dr. J. B. Baldwin.

CALLING OUT THE VOLUNTEERS. 257

"The call 'To arms!' resounded through the city broad and fair,
And volunteers in masses came, prepared to do and dare ;
Young lads, whose cheeks scarce showed the down, men bearded, stout and strong,
Assembled at the first alarm, in bold, undaunted throng.
'I'll volunteer!' an old man cried, 'I've served the Queen before ;
I fought the Russ at Inkerman, the Sepoy at Cawnpore ;'
And as he stood erect and tall, with proud and flashing eye,
What though his hair were white as snow ? He could but do or die.
'You are too old,' the answer was ; 'too old to serve her now.'
Then o'er his face a wonder flashed, a scowl came on his brow,
And then a tear stole down his cheek, a sob his strong voice shook,—
'Sir, put me in a uniform, and see how old I'll look !'"

Nor was the military ardour confined to those who were further to share it. It was but a day's work to change the usual aspect of tranquil industry over the country, and to fire the populace with "war's fitful fever." As the trains sped on their way from Toronto with the several contingents, the people, catching the excitement of the time, turned out in whole towns'-strength to see the expeditionary force pass by, and with cheers and God-speeds! to relieve surcharged feeling. A people, whose military enthusiasm could be so profoundly stirred, must have had an ancestry not unfamiliar with martial deeds. Here was a young nation that had heard little of the cannon's roar save in the *feu-de-joie* on some gala day, when the troops mustered for inspection by the reviewing General, suddenly infected with the death-thirst of the battle-field, and its young life eager to launch itself on the tide of war, and win the fame which is the hero's meed. Surely, it will be said, there is a bright future for a nation whose pulses can be so quickened at the summons of patriotism, and whose young men respond so eagerly at the call of duty.

But these gallant youths are the sons of no pampered soldier ancestry ; for the most part, their sires were the rough toilers of the land, the sturdy pioneers of the once wilderness their offspring are now passing through. The names of the stations on the Canadian Pacific, just east of Toronto, recall the wrestlings of their fathers in founding a nation in the backwoods once entirely peopled by the red Indian. Through the region opened up by the iron highway to the Ottawa, the stealthy Iroquois was wont to find his way to the sheepfold of the Huron; and down its waterways the descending birchbarks of the latter would occasionally steal to wreak Wyandot vengeance on the tribal enemy. Of these days we have left us but the tradition, and, in the region, the beautiful Indian nomenclature. Happily both are being treasured. Canadian literature, in the researches of its later writers, is recounting, often with infinite charm, the story of that early time. In the district through which the Toronto contingent was now speeding, a Canadian Parkman* has preserved for us, with inimitable literary grace, the chief incidents of the local history. Let us interrupt our narrative for a little with an extract:

"Of the Trent Valley, as it was two hundred and seventy years ago, Champlain gave such glimpses as must have stirred the sportsmen at the Court of Mary de Medici and Louis XIII. No part of Canada owes more to its pioneers than this charming and now most healthful lake-land. Some of the finest towns were, two generations ago, jungles reeking with malaria, and infested by wolves, black-flies, black snakes, and black bears. All honour to the men whose hands or brain wrought the transformation! . . Of the Iroquois domination, but few traces remain—a few sonorous names. The race of athletes who lorded it over half the Continent, whose alliance was eagerly courted by France and England, were, after all, unable to maintain their foothold against the despised Ojibways. Of these the Mississagas became specially numerous and aggressive, so that their *totem*, the crane, was a familiar hieroglyph on our forest trees from the beginning of last century. The

---

* J. Howard Hunter, M.A., in the article on "Central Ontario," in *Picturesque Canada.*

Mississagas so multiplied in their northern nests, that presently, by mere numbers, they overwhelmed the Iroquois.

"The Mississagas, though not endowed with the Mohawk verve or intellect, were no more destitute of poetry than valour. Take the names of some of their chiefs. One chief's name signified 'He who makes footsteps in the sky;' another was *Wawanosh*, 'He who ambles the water.' A local Indian missionary was, through his mother, descended from a famous line of poetic warriors; his grandfather was *Waubuno*, 'The Morning Light.' On occasion, the Mississaga could come down to prose. *Scugog* describes the clay bottom and submerged banks of that lake, which, taking a steamer at Port Perry, we traverse on our summer excursion to Lindsay and Sturgeon Lake. *Chemong* aptly names the lake whose tide of silt sometimes even retards our canoe when we are fishing or fowling. *Omemee*, 'the wild pigeon,' has given its name, not only to Pigeon Lake and its chief affluent, but to the town where Pigeon Creek lingers on its course to the lake. Sturgeon Lake is linked to Pigeon Lake by a double gateway. This 'rocky portal' the Mississagas described by *Bobcaygeon*. In our time the name has been transferred to the romantic village on the upper outlet, and the latter is now the 'North River.' By a reprehensible levity, the lower outlet is now called 'The Little Bob.' The steamer *Beaubocage*, which plies between Lindsay and Bobcaygeon, would evidently take us back for the latter name to the old French explorers, and to their outspoken admiration of the *lovely woodlands* on these waters. At the south-west corner of Stony Lake the overflow of the whole lake-chain is gathered into a crystal funnel, well named 'Clear Lake,' and thence poured into Rice Lake through the Otonabee.

"On Rice Lake, the chief Indian settlement is Hiawatha,— named after the Hercules of Ojibway mythology, which the American poet has immortalised in his melodious trochaics. At Hiawatha and on Scugog Island, you may still find, in the ordinary language of the Ojibway, fragments of fine imagery and picture-talk, often in the very words which Longfellow has so happily woven into his poem. And the scenery of this Trent Valley reproduces that of the Vale of Tawasentha. Here are 'the wild rice of the river,' and 'the Indian village,' and 'the groves of singing pine-trees, ever sighing, ever singing.' At Fenelon Falls we have the 'Laughing Water,' and not far below is Sturgeon Lake, the realm of the 'king of fishes.' Sturgeon of portentous size are yet met with, though falling somewhat short of the comprehensive fish sung by Longfellow, which swallowed Hiawatha, canoe and all!"

Leaving the lacustrine beauty of the region of these rich Indian appellatives, the face of Nature puts on a visible frown, and closing day brought the expedition to what the imagination might fitly conceive as the confines of an Inferno. Still eastward, the railway train, with its martial freight, rushes like some weird spectre through belts of hardy pine, to which the granite soil gives but a sparse sustenance, and over the borderland, which it now crosses, "between the oldest sedimentary rocks and the still more ancient Laurentian series." By midnight Carleton Place and an appetising supper were reached. Here an incident occurred which we may well stop to chronicle. In expectation of the arrival of the Toronto detachment, a number of patriotic Members of Parliament, hailing from the west, had for the afternoon left their arduous legislative duties at Ottawa to speed on the way the young martial life of the Provincial capital. In meeting the troops at Carleton Place, they had also this object, to present a flag to the Toronto Contingent, which was to be donated by the graceful hands of a lady,—Mrs. Edward Blake, wife of the honourable, the leader of the Opposition. After supper, the men were drawn up on the platform, under Colonel Otter, and the Commandant and officers of the Queen's Own and Grenadiers, were introduced to Mrs. Blake, by Mr. W. Mulock, M.P. Mr. Mulock, addressing Colonel Otter, spoke as follows:

"I have been desired by a number of the Members of the House of Commons to assist in the presentation of this flag for your command. In discharging this pleasing duty, let me say that this act has no significance, except as evidencing the fact that whatever differences Members of the House may have in other matters, they are a unit in support of law and order, and will, I am sure, co-operate in every possible way for the restoration of peace and quiet in our land. May this flag ever float over a law-abiding people; and may the brave citizen soldiers under your command return in safety to their homes after a speedy accomplishment of the object of the expedition."

Mrs. Blake then presented a handsome Union Jack to the Commanding Officer, with the few following heartfelt words:

" A number of my friends in the House of Commons, desirous of expressing their sympathy and good wishes for the men under your command, and on the expedition on which they have now started, have desired me to present you with this flag. I do so with great pleasure, and at the same time would like to add my own heartfelt prayer for your speedy success and safe keeping."

In acknowledgment of the gift, Colonel Otter made the following observations:

" Mrs. Blake and Gentlemen: I accept this flag from your hands as indicating, as you have said, that the House of Commons is a unit in the maintenance, not only of the integrity of Canada, but of the Empire of which she forms so considerable a part. I hope the men under my command will successfully accomplish the object of the expedition, and shortly return to their fond ones at home in safety, and will serve their country as Britons always do. On an occasion such as this, nothing more fitting could be presented than the British flag—the emblem of law, justice, and freedom. It will be ours to preserve it, and guard it carefully, as a reminder that the people of Canada are with us in our undertaking. I acknowledge the kindness which has prompted the representatives of the people to make this presentation to us, and I thank you as the bearer of the gift."

This graceful and patriotic act, we can well believe, had, as was observed, no political significance. As Colonel Otter happily remarked, on such an occasion, and, we might add, to such a body of men, nothing more fitting than the nation's flag could be presented. We should like to believe that the assurance which accompanied the flag was genuine, viz., that Parliament was a unit in desiring to maintain the integrity of Canada and the Empire. We do not churlishly call the assurance in question; but "acts speak louder than words," and the intensity of party and sectional feeling that finds frequent and acrid expression in and out of the national Parliament, is not favourable to the maintenance of Confederation or to the increasing adhesion of the people. To seek to limit the license of party objurgation, we know, is like seeking to control the four cardinal winds. Nevertheless, it is to be said, that the violence of party in Canada, is a disruptive force which, if not in danger of breaking up the Dominion into fragmentary Provinces, is in danger at least, of sapping the foundations of order and destroying confidence in the future of the country. This is a danger which politicians, we know, deride; but it is a danger, nevertheless, and one which partyism, for its own sinister end, conceals, and has an interest in concealing.

Our remarks may seem inopportune as a pendant to a loyal and kindly act; but we have only to look a little way ahead in the records of Parliamentary proceedings at Ottawa, from the period when the flag was presented, to discover how far the country's banner symbolised unity of patriotic feeling, and regard for the nation's weal over the pettiness of party conflict and the incendiary declamation of faction. We desire to draw no line between the existing parties that would separate them into loyalists and non-loyalists, into patriots and non-patriots, into nationalists and anti-nationalists. There is no such distinction to be made; for true patriotism exists among both parties; and, so far, the flag might fitly wave over both camps, as from both camps it came. The exception we take is to the disloyalty of party in the concrete, not to the disloyalty of either party in the abstract; for both are tainted with the virus of faction. It is disloyalty, not to the Crown, but to the individual, and to the public conscience of the nation which the individual represents. It is disloyalty to the high ideals of public life which party dethrones, and to that high sense of duty and keen sense of honour which partyism and the arts of partyism set at nought. The moral injury to the nation which this atmosphere of party scuffling inflicts, and the deterioration of public character for which party is responsible, few adequately estimate. Nor does the evil stop with Parliament; the press of the whole country is more or less infected with the poison; and the clear streams of political life that should flow from it are too often foul with the vapours of vituperation and unclean with the sewerage of invective.

CHAPTER XVII.

OVER "THE GAPS" TO QU'APPELLE.

DESPITE the noisome influences referred to in our last chapter the national heart is ever warm, and, on great occasions at least, the national brain is clear. The attitude of the nation towards disaffection in the North-West, it is safe to say, was manly, healthy, and vigorous. In the fullest and freest sense, it was patriotic. Parliament, too, shared the national feelings of the country. If there was guilt to be charged against the Administration, if there had been a flagitious use of patronage, if there was criminal neglect of protests and complaints, in the presence of revolt neither Parliament nor the country stopped to be querulous or censorious. There was no sympathy with the feeling that cropped out in some quarters to hold up our public men to public reprobation. Faction might choose an inopportune moment for its firework, but the nation was in no mood just then to encourage it. At another time it might hector and vituperate, and rise to the screaming level of captious criticism. But at present it was too indignant at armed revolt to listen to grumbling Cassandras; and only a persistent optimism would mollify it. A great emergency called for the exercise of higher powers than the Parliamentary picking up of pins; and

LIEUT.-COL. GEO. T. DENISON
Commanding Governor-General's Body Guard.

the country addressed itself to the duty of the hour with the coolness and self-possession of one who had not lost his head.

Other cries were now heard of an aspersive and mischievous character. Disloyalty and faction had not yet done their work. Permission, it was urged, should have been sought at Washington for the transport of the troops to the North-West through United States territory, rather than expose them to the hardships of transit over the incompleted portions of the line of the Canadian Pacific. Relying on the enterprise and activity of the Railway Company, the Government, fortunately, otherwise determined; and the country was saved the humiliation of reaching its western domains over other avenues than its own means of access. The Militia Department then came in for its share of criticism. The Volunteers, it was said, were inefficiently armed and indifferently equipped. The labour that at this time fell upon the Department was of a kind to stagger an indolent imagination. Yet, admirably as the strain upon its resources and strength was met, there were not a few to withhold from it its well-earned meed of praise, and to harass it with the jibes of untimely comment. Well has it been said that "what most recommends party government is that it enables its opponents to slander the country's rulers without sedition and, at times, to overthrow them without treason."

In other quarters fell the floutings of detraction and ill-timed criticism. Even the militia of the country did not escape. It had been said, that it was not a good instrument to employ in keeping the peace, "as it lacks that perfect self control which belongs to discipline, and shares the political passions of the combatants." Well, twelve years' experience of militia service, in the closest relation that officer and men could come to, in trouble and in peace, enables the writer to say that, so far as Ontario is concerned, the statement libels the force.

Nor would it be difficult in other Provinces to show, that when the Canadian volunteer is on active service he loyally does his duty. The same may be said of the much maligned Irishman, who, in the ranks of the British army, as well as in the Canadian militia, has been no whit less loyal and true than his comrade of Albion and Scotia.

But the charge, on one occasion, was more explicit. It was said that "a summons to the militia of the Dominion to take the field would meet with a strange response from the French Province: there, national enthusiasm would grow pale at the prospect of fighting its own race." How far the writer was mistaken in this prognostication, recent events overwhelmingly prove. The service which "A" Battery, from Quebec, has rendered in the North-West, and the loss it has nobly suffered, amply refutes the charge. Had signal opportunity in the field offered, we are sure the gallant 65th, the 9th Quebecers, and "A" troop, Cavalry School Corps, would have given equally good account of themselves. In the sister Province, we know that national traditions are closely and laudably cherished, but honour is no less cherished. It was perhaps a vain boast, that "the last shot fired in the New World for the maintenance of British connection would be fired by a French Canadian;" but in the case of many of our French compatriots there is more than a sentimental basis for the historic remark. Invidious comment of the kind we have referred to is to be deprecated, as it tends to incite bad blood, and to introduce into the service class and sectional feeling which should be wholly blended in the national militia. Equally to be deprecated is the foolish talk that exalts the deeds of one regiment at the expense of another, and leads the men to beat the tom tom of a section of the community or a part of the country rather than the Canadian people as a body and Canada as a whole.

In interrupting the narrative with these observations, we trust that we shall not be thought wanting in sympathy with Her Majesty's Loyal Opposition, in their often thankless task of keeping a watchful eye on the Administration. Doubtless, when the causes of the trouble in the North-West come to be finally determined, it will be found that our rulers have not acquitted themselves fully of their duty. But until the facts are all before us, or until there was an actual break-down in our Militia organisation, the Opposition obviously but wasted their powder in making premature and unsupported attacks. The feeling, we confess, however, was a natural one, that un-accustomed as was our Militia Department to meet the emergency of civil war, it was therefore supposed that everything was going wrong, and that men were being sent to the front ill-prepared for the services required of them. Happily, such was not the case; and Mr. Blake must have been reading the history of Whitehall maladministration in England, at the outbreak of the Crimean War, to have supposed there was occasion in Canada for his daily fusilade of interrogation, and the expenditure of his virile energy in criticism of the Department and the Government. In England, in 1854, there was need of Mr. Layard to badger Lord Palmerston and his Minister of War; but just then in Canada there was no need of a Mr. Layard. Mr. Blake's good sense enabled him speedily to see this, and led him to reserve his strength for a fitting time of reckoning.

Meanwhile the North-West expeditionary force had begun to feel the real stress of the situation. The trains had ploughed their way to the frontier of that realm of solitude, the upper shores of Lake Superior; and the batteries had already tackled the "gaps." Over the desolate region was still spread the white garment of the north, and its folds hung heavily upon the outstretched arms of hemlock and pine. The troops had now an opportunity, not of "conquering nature for political purposes," as a certain well known and brilliant writer had termed the work of constructing the railway to the north of the lakes, but of conquering nature for the purposes of war. On their dread mission, nature seems to have confronted them with every obstacle that would inure them to hardship, and steel their hearts for the coming conflict. Stern was her look on these early days in April when, amid the disarray of construction trains and all the impedimenta of the incompleted road, the tenderly reared city volunteer had to pick his path over a region that would have appalled a Cyclops to face. And what relief was there to ride, for the conveyances were open platform cars and uncovered sleighs; while the thermometer registered 20° and 30° below zero? Yet there was but choice of these and the alternative of a bleak tramp on the shore-ice of Lake Superior, where, when the sun came out, the glare on face and eyes blinded and blistered hundreds of the marching column. What wonder that a few, becoming delirious on the march, dropped by the way from pain and utter weariness! But of murmuring there was little or none: the spirit of the men was heroic.

But let us get some idea of time and distance—of the length and difficulties of the route, and the short period in which it was traversed. To any reader of our work outside the Dominion, this information will be helpful. We have said that the decision of the Government was to transport the troops by the all-rail route, so far as completed, of the Canadian Pacific Railway. On the north shore of Lake Superior, parts of the road—72 miles in length—were at the period incomplete. Had navigation been open, advantage would have been taken of the Company's fleet of steamers on the Upper Lakes, and the troops forwarded by the Georgian Bay and Lake Superior to Port Arthur, thence to Manitoba and the Far West. But the lakes were still in the grip of the Frost-King, and the only alternative was to make the circuit from Toronto to the Ottawa, thence directly eastward, in the line of the trapper's route to the old regions of the fur-trade, the new territories acquired by the Dominion. We append a table of distances in the route 'to the front.'*

Of the 1842 miles from Toronto to Qu'Appelle, only 72 miles of track were unfinished, and had to be traversed on sleighs or on foot.† This break consisted of three gaps, the bridging over of which was the chief difficulty in the path of the troops. The first gap began at Dog Lake, north of Michipicoten River, and extended 42 miles west, to near Jack Fish Bay. Then came a completed stretch of 15 miles; then a gap of 15 miles; after which were 150 miles of track, and, finally, another gap 15 miles in length. Leaving Toronto at noon on Monday, the 30th of March, the expedition took supper, as we have seen,

	Miles.
*Toronto to Carleton Place Junction.,	234
Carleton Place Junction to Sudbury	265
Sudbury to Dog Lake (first gap in the rail)	261
Dog Lake to Nepigon (due south of Lake Nepigon)	255
Nepigon to Port Arthur (formerly Prince Arthur's Landing)	68
Port Arthur to Winnipeg (capital of Manitoba)	435
Winnipeg to Qu'Appelle Station	324
Total distance, Toronto to Qu'Appelle	1842
Qu'Appelle, via Prairie trail to Clarke's Crossing, on the N. Saskatchewan	208
	2050

† Since April of the present year, this portion of the track has been laid, and the line completed 500 miles west of Qu'Appelle to Calgary, and about 150 miles further, to Stephen, the station on the summit of the Rocky Mountains. The line on the Pacific side of the Rockies is also well under way, and the links in the chain from sea to sea all but meet.

at Carleton Place towards midnight of the same day. Within twenty-four hours, the transport train was speeding past Sudbury in a snow storm, some 250 miles north-west of Toronto, and 500 miles round by rail. On the 5th inst. (Easter Sunday !) the head of the brigade marched twenty miles over the frozen surface of Lake Superior, from Port Munro westward. By dawn of Monday, the 6th, the column passed through Port Arthur; and on the following morning arrived at Winnipeg. This portion of the Brigade, composed of the Queen's Own and " C " Company of the Toronto Infantry School, rested at Winnipeg on Tuesday, and proceeded the same evening to Qu'Appelle.

The balance of the brigade, consisting of the Grenadiers and Capt. Todd's company of Ottawa Foot Guards, reached Winnipeg at 1 A.M. on Wednesday, the 8th inst., and on the morrow joined their Toronto comrades at Qu'Appelle Station. The men were all in good health, though much weather-beaten and fatigued. Some portions of the march severely tested the strength and endurance of the column ; while the whole passage of " the gaps " was monotonous and trying. Old campaigners were loud in their praise of the men: one man who had been in the Soudan affirmed that the march across the sands of the desert was not more trying than had been the tramp over the ice and snow of Superior. Sleet pelted them, and driving snow blinded their steps ; while faces were blistered and eyes inflamed from the glare of the sun on the frozen surface of the lake. Not a few were badly frost-bitten, and all were footsore and weary. The casualties were nevertheless slight; only two men were unable to keep up with the column. One officer, Lieut. Morrow, was disabled by an accidental pistol shot, and a private of the Grenadiers fell and broke his arm. The latter pluckily insisted, however, on going forward with his comrades, though Lieut. Morrow, and one other invalid, Capt. Spencer, of the Grenadiers, were compelled to return. Here are some passages culled from newspaper correspondence, and from letters of the men *en route*:

"Crossing the gaps in the railway, we had a taste of what we might expect later on in our journey to the front; but the courage of the men never failed, and the tramp, tramp of the column, as it wended its way, amid the silent woods or trackless wastes of Lake Superior, was a weariness to muscle and brain. But the most severe trial occurred in the night march from Red Rock to Nepigon, a distance of only seven miles across the lake. Yet it took nearly five hours to accomplish the task. After leaving the cars, the battalion paraded in line, a couple of camp-fires serving to make the darkness visible. All the men were anxious to start, and when the word was given to march, it was greeted with cheers. It was impossible to maintain the formation of fours, therefore an order was given, "left turn, quick march!" We turned obedient to the order, but the march was anything but quick. Then into the solemn darkness of the pines and hemlock the column slowly moved. On each side the snow lay four feet deep. It was impossible to keep the track, and a mis-step buried the unfortunate volunteer up to his neck. It now began to rain, and for three mortal hours there was a continuous downpour.

"The lake was reached at last, to the extreme pleasure of all in the corps. The wildness of the afternoon, and the rain turned the snow into slush, and at every step the men sank half a foot. All attempts to preserve distance were soon abandoned by the men, who clasped hands to prevent each other from falling. The officers struggled on, arms linked, for the same purpose. Now and then men would drop in the ranks, the fact being discovered only by those in the rear stumbling over them. Some actually fell asleep as they marched.

"One brave fellow had plodded on without a murmur for three days. He had been ailing, but through fear of being left behind in the hospital, he refrained from making his illness known. He tramped half-way across last night's march reeling like a drunken man; but nature gave out at last, and with a groan he fell on the snow. There he lay, the pitiless rain beating on a boyish, upturned face, until a passing sleigh stopped behind him. The driver, flashing his lantern on the upturned face, said he was dead. 'Not yet, old man,' was the reply of the youth, as he opened his eyes. 'I'm not yet even a candidate for the hospital!' He was placed on a sleigh and carried the rest of the journey; and next morning, after a good sleep and warm breakfast, he was as lively as a cricket, and ready for the fray."

Such are a few of the incidents of this eventful and trying march. It is but just to say that the officials of the Railway Company did everything that was possible to mitigate the discomforts of the passage. The supply officers on the line of march also did their duty in providing the men with the creature comforts. The strain on the resources of the railway, involved in the movement of the eastern volunteers to the front, was great, but great as it was the staff was equal to the demands upon the road. In the first twenty days of April, the Railway Company conveyed over its nearly two thousand miles of track 3,000 officers and men, 150 horses, and four guns, in addition to the Winnipeg regiments and other local organisations moved to various points in the west.

CHAPTER XVIII.

MIDDLETON'S MARCH TO CLARKE'S CROSSING.

TO mass two or three thousand troops, on war's horrid mission, in the peaceful valley of the Qu'Appelle seemed little short of an outrage. Had the season been summer, when the prairie flowers were in bloom, it would have been desecration. To have cut up that rich carpet of red lilies, white anemones, and purple pentstemons, with the great wheels of the cannon, and trampled its beauty under the heedless heel of armed men, would have been a great wrong to Nature, and wakened keener sorrow than that which stirred the heart of the Scottish poet when his ploughshare upturned the Mountain Daisy and crushed it " beneath the furrow's weight." But Nature's protecting covering was still over the region, and the rich soil had not yet thrown up its scented life to be mangled under foot. No matter were winter's robe soiled by the tramplings of the troops, and its beauty marred by the movement of three or four hundred transport carts, for the storm-king was abroad as the troops mustered at Qu'Appelle, and the day's soilings would be heavily coated by the night's white shroud.

> " The night sets in on a world of snow,
>   While the air grows sharp and chill,
> And the warning roar of a fearful blow
>   Is heard on the distant hill ;
> And the norther, see ! on the mountain peak
> In his breath how the old trees writhe and shriek !
> He shouts on the plain, ho-ho ! ho-ho !
> He drives from his nostrils the blinding snow,
>   And growls with a savage will."

But the valley of the Qu'Appelle had seen strife ere now Long ago its plains had often witnessed the shock of intertribal encounter. Between the Crees and the Blackfeet there had been years of feud, though the presence of the Mounted Police and the influence of a better day had now taught them peace. Savagery was in truth giving place to civilisation. The beautiful district was fast becoming the favoured resort of the settler, from the issue of the river at " The Elbow," on the South Saskatchewan, to its junction with the Assiniboine, at Fort Ellice. The region, geographically, belongs to the Second Prairie Steppe, succeeding that of the Lake Winnipeg basin, which forms the First. It extends from the Souris River on the south, and circling round the Pheasant, File, and Touchwood Hills, bears away northward to the Birch Hills, this side of Prince Albert. On the east it is bounded by the western limits of the Province of Manitoba, in long. 101° 30', and extends to the Lignite Tertiary Plateau, in about long. 107° W. North-westward of this great tract lay the scene of the insurrection. In that quarter, also, stretched the line of loyal settlement along the North Saskatchewan that was in jeopardy from the outbreak. Hither had General Middleton and his staff* come, with the Winnipeg volunteers, to organise the

---

* The following officers composed the General's Field staff : Lord Melgund ; Hon. Maurice Gifford, brother of Lord Gifford, of Ashantee fame ; Hon. C. Freer, grandson of Lord Saye and Sale ; Capt. Wise, and Lieut. Doucet, A.D.C. Capt. Buchan, of the 90th Winnipeg Rifles, and formerly of the " Queen's Own," Toronto, acted as Field Adjutant.

North-West Field Force and determine the plan of the campaign. The date of the encounter with the rebels at Duck Lake, it will be remembered, was the 26th of March. On the 23rd, anticipating trouble in the North-West, the Major-General in command of the Militia, left Ottawa for Winnipeg. On the 26th he reached the Prairie Capital, and the following day left, with the Manitoba troops, for Qu'Appelle. Here was the military rendezvous and the base of operations.

The morning of the 30th of March saw the first, though a precautionary, movement of the Field Force. On that day the General sent forward from the Fort three companies of the Winnipeg Rifles and the Armstrong gun, to protect the northern approaches to the rallying-place, to gather news of the rebels and of the threatened rising of the Indians in the neighbourhood, and to extend succour to such of the northern settlers as were fleeing from their homes to a place of safety. With the rebels, it was thought, there would be a speedy reckoning, though the character of the country was favourable to guerilla warfare, and the half-breeds knew every nook and covert of the region. The chief alarm was as to the attitude of the Indians. All eyes were turned upon their reserves, and the restless movements of the young braves of the several tribes gave occasion for much uneasiness. Where the Indians were likely to be approached by the disloyal half-breeds, it was feared they would go on the war-path. In the isolated districts in the north, where hunger was not satisfied, it was considered certain they would make descent upon settlements and raid Hudson Bay posts for food and provender. Battleford and Prince Albert were known to be in especial danger. Hence the campaign had in view, not only to suppress the half-breed insurrection, but to relieve the settlements on the North Saskatchewan from apprehended attack. The more speedy the attainment of this dual object, the less danger there would be of a general Indian uprising.

With wise and prompt decision, General Middleton's design was to make an instant movement on the heart of the insurrection. Not an hour had been lost in reaching the base of operations; and with cool impatience the General awaited the arrival of the troops from the East. Nor had the latter tarried on the way; in ten days, thanks to the railway facilities, two thousand miles had been covered, *plus* the weariful march over "the gaps" on the road. This, it will be remembered, was a greater distance than that traversed in 1870 by General Wolseley's expedition, which consumed the whole summer of that year in its transportation from Toronto to the Red River. But toilsome as had been the journey of the troops to Qu'Appelle, a forlorn two hundred mile march lay before them ere they could look upon the foe.

The period of the year, as it happened, was the worst the Fates could have chosen for moving a body of men over the Prairie trail to the front. Earlier, or later, in the season travel over the region would have been shorn of its discomfort and difficulty. From the arsenals of the north, the hoar monarch was discharging the last of his wintry weapons. Snow still lay heavy on the plains, and the warm spring sun melted down earth's white covering to be frozen over night and again thawed the next day. The line of march was either spongy with sodden earth or covered with water a foot deep. Such was the condition of the country the Field Force had to traverse, in this "land of magnificent distances."

Pending the arrival of the Eastern troops there was much to be done. The organisation and equipment of an army in the field was no light task, with every contingency to be provided for, and provision made for a distant march from the base of supplies. Each arm of the service had to be instructed in its duties, if not actually called into existence. There was, first, the Intelligence Department, which had to be organised *ab initio*. Fortunately, as the corps of Scouts and Rangers were raised in the territories, they wanted little drill in their duties. Then came the Commissariat and Transport service, which needed the expenditure of no little energy and foresight to make efficient. Following these, came the Hospital and Ambulance brigade, provision for whose important duties much care and forethought were demanded. Finally, there was the fighting arm of the force, which, to be effective, called for the careful inspection of the Major-General in command, and his constant oversight in drill and discipline. In addition to all this work, disposition had to be made of the various brigades to take the field, and corps stationed to keep open the lines of communication and supply. That everything went well during this period of hasty labour, and its attendant excitement, is its own tribute to the thorough work of the Commanding Officer and his staff, as well as to the energy and spirit of all ranks.

The immediate task was to get the troops, ammunition and forage, over two hundred miles to a rallying point on the South Saskatchewan. The route of the main column was the line of telegraphic communication from Qu'Appelle, *via* the Touchwood hills and Humboldt, to Clarke's Crossing. At the Crossing a junction was to be effected with another column, to be forwarded by boat on the South Saskatchewan, from the neighbourhood of Swift Current, thirty-two miles westward by rail. At the present time of writing we are without reasons for this division of the Field Force, and can only infer the following as necessitating the movement. First, the difficulty of transport over a single trail for so large a number of troops. Secondly, the obvious advantage of approaching the enemy from two different points. And, thirdly, the urgency of early relief reaching the settlements on the North Saskatchewan, and the fear that this might not be practicable if the half-breeds and Indians successfully withstood the advance of the main column. But whatever were the General's reasons, we may be sure he fully weighed them.

By the 5th of April "A" and "B" Batteries reached Winnipeg, and proceeded at once to Qu'Appelle. Within three days the Ottawa and Toronto volunteers were expected forward. The General now prepared for an advance. The transport service had been organised under Capt. S. L. Bedson, late Warden of the Manitoba Penitentiary, with the assistance of Messrs J. H. E. Secretan and Thos. Lusted. Some six hundred teams were pressed into service, and supplies drawn from the resources of the Hudson Bay Company and other contractors in Winnipeg. Already some two hundred teams had been despatched with rations and forage for the use of the column until it reached Humboldt, nearly two-thirds of the way to the river-crossing. The remainder of the teams were grouped into two grand divisions. These were again broken into subdivisions of ten teams each, over which were placed responsible headmen. Each head teamster was supplied with cooking kit for so many men, and given directions for camping and messing. Nightly camping sites, some twenty miles apart, were determined on; and, so far as the roads would permit, these were to be adhered to. Regulations were also issued to guide the order of march, and instructions given in the formation of corrals at the various encampments.

At last came "route orders," which were received by all ranks with glee, a glee that neither the condition of the roads nor the storm that was blowing could check. After a hasty breakfast, on the morning of Monday, the 6th, the troops paraded at 5.45 A.M., and were inspected by the General, who addressed them in a few stirring words of admonition and encouragement. An hour later, the column filed away to the northward, and the blinding snow soon hid Fort Qu'Appelle from view. The scouts led the way on each side of the trail; then came half a company of the 90th, as advance guard, with one field piece; then the main body of the North-West Field Force; after which came the baggage with the other field piece, its accompanying guard bringing up the rear. The trail was found to be in a frightful condition; and the march was impeded, not only by pools of water and heavy roads, but by a stiff gale from the north, blindingly freighted with sleet and hail.

The route lay due north, a little east of long. 104° W., and across the 51st meridian. On the right rose the File Hills, and to the north of these the Beaver Hills. Opposite the latter, lay the Little and Big Touchwood Hills, the line of march trending off westward between these two elevated plateaux, where it enters a great saline depression, full of white mud swamps and brackish marsh. This Salt Plain extends from the Touchwood Hills to near Humboldt, some sixty miles from the Saskatchewan. To the west of the plain are the Quill Lakes, and to the east is the head of Long or Last Mountain Lake, the haunt of innumerable pelican, water-hen, grebe, snipe, and plover. Long Lake lies due north of Regina, the capital of the North-West Territories, and is the favourite resort of the Indian for fish as well as of the white sportsman. The lake is forty miles in length, and about one and a half in breadth. The projected Prince Albert railway, a northern branch of the Canadian Pacific, will skirt its western shores, and connect the settlements on the North Saskatchewan with the capital of the

Territories. Of the country lying between Fort Ellice (at the confluence of the Qu'Appelle and the Assiniboine) and "The Elbow" of the South Saskatchewan, we get a pleasing description from the facile pen of Principal Grant, of Queen's University.* It is thus described by Doctor Grant:

"Between the mouth of the Qu'Appelle and any point on the Saskatchewan every day's ride reveals new scenes of a country, bleak enough in winter, but in summer fair and promising as the heart of man can desire; rolling and level prairie; gently swelling uplands; wooded knolls; broken hills, with gleaming lakes interspersed. One trail leads to the Elbow of the South Saskatchewan, and thence to Battleford; another to Fort Carlton; another to Fort Pelly. The most beautiful section of this region is the Touchwood Hills—a succession of elevated prairie uplands extensive enough to constitute a province. At a distance they appear as a line of hills stretching away in a north-westerly direction, but the rise from the level prairie is so gentle and undulating that the traveller never finds out where the hills actually commence. There are no sharply defined summits from which other hills and the distant plain on either side can be seen. Grassy or wooded knolls enclose fields that look as if they had been cultivated to produce hay crops; or sparkling lakelets, the homes of snipe, plover, and duck. Long reaches of fertile lowlands alternate with hillsides as fertile. Avenues of whispering trees promise lodge or gate, but lead only to *Chateaux en Espagne.* Beyond the Touchwood Hills we come to the watershed of the South Saskatchewan; another region that may easily be converted into a garden; now boldly irregular and again a stretch of level prairie; at intervals swelling into softly-rounded knolls, or opening out into fair expanses; well-wooded, and abounding in pools and lakelets, most of them alkaline."

But we return to the North-West Field Force, which we saw setting out to cross the country we have been describing, under a terrific snow storm. Hayward Creek, some twelve miles from Fort Qu'Appelle, was as far as the wearied column had been

---

*See *Picturesque Canada,* article on " Winnipeg to the Rocky Mountains."

able to gain on the first day's march. The country was covered with water, the meltings of the winter's snow which before the thaw set in had been three feet deep on the level. What the force suffered on this first day's tramp may in part be gathered from the following jottings of a journalist who had been permitted to accompany the column :

"All day Monday it blew a hurricane from the North, and the men had to get out of the waggons and foot it to keep from freezing. They suffered terribly from snow and cold. At noon it was 60° above zero, but the cold then set in, and before 4 P.M. it was 10° below zero. The wind in the afternoon blew 40 miles an hour, and when it abated at sundown the glass fell to 20° below zero. The men spent a miserable night, but stood it pretty well. The waggons were formed into a corral, and the troops slept in their blankets, the tents being generally discarded, as the wind blew them down or ripped them. The trail is exceedingly heavy. We have been going through an undulating country with scrub up to the present, but our next camp will be in the Touchwood Hills. The weather to-day is bright but extremely cold, and the men will have another bad night of it. At parade to-day many of the men were limping with cold and rheumatism, from the wet march yesterday and the exposure over night. But there was no grumbling, and cold is better than rain."*

As the column passed through the File Hill country, the Indians were found to be pacific, and were doubtless whole-

---

*In these narratives from the front we shall find ourselves under repeated obligations to the representatives of the Toronto *Globe* and *Mail*, as well as to the correspondence appearing in the Toronto *World*, *Telegram*, and *News*. We shall also be indebted to writers in the Toronto *Week*, *Truth*, and *Monetary Times*, to correspondents in the field of the *Illustrated War News*, and to representatives of the Montreal *Star*, *Witness*, *Gazette*, and *Herald*, and the Winnipeg *Times*. But our indebtedness will chiefly be to Mr. Ham, the able and intelligent correspondent of the Toronto *Mail*, whose initials, "G. H. H." will be very familiar to readers of that enterprising journal. The author will also owe his acknowledgments to Mr. W. P. McKenzie, to "W. W. F.," and particularly to "J. B. A.," of St. Boniface, whose impartial and instructive letters on the situation in the North-West also appeared in the *Mail*. To all, the author proffers his grateful thanks.

R

somely impressed by the martial appearance of the Field Force. At the outbreak of the insurrection fears were entertained of a rising among the Crees in the neighbourhood, there having been threatening movements on the reserves at Crooked Lake, on the Qu'Appelle river; and Chief Pie-a-pot had been restless on the Indian Head hills. Fortunately the Indian agent of Treaty No. 4 (Lt.-Col. Allan Macdonald) was able to "soothe the savage breast," and, by timely doles of tea and tobacco, to lull to quietness Pasquah, Loud Voice, O'Soup, Little Child, Star Blanket, Little Black Bear, and other local chieftains of the dusky clans.

But if tea and tobacco—the proverbial weaknesses of the Indian tribes—had lost their soothing charm for the native denizens of the Qu'Appelle district, and if Middleton's column had failed to awe them with the passing pageant, there now came the stirring spectacle of "the guns." Three hours after the column had marched out of Qu'Appelle, a train steamed alongside the station, south of the river, with "A" and "B" Batteries, under Col. Montizambert, and a battalion that had been recruited to accompany the two field-pieces that were to follow the General. By the latter's instructions the artillery brigade was here divided. "A" Battery, from Quebec, had orders to follow the main column, and "B" Battery was directed to await Col. Otter's arrival and be attached to his command. The brigade consisted of the two batteries, with a foot battalion to protect them, in all 230 officers and men, thirty-five horses, and four field guns. The men were armed with short Enfields. Closely in the wake of the battteries, there arrived at Qu'Appelle the Toronto Expeditionary Force, consisting of the "Queen's Own," the "Grenadiers," "C" Company Infantry School, with Capt. Todd's sharpshooters of the Ottawa Foot Guards. With the arrival of this additional force, the Second

Field Column, under Colonel Otter, was now made up and despatched to Swift Current. The additions to the main Field Force were the first to move off the ground. These consisted (1) of 60 Mounted Infantry, a body of Scouts under Major Boulton, a loyal officer who figured in the Red River Rebellion of 1869-70, and at one time under sentence of death by Riel; (2) "A" Battery,* 115 men and two guns; (3) Colonel Grasett's battalion of the 10th Royal Grenadiers, 15 officers and 248 men; and (4) half of "C" Company (35 men) Toronto School of Infantry, under Major Smith and Lieut. Scott. Accompanying the latter, and in temporary command, was Major-General Laurie, of Nova Scotia. Lt.-Col. Forrest, who had been acting as Supply Officer to the Battery, was appointed Paymaster to the force in the field, with his headquarters at Qu'Appelle. A mail service was now organised by Mr Nursey, and a telegraph field staff, by Mr Geo. Wood. Two hospital field corps were also organised, one to accompany General Middleton, and the other to be attached to Colonel Otter's column.† There was also to go forward, and

---

*The following are the officers of "A" Battery, Quebec, ordered to overtake General Middleton, with four companies and two guns. Lt.-Col. C. E. Montizambert in chief command. Major C. J. Short and Capt. C. W. Drury in charge of the Battery; Capt. Jas. Peters in command of the battalion. Company officers : No. 1, Lt. J. A. G. Hudon; No. 2, Lt. V. B. Rivers, with Lt. O. C. Pelletier, of the 9th Batt. attached; No. 3, Capt. A. A. Farley, with Lt. Prower attached; No. 4, Lt. Imlah, with Lt. Cimon attached. Lt. W. H. Disbrowe, of the Winnipeg Cavalry, accompanied the battery as a supernumerary. The acting Surgeon was Dr. J. A. Grant, of the 1st Batt. Gov.-General's Foot Guards.

†The following is the Field Staff of Hospital Corps, No. 1 : Surgeon-General D. Bergin, M.D., M.P., Cornwall ; Deputy Surgeon-General T. G. Roddick, M.D., Montreal ; Surgeon-Major C. M. Douglas, V.C., Montreal ; Surgeons, Dr. Jas. Bell, Montreal, and Dr. E. A Gravely, Cornwall ; Assist. Surgeons, Dr. Pelletier, Montreal, Dr. Allyne, Quebec, Dr. Powell, Ottawa ; in charge of hospital and medical stores, Dr. Roddick, of Montreal ; Purveyor, with headquarters at Winnipeg, Dr. Sullivan, of Kingston. The following compose Field Hospital Corps, No. 2 : Surgeon-Major, Dr. H. R. Casgrain, Windsor ; Surgeons, J. F. Williams, Barrie, A. Schmidt, Montreal, M. McKay, River St. John, N.S., F. J. White, Newfoundland, W. McQuaig, Vankleek Hill, and R. Turnbull, Russell.

take a prominent part in the operations at the front, two Gatling guns, from Colt's Firearm Manufactory, Hartford, Conn. One of these was assigned to Colonel Otter's Field force, and the other was attached to General Middleton's column, with Lieut. Howard, of the Connecticut National Guards, New Haven, in command of the gun platoon.

This exhausts the catalogue of the provision so far made to take the field. Alas! that it was a provision necessitated by civil war. This fact humbles the nation's pride in the success of its efforts to place a competent force in the field. It will be seen that the arrangements were not left to chance; all manifestly had been well planned. For this the country's thanks are unquestionably due to the Minister of the Militia, to the officials of his Department, and, above all, to the Major-General in command. The latter, as we shall see later on, is a strong figure in the picture. General Middleton is an old campaigner, and has reached that age when maturity usually brings discretion, good judgment, ready resource, and strong common sense. The harness of his duties sits easily upon him; and he works well himself and all works well with him. What was specially to commend him to the nation, was his care of the lads under him, his sympathy with them in their heroism as well as in their fatigues, and his admirable conservatism (we use the term in its highest non-political sense) in handling his men. He remembered that he was sent to suppress an armed insurrection, not aggressively to take the field, or to repel invasion. He also remembered that he was leading, not paid regulars to battle, but civilians for the time being enrolled as militia volunteers. Nor is there anything about him of the martinet, and less of that official *rigeur* of manner that so often offensively marks the relations of the "regular" officer with the rank and file of the volunteers. With this brief introduction to the leader of the North-West army in the field, let us rejoin the column: we shall see more of this able officer by-and-by.

Thirty miles north of Qu'Appelle, the column halted for a day or two to recruit strength, and to allow the battery to overtake the main body. The men needed the rest. They were well nigh exhausted from cold, discomfort, and fatigue. They had marched nearly all the way, for the terrible condition of the trail, and the intense cold and fierce head wind, made it almost impossible to make use of the waggons. The stress of the march told severely on not a few of the men. They suffered chiefly from swollen feet, and from rheumatic pains in body and limbs, occasioned by sleeping, or trying to sleep, on wet ground, which by morning was frozen hard. As they proceeded northward their plight grew worse; for each day the sun's rays gained in strength, and the increasing warmth softened the trail and made the marching heavier.

The tramp over the Great Salt Plain added to the prevailing discomfort; but the endurance of the men was beyond praise, and Humboldt at last was reached. The date was April the 12th. Here the column was once more considerately permitted to rest. The few days' halt enabled the Grenadiers and Boulton's Scouts to overtake, and be merged in, the main body. The parade-state now showed a strength of about 950 men, made up as follows: artillerymen 183; infantry 617; cavalry and mounted scouts, close upon 150.* With the now combined

---

*The combined column, up to this date, was, in addition to the armed teamsters, composed of the following : General's staff, 5 ; Capt. French's Scouts, 36; Major Boulton's Scouts, 60 ; Major Jarvis's Winnipeg Battery, 68 ; Capt. Knight's Cavalry, 38 ; Col. McKeand's 90th Battalion, 325 ; Col. Grasett's 10th Grenadiers, 265 ; Col. Montizambert's "A" Battery, 115 ; and Major Smith's "C" Co. School of Infantry, 35,—a total of 950 officers and men. In addition there was a small hospital corps, which had been organised in the prairie capital, under the command of Drs. Whiteford and Codd, of Winnipeg.

force a dash was to be made for the river crossing. On reaching the Saskatchewan the General hoped to have more definite news of the rebel movements, and thus see his way clear to give effect to his own plans. So far as he could rely upon his Intelligence Department, it was ascertained that Riel was fortifying himself at Batoche, and had with him about 250 Métis and a like number of Teton Sioux. Batoche is a half-breed village in the centre of the St. Laurent district, on the South Saskatchewan. It is situate about sixty miles from Humboldt and forty from Prince Albert. The village is surrounded by heavy woods, which would be favourable to the insurgents; and it was known that they were actively entrenching themselves.

The troops being now rested, the order came to move on to the telegraph crossing at Clarke's. On this march both wind and weather were more favourable. The trail, in some respects, also improved. The alkaline swamps were passed, and any ponds to be met with were of sweet water. The blustering cold winds also moderated, and the prairie became more free of snow. It was now possible to get a dry place for the night's encampment and wood for a cheery camp fire. The region, otherwise, was still bleak and desolate, for the rebels had effectively scoured the country, and swept it clean of cattle and emptied the barns of fodder and grain. But in a little over two days the fifty-five miles were covered, and the General and the head of the column reached the objective point on the Saskatchewan. Here, for a while, we shall leave the main Field Force, and accompany the Second Division in its march to the north.

CHAPTER XIX.

OTTER'S FLYING COLUMN—THE DASH TO
BATTLEFORD.

THE measures devised to meet the interruption of the general tranquillity of the North-West could hardly be said to be lacking in any particular. But the completeness of the military arrangements was not their sole merit. Both the Militia Department and the Commander of the Forces showed a genius for anticipating wants and for taking a comprehensive survey of the situation. Everything that human foresight could well devise seems to have been thought of and put in the way of immediate execution. Not only was the main column, which was to march upon the rebels, placed efficiently in the field, but, on their arrival, other brigades were despatched to relieve settlements in jeopardy in other parts of the country. Disposition was also made of the troops at central points, to prevent the possibility of a general Indian uprising.

The region of actual armed insurrection was as yet comparatively a small one; how large it might become no one knew and few dared to think. Grave fears had for some time been entertained for the safety of many an isolated post, while hope was almost abandoned in the case of not a few beleaguered settlements. From along the North Saskatchewan news had come of the restlessness of the Indians; and already it was known that there had been a massacre of white settlers at Frog Lake, to the north-west of Fort Pitt. From the latter post the small garrison of Mounted Police had escaped down the river in a leaky scow, while the settlers and their families were flying for succour to any place of safety. The frozen blasts from the north were freighted with the cry of women and children in distress, while every scout brought news of some cold-blooded murder, of raiding of farms, burning of homesteads, and general devastation. It was a time of license for barbarism. In the region no white man was now sure of his life. However friendly had been his relations with the Indian, and no matter what kindness he had shewn him, there were Indians bad enough to forget the claims of gratitude, and cowardly enough to shoot a man in the back. In this dread time even the agents of civilisation fell unoffending victims at their post. Payne, a Government Farm instructor, on a reserve of the Stoneys near Battleford, was brutally murdered, and his mutilated body strewed the barnyard of the farm.

In such a time of anxiety and trouble did the Second Field Force concentrate at Swift Current, whither it had come from the general rallying-point at Qu'Appelle. It was General Middleton's design that this column under Colonel Otter should disembark at Swift Current station, march to the South Saskatchewan, and there take the river route to Clarke's Crossing, thence by prairie trail to Battleford. This plan however was interfered with, in consequence of the water being low in the river. To go by boat, it was feared, would be risky and tedious, while relief would be delayed in reaching Battleford. It was therefore determined to make a dash across the prairie and carry instant relief to the beleaguered town. The situation of the once capital of the North-West Territories was at this time a very critical one. We shall best get an idea of this by quoting from a Battleford journal, whose editor thus comments on the condition of things in the embryo city just before the arrival of the Flying Column. We quote from Mr. P. G. Laurie, of the *Saskatchewan Herald*:

"Most outsiders," writes Mr Laurie, "do not properly appreciate the dangers of the situation in which for so long a time we were placed. In the Fort were well nigh six hundred souls. Of these only about two hundred were capable of action in case of attack. The palisade environing the fort is about ninety by one hundred yards in length. But one gun, the Mounted Police seven-pounder, was in the fort, and this could only be relied on to protect two sides of the bastion. Fifty men for each side was certainly a weak garrison; and if stormed simultaneously from all quarters, by determined men in sufficient numbers, it is questionable if the attack could have been successfully resisted. It was impossible to tell at what hour such an attack would be made, and equally impossible to estimate correctly the force that might be collected from the disloyal reserves all along the Saskatchewan Valley. It might be two hundred; it could well be many times that number. Suppose, too, the enemy had been sufficiently strong to prevent our access to the river, not a drop of water could be got in the fort, and without access to the river our capitulation would have been a matter of a few days at the furthest. It was indeed a trying situation!"

The situation was fully apprehended by Colonel Otter and his staff. The position was critical, and there was urgent need of an expeditious movement. Colonel Otter was the very man to respond to the need, and the troops that composed his column were but too eager to distinguish themselves. The opportunity of making a memorable march, we need hardly say, was readily embraced, and the force prepared at once to set out. The signal success achieved by the column, in covering a distance of one hundred and eighty miles in five and a half days, is almost without a parallel in military annals. But where the martial enthusiasm and stirring impulse of a Queen's Own movement are manifested, as they were manifested on this march, we were sure of witnessing some feat of distinction. This was certain to be the case with a corps that had been trained under the inspiriting influences of commanding officers such as Colonels Gillmor and Otter.

Nor were the other component parts of the Division less eager to distinguish themselves. Capt. Todd's Ottawa Foot Guards, a splendid body of men, were anxious to acquit themselves with honour; and "B" Battery, the School of Infantry, and the Mounted Police, were all anxious to do their duty. The force reached Swift Current from Qu'Appelle on Saturday, the 11th of April, and encamped over the Sunday on the line of the railway. The place derives its name from a stream, Swift Current Creek, which rises in the Cypress Hills, to the southwest, and flows into the South Saskatchewan. On Sunday there was a Church parade for service on the plain, which was conducted by Pte. Acheson of "G" Co. Q.O.R., and who, as a student of Wycliffe College, Toronto, naturally chose the Anglican form of worship. A correspondent of the Toronto *Globe* supplies us with the following account of the impressive service:

"That portion of the service specially prepared for military campaigns was read, and its beautiful and touching language seemed to bring home to the men with double force the reality that they were on active service, and that the dangers of their position were not insignificant. The eye of the King of Kings and Lord of Lords was upon them, and to Him they had turned to supplicate blessings, protection and guidance in the conflict to which they were hastening. The grand old hymn, ' Nearer my God to Thee,' was sung with spirit, and its touching melody seemed doubly impressive as it was caught up by the winds and its solemn cadence carried out over that boundless prairie. The sun was shining brightly, and the day would have been hot had it not been for a tempering wind that blew in from the south-west."

And well might the force reverently supplicate protection from Him who is a "strong tower of defence," for already the "flapping of the wings of the Angel of Death" might be heard over the plain, and to their comrades of the First Division only a few more shadows brought the sharp summons of the last enemy. Before three Sundays had passed, the dread summons was also to come to eight of those now in the encampment, who were to meet death on the battle-field, while twelve others of the force were to be counted among the casualties of the engagement.

Nearly the whole of the following week was consumed in the march from the railway to the South Saskatchewan, and in ferrying the troops across the river, with some two hundred teams, heavily loaded with stores, forage and ammunition. On arriving at the river it was found that the transport service could not be relied on for an expeditious moving of the force northward by boat. The water was low, and as yet only *The Northcote*, of the Hudson Bay Company's service, had been able to get down the river from Medicine Hat. It was therefore determined to take the prairie trail to Battleford, and to send the supplies for General Middleton's division by boat. In this latter undertaking Messrs G. H. R. Wainwright, and H. Galt, of the North-West Navigation Co., were to render important service; while the Midland Battalion, under Col. A. T. Williams, was to accompany the steamer as an escort. This expedition on the Saskatchewan had a trying ordeal to go through, from the difficulties of navigation and the assaults of disloyal half-breed scouts on the banks. The boat, though banked with bales of hay and flour sacks, was in repeated danger from the covert firing of the breeds in the woods; while its living freight was in constant peril from the attacks in the run down the river. The transport brigade for Battleford was organised and superintended by Messrs E. N. Armit, and George Murphy, of Winnipeg, who by the morning of the 18th inst., had the waggon train ready for the march to the north. On the route the transport was in charge of Mr. M. W. White, member for Regina of the North-West Council, and formerly of Hamilton, Ont.

At two o'clock on Saturday, the 18th of April, the bugles of the Queen's Own struck up an enlivening march, and the Second Division of the North-West Field Force filed away over the prairie.* The route of march lay almost due north on the line 108° W. of Greenwich, and across the 51st and 52nd north meridians. The country through which the column passed was an untenanted plain, and the incidents of the march were thus few and uninteresting. One day was like another, as happens often at sea, save that each day the pace quickened, and the night's rest was more and more keenly sought to recruit the exhausted strength of the rapid flight over the prairie. Happy the volunteer who had not to go on picket or guard duty when the curtain of night fell on the plain; and happier he who could get "a lift" on the waggons when the day

---

*This Division, under the command of Lt.-Col. Otter, consisted of 50 Mounted Police, under Col. Herchmer, who also acted as chief of the Field Staff; 50 Ottawa Foot Guards, under Capt. Todd; 30 of "C" Co. School of Infantry, under Lts. Wadmore and Sears; 268 officers and men of the 2nd Batt. Queen's Own Rifles, under Lt.-Col. Miller; and 112 officers and men of "B" Battery, under Major Short. The Red Cross Ambulance corps, patriotically organised by Mr. E. W. Wragge, of Toronto, and in charge of Dr. Nattress, of the Queen's Own, accompanied the brigade. A Gatling gun also formed part of the equipment of the column.

dawned and the column was once more on its way. Of the march we gather the following incidents from the *Globe's* correspondence—dated "In Camp on the Prairie, April 22d:"

"We have been marching about thirty miles a day since we left the Saskatchewan, and expect to reach Battleford on Friday, the day after to-morrow. We left our Camp at the Saskatchewan on Saturday and marched all Sunday. There is a waggon for every ten men; but when all our baggage and tents are put on only two or three can ride at a time: as some of the boys are used up and not able to walk at all, most of us have to tramp all the while. We reckon to have come 140 miles, and I have not been in the waggons more than twenty miles altogether, so have walked fully twenty miles a day, and been on outpost and guard duty all night for two nights. This is my second night. I go on guard as soon as we get into camp, two hours on and four hours off, so have four hours walking during the night. The guard is not as hard as picket duty, for we can stay in the tent four hours out of every six, while the pickets are out all night about a quarter of a mile from camp.

"I will give you my work for twenty-four hours, so you will have some idea of what we have to do. On Monday night I was told off for duty after marching all day. We had to go out on picket without any supper as it was late when we halted, so taking a few 'hard tack' in my pocket I went on with the others. We formed a line of men round the camp with four main posts, twenty-one on each post. Fourteen stayed at the post, and seven went out scouting for two hours. I went on at eight o'clock, stayed till ten, went back to the post till two A..M, then on again till four, so had four hours walking during the night. The night was cold, and it was impossible to sleep on the post, as we had no tent, and of course could not light any fires. We went back to camp at 5 A.M., and a worse broken up lot of fellows it would be hard to find. The tents were all struck when we got back ready to start; and all the breakfast we got was some tea, almost cold, and hard tack. Fully half of the picket were so used up they could not walk. Some of them had to be helped on the waggons. I was able to walk, so had to do it, all the waggons being more than full. We marched sixteen miles and halted two hours for dinner, and I had a good sleep during that time. I got a chance to ride for an hour, and then walked again till we halted for the night, doing twelve miles in the afternoon. After supper and getting baggage off and tents up, I turned in at nine o'clock and never moved till four this morning."

By Tuesday night the wearied column had reached the neighbourhood of Eagle Creek, about midway between the South and North Saskatchewan. Over the creek a bridge was extemporised, and the force, crossing the stream, proceeded on its way. Thursday morning brought the column to within sight of the Indian Reserve of Mosquito's band, where Payne, the white Farm Instructor, met his foul death at the hands of those whom he was instructing in the peaceful art of the farmer! The afternoon march took the column through the deserted reserve and past the desolate home of the unfortunate Farm Instructor. The mutilated body of the poor Indian Agent was found in an outhouse with his head smashed in, and the lifeless body of another white man, a Belgian rancher, was discovered near by. Nightfall saw the Division approach the low range of mountains, known as the Wolf and the Sliding Hills, which hem in Battleford on the south. As these hills are more or less covered with timber, in which the Indian marauders of the region could find cover from which to fire on the troops, a halt was called for the night on the borders of the prairie. The men slept under arms, while the sky was illumined by the Indian vandals setting fire to the houses in Battleford, a piece of parting pleasantry on the approach of the troops.

The excitement which this grim devastation created in the ranks of the relieving column was intense. The men, tired out as they were, clamoured to make a dash through the three miles of poplar and underbrush that intervened between the camp and the high banks of the Battle River, and, descending to the plain, to rush upon the Indian miscreants. But gallant as was the intent, Colonel Otter saw that the risk was too great to permit him to give the men their way. There was not only the risk of conflict with the Indians on the plain; there was danger in being ambushed in a locality unknown to himself and the troops. Had he yielded, and the charge been made, it might have been said of it, as General Bosquet is reported to have said of the headlong rush of the English Light Brigade at Balaklava, "It was magnificent, but it was not war!"* And Colonel Otter was right; the lives of his men were more to him than the safety of a few houses and stores, or even a decamped Judge's residence. Of the arrival at, and entry into, Battleford on the sixth day of the unparalleled march across the plains, we have the following record from a volunteer correspondent:

"On Thursday evening we arrived within three miles of Battleford, where we camped for the night. The Indians were between us and the town, and all ranks were anxious to get on; but the Colonel decided to wait till daylight before making an attack. That night the Indians burned the Hudson Bay store and the Government House, and sacked the town. The Mounted Police were out scouting, and a young fellow who was with them was killed. I was on outpost duty that night and could plainly see the blaze from the burning houses. About one o'clock in the morning the Indians tried to surprise our camp, but retired when they found us on the watch. We gave them a few bullets, but could not tell whether we killed any of them or not. Next morning we marched into Old Battleford; but not an Indian was to be seen. The stores we found plundered, and many of them burnt. All the people are in the Fort on the other side of the Battle River and between the latter and the Saskatchewan. The Indians have stolen or destroyed, I should say, over $50,000 worth of goods, and got off clear, and we only a few miles away. We were all wild to

---

*C'est magnifique, mais ce n'est pas guerre !

get after them, but had to go into camp. On Friday night some twenty police joined us here from Fort Pitt, with the news that it had been taken by the Indians. The police escaped by the help of a friendly Indian; but two of them were killed during the retreat. The Stoney Indians who sacked this place have joined Poundmaker, and are at his reserve, some thirty-five miles from here. To make a descent upon them, we expect, will be our next move."

The march of Colonel Otter's column to the relief of Battleford may not inaptly compare with incidents in the military annals of the Old World. It would be foolish to liken it to the relief of Poona or Cawnpore, for it lacks the tragic incidents which marked the relief by the British troops of these Indian cities. But it was lacking only in this particular. The rapidity of the forced march, the toil undergone by our volunteers *en route*, and the eager anxiety of all ranks to reach Battleford before savage lust of blood would be slaked in the massacre of the white refugees in the Fort, were features in common with the famed relieving expeditions of the barbaric East. "The looting of the town," writes a journalist after the arrival of Otter's column, "was about as complete as the Indian could make it. Nothing escaped his rapacity. The devil in his nature had full vent. The contents of the houses were smashed and strewed about with a fury as fiendish as it was vain. Household gods—treasures infinitely more of the heart than of the pocket,—were tumbled about in indescribable confusion; and cosy comfort, which years had fashioned and time had rendered doubly dear, was converted into desolation. Vast stores of provisions were carted away, and what the marauders could not carry off they destroyed." Nor was this riot of pillage and purposeless wrecking of stores and houses confined to the town. Similar rapine had been going on over the district, alike in the residence of the well-to-do, and in the

LIEUT. A. L. HOWARD.
Commanding Machine Gun Platoon Second Connecticut National Guard

modest home of the poor settler. "Humanitarian critics in the east," writes an indignant resident of Battleford, "may counsel clemency in dealing with the Indian; but these peace exhorters should be here to witness the wreck of all our possessions, and undergo the mental strain of many weeks' dread of nightly massacre, before they are competent to say what shall be the fate of those whose hands are red with the blood of the settler, and whose lawlessness was restrained only by innate cowardice and the approach of the troops."

Fortunately this carnival of license ended with the appearance of the relieving column on the heights over-looking the Battle River and the low, rich plain on which stood New Battleford. To the townspeople and settlers of the neighbourhood, who had for weeks been immured in the Police Barracks at Battleford, the dawn of Friday, the 24th of April, was freighted with joy. At sight of the troops all turned out to greet them with cheers; and the citizens and relieved garrison hastened to make provision for their rest and refreshment. Colonel Morris, of the Mounted Police, who had been in charge of the Fort, was hearty in his welcome of Colonel Otter and his command, and no less hearty in extending the courtesies of the post to his old comrade, Colonel Herchmer, and his mounted detachment. For a time all was bustle and excitement; but a day or two saw the Second Field Division settle down to routine camp duty, varied by the occasional excitement of camp sports, or of news of Indians on the war-path, brought in by the ubiquitous scout. Camp was pitched on the plain between the Battle River and the North Saskatchewan, and the men for a time worked off their superabundant vitality in erecting earthworks to protect it, and in building a bridge over the Battle River. A daily garrison was also told off for duty at the Industrial School on the heights, at

s

occupy that commanding post of observation, and on occasion to give note of warning.

The inaction that followed soon chafed the eager spirits of the camp. All were anxious for a brush with the Indian, the more so as news had reached the garrison of fighting on the South Saskatchewan, and of the heroism of comrades at the Battle of Fish Creek. But orders came not. The men grew tired of nursing their abraded heels and of mollifying with ointment each other's sun-scorched faces. Soon, too, the mending of rents in their uniform palled, though the exhilaration of this necessary task was not without its relief. Its comical aspect is thus portrayed in a letter from a young divinity student in the ranks to his father, a well-known and worthy clergyman, whose parish is in the north-west suburb of Toronto. As the letter appeared in the Toronto *Mail*, we have no scruple on the score of delicacy in transferring it to our pages. Nor, in doing so, shall we be charged, we hope, with making an oblique partisan attack upon the Government. The innocent, clever fun in the extract should relieve the writer and ourselves from a charge so false.

"Our clothes," writes this militant Churchman, "are beginning to show signs of wear, especially the rear of our unmentionables; mine gave out entirely. One sleeve came out of my overcoat, and I made use of the latter to make up the former deficiency, or, as I told an officer last night who asked me what had become of my sleeve, 'I took a detachment from the right subdivision of my overcoat to reinforce the rearguard of my trowsers.' However, the strength of the reinforcement only serves to show the weakness and utter demoralisation and rottenness of the said rearguard; and, consequently, I have applied to the Colonel for their superannuation, and for the attachment to my command of one of a hundred new pairs daily expected from headquarters. One night on picket I felt a little cool for want of this rearguard, and to supply its place I took off my rifle sling, fastened it to my waist belt before and behind, passed it through my legs, and thus pressed the tail of my overcoat into service as a substitute, and a very good one it proved! Otherwise, I have in no way suffered from the cold since leaving Qu'Appelle, and very little then, the north-shore trip having done much in hardening us. Life as a soldier is by no means bad, in fact, it improves as we go on, and would be first rate if we could only drop into Toronto occasionally, or even get the mails regularly."

Such was the spirit and good humour, not only of the "Queen's Own," but of all the Battleford troops, as well of their comrades in other portions of the North-West. From all quarters came the same note of cheerfulness, the same manly undergoing of hardship, and, from the battle-field, a courageous facing of death! In closing this chapter, let us signalise the great march we have attempted to describe by quoting the compliments it elicited in Parliament, and the well-merited praise awarded to the whole force in the field. On the 27th of April, after the march to Battleford, and the gallant conduct of the troops at Fish Creek, Mr. J. D. Edgar, M.P. for West Ontario, rose in the House and made the following remarks, with the accompanying enquiry of the Minister of Militia:

" While the whole country has been excited about the troops under Gen. Middleton, all Canadians, I am sure, are filled with admiration at the extraordinary and brilliant march made by Col. Otter's column from the Saskatchewan to Battleford, and everybody is interested in knowing how the troops have stood that extraordinary strain. I have no doubt the Government have informed themselves of the general health of that column, and I would like to know from the Minister what the report is.

Hon. Mr. Caron—It gives me very great pleasure, indeed, in answer to the question, to state that the hon. gentleman has qualified the march of Col. Otter's column as it should be qualified. That march is considered by those who are authorities in such matters—I mean military men—to have been a march deserving of all the encomiums that can be given to a feat of that kind. We always knew Col. Otter to be one of the very best men we had in the Canadian service, and in the opportunity which has been given of showing his great value he has not been found wanting. I am happy to state that from the telegram I have received from Battleford, I have reason to believe the troops are in the very best possible health and spirits, and that they have stood that wonderful march (for it was a wonderful march) in a manner that could not have been expected from them. I received yesterday a cipher telegram from the Major-General, in which he speaks in the highest possible terms of the behaviour of the troops in their first engagement. He confirms the news which appeared in the press of this morning of the encounter, and mentions the names of our brave volunteers who have fallen on the field. I am sure I am merely expressing the views and the opinion of the whole country in saying that we all deeply regret the loss we have suffered. They died the death of soldiers, and I am sure the country must be proud of the manner in which they have done their duty." (Cheers.)

CHAPTER XX.

THE FROG LAKE MASSACRE.

HILE the tender blades of the prairie grass in the North-West were springing rapidly from the womb of earth, and

" The mother of months in meadow and plain
Filled the shadows and windy places
With lisp of leaves and ripple of rain,"

a deed of horror was being enacted in an isolated region beyond the frost-liberated waters of the North Saskatchewan. The scene was Frog Lake, in the neighbourhood of Fort Pitt. For a time the facts of the tragedy did not transpire, and in the absence of reliable information, as often happens, idle rumour exaggerated the report. The first startling intelligence was of the wholesale massacre of the Government Indian Agents of the district, the Farm Instructors and Hudson Bay officials, with their wives and families, the Priests of the Roman Catholic mission, and the garrison of mounted constabulary at Fort Pitt. A later report still further exaggerated the facts, with the tidings that all of one sex had been butchered, and the other reserved to suffer the nameless horrors of Indian indignity and savage lust. Calamitous as was the occurrence, the facts were not quite so incredible. The truth was finally got at, and the enormity of Big Bear's crimes reached the outer world. In brief these crimes consisted in the murder, in cold blood, of two Oblat Fathers of the Catholic Mission; one Lay Brother; one chief Indian Agent; two Farm Instructors; two Mounted Police; two Hudson Bay Company employés, and the capture and detention of some thirty others, men, women, and children. The indictment further included the wrecking of the settlements; the raiding of the posts; the burning of the Mission Church, the bodies of the Priests being flung upon the pyre; and the seizure of cattle and stores, wherever marauding hands could reach them. The captives, for the space of two months, were in hourly fear for their lives. Dragged to and fro over a wild and desolate region, they for a time lived a living death.

The region of the Indian rising, in the Fort Pitt Agency extends from Fort Pitt on the Upper Saskatchewan, north-westward to Frog Lake on the western flank of the Moose Hills, and south of the Beaver River. Roughly speaking, the meridians 110° W. and 54° N. may be said to intersect each other at the north-east angle of Frog Lake. The Indian reserves at the Lake were occupied by the small bands of Chiefs Weemis-ti-co-wa-sis, Ne-paw-hay-haw, and Puska-ah-go-win, in all less than two hundred souls. But the region, of late, had become the stalking ground of the large and restless tribes of Big Bear, Lucky Man, Little Poplar, and Wandering Spirit, some six or seven hundred in number. At Fort Pitt the band, nearly two hundred strong, of See-kas-kootch had a reserve, and at Long Lake, a considerable distance to the northward, a hundred troublesome Chippewyans were located. Over all these bands Big Bear dominated, and his malign influence and the fear of his name disaffected the whole district, and finally led most of them to go forth with him on the war-path.

The action of Big Bear, and the insurrection of Riel and his half-breeds, incited other bands, if not to murder, to acts of thievery and lawless intimidation. Not less than five thousand Indians, on the North Saskatchewan, were known to be more or less disaffected. Besides the bands we have mentioned, and Beardy's Duck Lake following, all the Indians round Battleford were actively hostile. These included the Eagle Hill Indians, under Chiefs Mosquito, Bear's Head, Lean Man, and Red Pheasant; with the bands under Poundmaker, Little Pine, and Sweet Grass, or Strike-him-on-the-back, all situate in the neighbourhood of the Battle River. On the reserves at Jack Fish Creek, the bands of Moosomin, and Napahase, were also feared to be unfriendly, together with the following of Mistawasis and One Arrow.

The sedition of Riel was the signal for the rising of this mass of disaffection. His runners carried news of the halfbreed revolt throughout the district, and the Indian nature could not resist the contagion. We have seen what part the Willow Crees of Duck Lake played in the first uprising, and we have been witness to the devilment of the marauding bands round Battleford. Let us now move westward to the troubled region of Fort Pitt and the lair of the Pontiac of the North-West, the notorious rascal Big Bear. His stalking ground was the whole district between Edmonton and Battleford, but lay chiefly round Long, Frog, and Stoney Lakes, north of the Saskatchewan. In this district Big Bear had long been a source of anxiety to the Government Agents at Fort Pitt, as he had formerly been troublesome at Fort Walsh, in the Cypress Hills. At the latter Fort he refused to take treaty in the summer of 1879, when Little Pine and Lucky Man, chiefs of his own tribe, became adherents to Treaty No. 6, made at Forts Carlton and Pitt in the Fall of 1876. The reason assigned for refusing treaty was some scruple he had to the indignity of hanging for murder, a punishment he was richly to merit by his subsequent acts. Towards the close of 1882 he signed adhesion to treaty and agreed to go on a reserve in the neighbourhood of Fort Pitt. Here, as a correspondent remarks, it was thought that amidst hitherto quiet and peaceful bands of his own nation in the district, and hemmed in on the south by the Upper Saskatchewan, he would settle down and give no further trouble. But trouble from the first he has given and continued to give, and has repeatedly been guilty of acts of violence and intimidation. Time and again he has attempted to overawe the Police at the Pitt Agency, and summoned the various bands in the district to take up the hatchet and tomahawk. At repeated pow-wows he has incited his followers to acts of sedition, and endeavoured to persuade his braves to exterminate the settlers. He also revived the "Thirst Dance" with all its revolting features.

Fort Pitt is a fort only in name. It lies unprotected on a low, rich flat somewhat back from the north shore of the Upper Saskatchewan, and is situate about a hundred miles from Battleford on the East, and two hundred miles from Edmonton on the West. Here, on Good Friday, the 3rd of April, Henry Quinn, nephew of the local Government Indian Agent, who had escaped from Frog Lake with his life, brought the news to the Fort of the massacre of the whites at the Lake, and of the capture by Big Bear of those he wished to hold as prisoners. The horror occurred on the previous day, Big Bear, Wandering Spirit, and Little Bear and their bands, being its chief actors. The victims of the massacre, it was reported, were Thomas Quinn, resident Indian Agent; John Delaney, Farm Instructor; John A. Gowanlock, millwright; Fathers Farfard and Marchand, of the Indian Mission; J. Dill, a storekeeper; W. Gilchrist; J. Willscroft; and C. Gouin.

The ill-fated missionaries were Oblat Fathers engaged in the self-sacrificing duties of the Indian Missions in this outlying portion of the diocese of Bishop Grandin, of Prince Albert. Father Farfard was a Lower Canadian, and for the past nine years had been occupied in missionary work in the North-West. Father Marchand was a native of France. He came to Canada two years ago, and, accepting duty in the Battleford Missions, had recently settled at Frog Lake.

Thos. Quinn, the trusted Indian Agent of the Government, was a native of Red River. His father was an Irish trader in that region, and his mother a Cree half-breed. Physically, Quinn was a fine specimen of humanity: he was a thorough frontiersman, an accomplished horseman, and an expert canoeist. He is said to have laboured long and zealously for the conversion of his Pagan brethren, and to have earnestly sought the amelioration of their condition. His fate at the hands of those to whom he had been kind is a grim commentary on the results anticipated from Indian evangelisation. But, in a reflection of this sort, the agitated condition of the country, and the example of the seditious half-breeds, have to be borne in mind, and allowance made for their effects on imperfect civilisation.

John Delaney, the Farm Instructor, had in 1882 come with his wife from the neighbourhood of Ottawa, and had the supervision of four bands of Indians in proximity to Frog Lake. His official duties were also to attend to the issue of Government rations to the followers of Big Bear. We are told that he was engaged in the performance of this humane duty when the outbreak took place. A like beneficent work had brought Mr. J. A. Gowanlock to Frog Lake: he was engaged in erecting a mill for the benefit of the Indians of the district. Mr. and Mrs. Gowanlock belonged to Parkdale, the western suburb of Toronto. Theirs is a sad tale. The young couple had been but a few months married, and had come to Frog Lake in the previous December. The story we have to tell of the massacre is taken from the lips of the surviving-wives of Delaney and Gowanlock.* After the shooting of their husbands, these unfortunate gentlewomen were dragged from the lifeless bodies of their loved protectors, and for two months were the terror-stricken captives of the Indian murderers. For this long period they were in ignorance of what had happened elsewhere in the Territories, and were unaware that their fate had become known to their kin and the people of Canada. Not knowing this, how sad was their plight in their forced marchings and counter-marchings with their hunted Indian captors, for hope of freedom or rescue never came to relieve or buoy their minds!

The dread incidents of the massacre are briefly as follows: On one of the closing days of March a message reached the home of the Gowanlocks, informing its inmates that Mr. Quinn, the Indian agent, had fears of a rising among Big Bear's band, and advising Mr. and Mrs. Gowanlock to come to Quinn's house, and from there the small colony of white settlers would proceed to Fort Pitt for safety. The Gowanlocks, thus warned, set out for the rendezvous. On their way they called at the homestead of Delaney, the Farm Instructor, where their fear of pending trouble was allayed, and they abode with the Delaneys two nights. At dawn on Thursday, the 2nd of April, the household was startled at seeing the place surround-

*For the basis of this narrative we are indebted to "A. S. O. E.," the *Globe* special correspondent, who transmits the combined story of Mrs. Delaney and Mrs. Gowanlock to the Toronto *Globe*, under date. Battleford the 12th of June.

ed by some thirty armed Indians, most of them mounted on their prairie ponies. The leaders forced their way into the house, and took possession of all the arms and ammunition they could find, informing the Delaneys and their guests, the Gowanlocks, that they had need of the weapons. They then required the inmates of the homestead to go with them, for they wished to save them—such was the pretext,—from halfbreeds who were coming to attack them. In their fear, though not suspecting molestation, they complied with the Indians' wishes, and set out for Quinn's home, and from Quinn's to the Mission House. At Quinn's a like demand was made for all the arms at the Agency, and the story was repeated of threatened attack by the breeds. At the mission morning mass was being celebrated, which the Indians interrupted, and all were ordered back to Delaney's, together with the half-breeds who had been taken prisoners by the Indians, and had sought the shelter of the Church.

At the Delaney's all were left for a time in quiet. The Indians soon returned, however, after looting a couple of stores in the neighbourhood; and some, it is supposed, gaining access to the sacramental wine at the Priests'. Big Bear now appeared on the scene. To the Delaneys the Chief, with affected guilelessness, imparted his fears of the hostile intent of his young braves. He assured the Instructor, however, that he and his wife would be safe. The whole were now ordered to the Indian camp, though as yet none apprehended serious trouble. The tragic events that followed we shall leave Mrs. Gowanlock to relate:

" We all left Mrs. Delaney's house together. When we left no one knew what was going to happen, and I do not think it was really supposed any of us were in danger. As we left the house my husband took me with him and we walked on together. We had gone only a few paces when the Indians began firing. Mr. Dill, Mr. Quinn, and Mr. Gilchrist were shot first, though I did not see them shot; but as soon as I saw Mr. Willscroft, an old grey-headed man, fall in front of us, I then knew all were being killed. I became greatly alarmed. I saw an Indian aiming at my husband by my side. In a moment he fell, reaching out his arms towards me as he sank. I caught him, and we fell together. I lay upon him, resting my face upon his, and his breath was scarcely gone when I was forced away by an Indian. It was not the Indian who fired that dragged me from my husband. I was almost crazy with grief; but I remember seeing the two priests shot and also Mr. Delaney. They were in front of me. One of the priests, when shot, was leaning over Mr. Delaney. I saw them fall, but it appeared to me like some terrible dream. I did not seem to know what it all meant, and I went through it dazed and stunned, with only the power of my limbs left me to follow after the Indian, as he dragged me after him. I was pulled through the sloughs and coarse brush, which wet me through and tore my clothes and flesh, and I must have suffered intensely from rough treatment, though my grief and terror rendered me unconscious of much of my suffering. . . After this I was not subjected to any very severe hardship, but my mental anxiety, verging on derangement, was my worst trouble. I never knew what next was coming; 1 did not fear actual death at the hands of the Indians, but I dreaded ill-treatment and abuse a thousand times worse than death itself."

Mrs. Delaney's personal experience is as unspeakably sad. After reciting the facts connected with the early morning's proceedings, in which she took part, she enumerates those who fell, among whom were Mr. Dill, Mr. Quinn, Mr. Willscroft, Mr. Gouin, Mr. Gilchrist, and Mr. Gowanlock. The latter she saw fall. Here is a portion of her piteous narrative :

"Mrs. Gowanlock was beside her husband when he fell, and as he dropped she leaned down over him, putting her face to his. As two shots had been fired at her husband some supposed that she had fallen at the second shot. When I saw Mrs. Gowanlock fall I saw some hideous object, an Indian got up in frightful costume, take aim at my husband. Before I could speak my husband staggered away, but came back and said to me, 'I am shot.' He then fell, and I called the priest and told him what had happened. While he was praying with my husband the same hideous Indian fired again, and I thought his shot was meant for me, and I laid my head down upon my husband and waited—it seemed an age—but it was for my poor husband, and he never spoke afterwards. Almost immediately another Indian ran up and ordered me away. I wanted to stay, but he dragged me off, pulling me along by the arms through the brush and brier and through the creek, where the water reached to my waist. I was put into an Indian tent and left there until nightfall, without anything offered me to eat, though I could not have eaten anything. I was not allowed outside of the tent, and so had no opportunity of returning to my dead husband, and have never seen him since."

Escape from the heart-rending situation which had so suddenly environed these poor women was not to come for two months after these events occurred. Thanks to the humanity of their fellow-prisoner half-breeds, relief, however, was in some measure to be theirs. To their protection and incessant interposition, they owed their lives and all that a woman holds dear. In their trying situation Heaven's mercy seemed miraculously extended to them; for at nightfull on the day of the massacre, while Mrs. Delaney and Mrs. Gowanlock were confined in separate tepees among the Indians, some half-breeds in the camp purchased their release by giving up their horses and a little money they had concealed upon their persons. The names of their half-breed liberators are John Pritchard and Adolphus Nolan, with two others, named Blondin and Goulois. To Pritchard, especially, do the women acknowledge their eternal gratitude. By the purchase, the women came together, and in their common captivity were tenderly cared for. At Pritchard's interposition they were also permitted to travel with the half-breed prisoners,.

"Every other day," observes Mrs. Delaney, "we were moved with the entire camp from one place to another. Big Bear's treatment of us would have been cruel in the extreme, but Pritchard saved us from the agony and torture of forced marches through sloughs, brush, and rough land. Frequent attempts were made to reach us by the Indians, but the half-breeds watched night after night, armed and ready to keep off any attempt to ill-treat us. Four different nights Indians approached our tent, but the determination of our protectors saved us. There is no telling what abuse we might have been subject to but for their presence."

Mrs. Gowanlock's testimony to Pritchard's fidelity and constant thoughtfulness is equally heartfelt and sincere. She remarks:

"I dread to imagine what would have been done to us had it not been for John Pritchard and those who were with him. We were not compelled to march on foot, although once or twice Mrs. Delaney and I walked off together when the cart was not ready. John Pritchard often made his children walk that we might ride. I had no idea where we were being taken to, or what was going to be done with us, but I kept up as best I could. We had heard nothing of troops coming, nor had we heard anything of Riel's rebellion, further than early in March that there was likely to be one. We had nothing at all to look forward to, and hope was not entertained for a moment. Sometimes John Pritchard encouraged me and would tell us that he would do what he could to get us to our friends, but this, our only hope, was only of momentary comfort, and the terrible present would drive away all expectations of ever again seeing home and friends. For two months we travelled on, going long and short distances by daylight, according to the inclination of Big Bear. I frequently saw him. He would come into our tent and talk to us. Mr. Pritchard would interpret, and Big Bear professed sorrow, telling us it was all the fault of his braves whom he could not control. I did not believe this altogether, although he had very little control over his band. Wandering Spirit seemed to have more influence with the tribe than anyone else. He was one of Big Bear's councillors, and the man who fired the first shot, the shot that killed Mr. Quinn. The Indians would contend with one another for the honour of having killed the whites, and would even quarrel over the disputes that would arise between themselves on this account. The squaws would come to our tent—not a tepee such as the Indians used—and jeer and laugh at us and ask us how we liked it; and shortly before we escaped they kept saying they wanted to kill us."

We shall anticipate events if we here give the sequel to this lamentable story. But it will be better to complete the sad narrative in the present chapter; and we do so more willingly, as what we have now to tell has a measurably happy ending in escape and succour. About the time General Middleton's Field Division reached Humboldt, on the way to the seat of insurrection, Big Bear's band, in their wanderings to and fro with the Frog Lake captives, threatened a descent upon Fort Pitt. This post at the time contained a small garrison of Mounted Police, a few Hudson Bay Company officials and their families, together with the Missionary and the Farm Instructor of Onion Lake, who, in the disturbed state of the district, had sought the protection of the Fort for themselves and their households. In anticipation of attack by Big Bear's young braves, willing hands within Fort Pitt were busily employed pulling down all outside buildings, blocking up windows, making loop holes for musketry, erecting bastions, and generally fortifying the defences of the post. Before two weeks in April had passed over, word was brought to the Fort of the approach of Big Bear, Little Poplar, and Wandering Spirit, with some ten or twelve lodges of Indians. On the 14th inst., they were descried on an eminence, some eight hundred yards from the post, where they made night hideous with the war-dance, and frightened the garrison by firing stray shots into the Fort, and by scouting round its defences

Double sentries were now mounted all day, and during the night the whole garrison was under arms. Even young girls, inmates of the Fort, pluckily stationed themselves at loopholes, rifle in hand, ready to withstand attack. Next morning a message was received from Big Bear requiring the garrison to evacuate the Fort and give up arms. A council was now called, and it was decided that Mr. Maclean, the Hudson Bay Factor at the post, should seek an interview with the Indian Chief, and learn from him whether he would protect life on the post being surrendered to pillage. At the parley that ensued, Maclean was told that the Indians wanted to raid the fort, and not to kill the inmates. Protection was guaranteed to the Hudson Bay officials and their families, if they at once surrendered themselves; and a personal message was sent by Big Bear, urging the Mounted Police to make good their escape from the Fort. They were also informed that he would not be answerable for the actions of his followers if they continued to defend the place. Maclean, meanwhile, was held a prisoner.

In view of the situation, and anxious for the safety of his wife and family, of ten children, as well as for the other inmates of the Fort, Maclean took Big Bear at his word, and sent a letter directing his family to join him, and urging all the Hudson Bay Company employés to do the same. As the latter numbered only twenty-eight souls, men, women, and children, and the Mounted Police, all told, were but fifteen men, with Inspector Dickens in command, the impossibility of holding the Fort against two hundred and fifty Indians, was patent to everyone. The Hudson Bay people therefore marched out of the Fort, and proceeded to Big Bear's camp on the hill, where they gave themselves up. The garrison being thus depleted, the Police saw discretion lay in making speedy escape from the beleagured Fort. They were hastened in this, act by the killing of one of their number (Constable Cowan*), and the wounding of another (Constable Loasby), who were shot while scouting on the plain. That evening, the night of the 15th inst., the intrepid Police stole from the Fort, carrying with them the colours and their wounded comrade. With difficulty the fugitives crossed the ice-choked river, and camped till dawn on the southern bank of the Saskatchewan.

At four o'clock the next morning, in a heavy snow storm, and with ice running very strong in the river, the gallant troopers boarded a scow and set off for Battleford. For days they kept to the river, not daring to land on the banks, for fear of capture by hostile Indians. Only when they reached some island on the way, were they able to get under canvass over night and to start a fire to thaw their half-frozen limbs. In the passage down the stream they were in constant peril from ice-jams, and occasionally got caught on sandbars at bends in the river. On the eighth day out, their troubles happily ended, on arriving at Battleford, where they were enthusiastically greeted by their comrades in the garrison, the Police band playing them into fort.

The whites, who surrendered themselves prisoners to Big Bear at Fort Pitt, besides Maclean, the Hudson Bay Factor, and his family, were the Rev. Charles Quinney, of the Church of England Mission, at Onion Lake; his wife; Mr. Mann, the local Farm Instructor, and family of five children, Mr. Stanley Simpson, Hudson Bay Clerk, with a number of the Company's

---

* A correspondent of the Montreal *Witness* states that Cowan's mutilated body was found some weeks afterwards in a little clearing in the bush close to Fort Pitt. He relates some horrible details in regard to the fate of this and other victims of Indian malignity in the district. "Cowan's heart," he describes, "had been cut from the body, the limbs had been gashed by knives, and the red-skinned fiends had finished by carrying off the scalp of the dead constable. A pair of handcuffs," he adds, "had been put on his wrists by way of special indignity."

T

servants, some few French Canadians, and friendly Indians. These prisoners, with those who had fallen into his hands at Frog Lake, Big Bear took away northward with him, and were unwilling witnesses of the plundering operations of his band over the region as far west as Victoria and north to the Beaver River. For weeks they had to tramp through swamps and muskegs, and over a wild unbroken country; for the Indians avoided the ordinary trails, lest they should meet with Major Steele's loyal scouts who were on their track, and the forces of General Strange, who had set out from Edmonton to operate against them. Towards the end of May the troops got repeatedly on the track of the fugitives, and had several engagements with the Indians. Advantage, by the white prisoners, was always sought to be taken of these fights to make good their escape; and the half-breeds and not a few of the Indians, who had been forced by Big Bear to rise against the whites, were also eager to part company with their captors. But for a time they were too closely watched. The Plain Crees made themselves particularly officious in preventing escape, and but for the Wood Crees they would ere this have massacred all the prisoners.

But to some of the prisoners escape, providentially, was soon to come. While the Indians were holding a " thirst dance," about the 28th of May, scouts brought news to the camp of the approach of an armed force,* which for some hours had a hot engagement with the young fighting braves of the band. In the fight the Indians pursued their usual tactics of drawing the troops on to an ambuscade; but fortunately the ruse was

---

*This force was a portion of General Strange's Division from Edmonton, that had been detailed to seek to rescue the white captives. It consisted of three companies of Col. Osborne Smith's Battalion of Winnipeg Light Infantry; two Companies of Col. Ouimet's 65th Regiment, of Montreal; Major Hutton's local Mounted Rifles ; and some fifty men of the Mounted Police and Scouts, under Major Steele,

detected, and the troops were withdrawn to the rear, before being surrounded and cut off. This enabled the Indians again to get away with their captives, when they took to still more unfrequented paths, and to a region of muskeg and swamp where it was impossible safely to follow them. Mr. Quinney, the missionary, states that camp was formed that night about sixteen miles from the scene of the engagement, and not far from Red Deer Creek. A few days after this, some of the Indians who were restive under Big Bear's leadership, and notably a friendly Indian, named Long Fellow, facilitated the escape of Rev. Mr. Quinney, his wife, Mr. Cameron, a Hudson Bay Clerk, and Francis Dufresne, an employé of the Company, with a few half-breed women. After a fatiguing march, of about twenty miles, they came to the North Saskatchewan, and were gratified to hear two prolonged whistles from a steamboat on the river. By this time it was dark. The party took to shouting, and finally their cries met the response of a friendly cheer, and the whole were soon in safety.

About the same time, the Indians becoming excited at the daring of loyal scouts who were constantly on their track, hastened their movement northward, and the half-breed protectors of Mrs. Delaney and Mrs. Gowanlock, watching their opportunity, and taking advantage of the morning fog over the lakes of the region, turned into the woods and made off with all speed for the south. For a time they moved backwards and forwards, so as to avoid their trail being discovered; but finally were able to strike a scout, named Wm. McKay, of Battleford, who with eight others conducted the whole party in safety to Fort Pitt. Here the sufferings of the two poor gentlewomen, and the toils and anxiety of their humane half-breed deliverers, were happily forgotten in the welcome they received from the garrison, and the thoughtful provision made for them by Colonels B. Van Straubenzie, and A. T. Williams.

Another fortnight was to elapse ere the remainder of the white prisoners effected their escape. Big Bear was now being hard pressed by General Strange's troops, and these had had engagements with his band at Frenchman's Butte and at Loon Lake. After these fights there were repeated quarrels between the Wood Crees and the followers of Big Bear. The former determined to separate from the band, and to take the white prisoners with them. The plight of the latter was now pitiful. Utterly weary of the incessant marching, it is said that the young girls repeatedly fell down exhausted at the feet of the mounted Indians, and begged to be allowed to die where they fell. But their captors kicked them up and forced them on. Provisions were now also getting scarce, and the daily allowance was not sufficient to enable them to continue the march. Their friends, the Wood Crees, here again interfered, and when the party was near Lac des Iles, they gave them their freedom, with one or two horses to enable them to make good their escape. For a time, it seemed, they had secured release only to perish from hunger by the way. One morning all they had for breakfast was one rabbit for twenty-eight people. But their trials were soon over, for on the 18th of June one of their number reached an outpost of the troops not far from Beaver River, and a relieving party set out instantly to bring them in. Canon Mackay, who was with the outpost of scouts, secured their transportation to Loon Lake; and Captain Bedson, on Mackenzie, the *Mail* correspondent's riding in to Fort Pitt with news of the release of the prisoners, was sent off by the authorities to take provisions to them and to convey them to the Fort. The party arrived at the Pitt Agency on the 22nd of June.

CHAPTER XXI.

OTTER ATTACKS POUNDMAKER—THE FIGHT AT CUT KNIFE HILL.

BEFORE leaving the North Saskatchewan, and returning to General Middleton's column, in the hot contests with the Half-breeds on the South branch of the river, let us chronicle a movement of Colonel Otter's force against Poundmaker's band, which occupied a strong position some thirty-five miles distant from Battleford. The engagement took place on Saturday, the 2nd of May, between a flying column of 300 men, under Colonel Otter, and about 600 Indians, posted near Poundmaker's reserve, close by Battle River. Brief telegraphic despatches reached the East on Tuesday, the 5th inst., stating that the fight began at five o'clock in the morning and lasted till noon. Our loss was seven killed and twelve wounded. The casualties of the Indians were supposed to be not far short of eighty. The despatches closed with the following words: "Colonel Otter covered, including the engagement, seventy miles, fought the battle and returned inside of thirty hours."

On reading the despatch our first emotions were of pity. In our heart there was no response to the strain of heroics that announced the achievement. Whatever military necessity existed for the movement, we regretted that the forces of civilisation had to be used for such a purpose. To enforce respect for law and order upon savage life at the mouth of Gatling guns and seven-pounders, we could not help reflecting, was a grave step in the history of the insurrection, and a dire calamity. From a military point of view it was doubtless necessary to overawe Poundmaker by a display of our strength on the field, and if possible, happily, to hem in the insurrection. Moreover, there were scores to be settled with his band for their plundering and intimidation in the region, for the murder of Payne and Applegarth, the local farm instructors, and for the shooting of at least two of the settlers. There was also the need of keeping Poundmaker from joining Riel and his half-breeds, and of giving aid to Big Bear and his bands in the west. But whatever justification there was for sallying out with an armed force against the Indians, we could have wished that Colonel Otter had met Poundmaker anywhere but on his own reserves and surrounded by the tepees of his women and children.

It is little palliation to say that the Indians fired the first shot: this they naturally would do on the advance upon their encampment of an armed force. There is a sounder plea, in what seems to be the case, that the band was about to take part in extending the flame of insurrection, and in joining the forces of Big Bear or Riel. In preventing this, the presence of the flying column may be said to find its true justification. But it is to be borne in mind, that the insurrection in the North-West was not a rising of Indians, though the Indians, unhappily, were led to take part in it. Their part in it, however, has been singularly slight; and considering the example that had been set them by the half-breeds, it is a marvel that the flames of the contest did not envelop the whole territory. But in these remarks we have no desire to criticise Colonel Otter's action, or to question the expediency of his military operations. No doubt, he considered the step a necessary one; though the embittered condition of the local mind at Battleford, if he listened to that, was at the time, we fear, perilous to the retention of a calm and pacific judgment. In the absence of official reports of the engagement, or of the reasons that led to it, we are content to rely upon the Commanding Officer's caution and good feeling, as well as on the motives of humanity.

Poundmaker, against whose band the movement was directed, has the reputation of being one of the most sagacious Indians in the North-West. The Cree Chief, moreover, is a particularly handsome and refined-looking specimen of his race. Through his veins courses the blood of the Cree, the Blackfoot, and the Assiniboine or Stoney; though at one time each of these tribes was the hereditary enemy of the other. It was mainly at his interposition that they all buried the hatchet. In 1881, when Lord Lorne went across the plains, Poundmaker, it is known, joined the party for the purpose of interpreting the language of the Blackfoot into Cree, as the Governor-General's Cree interpreter did not understand Blackfoot. He was also of service as a guide to the party, for Poundmaker knows the North-West as the sailor knows the sea. Cut Knife Hill, the scene of the conflict, is an elevated ridge on his reserve, flanked by scrub-covered ravines and almost impregnable coulees. It derives its name from a raiding Chief, Cut Knife, whose followers were here once set upon, and paid the penalty of their career of plunder and scalping by the death of their leader and the extermination of the band. The hill was now to receive a further baptism of blood.

On a bright May day afternoon (Friday, the 2nd inst.), Colonel Otter's column crossed the Battle River, and gaining its southern heights turned westward towards Poundmaker's reserve, through an undulating country, interspersed with high bluffs, thickly covered with sedge, elm, and small poplar. The fighting force, in addition to the armed teamsters, who had charge of the provisions, ammunition, and forage, numbered about 320 men. The order of the column was as follows: a small force of scouts on horseback, under Mr. Charles Ross; 75 Mounted Police, under Colonel Herchmer and Inspector Neale; 30 men of "B" Battery, with two seven-pounders and the Gatling gun, under Major Short, with a garrison division under Capt. Farley; 45 men of "C" Co. Infantry School, commanded by Lieuts. Wadmore and Sears; 20 Ottawa Foot-Guards, under Lt. Gray; 50 men of the Queen's Own, Capt. Thomas Brown, and Lieuts. Hughes and Brock in command; the line of teams, with tents, provisions, and forage; and, finally, 50 of the Battleford Rifles, under Capt. Nash, late of the Queen's Own. Accompanying the column were the Signal Corps, of the Queen's Own Rifles, and the Ambulance Brigade, the latter under Surgeons Strange and Lesslie. The force marched some sixteen miles before sundown, when a halt was called for supper and a rest until moonrise.

At eleven o'clock the column resumed the march, the scouts carefully feeling the way. Most of the men on foot were taken up on the waggons and refreshed themselves with what sleep they could obtain in the lullaby of creaking wheels and under the soporific influence of the moonbeams. At daybreak all were astir momentarily expecting to come across the enemy. Passing through a deserted Indian encampment, the trail seemed to end in a series of scrub-covered elevations, towering above which rose Cut Knife Hill, flanked by a succession of gorges. A herd of cattle was peacefully grazing on the near hillsides, while, across the trail, brawled a winding creek, in a deep depression of the land. As yet there was no sign of the Indians. Fording the brook, and toiling up the heights on the further side, the column suddenly pulled up at sight of the mounted scouts falling back on the gallop with news of the enemy. A moment later a flight of bullets whistled through the air, and told its own story, that the fight had begun.

The videttes of the Mounted Police, who had nearly reached the summit of Cut Knife, instantly dismounted, and were joined by their comrades from the head of the column. They extended on the double, and rushed to the crest of the hill; while "B" Battery dashed after them with two seven-pounders and the Gatling. Gaining the ridge, the Police poured a withering fire upon the advancing Indians, while the guns unlimbered and prepared for action. Undaunted by the fire of the skirmishers, a posse of yelling braves made a rush to capture the field-pieces, but were checkmated by a volley from Farley's foot division of the battery, which had been ordered up in support. To the right of the guns "C" Co. extended to the edge of the hill; and No. 1 Co. Queen's Own, in skirmishing order, deployed to the left of the Police. In a minute or two the seven-pounders belched shrapnel shell at the enemy; and, with appalling effect, the Gatling raked the coulees with a thousand shot. Above the din of the guns was now heard the war-whoop of hundreds of advancing Indians, and from the ravine, served by the Gatling, came the death-wail of a score of prostrate braves. Despite the noise, the Indian fire was hot and incessant; and it seemed to come from every quarter.

For a time the safety of the column was in doubt. But under the steady fire of the skirmishing line the confusion, incident to the sudden opening of the fight, passed away, and confidence was restored by a good disposition of the force. The Indians now made an effort to surround the troops. This action was observed, however, by their wary commander, and the Ottawa Guards and the Battleford Rifles were ordered into positions to foil the movement. The latter were subsequently recalled to act as reserves, to guard the kraal of Police and Battery horses, and to protect the laager of waggons, the ammunition, and the Field Hospital. In these important duties the Rifles did good and efficient service. Once more, however, the rear was threatened, as far back as the creek, and once more the Battleford Company was called on to show its mettle. Dashing into the scrub at the ambushed enemy, they gallantly cleared it of the half-breeds who had taken possession of it and kept the trail open to the crossing.

The enemy's fire continued to play hot on the ridge. The heights in front of Cut Knife were reinforced by the Indians, and showers of bullets sped across the ravine and fell thick in the skirmishing line. On both flanks of the hill the coulees were packed with redskins, and from the brushwood cover white puffs of smoke would disclose the hiding-place of Indian marksmen. Already their fell work had made many demands on the ambulance, and not a few had passed need of a surgeon. A Mounted Policeman, Corporal Sleigh, who had escaped from Fort Pitt, was the first to fall, mortally wounded. A bullet entered his mouth, and passed out at the back of his head. The brave fellow is said to have raised himself on one knee, while the blood streamed forth from the wound, and, taking aim at an Indian, fired and fell dead. Private Arthur Dobbs, of the Battleford Rifles, had also fallen, and rendered his last account. So had Pte. John Rogers, of the Ottawa Foot Guards, and Brigade Bugler Herbert Foulkes, of the School of Infantry. Among the wounded were Lieut. Pelletier, Sergt. Gaffney, Corp. Morton, and Gunner Reynolds, all of "B" Battery; Sergt. Winters, and Pte. McQuilkin, of the Foot Guards; and Sergt. Ward, of the Mounted Police. Four men of the Queen's Own were also carried from the field, viz., Col.-Sergt. Cooper, Ptes. Lloyd, C. Varey, and Geo. Watts. Bugler E. Gilbert, of the Battleford Rifles, was also borne to the rear; and Brigade Sergt.-Major Spackman, of "C" Co., received a flesh wound in the arm. Meanwhile the morning hours passed, and heaven's unruffled blue vault looked down on the carnage on hill and plain.*

Whatever were our compunctions in regard to the attack upon the Indians, there was no doubt now of their own murderous intent, either in moving to assault Battleford, or to join Reil in his defence of Batoche. That they were well prepared to receive Colonel Otter's troops, and had designedly endeavoured to entrap them to ruin, the morning's fight, and the tactics pursued, sufficiently attest. Even the grazing cattle on the hillsides was seen to be a ruse, for the ravines were alive with redmen, and every covey had its marksman. Even Indians of tender years were armed, and with bows and arrows offered a menacing resistance. But for the cannon it would have gone hard with Otter's Flying Column. For the musketry fire the enemy cared little: only the shrieking shrapnel held them in check, and the Gatling fast reduced them to carrion.

---

* For the details of this engagement we are indebted to "W. W. F." correspondent of the Toronto *Mail*; but we are specially beholden to "W. A. H.," whose long and graphic account of the fight appeared in the columns of the Montreal *Star*. We have also had the advantage of listening to the recital of the main facts by a gallant non-commissioned officer who was present. We refer to Sergt. F. Kennedy, of the "Queen's Own."

In clearing the coulees and protecting the guns, more than once there was a hand to hand conflict, in which Indian disregard of life had at times the advantage. Then only the stubbornness of true heroism saved the column from disaster. Every man stood nobly to his post. The scout, Ross, seemed omnipresent; and his experience of Indian fighting, as well as his personal bravery, contributed in no little degree to the success of the day. Colonels Otter and Herchmer, and Adjutant Sears and Capt. Mutton, of the staff, constantly exposed themselves in their trying position. Colonel Otter, himself, was ever in the thick of the fighting, and his cool watchfulness of the weak points of the field, and ready resource in meeting them, gained him the admiration, as well as the increasing confidence, of his men. While the Mounted Police and the Battery were gallantly holding the often threatened crest of the hill, the flanks were repeatedly the object of attack. Again and again it was necessary to clear the coulees of the crouching Indians who infested them; and when a warrior was struck he could be seen making a death-leap into the air from behind his retreat. On the right, " C " Co., the Police, and the foot battery, performed the hazardous duty of clearing the coulees; and on the left, the posts of danger were held by the Guards and the Queen's Own. From a hill on the left the enemy were gallantly dislodged by the Ottawa and Toronto Companies, Lt. Gray of the former and Capts. Brown and Hughes, and Lieut. Brock of the latter being in repeated danger.

The position of the sun now indicated the approach of noon, but the fortunes of the day were not yet decided. Both sides stubbornly held their ground, though the troops had gained strong positions on the adjacent heights. Two hills on the right, beyond a pond in the ravine, were taken by the Guards, "C" Company, and " B " Battery. The enemy's camp in the distance, and an elevation on the left, from which the Indian movements were directed, were now shelled and cleared by the seven-pounders, at a range of 2,000 yards. Other advantageous positions were also being fought for and occupied. Just then, unhappily, the gun carriages broke from the strain of the recoil, and could not be moved forward with safety to follow up the attack. There was much risk also in further pressing the fighting, for the Indians had two to one of a fighting force. The losses of the troops were moreover heavy, and they were beyond timely reach of fresh support. The force was also exhausted, and no one had eaten breakfast. A withdrawal from the field was therefore wisely determined. True, much of the moral effect of the morning's engagement would be lost by a retreat. But wisdom seemed to counsel it, and though there was danger in withdrawal, it was admirably managed. A further reason for retreat was the difficulty of successfully holding the positions occupied after nightfall, and the probability that the enemy would receive large reinforcements before morning. Already Indian signal fires had been lighted on the heights, with the apparent intention of attracting aid.

It was close upon one o'clock when the order to withdraw was given. The difficulty of calling in the gallant force, and getting it back over the gully through which ran the creek, was obviously great. It was a crucial test of Otter's generalship; but luck, as well as strategy, attended the movement. The first to be convoyed from the field were the waggons containing the dead and wounded. Then followed a field-piece, in charge of Captain Rutherford, who after repairing the break in the carriage, got the gun in position to cover the retiring column. The other field-piece and the Gatling Major Short adroitly withdrew, and posted them on a sandhill to the rear of the creek, commanding both ravines. The advanced line of skirmishers, which now became the rear-guard, slowly left Cut Knife Hill, skirmishing in alternate lines down to the creek. The Indians, realising the movement instantly began to pour over the crest of the hill. Here they were exposed to the fire of the guns from the sandhills in rear, and to volley-firing from the retiring troops. The Gatling at this time, served by Major Short, did terrible execution, and caused many a brave to sing the death-song and the squaws to howl their lament.

From scores of lurking-places the Indians now intrepidly came forth; but they evidently had had enough of the fighting, for they did not follow the column. Withdrawing the flanking parties, the force was compactly concentrated in the line of the trail, with a strong rear-guard told off to cover the retreat, and to fire the prairie to prevent pursuit. Passing through a ravine to overtake the column, the scouts, it is said, counted twenty dead Indians in one spot, where a shrapnel had burst. The loss of the enemy, the scouts estimated, at from a hundred to a hundred and fifty lives. Our own loss was eight killed and thirteen wounded. One poor fellow, Pte. Osgoode, of the Ottawa Foot Guards, was reported missing, and though he was seen to fall, he was inadvertently left on the field. Teamster Winder was killed just before the retire. Corporal Lowry, of the Mounted Police, died in the waggon which conveyed him from the field; and Trumpeter Patrick Burke, of the same corps, died at Battleford next day.

At ten o'clock on Saturday night, through the inky darkness, the lights of Battleford could be descried, and half an hour later the last of the waggons filed in to Fort Otter. There had been but one halt, for dinner, from the battlefield to the camp, the thirty-five miles having been covered during the afternoon and evening. Reaching camp, the wearied column sought needed rest, though the eagerness of comrades to learn news of the battle, and the no less eagerness of those who had come from the field to recount modestly their share in it, delayed retirement. The wounded were taken to the Industrial School, which had been extemporised as an hospital, and the surgeons were busy with their sad task all night. Thanks to careful tending, all of the wounded lived, save Burke, who died on the Sabbath morning. A sad incident is related in connection with the death of this gallant trooper. It seems he had a wife and seven children then in Battleford. On the Sunday morning, learning that her husband had been wounded, she crossed the river to the hospital, and on the way passed a waggon with her husband's remains. The sad story is thus told by the Montreal *Star's* correspondent:

"Before nine o'clock, Burke of the Mounted Police expired. His wife crossed from the fort at an early hour to the Industrial School. Buoyed up with the false hope that her wounded husband would recover, she drove towards the temporary hospital when she was passed by a waggon actually conveying his lifeless body to an unoccupied house. Her companions unable to keep up the ruse longer, immediately communicated the painful intelligence. With an agonised wail, which moved the uniformed spectators to tears, the bereft widow alighted and following the waggon she threw herself upon the prostrate form as soon as it was laid beside the other dead. Two children of tender years, unable to comprehend the outburst of grief, clung crying to their mother. Such was the sad scene witnessed by a score or more of sympathetic spectators on that bright May morning. All day long an endless throng wended their way towards the little house near the ferry to have a last look at the victims of Cut Knife Hill. The countenance of each unfortunate man lay composed in death. A peculiar feeling of gloom pervaded the camp until the final interment took place. Volunteers moved about in groups of threes or fours conversing in low tones of the fate of their companions, or discussing the possibility of prompt and effective vengeance."

CHAPTER XXII.

THE CAMPAIGN ON THE SOUTH SASKATCHEWAN.

With Middleton at Fish Creek.

LET us now return to General Middleton, in his operations against the insurgent half-breeds on the South Saskatchewan. It will be remembered that we left the main division of the North-West Expeditionary Field Force at Clarke's Crossing, where the General in command awaited supplies at the Ferry, the Gatling gun, and the Midland Battalion, that was to convoy the *Northcote* down the river from Swift Current. But the river stern-wheeler was expected for another and a military purpose. The General wished to make use of it in co-operating with his land force in the attack upon the enemy. In this desire he was for a time baulked. The craft, at this period of the year, when the water was low, was not given to rapid transit. Moreover she was heavily loaded with military stores and supplies for the troops, in addition to her armament of strong two-inch plank, doubled round her lower deck and bulwarks to protect her boilers and to shield the troops from anticipated attack. She had on board four companies of the First Provisional Battalion under Lt.-Col. A. T. H. Williams, M.P., of Port Hope. This battalion, composed of town and country yeomen, drawn from the region lying between Bowmanville and Kingston, including the counties to the rear, was, under its able and soldierly commander, to give a good account of itself.* Besides the companies of the "Midlanders," the *Northcote* had on board Lt. Howard, in charge of the Gatling gun; a veteran of the Crimea, Lt.-Col. B. Van Straubenzie (late Major 100th Foot), Deputy Adj.-Genl. of Military District No. 5 (Montreal); Surgeon-Genl. Roddick, with additions to the hospital staff at Saskatoon, where, after the fight at Fish Creek, the large number of wounded at that and subsequent engagements were taken.

So great were the difficulties of navigation that the *Northcote*, though she left Swift Current on the 22nd of April, did not reach Clarke's Crossing until the 5th of May. In the meantime General Middleton determined to advance. The fighting force now at his disposal was, as we have seen, not far short of a thousand men. As many more had assembled at Winnipeg, waiting orders to proceed to the front, in addition to the troops that had gone west to Calgary, and those that were now at Battleford. At Prince Albert there was also a

---

*The following are the staff and company officers of the First Provisional (Midland) Batt., under the command of Lt.-Col. Arthur T. H. Williams, of the 46th East Durham Infantry. Majors H. R. Smith, 47th Batt. Kingston, and Lt.-Col James Deacon, 45th Batt. Lindsay. Adjt. E. G. Ponton, Belleville; Paymaster, Capt. J. Leystock Reid; Quartermaster, Lt. J. P. Clemes, Port Hope; Surgeons, Dr. Horsey, Ottawa, and Dr. Jas. Might, Port Hope. 15th (Belleville) Capt. and Adj. T. C. Lazier, Lts. J. E. Helliwell and C. G. E. Kenny. 40th (Northumberland) Capt. R. H. Bonnycastle and Lt. J. E. Givan. 45th (West Durham) Capts. John Hughes, and J. C. Grace. 46th (East Durham) Capts. R. Dingwall, Port Hope, and C. H. Winslow, Millbrook; Lts. R. W. Smart, Port Hope, and J. V. Preston, Lifford. 47th (Frontenac) Capt. T. Kelly; Lts. Sharp and Hubbell. 49th (Hastings) Capt. E. Harrison; Lts. H. A. Yeomans, and R. J. Bell. 57th (Peterboro') Capts. J. A. Howard, and Thos. Burke; Lts. F. H. Brennan and J. L. Weller (R.M.C.) The following were also attached as 2nd Lieuts.: R. J. Cartwright, C. E. Cartwright, G. E. Laidlaw, H. C. Ponton, A. T. Tomlinson, and D. C. F. Bliss.

large detachment of the Mounted Police, under Colonel Irvine, a portion of which the Major-General hoped might be free to strike the rebels in the rear. Dividing his force into two columns, on the 22nd April, General Middleton placed the left one under Col. Montizambert and despatched it across the river to move on the enemy along the opposite bank. This force, besides 80 armed teamsters, consisted of 250 of the Grenadiers; 50 men of the Winnipeg Battery; and 25 of French's Scouts. Lord Melgund accompanied it as chief of staff. The right column, under General Middleton, with Lt.-Col. Houghton as chief of staff, was composed of the following troops: 300 of the 90th Batt.; 40 of "C" Company; 120 men of "A" Battery; 40 of Boulton's Mounted Scouts, and about 60 teamsters. On the General's staff were his two A.D.C.'s, Lts. Wise and Doucet. With each battery were two nine-pounders, muzzle-loading rifled guns, with fuse shrapnel, percussion shells and case shot.

On the afternoon of Thursday, the 23rd of April, the command was given for both columns to advance. Communication across the river, which is here over 200 yards wide, was kept up by means of flags. Instructions had been issued to proceed with caution. The two divisions marched to within twenty miles of Batoche, where they halted for the night, strong scouting parties being thrown out to feel the ground for the morrow's advance, and to ensure the safety of the camps. The Friday morning opened with rain; but spite of its discomfort the order was again given to advance. Reaching a point about fifteen miles south of Batoche, the Mounted Scouts under Major Boulton encountered the rebels, who instantly opened fire. The time was nine o'clock A.M. The shots came from a body of half-breeds on horseback, who, after delivering their fire, wheeled about and galloped under cover within the ravine. The ravine is an abrupt, wood-clad depression, skirting the northern slope of the prairie, within a mile and a half of the Saskatchewan. A stream winds through it, which must become historic in our native annals, as Fish Creek. On the northern rise of the ravine are a few rebel farm-houses, while its eastern end is heavily wooded. Its width is about two hundred yards. On a series of ledges sloping down to the creek, the half-breeds had dug in parallel lines well-covered rifle-pits. These were constructed at such points as would best shelter their inmates, and effectively mask the fire. Only the bayonet could adequately cope with the enemy so entrenched.

When the loyal scouts fell back on the column, the latter was divided into two wings, half of the 90th, "A" Battery, and "C" Co. School of Infantry, forming the right wing; the remainder of the Winnipeg Battalion, with Boulton's Mounted Corps, forming the left. The whole advanced, in extended order, and circled round the entrance to the ravine, in a sort of half-moon formation. "A" Battery, under Capt. Peters moved to the front at the gallop; but had difficulty at first in bringing the guns into position. The garrison division of the Battery, under Lieut. Rivers, closely followed the guns in support. The left wing was the first to come under fire, and was for a time alarmingly exposed while unable effectively to return a shot. The brush was densely thick, and as the rain was falling, the smoke hung in clouds a few feet above the muzzles of the rifles.

The evident intention of the enemy was to draw the troops into the ravine, and there pour upon them a murderous fire. Had the men's eagerness to get at the breeds not been checked, the ravine would have become a veritable valley of death. As it was, the men recklessly exposed themselves, and for a time to little purpose, as the natural advantages of the enemy's position, in the hell-pits they had dug for themselves, effectually shielded them from danger. The brunt of the fighting fell disastrously upon the gallant Ninetieth. From the outset they were incessantly exposed to the concealed fire of the dusky foe. But they stubbornly held their ground; and, taking advantage of whatever cover was available, they spiritedly gave back the fierce fire of lead. Round the mouth of the ravine, where the enemy had their stronghold, a terrific fusilade was kept up throughout the morning; while a desperate conflict was raging in the bluffs on either side. Here the black coat of many a prostrate Winnipeg rifleman showed how fierce had been the strife.

The morning's death-roll and other casualties of this gallant regiment, which was to bear so noble a part in the now opened campaign, attest the heroism which actuated its ranks. Two of its officers, viz., Capt. Wm. Clark, and Lieut. Charles Swinford, were to fall, the latter subsequently dying of his wounds. Among the first of the rank and file of the 90th to give up their life on the battle-field, were Privates Ferguson and Hutchinson, of "A" Co., who fell in the opening charge, and were both shot in the heart. The death missive was also to come to Privates Wheeler, of "B" Co., and Ennis of "D" Co. The 90th, during the day, had fourteen wounded, viz., Corps. Thacker, Lethbridge, and Code; Ptes. Kemp, Matthews, Lowell, Swan, Jarvis, Johnson, Chambers, Canniff, Bowden, Hislop, and Blackwood —a glorious list of casualties!

The death-roll of "A" Battery comprised three gunners— Demanolly, Harrison, and Cook; with the following wounded: Sergt.-Major McWhinney; Gunners Moiseau, Ainsworth, Asselin, Imrie, Woodman, Langarell, Ouillette, and McGrath; Bombardier Taylor; and Drivers Turner and Wilson—a proud total of three dead and twelve wounded! "C" Company, Infantry

School, lost one killed—Pte. A. G. Watson—and six wounded. The names of the latter are as follows: Col.-Sergt. R. Cummings; Ptes. H. Jones, R. Jones, E. Harris, R. H. Dunn, and E. Macdonald. Capt. Gardner, of Boulton's Mounted Scouts, was also wounded; and the troop suffered the following losses: Sergt. Stewart, and Troopers Langford, Perrine, King, Bruce, Thompson, and D'Arcy Baker—all wounded.

But the engagement was not yet over. Though hemmed in on three sides, the half-breeds stubbornly kept to their rifle-pits, from which the hurtling shell and enfilading musketry fire failed to dislodge them. So closely were they now beset that the encouraging voice of Dumont, their half-breed leader, could be distinctly heard. It was now past noon, and the state of affairs, if not critical for the Métis marksmen, was decidedly unpleasant. More than one rifle-pit had become the grave of a half-breed; while, in the bush, many of his dusky kin had gone to the happy hunting-grounds of the race. But the rebel commander kept his head, and had well gauged the strength of the force opposed to him. His only fear was of the crossing of Montizambert's force from the west side of the Saskatchewan, and cutting off his retreat. But this force, though it had been signalled early in the day, had not yet joined Middleton.

Meanwhile death was reaping his harvest; and, outside the crowded hospital tents, the pitiless rain beat on the fevered faces of the wounded.

> " The fight rolls on, Death stalks around,
> And blood-red gashes drench the ground."

Middleton's force continued to close in upon the enemy. The guns took up new positions; and the battery supports, and the thin red line of "C" Company, under Major Smith, pressed on to secure possession of a knoll some distance up the ravine. On the left, a company of the 90th, under Capt. Forrest, an

Lt. Hugh J. Macdonald, the gallant son of the Dominion Premier, made a dash across an open stretch of prairie, and gained the top of the gully. In other parts of the battle-field, Capt. Peters of the Battery, Major Boulton, of the Mounted Scouts, and Majors Buchan and Boswell, of the Rifles, were pluckily contesting points of advantage with the enemy. The latter, now hard pressed, sullenly withdrew, but still showing too bold a front for defeat. The gunners, getting the position of the rebel farm-houses, now hotly played upon them, and drove the half-breeds further up the ravine. The houses were then set on fire, and the guns brought to bear on the Indian ponies, that were coralled in the woods. In ten minutes the equine Bartholomew was complete.

At last our Canadian Blucher came up. Montizambert's Column, with difficulty had got punted across the river, and Capt. Mason's Co. of the Grenadiers was the first to appear on the scene. It was quickly followed by the remainder of the battalion, by the Winnipeg Artillery, and by Lord Melgund and the Scouts. The fresh troops were sent to relieve the fatigued advanced skirmishers, but the guns were ordered to the rear. From now till dusk the firing was weak and desultory, the half-breeds having melted away from the ground. Presently the bugles sounded the recall, and the rain damped the waning ardour of the troops. The fight was over, though the day can hardly be said to be won. It brought no signal victory.

What were the decisive results of the day's engagement could at least be counted under the white sheets, and their country's flag, by the hospital door. Of the 350 men actively engaged in the heat of the strife, close upon 50 were *hors-de-combat*. How many more hearts were to be pierced, when news of the day's conflict reached the friends of the fallen, one shuddered to think. To one man in the field the cessation of the fight must have brought infinite relief. Old campaigner as he was, the strain of the day's anxieties on General Middleton must have been intense. Through the varying fortunes of the day he bore himself valorously, and personally directed each movement, no matter into what danger it led him. Frequently, while riding along the front lines, giving orders and encouraging the men, he exposed himself recklessly. Early in the fight a bullet pierced his cap. Equally heroic was the bearing of his two aides-de-camp, Capts. Wise and Doucet, who were both wounded. The former had his horse shot under him; as had Major Buchan, Field Adjutant, and Major Boulton, in command of the Mounted Scouts. Cool and soldier-like was also the conduct, during the day, of Col. Houghton, chief of the General's field staff, and of Capt. Haig, R. E., acting Q.M.G.

To be "mentioned in the despatches" is an honor that fell to the lot of a young hero in the fight, which, before closing this chapter, we must not omit to chronicle. Says General Middleton:

"I cannot conclude this report without mentioning a little bugler of the 90th regiment, named Wm. Buchanan, who made himself particularly useful in carrying ammunition to the right front when the fire was very hot. This he did with peculiar nonchalence, walking calmly about crying, 'Now, boys, who's for cartridge?'"

The number of rebels known to be present at Fish Creek, under Gabriel Dumont, was 280 men. They had eleven killed or died of wounds, and eighteen wounded,

CHAPTER XXIII.

THE CRISIS AT HAND.

THE battle of Fish Creek was the prologue to a three days' hot fighting before Batoche, which was happily to end the insurrection and dash the hopes of the madman, Riel, and his lawless half-breeds. For a fortnight after the affair of the 24th of April, there hung over the region a heavy electrical atmosphere of pent-up war feeling and military preparation, soon to discharge itself on the wooded ravines that encompass Batoche. With even greater activity and excitement did the breeds prepare to make a determined stand round the homesteads their sedition had emperilled; and Nature helped them in their work. Her hand, in seeming kindness, had raised a rampart of woods around her wild and wayward children, and locked them in the fastnesses of Mother Earth. From Dumont's Crossing to Batoche, the whole country is a mass of wooded ravines, often fifty feet deep, and the valleys are covered with underbrush. In these ravines tribal instinct and tactical skill planned a defence well calculated to keep the loyal troops at bay. "The half-breeds," it has been remarked, "adopt the Indian mode of fighting, but they graft upon it something they have learned from the white man. A guerilla warfare, carried on in ambush, is distinctly Indian; but the addition of artificial rifle-pits is the utilisation of a lesson which the half-breeds have learned from the whites." Nor was courage wanting when the time came to defend these rifle-pits. Still less was courage wanting to attack them. "If these brave lads of mine were only regulars!" General Middleton is reported to have said, he would not have restrained the eager desire of the volunteers to charge the pits and drive out the enemy. But as this would have involved too great a sacrifice of life, he acted discreetly in checking the valour of his men.

What valour had been permitted to display itself on the battlefield, the high Cairn and rustic Cross erected on the banks of the Saskatchewan, where the heroes of Fish Creek lie buried, will ever remain a witness. On the day following the battle, the last sad rites were paid to the fallen volunteers, in the presence of the whole camp. When their sorrowing comrades consigned the dead to their last resting-place, General Middleton read the burial service, and the firing-party paid their remains the honours of a parting salute.

"Not in the quiet churchyard, near those who loved them best;
  But by the wild Saskatchewan they laid them to their rest.
A simple soldier's funeral in that lonely spot was theirs,
  Made consecrate and holy by a nation's tears and prayers.
A few short prayers were uttered, straight from their comrades' hearts—
  A volley fired in honor, and the company departs.
Their requiem—the music of the river's surging tide;
  Their funeral wreaths—the wild flowers that grow on every side;
Their monument—undying praise from each Canadian heart,
  That hears how, for their country's sake, they nobly bore their part.
So, resting in their peaceful graves, beneath the prairie sod,
  Enshrined in golden memories, we yield them up to God."*

---

* E. C. P. in the Toronto *Mail* of May 6th.

Before dismissing the troops from the solemn scenes of which they had been witness, the General addressed them in a few brief words characteristic of the soldier: "Well, men," said he, "your comrades have found a soldier's grave; let us hope we shall have an opportunity to avenge their deaths!" In the determination to seek that opportunity all ranks prepared for the coming march to Batoche.

For some days the many wounded received the tender consideration of the General-in-Command, and the skilful tendance of the surgeons and volunteer nurses on the field. Nor were they forgotten at home. The results of the engagement touched the nation's heart with a thrill of pity. Throughout Ontario, relief committees, organised chiefly by the gentler sex, went to work with a will, and poured creature comforts and the thoughtful needs of the hospital wards, in rich abundance, into the North-West. One of the first and most substantial of these services was rendered by the "Toronto Volunteers' Supply Fund," in kind charge of Mrs. Edward Blake, by whose instrumentality, and that of other willing workers, some car loads of most acceptable necessaries were forwarded in the care of Lieut. Hume Blake. In other towns of importance, in and out of the Province, similar relief associations were organised for the benefit of those who had stepped into the breach in the hour of the country's peril. Military chaplains were also sent forward. Toronto liberality was further to show itself in the organisation and despatch to the front of the Red Cross Ambulance Corps, the energetic mover in which was Mr. Edmund Wragge,* local manager of the Grand Trunk R.R., assisted by Dr. Ellis and Mr. A. H. Smith.

---

*This Red Cross Ambulance Corps, which left Toronto for the North-West on the 16th of April, consisted of seven Surgical dressers, under the direction of Dr. Nattress. The following are the names of those selected for the duty: D. O. R.

Pity for Canada's wounded sons also stirred the tender heart of a lady near the throne of her for whom they had bled. With characteristic thoughtfulness the Princess Louise initiated a movement in London for sending to the North-West ambulance appliances and the cordial of other comforts for the wounded. This graceful act, we can well imagine, brought the poet's couplet to the mind and tongue of many a tossed sufferer, as he partook of the cheer which royal hands had forwarded—

"When pain and anguish wring the brow
A ministering angel thou!"

Nor were Winnipeg's gallant sons forgotten. At such a time when pride in the heroic deeds of the dark-coated 90th well nigh extinguished sorrow for those whom death had called out from the ranks, the suffering wounded were forwarded many tokens of kindness and remembrance. From other sections of the Prairie Province also came the healing balm of kind offerings, and a common pride in the achievements of the regiment. One of the latest battalions to be enrolled in the Canadian Militia, the Winnipeg Rifles had won a name for themselves for well-approved valour. When the regiment took the field, its first Colonel, Wm. Nassau Kennedy, lay dying in a London hospital on his way home from the Soudan, whither he had gone at General Wolseley's request in charge of the Canadian Voyageurs on the Nile. The death of this estimable officer, in Britain's service in the Far East, appeared specially to consecrate his late regiment to a high and honourable mission in the campaign just opened; and his gallant spirit seemed to pervade all ranks.*

Jones, M.D., Hospital Surgeon; O. Weed, B.A., W. Mustard, B.A., and R. J Wood, of Toronto, J. F. Brown, B.A., Guelph, D. Patullo, M.B., Brampton, and J. R. Robertson, of London, Eng.

*The following are the staff and company officers of the 90th Batt., "Winnipeg Rifles," Lt.-Col. Alfred Mackeand in command. Majors Chas. M. Boswell,

By this time May had come, though the *Northcote* hadn't. She was still aground in the river, though now daily expected. Humboldt had been garrisoned by the Governor-General's Body Guard; and the York and Simcoe Battalion, commanded by Lt.-Col. W. E. O'Brien, had reached Qu'Appelle. This fine regiment was composed of part of the York Rangers and the Simcoe Foresters. The York Companies were drawn from Parkdale, Seaton Village, Yorkville, Riverside, Newmarket, and Aurora: the Simcoe Companies from Barrie, Bond Head, Collingwood, Penetanguishene, Orillia, Alliston, Tay, Vespra, and Cookstown.* Though expecting to be ordered to join the column under Middleton, this battalion was meanwhile guarding the base of supplies on the line of railway. The Body Guard occupied an important point, overlooking the main approach to the rebel positions, and in the line of communication north, south, and west. Under Lieut.-Col. G. T. Denison, its able and experienced commanding officer, the Body Guard did important scouting and outpost duty; and, by an elaborate series of entrenchments, had converted the simple telegraph

---

and Lawrence Buchan; Paymaster A. H. Witcher; Quartermaster H. Swinford; Surgeon Dr. Geo. T. Orton; Assist.-Surgeon Dr .J. W. Whiteford. Capts. C. F. Forrest, H. N. Ruttan, W. A. Wilkes, C. A. Worsnop, R. G. Whitla, Wm. Clark; Lts. Hugh J. Macdonald, G. W. Stewart, H. Bolster, Zach. Woods, E. G. Piche, F. L. Campbell; 2nd Lts. R. L. Sewell, J. G. Healy, C. Swinford, H. M. Arnold, A. E. McPhillips, and R. C. Laurie.

*The following are the staff and company officers of the York and Simcoe Batt., under the command of Lt.-Col. W. E. O'Brien, M.P., (35th Batt.), of Barrie. Majors, Lt.-Col. R. Tyrwhitt, 35th Batt , and Lt.-Col. A. Wyndham, 12th Batt; Adjt. Major Jas. Ward, 35th ; Paymaster, Capt. Wm. Hunter, late 35th; Quartermaster, Lt. Lionel F. Smith ; Supply Officer, Lt. G. H. Bate, G.G.F.G. ; Surgeon, Dr. John L. G. McCarthy, 35th Batt. Captains (35th), Majors W. J. Graham, and Peter Burnet, Allison Leadly, R. G. Campbell; (12th), Jno. T. Thompson, Geo. H. C. Brooke, and Joseph F. Smith. Lieuts. (35th), Capt. John Landrigan, Thos. H. Drinkwater, Chas. S. F. Spry ; (12th), Lts. Geo. Vennell, John T. Symons, Thos. Booth, and John K. Leslie G.G.F.G., Lt. S. L. Shannon. 2nd Lieuts. (35th) Thos. H. Banting, K. L. Burnet, I. T. Lennon, and R. D. Ramsay ; (12th) 2nd Lts. Wm. J. Fleury, and John A. W. Allan.

station of Humboldt into a fortified military encampment. The labour and tedium of this work was occasionally relieved by a scamper over the prairie, to gather news of the rebel half-breeds, and watch the movements of the Indians. In this roving, free-lance work Lord Melgund had already distinguished himself, by capturing, and, with the assistance of Capt. French's scouts, bringing into camp some of Riel's "runners" with messages for one or two of the unfriendly neighbouring tribes. In this risky service, Lieut. Wm. Hamilton Merritt, with a detachment of the Body Guard, was also successful, after an exciting chase, in capturing on the plains a strong party of disaffected Sioux, of White Cap's band. These Indians had sought an asylum in Canada, after participating in the Minnesota massacre in the year 1862, and had been given a reserve on the South Saskatchewan. Ungratefully violating the country's hospitality, by various acts of lawlessness and sedition, a roving band of them fell in with the picturesque Nemesis of a gallantly led troop of the Body Guard, and were taken prisoners.

At last the *Northcote* arrived, having crutched rather than steamed her way down the river. With her came the needed supplies, the Midlanders, and the Gatling. In her wake also came some ten barges, built at Swift Current, that had been despatched to the front, to facilitate, if need be, the crossing of the river, and to be of assistance in operating against the enemy. The water was now rising in the Saskatchewan, and the supply difficulty was solved. It remained now but for General Middleton to relieve himself of the wounded, and to move his lines closer to Batoche. A number of ambulances were extemporised, by stretching buffalo skins tightly across the waggons, on which the wounded were carefully placed, and thus conveyed to Saskatoon. Here the hospital corps, under Surgeon-Genl. Roddick, and Dr. Douglas, V.C., an old army surgeon, decorated for personal bravery in the field, were ready to extend to them the skill of their professional services.

Finally, on the 7th of May, the lagging camp was struck at Fish Creek, and a forward movement made to Gabriel Dumont's Crossing, about eight miles south of Batoche. The advance was unopposed. There now joined the General's personal staff Lieut. Frere, a son of Sir Bartle Frere, who assumed the duties of one of the wounded aides-de-camp. A strong reconnaissance was now made as far north as the Crossing, through the beautiful hilly country of the French half-breeds. "What fools these mortals be!" is the borrowed phrase made use of by a press correspondent with the column, as the troops marched by the deserted homes and neglected farms of this fertile valley. For the sham glory of cutting a figure in a wicked rebellion, which was sure to bring ruin to the individual Métis, and desolation to as fair a region as ever man owned for a home, these misguided half-breeds sacrificed every comfort and recklessly imperilled their lives. The whole district was deserted. "It is now a Great Lone Land with a vengeance," writes the correspondent we have just referred to,[*] "and yet in the bright May sunshine the grass grows green, the wild crocus and anemone dot the prairie, the trees begin to bud, and bluff and wood and lakelet combine to make as pretty a picture as painter or poet ever saw. But it is beauty without life, except that of the prairie chicken, the wild gopher, and the song birds that are greeting the sunshine." Before night the column made a detour to the eastward, away from the river and the wooded bluffs at the Crossing, so as to reach a clear site on the prairie for the evening's camp, and from which to advance on the morrow the contracting lines around Batoche.

---

[*] Mr. G. H. Ham, Special Correspondent of the Toronto *Mail.*

CHAPTER XXIV.

THE LINES BEFORE BATOCHE.

MAJOR Boulton's Mounted Scouts led the way. Then came the Grenadiers, with Capt. Caston's company as advance guard; following which was the Gatling, in charge of Lt. Howard; then the 90th Battalion; and "A" Battery, with two guns. In the centre of the advancing column was the Ammunition train, followed by the Ambulance Corps. Next came the Winnipeg Battery, with two guns; two companies of the Midland Provisional Battalion, under Col. Williams, bringing up the rear. The flanks were protected by Capt. French's Mounted Scouts. Such was the order of the unobstructed advance upon Batoche, on the morning of Saturday, the 9th of May.

The column, which had rested over night about eight miles east of the village of Batoche, paraded after a hasty breakfast at 5 A.M. on Saturday, and half an hour later was under way. The total strength of the column was a trifle over 900 men. Since it first took the field it had to some extent been depleted by the casualties at Fish Creek; but these had been made good by the arrival of two companies of the Midland Battalion. To support the column, and divert the attention of the rebels, it was arranged that the *Northcote*, flanked by two barges, and having on Board " C " Company, School of Infantry, in command of Major Smith, should go down the stream to Batoche, and on a preconcerted signal engage the enemy from the river. The difficulties of this undertaking, and the miscarriage of the arrangements, we shall subsequently relate.

Meanwhile Middleton's force reached the deserted reservation of the band of Teten Sioux, under One Arrow, and presently came in view of the Parish Church of St. Laurent, and a neighbouring school, on the heights. The cross-crowned belfry tower of St. Antoine de Padone looks down, on one side, over the prairie trail to Humboldt, and on the other, on the curving line of the Saskatchewan and the sleeping plain of the village of Batoche. Nearing the outskirts of the settlement, the Scouts fell back and " A " Battery moved to the front. A well-directed shell was now fired at a house by the side of a ravine on the right, and a number of rebels were seen to scamper off to the bush. Some days previous to the approach to Batoche, the General-in-Command had issued a proclamation in French to the inhabitants of the region, requiring them to surrender to the troops or take the consequences. The proclamation the General caused to be distributed by the agency of a few Sioux prisoners, whom he released for the purpose.*

The Gatling was now ordered to the front, under an escort of Boulton's Horse. When within a hundred yards of the church and schoolhouse, and just as the gun was sighted for the latter, the door of the church opened and a priest came

---

*Translation of General Middleton's Proclamation: "Those half-breeds and Indians who have been forced to join the rebels, and also those mistaken Indians who have joined voluntarily, are informed by this that if they give up at once and return to their houses and reserves they will be protected and pardoned. The troops sent by the Government do not desire to make war against these men, but only against Riel, his council, and his principal accomplices. (Signed) Middleton."

forward and waived a white handkerchief. The General and his staff at once rode up, when four priests, five nuns, and some few loyal inhabitants of the district, who had taken refuge in the church, advanced and claimed the protection of the troops. The forlorn refugees were instantly taken care of, and appeared extremely thankful for their rescue. From the priests some information was gleaned of the strength and disposition of the rebel forces. The sad story was also gathered of what both priests and nuns had suffered by discountenancing rebellion, and in exerting themselves to keep the Métis quiet. Their lives, it was learned, had been repeatedly threatened by the half-breeds. But for the interposition of one of the rebel leaders, who insisted that the church should not be desecrated by murder, they would have fallen victims to the enmity of Riel and his reckless following.*

During the conversation with the priests, a reconnaissance had been going on, in the endeavour to find advantageous positions for shelling the rebel stronghold. The church and schoolhouse, as we have said, occupy a prominent position commanding the village and the approach to it from the south. They stand on a ridge some two hundred yards back from the river. This

---

*Here are the names, so far as can be ascertained, of the men who composed Riel's Provisional Government, with the chief rebel leaders. A few are irreconcilables from the period of Riel's first insurrection, at Red River. Gabriel Dumont, who may be styled the rebel Commander-in-chief; Andrew Nolin, Commissariat Officer; his brother Charles, said to be one of the chief instigators of the insurrection; Albert Monkman, accused of inciting the Indians to revolt, a member of the Council, and present at the fight at Duck Lake; Alex. Fisher, Receiver-General of the rebel government; W. H. J. Jackson, Riel's private secretary; Maxime Lepine, and M. Jobin, members of the Council, and A. Lomborbark, Sioux Interpreter. The following are known to have taken a prominent part in the insurrection, to be captains of companies, or guards over prisoners: Delorme, Dumais, Tourand, Gervais, Poitras, Fider, Pilon, Parentot, Dubois, Pochelot, and Vendue, In some instances, two or more of the same family, brothers, or father and son, were in revolt; and, in not a few cases, were recognised in fights, or were seen by loyal scouts, with arms in their hands.

V

ridge which, to the south of Batoche, towers in high bluffs over the river, curves away to the east at the church and the cemetery, and forms what may be termed the secondary banks of the Saskatchewan. Between this lofty ridge and the lower wooded bluffs that border the river, there is an oblong open plain, the site of the village. Through the middle of this plain winds the trail, from the south and east, to the river crossing. On the plain are a few stores, Riel's Council Chamber, Batoche's house, and several half-breed dwellings. Close by the river, at the upper end of the plain, and concealed by a skirting of woods, was the half-breed and Indian camp. On the west side, at the foot of its sloping wooded banks, were also a few houses and the gaudily coloured tepees of Indians. Grazing on the slopes were some cattle and Indian ponies.

In the bluffs surrounding Batoche, which nestles prettily in an elliptical basin, the rebels had entrenched themselves in rifle-pits. Wooded ravines break the continuity of the surrounding ridge, and from the east afford glimpses of the slumbering village. But the Gatling disturbs its quiet, though as yet the half-breeds are nowhere to be seen. Suddenly, while the staff on the ridge was watching the effect of a shell from the battery, a volley of musketry and the whoop of Indians and half-breeds came from the bush immediately in front of the group. Fortunately, the bullets went high, and no one was hit, though the suddenness of the fire almost caused a panic. The Battery guns were speedily withdrawn, though not before there was danger of their capture. But Captain Peters here galloped up with the Gatling, and Lt. Howard, at great personal risk, rushed it to the front, and, turning the cylinder, discharged a torrent of lead.

Simultaneously with the advance of the Gatling two companies of the Grenadiers were ordered to take up a position in rear of the schoolhouse, and to the right of the spot where the action began. Detecting this movement, the rebels made an effort to turn the left flank of the 10th, by concentrating a heavy fire from the bush, overlooking the high banks of the river, on the advanced line. But as the enemy seemed here to be armed only with shot-guns, their fire fell short. The skirmishing line was now strengthened by the dismounted men of "A" Battery, and by the sharpshooters, armed with Martini-Henry rifles, of the 90th. Both of these corps took up a position on the crest of the rising ground near the church, and for a time kept up a smart fire on the ravine in front and on the bush on the hill. The main body of the 90th was deployed in rear, and held in readiness to move in any direction. Presently part of it received orders to support the right centre, upon which a hot fire now poured from a hitherto concealed row of rifle-pits on broken ground to the right. The remainder advanced to support the left centre and left. The Winnipeg Battery took up a position on the right; and, on the extreme right, Boulton's Horse looked after that flank.

"A" Battery men, supported by French's Scouts, now made a movement towards the river, rounding the edge of the ridge on which they had previously been stationed, and into a coulee that winds down to the plain. Here they encountered the enemy in strong force, and were compelled to fall back, with the loss of one killed and two or three wounded. The rebel fire now became general, and the troops began to realise the extent and ramifications of the rifle-pits. A more formidable lurking-place of danger could hardly be conceived; but Fish Creek had taught the troops to be wary of these death-traps, and the General was careful to caution the men against unduly exposing themselves. But there was more danger than from the enemy's fire; for, at this time, the underbrush along the skirmishing line was ignited by the flame of fire which was maintained on the rebels, and dense clouds of smoke rolled along the ground. The next hour was an uncomfortable one for the troops; but they never flinched from their positions, until ordered to fall back a little, when the fighting was renewed with vigour.

The steady play of the guns, which had continued with little interruption since the morning, and in which the Winnipeg Battery had taken an active share, had by 2 P.M., in great measure, subdued the enemy's fire. Taking advantage of a lull in the fighting, a company of the Midland Battalion was sent up the ravine, with a stretcher in charge of Dr. Codd, of Winnipeg, to recover the body of Gunner Phillips, of "A" Battery, who had fallen early in the day. The Midlanders met with a hot fire in the coulee, but were successful in bringing out the body, without loss to themselves. The poor Gunner's remains were carried to the rear, and in the evening were buried by his comrades of the Battery, Chaplain Gordon, of Winnipeg, officiating. It is related that while the reverend gentleman was reading a portion of Scripture at the grave, his words were punctuated by a volley from the enemy's sharpshooters, while "the staccato crashes of the Gatling broke in on his voice, but did not drown it."

> ' Hark! the muffled drum sounds the last march of the brave,
> The soldier retreats to his quarters—the grave.
> Under Death, whom he owns his commander-in-chief,
> No more he'll turn out with the ready relief;
> Yet spite of Death's terrors or hostile alarms
> When he hears the last bugle he'll stand to his arms."

From now on till evening the firing languished, and, as little was to be gained by exposing the men to the fire of concealed marksmen in well-sheltered rifle-pits, the bulk of the fighting line was withdrawn. Arrangements were now made for the night's camp, and for protection from attack. Early in the afternoon some tents and waggons had been ordered up from the site of Friday night's camp, and the latter were formed into a zareba, outside of which the troops were busy throwing up entrenchments. A field hospital and the headquarters of the Commissariat were established; and the wounded were tended and the men had supper. While the men were at their meal, the brave Howard came into camp with the Gatling, and received the cheers of the men for his heroic act in saving the guns from capture in the morning.* This brave officer, to whom Canada owes much for his services on the field, in charge of the Gatling gun, was for five years in the United States Cavalry, and latterly was in command of the machine gun platoon of the Connecticut National Guard. At the time Dr. Gatling acquired his services, Lt. Howard was engaged in the Winchester arms factory, and he received leave of absence to accompany the guns to the North-West. He is well acquainted with projectiles and arms of precision, and, by his bearing under fire, was even reckless in practically exemplifying their use. Had the rebels had a Gatling or two, with a hero like Howard in command, it would have gone ill with the North-West Expeditionary Force.

---

*" The Gatling gun weighs about 1,500 lbs., and is precisely of the same design as the ordinary cannon. There are ten chambers that revolve in the barrel proper, and each chamber has an independent lock. The main barrel is eight inches in diameter. The size of cartridge used is that of the ordinary 45 government rifle calibre. Each feed drum contains 240 rounds. The firing is done by operating a crank; the cartridge is exploded by a hammer which works with such great rapidity that 120 cartridges are fired in a minute. The movement of the gun can be so adjusted as to make it either stationary or oscillating, so that the gun practice can become either scattered or centrifugal in its execution. At 700 yards the Gatling gun has been known to hit a 12×15 ft. target 396 times out of 400 shots. At 1,200 yards 413 out of 600 shots have struck a 9+25 ft. target. To show the rapidity with which the gun can be worked, it might be explained that the time occupied in coming into action front from trot and firing is 10 seconds; rear limber, mount and off, 13 seconds."

On the Sunday morning the camp was in motion at sunrise, the troops having bivouacked on the ground with their arms beside them. The column of attack was formed under the eye of the General. The Grenadiers marched out to occupy the centre and the left, while the Midlanders took up a position on the right. Beyond occupying the shelter trenches, and keeping up a desultory fire on the enemy, which was replied to without vim, little was done all day. In the afternoon a feint was made to draw the rebels from their rifle-pits, but only a few of the Métis marksmen left their hiding-places, and the skirmishing line of the 90th drove them quickly back. The only other incident of note was the shelling of the cemetery, by the Winnipeg Battery, where a number of half-breeds for a time had massed. The Mounted Scouts, under Capt. French, manœuvred for a while to the north-east of Batoche, and succeeded in capturing a number of Indian ponies. On their return to camp, the Scouts were joined by Dennis's Horse, a company of Mounted Surveyors that had galloped in from the south. Presently, the advanced lines were withdrawn, and night again fell upon the camp.

Monday was, in part, a repetition of the previous day, save that the 90th moved to the front, while the Grenadiers stayed in camp. The enemy was again found safely ensconced in his rifle-pits. In the seclusion of their position, the half-breeds were able to bid defiance to both musketry and gun fire; while the shells but further protected them by covering the pits with the *debris* of shattered timber. A strong reconnaissance was undertaken by the General north-eastward, accompanied by Boulton's and Dennis's Horse, and the Gatling. Here they found Batoche defended by a Sebastopol of rifle-pits. These were strategically located so as to offer opposition from whatever quarter the village was approached. We quote from G. H. H., the *Mail* correspondent, the following description of these rebel trenches:

"As a prominent military man remarked, an engineer could profitably take lessons from these untaught Métis of the west. The rebel position (it could not be called lines, for the pits run in all places and in all directions), demonstrated that the plans of defence were admirably conceived and excellently executed. It seemed as if they expected the troops to come along the river bank, and had prepared a ravine, a short distance up stream, to give us a warm reception. Weeks must have been spent in fortifying the place, since every conceivable point of vantage for a radius of a couple of miles was utilised. All their pits were deep, with narrow entrances, which widened at the bottom, thus giving perfect protection. Notched logs, the notches turned downwards, formed a parapet, earth being piled on top, and the notches cleared for loop holes. Lines of sight for the rebel marksmen were cleared in the brush. There were trenches of communication between the pits, arranged *en echelon* on the main road from Humboldt, but fortunately we did not come that way. Not alone in the field had the enemy prepared for a determined stand, but the houses in the village were also ready for an emergency. Even the tents in which some of the rebel warriors lived were not without protection. Almost every one had a rifle-pit, and under the cart or waggon—for some of these people have discarded the old-fashioned Red River cart—a parapeted hole was dug for defence. If they had prepared for us at Fish Creek, they had a thousand times more so at Batoche's. It was their last ditch. No trail, no pathway, however insignificant, was left unguarded; no ravine, no gully that was not made a point of attack or defence."

Nothing came of the reconnaissance save to bring home to the General's mind the fact that the defences of the revolted half-breeds could be carried only at the point of the bayonet. This was what the troops wanted. The harassing desultory fire, one day after another, all chafed under; and the return to camp each evening, with nothing accomplished, made the men sullen. Middleton's economy of the lives of the troops, however kindly intentioned, only fretted his gallant force. As the day's wounded were brought into camp, the limit of the men's forbearance seemed to be reached. To-morrow, despite orders, they would do something.

The three days' casualties were three killed and some sixteen or more wounded. Besides Phillips, the Batteryman, who was killed on Saturday, another and a young hero was to fall the same day. This was Pte. Thomas Moor, of C. Co. Grenadiers, who won the goal of a soldier's ambition—an honoured death on the battlefield. Of the same regiment Capt. Mason received a severe wound in the thigh, while Staff-sergt. Mitchell was struck by a bullet in the forehead. Of the gallant 10th, Corp. Foley, and Ptes. Cantwell, Martin, Brisbane, Stead and Scovell were also wounded. The 90th had one killed, Pte. R. R. Hardisty, a comrade whom the regiment sincerely mourned. The 90th wounded included Corp. Kemp, and Ptes. Baron and Erickson. "A" Battery had four wounded: Driver Stout and Gunners Fairbanks, Charpentier, and Cowley. Of French's Scouts, Troopers Allen and Cook were wounded. The latter was gallantly snatched from the hands of death by his intrepid commander.

CHAPTER XXV.

CHARGING THE RIFLE-PITS—ROUT OF THE REBELS.

"By heavens ! 'tis day indeed begun !
Yet once more gaze upon the sun,
For many here, now armed for fight,
Shall never see that sun at night.
In many a heart the blood beats high,
Flushed with the hope of victory ;
And ere the bell the hour repeat,
Shall many a heart have ceased to beat."

TUESDAY, the 12th inst., was the fourth day of the investiture of Batoche. In the three days desultory fighting the temper of the troops had been sorely tried. There had been no appreciable blow struck at the enemy; and at long range he was not even assailable. The force, in truth, was too weak for aggressive measures, unless boldly conceived and recklessly acted on. Moreover, both Colonel Irvine and the steamer had failed to co-operate ; and General Middleton, no doubt wisely enough, thought it wouldn't do to be precipitate. With the systematic deliberation which characterised all his movements, he was ready to give effect to his own plans ; but he was not willing to risk the troops in an unequal encounter. He acted, and acted rightly, on the good old military maxim: "Conquest is twice achieved when the achiever brings home full numbers."

But, if we may say it without offence, there was another factor on the field besides the General; and the kindly old warrior knew it. There was the ardour of youth, and, when the fight began, the unrestrainable impulse, with each gallant soul, to do a deed of daring. There was, moreover, in everyman's breast, a conscious realisation that he had right on his side, than which there is no higher impelling motive to fidelity and heroism. We may not be justified in saying that, on the rebel side, there was not a similar consciousness of right; for treason, like party rancour, sometimes puts on the cloak of patriotism and complacently felicitates itself on its well-doing. But if there was right on their side, by the close of the day there were many to deny it. Defeat, we know, brings weakness; but defeat in an honourable cause does not usually manifest itself in whining excuses for fighting, or exculpate itself on the plea that its actors, against their wishes, were forced to take up arms. But we are anticipating events.

Moving out with the mounted troops, the Gatling, and a detachment of "A" Battery, with one gun, General Middleton took up a position with his staff on the plateau, on the extreme right front, overlooking Batoche. Here Capt. Drury opened the memorable day's fight with a shower of shrapnel directed at the village and at the rifle-pits in the brush immediately in front. The fire was instantly returned; and Lieut. Kippin, of Dennis's Surveyor Scouts, was the first to fall, mortally wounded. The infantry, led by Colonel Van Straubenzie, meanwhile took up their daily position in the shelter trenches in the advanced lines along the front. The Grenadiers held the centre, the 90th the right, and the Midlanders the left. For a time the morning salute from the trenches occupied by the troops, was hot and vigorous—a premonitory symptom of the men's impatience. While coolly superintending these movements, and planning how best to strike the enemy a decided blow that day, the General observed a white flag flying at a point in the rebel lines. Presently, two prisoners on parole advanced with the flag, and a note for the Major-General. The note read as follows:

"SIR : If you massacre our families we will begin by killing Indian Agent Lash and other prisoners.
LOUIS DAVID RIEL."

To this first confession of weakness, on the part of the rebel chief, the General made the following response:

"MR. RIEL: I am most anxious to avoid killing women and children, and have always been so. Put women and children in some place and I won't harm them. I trust to your honour not to put men with them.
FRED. MIDDLETON,
Major-General Commanding."

Before the prisoner, Astley, had well got back to the rebel lines, the half-breeds in the pits took up the firing, which was hotly returned from our trenches. The morning passed in such manœuvring, and the General and his staff returned to camp. After the men had partaken of a hasty dinner in the trenches, Colonel Straubenzie informed the regimental commanders that the General wished to press the fighting, and to relax no discreet effort in pressing forward.

The beginning of the end now drew near. By this time Colonel Williams had extended the Midlanders to the extreme left of the lines and advanced to a position overlooking the river. Grasett and the Grenadiers now cleared the enemy from the high ground near the Church; while McKeand and the 90th, running a gauntlet of fire, pressed forward their right. The beleaguered line, on the extreme right, was contracting under the fire of Boulton's and Dennis's troopers, who had dismounted and were pressing the enemy hard on his flank. The General, who had meantime ridden forward to the church, now gave the order for a reconnaissance in force. Instantly, the whole line made a forward movement, and it was soon seen that the men were about to pass from the control of command. Already the Midland Battalion had taken the bit in their mouth. Pressing along the river bank, with unbending courage, and with a contagious cheer, they drove the half-breeds from the rifle-pits back to the cemetery. From the cemetery the Midlanders entered a small ravine, that wound round its base, and poured in on the rifle-pits a hot enfilading fire. Grasett, meanwhile, had swung round his right, and gained cover for his Grenadiers on new ground over the ridge. The Grenadier left, led by Straubenzie, also crossed the ridge and joined the Midlanders, bayoneting the flying breeds as they advanced.

The attack on the whole line being now fully developed, the rebels, who seemed to be much demoralised, and some say under the influence of a superstition, abandoned their fastnesses and fled. At this juncture, another note from Riel found its way to the General. This was its purport:

"GENERAL : Your prompt answer to my note shows that I was right in mentioning to you the cause of humanity. We will gather our families in one place, and as soon as this is done we will let you know.

" (Signed), LOUIS DAVID RIEL."

On the envelope was written the following:

"I do not like war, and if you do not retreat, and refuse an interview, the question remains the same concerning the prisoners."

The practical reply Riel got to his note was the ringing cheer of the victorious volunteers, and their hot dash into the key of the position. The formal reply was, that " the troops would cease firing when the enemy did, and not before." But there was work yet to be done. The half-breeds and Indians who held the inner defences, seeing the day lost, for a time fought with the courage of despair. But they could not withstand the bayonet; while the Gatling and the nine-pounder, catching the enemy now in the ravines, mowed them down with the iron hail. Still more closely did our long line of skirmishers converge upon the now doomed rebels. But there were ridges yet to get over, and gullies to cross; and many a young life fell out by the way—the stretcher and ambulance being in frequent requisition. This was the crisis of the day.

The din now became furious; for both the Quebec and the Winnipeg Batteries were plying their thunder, and there was the crash of the Gatling and the incessant fusilade of Snider, Martini, and Winchester. On the right, the 90th were having it hot; though they were gallantly supported by the batterymen and by Boulton's troopers. At the head of the latter, impetuously leading in the assault, fell Capt. E. T. Brown

"And round him gathers still the strife,
And death in every form is rife."

Again was the moment critical. The right skirmishing line had here to charge a series of rifle-pits, skilfully placed *en echelon*, to guard the trail from the East. But half an hour sufficed to clear them, and to drive their dark-skinned occupants back on the village. Had the enemy not been dazed at the unexpected turn of events, at one or other of the many formidable lines of defence they might have successfully stemmed the advance. But baffled in one quarter, the troops, now fairly furious, would have overcome in another; for nothing could withstand the headlong rush of the men.

At the southern end of the line, on went the Midlanders, unflinchingly led by their gallant Colonel and Major Hughes, and closely followed by Capt. French and his Scouts. On, too, went Grasett and his Grenadiers; but, alas! not all of them, for Death met the brave Lieut. Fitch in the moment of victory; while Major Dawson and Adjutant Manley fell wounded. Hardisty and Fraser, of the Winnipeg Rifles, were also summoned from the field. Stubbornly charging the centre, on, too, came McKeand, with Buchan, Boswell, and Ruttan, of the 90th, until the plain was reached, when house after house was carried—

"Then grim Death grew sated, and the field was won!"

Among the first to reach the village were two gallant officers who, now, alas! are both beyond earthly honour. One of these was Capt. French, who was the first to dash into Batoche's house, in quest of Riel's prisoners. Reckless of life, he rushed up a flight of stairs in the building, and, passing by an open window, received a bullet in his breast. Pressing on after him were some volunteers, into the arms of one of whom he fell, exclaiming: "Don't forget, boys, that I led you here!" Close behind him was Colonel Williams, with Capts. Young and Dennis. The former, entering a neighbouring house, wrenched the fastenings from a trap door, and there found and released the white captives. Thenceforward all was over.

The scene which ensued in the village baffles description. Over the ploughed field and the nearer plain came the rush of red coat and rifleman, and before them the flying Métis and Indians. Up, too, dashed the Gatling, and the Winnipeg ninepounder; while, in a heterogeneous mass, mixed Batteryman, Scout, Infantryman, and Trooper. To add to the medley, from every hole and corner trooped half-breed women and children while, limping along, came wounded rebel and painted savage. To complete the picture, up rode Col. Montizambert, gallantly leading the Quebec Battery; then the General and his staff; followed by black robe, nun, and surgeon.

At this stage of the exciting day's events, the whistle of the *Northcote,* with her consort the *Marquis,* was heard in the river. The latter had on board some twenty-five men of the Mounted Police. The main body of the constabulary was still shut up with Colonel Irvine at Prince Albert. The *Northcote,* with "C" Company, School of Infantry, about whose safety, and that of the sick and wounded on board, there had been much anxiety felt during the investment of Batoche, had had a perilous journey down the river. On leaving Gabriel's Crossing, on the morning of the 9th inst., rebel spies tracked the movements of the boat down to Batoche, and raked it with a continuous fire from the brush and timber that border the river. As the steamer was strongly bulwarked, few casualties occurred; and the troops, from behind their shelter, maintained a vigorous fusilade on the banks. Nearing Batoche, the craft got into the rapids, and was forced to run the gauntlet of the fire the Métis had prepared for her. At the village a storm of shot was directed against the steamer, and the ferry cable was lowered in expectation of coralling the stern-wheeler, and massacring its human freight. Fortunately, the cable did no more damage than bring down the smoke-stack, and strew the hurricane deck with the masts and spars. For nearly five miles the steamer was followed by half-breed and Indian marksmen, until spent with their fatiguing and profitless pursuit, they gave up hope of capture and returned to Batoche. The craft, in her hot chase down the river, was piloted by Captains Seager and Street, the former having a narrow escape from the enemy's fire. On board the steamer was Chief Transport officer Bedson, with Major Smith, and Lt. Scott, of the "C" Company. Lieuts. Elliott and Gibson, of the Grenadiers, were also on board; and Capt. Wise, A.D.C., and Lt. Hugh J. Macdonald, were in the saloon on the sick list. Proceeding some distance down the river for wood, the *Marquis* was met at the Hudson Bay ferry. After repairs to the *Northcote*, both steamers returned up stream with their marine guard in time to witness the capitulation of Batoche.

It is a well-worn saying, but a true one, that "next to defeat the saddest thing is victory." After the day's engagement came the drear duty of counting the cost. The casualties of the four days' fighting were eight killed and forty-five wounded.* The losses of the 10th and 90th, it will be seen, are specially heavy. In the gallant charge over the open ground both regiments suffered severely. Of the victory General Middleton wrote in the following terms to the Hon. M. Caron, Minister of Militia :—

"Have just made a general attack and carried the whole Settlement. The men behaved splendidly. The rebels are in full flight, and we are now masters of the place. Most of my force will bivouac here. * * Since my last evening's

---

* The official list of the entire number of killed and wounded before Batoche is as follows :—

KILLED :—French's Scouts, Capt. John French ; Boulton's Horse, Capt. E. T. Brown ; Dennis's Surveyors' Corps, Lt. A. W. Kippen ; 10th Grenadiers, Lt. Wm. Fitch and Pte. Thos. Moor ; "A" Battery, Wm. Phillips ; 90th Rifles, Ptes. Jas. Fraser, and Richd. Hardisty.

WOUNDED :—10th Grenadiers, Major Dawson, Capts. Mason, and Manley, Staff-Sergt. Mitchell, Corp. Foley, Ptes. Stead, Scovell, Cantwell, Martin, Quigley, Cook, Barbour, Marshall, Wilson, Brisbane, Eager, McLow, Bugler Gaughan ; 90th Rifles, Sergt-Major Watson, Sergt. Jackes, Corpls. Kemp and Gillies, Ptes. Baron, Young, Watson and Erickson ; Midland Batt., Lieuts. Helliwell and Laidlaw, Sergts. Wright, and Christie, Corp. Helliwell, Ptes. Barton, and Daley; "A" Battery, Driver Stout, Gunners Cowley, Charpentier, and Fairbanks; French's Scouts, Troopers Allan, Cook, and Gillen ; Boulton's Horse, Trooper Hay ; Dennis's Surveyors' Corps, Troopers Garden and Wheeler.

THE LATE LIEUT. FITCH,
10th Royal Grenadiers.

despatch I have ascertained some particulars of our victory, which was most complete. I have myself counted twelve half-breeds on the field, and we have four wounded besides in the hospital, and two Sioux. As far as I can learn, Riel and Dumont left as soon as they saw us getting well in. The extraordinary skill displayed in making rifle-pits at the proper points, and the number of them, are very remarkable ; and had we advanced rashly, I believe we might have been destroyed. After reconnoitring, I forced on my left, which was the key of the position, and then advanced the whole line with a cheer and a dash worthy of the soldiers of any army.

"The effect was remarkable. The enemy in front of our left was forced back from pit to pit, and those in the strongest pit, facing east, found themselves turned and our men behind them. Then commenced a *sauve qui peut.* * * The conduct of the troops was beyond praise, the Midland and Royal Grenadiers vieing with each other in gallantry They were well supported by the Ninetieth, and flanked by the mounted portion of the troops. The Artillery and Gatling also assisted in the attack with good effect. * * My staff gave me every assistance. The medical arrangements, under Brigade-Surgeon Orton, were, as usual, most excellent and efficiently carried out."

Thus terminated in complete success,—for a day or two afterwards Riel surrendered,—the military movement against the rebel stronghold, and with it the suppression of the half-breed insurrection. A melancholy interruption to the rejoicing of the force ensued, on learning of the death and wounding of so many brave comrades. But they had gained the summit of a soldier's ambition—to meet death, or the scars of battle, on the field of honour.

*　　　　*　　　　*　　　　*

" The great heart of the nation heaves
With pride in work her sons have done so well,
And with a smile and sigh she weaves
A wreath of bays and one of *immortelle !*

Baptized with fire, they stood the test ;
And earth, in turn, baptized with blood they shed ;
Canada triumphs, but her best
Are not all here—she mourns her gallant dead.

> A glorious death was theirs, a bright
> Unsullied ending to a cloudless day;
> They sank, as sinks the sun in sea of light;
> And in their country's memory live for aye!
>
> But flush of victory pales in pain;
> Tears fall for darkened homes where glad tones cease,
> Whose loved, that left, come not again—
> Heaven give the mourners and the nation—Peace!" *

Where the gallant bearing of all the troops engaged was so conspicuous, it would seem invidious to single out any for special mention. We may, however, be permitted to place on record in these pages an act of individual heroism which has come under our notice, and like that of Capt. French's, which occurred on the previous day, may be taken as an example of the general gallantry of the force. The incident we find recorded in the columns of the Toronto *Mail.* Here is the brief but noble story:

"There was one case of heroism which deserves mention. One of the Grenadiers was seriously wounded at Batoche, and would have bled to death had he been left any length of time. Col.-Sergt. Curzon, under a shower of rebel bullets, at once knelt down and stopped the hemorrhage and carried his wounded comrade to a place of safety, marching coolly away to the music provided by the guns of the enemy."

This act of chivalry and humanity, we trust, will not go unrewarded of the Government. Its action merits some signal token of the nation's honour. Referring to the incident, we are glad to observe that Dr. Ryerson, one of the regimental surgeons of the 10th, thus speaks of it: "Sergeant Curzon, of the 10th. Batt. Toronto, attended my Ambulance Class last winter, and learned how to stop bleeding. His knowledge enabled him to save the life of a man who was shot through the

---

* From a poem, entitled "Victory at Batoche," by Charlotte (Mrs. Edgar) Jarvis.

main artery of the arm and was fast bleeding to death. He did it under fire."

Very noticeable was the gallantry displayed during the day by Cols. Montizambert and Houghton, and by the General's Aide-de-camp, Lieut. Frere (38th Regt.). Capt. Young, of the Winnipeg Field Battery, and Capt. Peters and Lieut. Rivers, of "A" Battery, also bore themselves with conspicuous daring. The Chaplains, Revds. D. M. Gordon and C. C. Whitcombe, were also assiduous in their attentions in the field.

The rebel loss, in the four days' fighting at Batoche, is estimated at 51 killed and 173 wounded. Their total strength in the engagement, including Half-breeds and Indians, was nearly 600. Against this number, with every disadvantage of position, General Middleton had at his command a fighting strength of only 500.

CHAPTER XXVI.

AFTER BATOCHE—THE "BIG BEAR HUNT."

THE issue of the insurrection in the North-West had now greatly narrowed itself. The struggle was for a time doubtful, with a small, inexperienced, and necessarily scattered force to cope with the insurrection, and with an enemy strongly entrenched in rifle-pits, whose number and construction elicited the wonder and admiration of military critics. But at close quarters, the rebels, however courageously they fought, and with whatever skill they were generaled, were no match for the loyal troops. When the charge was made, and the bayonet came into play, neither half-breed nor Indian could withstand the assault. The valour and endurance of the troops, throughout the campaign, had been put to a severe test; but the Canadian Militia did not swerve from its duty, nor discredit its old-time honours.

The immediate task of General Middleton was now to relieve, as far as possible, the distress at Batoche, and to ensure the general pacification of the region. Measures were at once taken to reassure the well-disposed, and to remove for trial the ringleaders, and those who were still disaffected. In the former beneficent work, the troops did good and humane service. A correspondent of the Toronto *Globe* bears testimony to this fact. Says the writer:

"One of the most pleasant incidents in connection with the Batoche fight was the respect, courtesy, and kindness with which the men, flush with victory, treated the women who were found in the corral after the fight. Had they been their own mothers, sisters, or wives, they could not have shown them greater consideration."

All seemed thankful that the trouble was over, and with common consent, disavowed responsibility for the insurrection. The fighting, they affirmed, was forced upon them by the designing leaders, who, seeing the cause lost, had now left them to their fate. For Riel, no one seemed to have a good word, the women being particularly severe on his religious imposition, and on his effeminate bearing throughout the struggle. The old Latin maxim, *Mulier imperator et mulier miles,** in the present instance, did not hold good; for the fighting force of rebeldom was neither womanish nor softhearted.

But in the wicked, and, in the main, causeless outbreak, it was Dumont, and not Riel, who was the General. In the whole period of the rebellion, it is doubtful whether Riel ever fired a shot. Even now, the religious monomaniac, instead of making good his escape, in company with Dumont, his plucky Adjutant-General, was moodily haunting the neighbouring woods. Here, four days after the taking of Batoche, he was seen by some scouts and surrendered. The Jove of insurrection was found weak in the knees, and afraid of his miserable life. The taking of Riel happened in this wise. While the country was being scoured to see that no number of armed

---

* "A woman for a general and the soldiers will be women."

insurgents were still lurking in the woods, a rumour reached headquarters that the rebel chief was not far off. Three couriers, named Howrie, Armstrong, and Deale, who had diverged from the trail in an advance party of Boulton's Scouts, came upon four men at the edge of a wood. One of the four, Howrie recognised as Riel, though he was "coatless, hatless, and unarmed. His companions were young men, and they carried shotguns. The couriers rode up, and they called Riel by name, and he answered the salutation. They expressed surprise at his being there, and in reply Riel handed Armstrong a slip of paper—the note which General Middleton had sent him—informing him that if he would give himself up he would be protected, and given a fair trial. At the same time he said: 'I want to give myself up; but I fear the troops may hurt me.'"

The couriers relieved Riel's mind on this point, and undertook to smuggle him into camp without molestation. This was ultimately done, and the rebel chieftain soon stood, a prisoner, in the tent of the General. The "Exovide" was now a broken man, and his rebel flock was subjugated or scattered. The rest is soon told. Placed under a guard, the arch-traitor was sent off, with the other leading conspirators, for trial to Regina; and the General and the troops prepared to proceed to Prince Albert, thence westward, to join in the pursuit of Big Bear.

This part of our story need not long detain us; for, in the chapter on "The Frog Lake Massacre," we have already dealt with the chief events on the North Saskatchewan. The disaffected St. Laurent region once more assumed its normal quiet. Each day brought its quota of surrendering Métis, whose hearts must have smote them at sight of the want and wretchedness which their criminal folly had occasioned. Seeing their folly, most of them, it is to be said to their credit, set heartily to work to repair the evil they had done.

> "And men, taught wisdom from the past,
> In friendship joined their hands;
> Hung the gun in the hall, the spear on the wall,
> And ploughed the willing lands."

Meanwhile the distress had to be met by the humanity of the Government and the kindness of its agents and the troops. This was done with no niggard hand, and the latter set off for Prince Albert. To protect the region there was now within hail an increased force at Humboldt, for, in addition to the Body Guard, the united 12th and 35th Battalions had been called up from Qu'Appelle; while the Seventh Fusiliers* had been moved from Swift Current to Clarke's Crossing.

The 91st Winnipeg Battalion,†commanded by Lt.-Col. Thomas Scott, M. P., was guarding Qu'Appelle, while Capt. White's Auxiliary Scouts were to the south of it. The 92nd Winnipeg Light Infantry,‡ under Lt.-Col. W. Osborne Smith, C.M.G.,

---

*The following are the staff and Company officers of 7th Battalion, "Fusiliers," London, Ont. Lt.-Col. W. De Ray Williams; Majors, A. M. Smith and W. M. Gartshore; Adjut., Capt. Geo. M. Reid; Quartermaster, Capt. Jno. B. Smyth; Paymaster, Major D. MacMillan; Surgeons, Dr. J. M. Fraser, and Dr. J. S. Niven. Capts., Thos. Beattie, E. Mackenzie, F. H. Butler, T. H. Tracey, R. Dillon, and S. F. Peters; Lieuts. H. Bapty, C. B. Bazan, A. G. Chisholm, W. Greig, C. F. Cox, H. Payne, Jas. Hesketh, C. S. Jones, J. H. Pope.

† The following are the staff and Company officers of the 91st Batt. Winnipeg, Lt.-Col. Thomas Scott, M.P., in command. Majors, D. H. McMillan and Stuart Mulvey; Adjut., Capt. W. C. Copeland; Quartermaster, Capt. W. H. Bruce; Surgeon, Dr. Maurice M. Seymour, Assist.-Surgeon, Dr. Frank Keele; Inspector of Musketry, Capt. A. W. Lawe; Capts., J. A. Mc. D. Rowe, Thos. Wastie, Wm. Sheppard, S. J. Jackson, J. H. Kennedy, J. C. Waugh, R. W. A. Rolph, John Crawford; Lieuts., F. I. Bamford, E. C. Smith, R. C. Brown, J. B. Rutherford, Major A. Oates, Geo. A. Glinn, A. Monkman, A. P. Cameron; 2nd Lieuts., W. H. Saunders, R. Hunter, G. R. Reid, T. Lusted, H. W. Chambre, H. McKay, F. R. Glover. T. B. Brondgeest., Ed. Ellis, and F. V. Young.

‡ The following are the staff and Company officers of the 92nd Batt., the Winnipeg Light Infantry, Lt.-Col. W. Osborne Smith, C.M.G., in command. Majors,

had gone to Calgary, to join the 3rd Division of the North-West Field Force, under Major-General Strange. The latter, a veteran of the British service, had organised some local corps in the neighbourhood of the Rocky Mountains, with the design of keeping the Blackfeet Indians of the region from the disturbing influences of trouble on both branches of the Saskatchewan. When Big Bear took to the war-path, General Strange was instructed to place himself at the head of a Field Column, which would instantly be despatched to Calgary and Edmonton. This column was mainly composed of the Winnipeg Light Infantry, 300 strong, under Lt.-Col. Smith, C.M.G., and the 65th "Mount Royal Rifles," 317 strong, under Lt.-Cols. Ouimet and Hughes. It was subsequently strengthened by Major Stewart's Rocky Mountain Rangers; by 75 Mounted Police, under Major Steele and Inspector Gagnon, with the Police nine-pounder, under Major Perry, R.E.; and by 100 men of the Edmonton Volunteers, and 50 of the Alberta Rifles, under Major Hutton. The Calgary force was further supplemented by the 9th "Voltigeurs," of Quebec, under Lt.-Col. Amyot; and by the Quebec Cavalry School Corps, Lt.-Col. J. F. Turnbull, Commandant. The Montreal Garrison Artillery, under Lt.-Col. W. R. Oswald, was stationed at Regina, the capital of the North-West Territories; and the Halifax Provisional Battalion, commanded by Lt.-Col. Bremner, garrisoned Swift Current, Moose Jaw, and Medicine Hat.*

John Lewis, and W. B. Thibadeau; Adjut., Cap. Chas. Constantine; Paymaster, E. P. Leacock; Quartermaster, R. La Touche Tupper; Surgeon, Dr. J. P. Pennefather, Assist.-Surgeon, Dr. S. T. Macadam. Capts., W. R. Pilsworth, W. B. Canavan, F. J. Clarke, Dudley Smith, T. A. Wade, T. P. Vallancy, D. F¶ McIntosh; Lieuts., D. G. Sutherland, G. B. Brooks, T. G. Alexander, J. W. N. Carruthers, Augustus Mills,—Canwell, T. Gray; 2nd Lieuts., R. G. Macbeth, J A. Thirkell, W. R. Currie, F. T. Currie, Thos. Norquay, Thos. D. Deegan.

* In addition to calling out this force, and putting it in the field, the Militia Department placed the following corps under arms, in their several localities, as a

General Strange's Field Division consisted of 1,200 men of all arms. With this force he had to garrison Calgary, Edmonton, and Victoria, and to operate along the upper waters of the North Saskatchewan. On learning of the horror at Frog Lake, General Strange made his way, with a flying column, to Edmonton and Victoria, thence, to Fort Pitt. At the latter post he arrived on the 25th of May, and three days afterwards part of his force had a brush with Big Bear's band as narrated in our chapter on "The Frog Lake Massacre." During the whole of June the "hunt" for Big Bear was prosecuted with great energy, in the hope of releasing the white captives in his possession, and of bringing the Bear himself and his band to justice. The story of the hunt is too tedious, as well as barren of incident, to detain the reader with in the closing chapters of this narrative. We shall simply outline the operations of the combined military force directed against the barbarian fugitives in their native fastnesses. The escape of the white prisoners we have already dealt with.

General Middleton's force left Guardepuy's Crossing, on the South Saskatchewan, a few days after the taking of Batoche. Riel, we have seen, had been sent with his chief accomplices for trial to Regina. Dumont and Dumais had escaped into United States territory, and there gained their liberty. The half-breed trouble was at an end: now came the settling of scores with the Indians. At Prince Albert, whither the General had gone, Chief Beardy was the first to surrender. White Cap, the Sioux Chief, who had given material aid to Riel in the rebellion, was captured, with twenty of his band, at Dead

---

reserve, to be held in readiness in case of need: Toronto Battery of Garrison Artillery, under Capt. W. B. McMurrich; Toronto Field Battery of Artillery, under Major John Gray; and the 32nd Bruce Infantry (formerly Col. Sproat's Battalion), now commanded by Lt.-Col. J. G. Cooper, of Walkerton.

Moose Lake, by Lieuts. Merritt and Fleming and a few troopers of the Body Guard. At Battleford, after the raiding of some thirty supply waggons by the Battle River Indians, Poundmaker thought it discreet to feign penitence and give himself up a prisoner. Now came the disposition of the forces in the endeavour to capture Big Bear.

On the last day of May three steamers were loaded at Battleford for Fort Pitt.* There General Middleton wished to effect a junction with the 3rd Division, North-West Field Force, and together to move upon the marauding Indians who, under Big Bear, Wandering Spirit, and other types of the noble savage, had betaken themselves to their native wilds and defied the majesty of the law. The undertaking was full of difficulty, for the country was of the roughest, and almost impenetrable to an armed force. The hot season added to the difficulty of pursuit, in a realm of dense scrub and muskeg, made further repellent by myriads of mosquitoes and black flies. The pursuit occupied most of the month of June, the Bear leading the troops a fine dance through his all but impassable country. The whole district north of Fort Pitt, beyond the Moose Hills, beyond the Beaver River, and stretching as far as Cold Lake and Lac des Iles, south of the Athabasca River, was covered in the operations. But the chase was fruitless, save to intimidate the Indians, and lead them to release their prisoners, and finally to surrender themselves. As a fighting force, it was of course possible to beat them, even without the convincing rhetoric of the Gatling; but as a host of cunning fugitives, it was all but impossible to secure their

---

*The following are the corps that took part in this Expedition: The Midland Batt. (250 men); the 90th (275), the Grenadiers (250), with part of "A" and "B" Batteries, and two Gatlings. The following went by the south trail from Battleford to Fort Pitt: Dennis's Scouts (60), Boulton's Scouts (60), Mounted Police (50), Brittlebank's (late French's) Scouts (50).

defeat. The only hope was to hunt them down or to starve them out. For weeks the pursuit was kept up with hot ardour by forces under Generals Strange and Middleton. The aid of Colonels Irvine from Prince Albert, and Otter from Battleford, was also called into requisition. The former, with the Mounted Police, moved to the neighbourhood of Green Lake; while the latter, with the Queen's Own, the Ottawa Sharpshooters, and C. Company School of Infantry, pushed on to Jack Fish Lake, thence to Turtle Lake and the region about. Twice General Strange's command came upon the fugitives, and at Frenchman's Butte and at Loon Lake made it hot for the enemy. General Middleton, with his column of horse and the Gatlings, pressed the enemy hard along the Beaver River, and as far north as Cold Lake. But the Bear eluded all efforts to entrap him; so, spent with the toil of march, the bulk of the troops returned to Fort Pitt.

But hunger did what the troops were unable to do. At last it brought submission and a reasonable degree of penitence. First the Chippewyans surrendered, then some lodges of Little Poplar's band, and, finally, Wandering Spirit became a prisoner, followed, a few days afterwards, by Big Bear. The latter was taken near Carlton, whither, it is said, the outlawed Chief was proceeding to surrender himself. His following vanished into thin air; or, more prosaically, broke up into fragments, and took advantage of wild nature's concealment. The scouting parties were now all called in, and the campaign came to a close. After the trying marches were over, and the dangers and difficulties of the Indian pursuit were passed, the troops congregated at Fort Pitt, and were only too glad to have done with the campaign and get back to their homes. Well might the country now release them from their arduous and honourable service!

CHAPTER XXVII.

THE NATION'S HEROES—COUNTING THE COST.

"There is sobbing of the strong,
And a pall upon the land."

DUCK Lake, Cut Knife Hill, Fish Creek, and Batoche,—these are the engagements memorable in the history of the military operations against the now defeated insurgents in the North-West. But for the fact that these battles were fought in the course of a civil war, the names of at least three of them might fitly be blazoned on the country's banners. This is the one drop of bitterness in the cup we would quaff over the success of our arms. Only for the circumstance we mention, the engagements might take their place in the nation's history alongside Chateauguay, Chrysler's Farm, and Lundy's Lane. In no other particular are they less worthy of being held in perpetual honour, for the achievements of those who took part in them were characterised by an old-time valour.

But do we say there is only one drop of bitterness in the cup of joy? Ah, that that might be! Alas! there are those whose hearts have been torn by the conflict, and who, in the now joyous tumult of the returning troops, look with strained eyes and yearning souls for those who come not back.

> "O mothers, sisters, daughters, spare the tears ye fain would shed;
> Who seem to die in such a cause, ye cannot call them dead."

The total casualties in the four engagements amounted to 40 killed and 110 wounded. Besides these, over twenty lives fell a sacrifice to Indian bloodthirstiness, and almost as many more received injuries at various periods of the campaign. This calamitous loss of life and limb is the price the people have paid to suppress sedition and to secure returning peace to the country. The immediate and entailed cost, in treasure, though far from inconsiderable, is as nothing to this loss of life, for which Riel and his unprincipled confederates are primarily responsible. The pecuniary burdens of the campaign, however, are no light ones; and the sum of them will long remain an oppressive memory—to the country's rulers we hope an admonitory memory—of the conflict. Could those be coerced into settling the bill who use loose language in regard to the freedom of sections of the community, at will, to resort to rebellion, or who have in any way incited the wicked movement, it would be some satisfaction in contemplating the financial legacy of the strife.

But the cost in blood there is nothing to repay. No treasure can replace a single life; though the individual and the national loss may bring its compensations and be fraught with good. The insurrection has its lesson for the nation; and what it has cost the country may do more than any remonstrance, rational or irrational, could possibly effect. Not only will the ear of Government, henceforth, be more acute, and the official mind, we trust, be more alert, but, for a time at least, the public conscience will be quickened and the national heart become less apathetic. In the cause of humanity everyone must desire to see greater regard paid to the claims and the interests of the settlers in the North-West. In another direction we may also look for national gains as the result of the conflict. All sections of the country have participated in the common duty of suppressing the rebellion, or in limiting the area over which it has spread. In this national service the volunteers have been thrown together with beneficent results, for they have nobly emulated each other in acts of stirring heroism and self-sacrificing devotion to duty. Together they have shared the common danger, and, together, it is theirs to reap the common glory and the common reward. In a journal in one of the Maritime Provinces, the Halifax *Herald*, we find the following patriotic observations on the progress of Canada since the era of Confederation, and the welding influences which have come of closer intercourse in the nation's commercial and military life.

" Eighteen years," says the writer, " is but a brief period in the life of any nation ; but looking over the history of Canada since the first day of July, 1867, we seem to have achieved more in that time than many nations with whose history we are familiar. From being four disconnected Provinces, bounded westwardly by Lake Superior, we have assumed continental proportions, and now stretch one-fourth of the way around the globe, having three oceans for our boundaries. And we have not only grown big, but we have grown together. Eighteen years ago, few Nova Scotians had ever seen the St. Lawrence, and fewer yet had ever heard the name of the Red River of the North, of the Assiniboine, or of the Saskatchewan. To attend Parliament it was necessary for Nova Scotia and New Brunswick members to travel through a foreign country, and to take about a week in the journey. While for any Haligonian on the 1st of July, 1867, to have proposed to have crossed the continent of North America on Canadian (or rather British) soil, would have seemed about equal to a journey across Africa. But on the 1st July, 1885, what do we find ? Continuous railway connection on Canadian soil, from Halifax to the Selkirk

Mountains in British Columbia, and —with the exception of a comparatively short and rapidly disappearing gap—to the Pacific Ocean. Thousands of Nova Scotians now visit the Upper Provinces every year, and thousands of Upper Province men visit Nova Scotia. Hundreds of thousands of dollars of Nova Scotian capital are invested in the North-West; thousands of Nova Scotians have gone there to live ; and within the last few months, we have seen a Halifax battalion of militia holding the passes of the South Saskatchewan—500 miles west of Winnipeg—in a triumphant struggle to maintain peace and security in that country. These things are but some of the results of eighteen years of our united life."

Despite the political pessimists, there is hope for Confederation in the ring of such words. There is hope, too, when the youth of the land give their lives so ready a sacrifice on the altar of their country. Ill indeed we could spare them ; but they have fallen in no unworthy cause ; and the brain and heart of the nation will be enriched by their blood. At no epoch of its history has the country played so noble a part; and never has material so rapidly accumulated on which to found in honour the edifice of Canadian nationality. Referring to this period of strife in the North-West, and its irreparable losses, the following kind and considerate words of His Excellency, the Governor-General, may well find a place in this volume. The passage occurs in a speech made by Lord Lansdowne to the students of the College of Ottawa:

" You express your hope that during my term of office this country may enjoy the blessings of prosperity and of peace. That solemn prayer is one which I believe was never offered with greater sincerity than it is at this moment by every man and woman in the Dominion. The struggle in which we have been engaged in the North-West is an insignificant one compared to those great conquests with which your studies of the history of the old and the new world have made you familiar ; but it has cost us already many valuable lives, and has brought sorrow and suffering to many a happy family, and desolation to many a quiet homestead. Public order and confidence will soon be restored—perhaps on a sounder foundation than before; but there are many to whom victory will bring no consolation in the bitterness of their sorrow. We cannot forget them in the hour of success. By all of us the spring of 1885 will be remembered with mingled feelings—feelings of pain and regret that the peaceful career of this country should have been thus interrupted—feelings, too, I am glad to say, of pride at the thought that from every part of Canada, from Nova Scotia to the foot of the Rocky Mountains, without distinction of locality or of race, our soldiers have shown themselves ready to endure danger and hardship in a spirit of the truest patriotism when the service of their country required their presence in the field."

"We cannot forget them in the hour of success."—No, and since these words were uttered, we have greater reason not to forget them. Since then the mission of the troops has been fully accomplished, and the country greets their return with the trumpet note of honour. But with the peal of acclaim mingles the sad notes of the funeral dirge. Him of whom we were so proud, the Bayard of the North-West Expeditionary Force, has fallen by the way, and there is a "pall upon the land." In the lamentable death of Lt.-Col. A. T. H. Williams, the hero-commander of the Midland Battalion, the country mourns one of the best of her sons. In his person, our modern age seemed to "restore the ancient majesty of noble and true bearing."

" Praise of him must walk the land
  Forever, and to noble deeds give birth.
This is the happy warrior: this is he
  That every man in arms would wish to be.

Complaining of illness at Church parade, at Fort Pitt, on Sunday, the 28th of June, Colonel Williams retired to his tent On the Tuesday following he was removed to the steamer on the river for treatment by the Brigade Surgeons on board the *North West*. The next day inflammation of the brain set in,

THE LATE CAPT. E. BROWN,
Boulton's Scouts.

and typhoid fever showed itself. On Thursday the patient became unconscious; and on the morning of Saturday he passed peacefully to his rest. Colonel Williams was an accomplished soldier, an earnest Christian gentleman, and a true patriot. The hardships and anxieties of the campaign, in which he bore himself with conspicuous gallantry, had told on a frame never robust. His death was a sad ending to the triumphs of the North-West Military Expedition. Universal is the regret which his death has occasioned. We extract the following tribute from the Toronto *Globe*, which must be the more acceptable to Colonel William's friends, as it comes from the organ of the opponents of the political party to which the deceased officer gave his allegiance:

"The eulogies of Col. Williams, M.P., in the House of Commons last night were by no means overstrained. In him Canada loses a gallant son. Against a far more formidable foe than Half-breeds and Indians he would have demonstrated that the Dominion can give birth to a race of soldiers, in dash, in courage, in impetuosity, and in staying power, in no whit inferior to the best specimens of the iron races from which Canadians have sprung. It was not given him to die a soldier's death in battle. He fell a victim to a raging fever. Yet was his life as truly a sacrifice to his country as though he had fallen, shot through the heart, while in the van of the daring charge upon the rifle-pits of Batoche. Other lives than his also will wither away as the result of the terrific strain of these last exciting three months. Many a wife and mother will be anguished to see dear ones fading away day by day before their eyes, from illness contracted during exposure and over-exertion in this campaign now ended. War and tears go hand in hand. Many a home must yet be thrown into such heartrending grief as that which hangs like a pall over the now desolated household at Port Hope."

Our rapidly contracting space, we regret, prevents us from dwelling upon incidents in connection with the death of other gallant heroes of the campaign. Their names have been already

x

noted among the casualties of the engagements with which we have dealt in the preceding portions of our narrative. Their fame, however, holds by a surer title than any poor words of ours. May their memories long live in the heart of the nation, and the influence of their deeds never abate ! Each section of the country has had its loss; and throughout the land the memory of those who have fallen must remain a perpetual and an inspiring possession. Toronto mourns her Fitch and Moor, of the gallant 10th, and her Foulkes and Watson, of the School of Infantry. In Lieut. Fitch the Grenadiers had an officer endeared to every man in the regiment; and his name will be proudly inscribed on its roll of honour, for his chivalrous bearing on the battlefield and for resolute valour.

> "The good die first,
> Then those whose hearts are dry as summer dust
> Burn to the socket."

To Port Hope, Kingston, St. Catharines, and St. Thomas, death brought its victims of the fight. Quebec lost three of her gunners; Ottawa, Rogers and Osgoode, of her Foot Guards; London misses her Elliott; and Peterboro' her young but gallant son, Capt. Edward Brown, of Boulton's Horse. Prince Albert had her holocaust of dead from Duck Lake; and Winnipeg has been sorely bereft. Swinford, Hutchinson, Hardisty, Fraser, Ennis, Fergus, and Wheeler are among her fallen, to keep green the memory of the deeds of the brave 90th. Nor do we forget French and Kippin, and Smart, Burke, Sleigh, and Lowry, of the local Scouts and Mounted Police; nor the victims of Frog Lake; nor the true sons of the Church, the intrepid missionaries of the Cross, whose lives fell a noble sacrifice to Christian duty.

But fertile in heroes as the campaign has been who have died for their country, it has also been fertile in those who have bled for her. To the suffering wounded, though their lives have been spared, the nation's gratitude is no less due. The sight of Mars on crutches, or of young heroes with their arms in a sling, will no doubt be a familiar sight for many a day, to speak with eloquent tongue of the service rendered with touching enthusiasm by our patriot soldiers. If the memory of their deeds shall evoke a more active patriotism and a higher development of public spirit, the country will have little to regret in the perils her sons have braved or in the sad losses of the conflict. To the hospital and field corps, organised by the medical staff of the various divisions of the army of the North-West, the country's thanks are richly due. To this important branch of the service the wounded owe much for skilful treatment and kind tendance. But the poet here comes to our aid; and, with the touching lines of a lady who took the following despatches for a text, in her apostrophe to Saskatoon, we may fittingly close this chapter. "Saskatoon requested to be allowed the charge of the wounded."—April despatch. "The hospital at Saskatoon is now closed."—June despatch.

" 'Neath thy splendid Northern starlight, by the rushing of thy waves,
In thy warmth of summer gladness, there remain thee but thy graves.
All fulfilled thy tender mission, all bestowed thy generous boon—
And thy foster sons have left thee, lonely Saskatoon.

Weary, bleeding, faint, thou sought'st them ; from the very grasp of death
Thou hast snatched them, soothed and tended, and sustained their falling breath ;
From thy bosom, healed and strengthened, they are scattered far and wide—
He to mother's fond embraces, he to children, he to bride,
Owes to thee his restoration. Shall they ever, late or soon,
Cease to count thee as their mother, kindly Saskatoon ?

Cease to blend with dreams of mercy recollection of their pain !
Sigh to know that they may never see thee—breathe thine air—again ?'

Bless the hands that bound the burning wound, and bathed the fevered brow ?
And the voice that whispered comfort when the tide of life was low ?
Ah, to souls for kindred yearning, what the touch of stranger hand ?
What the word of hope and cheering spoken in an alien land ?
What the glories of thy starlight or the sunlight of thy June
To home-haunted hearts within thee, foreign Saskatoon ?

Grateful now for loving tendance, thou hast given them one by one
Back to life, and love, and labour, aud thy holy work is done.
They shall take thy memory with them as a dear and fond regret ;
Chide them not, if glad to leave thee, though they never may forget.
Fathers on their children smiling, lovers 'neath the summer moon,
Can but joy to think, ' Farewell forever, remember'd Saskatoon !'*

---

* (Mrs.) Anna Rothwell, of Kingston, in the Toronto *Mail*,

CHAPTER XXVIII.

REMEDIAL MEASURES—THE COUNTRY'S FUTURE.

THERE can be little question that the first of remedial measures is to give Riel and his accomplices a fair but speedy trial. The mistake of 1870 must not be repeated. We then sought to conciliate before we conquered. Had political exigencies at the time not interfered, we might not have had the trouble we have to-day. The sympathies of race and religion, right and proper in their place, are worse than wasted on such a miscreant as Riel. The duty of the Government is plain: the guilty must be punished. The public sentiment, no less than its righteous indignation, will insist upon this. It is confessedly difficult to deal with those who have been inveigled into rebellion, and whose sense of social duty does not rise above the level of tribal morality. But the case is different with the leaders and instigators of the revolt. With them there is no question as to responsibility for their acts; and for those acts they must be punished. Justice means no less than this, and the demands of justice are imperial.

We have no wish unduly to heighten the indictment against Riel and his seditious half-breeds; but there is little danger here of exaggeration. The enormity of their crime, and the utter recklessness and inhumanity of their conduct, can hardly be over-stated. To them we owe all the horrors of the period —the desolate homes, the stricken hearts, the foul murder at Duck Lake, the cowardly shooting of unarmed and trustful victims, and the long rows of new-made graves on the banks of the Battle River and the Saskatchewan. To them we owe, too, the atrocities of Frog Lake, the heaps of charred and unburied dead round the chapel of the mission station, the killing and mutilating of Farm Instructors and Mounted Policemen, the long and weary bondage of captive men, women and children, and all the murder and rapine which their cruelty has incited. For these things the leaders of the revolt must be brought to an account, and punishment will be salutary if it be sharp and decisive.

But the bringing of the culprits to justice is a matter the country must leave in the hands of justice. In view of the approaching trials, it would be unseemly in us to hand over to the law those whom the law has not dealt with. Fortunately, the Government has appointed a gentleman to conduct the trials in whose competence and fair dealing the country reposes every confidence, and whose private character sheds a lustre on the profession he adorns. Into the hands of Mr. Christopher Robinson, Q.C., we may leave Riel and his confederates, with those whom he has cajoled into rebellion, in the full assurance that they will be righteously dealt with. *

---

* The gentlemen associated with Mr. Robinson as Crown Counsel in the trial of the half-breeds and Indians implicated in the rebellion, are : Messrs. B. B. Osler, Q.C., of Toronto ; Burbidge, of Ottawa ; Casgrain, of Quebec ; and Scott, of Regina. The gentlemen retained as Counsel for the defence of Riel are : Messrs. C. Fitzpatrick and F. X. Lemieux, of Quebec. The presiding Judge is Col. Richardson, Stipendiary Magistrate for the N.W.T.

We have said that it will be difficult to deal with the rebellious Indians. That we have been spared a general Indian uprising, and that the half-breed insurrection has not entailed upon us a war of races, we have not to thank Louis Riel. In this matter there has been a signal deliverance. The greatness of the danger which Providence has averted from the country calls for profound thankfulness. Considering the natural restlessness of the tribes, the native propensity to steal and to murder, and the alluring prospect held out to them of plunder, it is a marvel that the demon of sedition has not wrought greater havoc. These and similar reflections will be present to every mind that gives a thought to the subject. Their prevalence, it is not too much to say, must have weight in extenuation of the crimes the Indians have committed.

But although favouring circumstances have limited and modified the disturbance, the direct and indirect consequences of the insurrection have been calamitous. What their effect will be upon the country will depend much upon the remedial measures now to be adopted for its pacification. The first, though a tardy step, was a wise one—the appointment by Government of a Half-breed Commission.* This act of justice, long delayed, has already, we believe, produced good results. Why it was delayed, party and the henchmen of party, according to the shibboleth of their camp, will find an answer. The correspondence between the party and the answer—need we say it ?—is sure to be uniform and intimate.

In this matter of delay lies the question of responsibility for the half-breed insurrection. To the heedless, to the criminal, inaction of Government we owe the recent troubles in the North-West. " The fault of the Administration," writes a well-

---

* The gentlemen who are acting on the Commission are : Messrs. W. P. R. Street, Forget, and Goulet.

known publicist, in a late issue of *The Week*, " lay in protracted inaction." The thoughtful writer goes on to say:

"The administration of the North-West, it is now certain, has been feeble, limping, and laggard. An army of officials has been sent from the East who were not always in sympathy with the people of the North-West; but the capital fault has been in a want of promptitude and vigour at the seat of the central authority. The North-West was not represented in Parliament; and the want of this safety-valve helped to make it possible for complaint to take the most objectionable of all forms, armed insurrection."

This is the language of truth, as well as of sobriety and moderation. But much of what is here said is practically admitted by the chief organ of the Government. The Toronto *Mail*, in a recent article remarkable for its judicial view of affairs, blames " a rusty Departmental system," for withholding justice from those to whom it ought to have issued. This frank admission settles the question of responsibility for the troubles of the North-West, though upon a previous Administration, of the Opposition party, the journal lays a portion of the blame which, speaking for its own side, it accepts. We cull the following sentences from the article referred to:

"It has never been denied by *The Mail* that the Métis had good grounds for complaint. * * * In spite of the manifest and unanswerable logic of the half-breed case, the Department for years and years steadily refused to move in the matter. It was a tangled question; it would involve the appointment of a commission and no end of trouble; St. Albert and St. Laurent were far distant dependencies without political influence; it was a claim that would be none the worse for blue-moulding in the pigeon-holes. This was the way in which the officials treated the just demands of the Métis, and we agree with Mr. Blake that their negligence was gross and inexcusable, and contributed to bring about the insurrection. But, and this puts him and his case out of court, Mr. Mackenzie was just as much to blame as Sir John Macdonald. The Métis say that they began pressing for the fulfilment of the agreement implied, if not expressed, in the Manitoba Act as far back as 1872; that they renewed their efforts in 1874-5. * * * But it was all to no purpose. Neither Grit nor Tory officials would attend to them. The *vis inertia* of the Department was immovable. * * * We repeat again that the Departmental system under which such callous and cruel neglect of the rights of a portion of the community was possible, was wrong and should be censured ; but as Reformers were responsible for it equally with Conservatives, how can one condemn the other ? The Métis were disgusted with both."

Need there be further wrangle over the question of responsibility for the insurrection in the North-West ? We think not. Both parties are implicated; and to both parties should come the lesson of honest and faithful governing. But the disaster is not a matter for parties now to fight over; it is a matter for the country's profit and instruction. We have seen where we have come short of our duty; and the enlightenment should be a guide to the future. There are problems in connection with the North-West still hard of solution, and difficulties likely to arise which the most assiduous efforts of Government will not avail to remedy. But luck may help when tact and good judgment fail.

For a time at least the North-West must be governed by force; and here is a source of peril. But it is a peril that can be overcome by putting the military administration, as well as the civil, in good and competent hands. Let us look with a careful scrutiny at the local officials we appoint, and with a still more careful scrutiny at those we send up from the East. This, in part, is the lesson of the insurrection. If good is to come out of evil it is a lesson it will be well to heed.

" Then the gazers of the nations, and the watchers of the skies,
　Looking through the coming ages, shall behold, with joyful eyes,
　On the fiery track of Freedom fall the mild baptismal rain,
　And the ashes of old evil feed the Future's golden grain."

To the evil of "making politics pay," not only in the North-West but nearer home, do we owe much of our humiliation and trouble. In one quarter of the country let us have done with the professional politician. To those who have not lost faith in our political systems, and who, above all things, desire the moral elevation of the community, the result will be welcome. If under our party system we must reward men for political services, let us agree to pension them rather than place them in positions for which they are unfitted, or where they are likely to abuse their trust. The suggestion will doubtless bring a smile to the faces of some of the liverymen of party, but it would be well for the nation did it bring a blush.

At the seat of the insurrection the situation for a time must be one of extreme delicacy. To meet the disorganisation, and heal the scars of the conflict, we must draw upon patience and conciliation, as well as upon the country's purse. To the ministration of kindness we must above all things look. To the white settler let us be kind, as well as helpful of his interests, and ready, with discretion, to ameliorate his lot. To the half-breed we can afford to be generous; and it becomes us to be patient with his weaknesses and tender towards his susceptibilities. To none should we do injustice, and from none withhold a ready and patient hearing. The Indian should be our especial care. In his management are wanted a union of firmness and compassionateness, with the accompaniment of a high Christian example and unwavering good faith. The present condition and future of the fast vanishing race demand our warm and active sympathies. Let us not forget that to the intrusion of the white man their whole destiny has been changed. Above all let us keep from them the diseases of our modern civilisation, and undeviatingly maintain our embargo upon intoxicating liquors. Despite their material and moral squalor, the Indians have a tribal life which it is fitting we should respect. They have also claims to the sovereignty of the land which, as colonists rather than conquerors, we cannot with justice wholly set aside. Pursuing our traditional policy of kind treatment, we may win many of them to civilisation, and lead all of them, we trust, to renew their attachment to Queen and Country.

"We must, however, be reasonable in our expectations. We must remember that the Indian has never been habituated to steady labour, and it should not be a matter of bewilderment if he is vacillating and irregular in accepting that condition. For countless generations his life has been nomadic. He has been lord of the soil, bred a warrior, and the white man who has been the cause of the change in his condition should bear with him and be patient, and extend him help and aid. He has much of his former life to unlearn; he has to struggle against the instincts of his blood; he has to accept the great truth that labour is honourable. * * No doctrine is more recognised than that every right is coexistent with a duty. The Indian has to reach the condition of understanding that he can only hold his place by the side of the white man by fulfilling the obligations attendant on the position he claims."[*]

While not impatient of results, and pursuing the policy which has long been our proud boast, we may hope that the animosities of the conflict will soon pass away, and that the great domain of the Canadian people will take a fresh start in a bright career of progress. Its prosperity, we believe, will receive a new impulse from the events of the past few months, and the nation at large will benefit in an accession of patriotism and national spirit from the effusion of blood. But as we pen these closing lines, we hear the bugles of the returning heroes—conquering heroes!—from the fields of their glory, and we take leave of our task to join in the plaudits, and add a voice to the chorus of acclaim.

---

[*] "England and Canada," by Sanford Fleming, C.E., C.M.G.

Conquering heroes! Yes; what is it they have not conquered?
Wearisome miles on miles up to the far North-West;
Limitless breadths of prairie, like to the limitless ocean;
Endless stretches of distance, like to eternity.
Farther still,—to their seeming far as the starless spaces
That loom in the measureless void above some desolate heart.
How the unnumbered miles threatened them like an army,—
Then perished in silence beneath the tread of resolute feet.

Not alone did they march, our brave Canadian soldiers,
Grim Privation and Peril followed them hand in hand;
Sodden Fatigue lay down with them in the evening,
And Weariness rose with them and went with them all the day
Inexpressible Sadness at thought of the homes they were leaving
Hung like a cloud above them, and shadowed the path before.
These, all these, were slain by our brave, our conquering heroes.
Ah! but the battle was long,—long and bitterly hard.

Crueller enemies still ;—treacherous, scarcely human,
Hard and fierce in look, but harder and fiercer in heart;
Versed in animal cunning, warily waiting in ambush;
Merciless in the purely animal power to smite.
Swift in their veins runs the hot, vindictive blood of their fathers;
Deep in their hearts lies a hatred, strong and cruel as death.
The heart of our country is beating against the knife of the savage;
But the knife has dropped to the ground, the heart is conqueror still.

Ah! but the brave boys wounded and dead on the field of battle,
Giving their brave young lives for a cause that was dearer than life.
Say you they who have yielded their all have conquered nothing,—
Nothing remains to them but the sad deep silence of death?
No, a thousand times, no! For them are the tears of a nation—
Tears that would fain wash out the pitiful stain of blood.
These are their victories; The love that knows no forgetting,
Measureless gratitude, and the fame that forever endures.*

---

* Agnes E. Wetherald, in *The Week*.

SUPPLEMENTAL LIST OF STAFF AND COMPANY OFFICERS OF CORPS SERVING IN THE NORTH-WEST.

[NOTE.--I wish here to express my thanks to Colonel Walker Powell, Adjut.- General of Militia at Headquarters, for courtesy in furnishing the following information, which I was unable to procure in time for insertion in the body of the book. My thanks are further due to the Hon. the Speaker, and to the Clerk of the House of Commons, Ottawa, for personal and official courtesies.

I am also under obligations for like courtesies, and other kindnesses, to my valued friend and old commanding officer, Lt.-Col. C. T. Gillmor, late of the Queen's Own Rifles. Though unable to take part in the duties and honours of the campaign, no one, I venture to think, has followed the doings of the troops on active service in the North-West with greater pride or with a keener interest than has this true soldier and veteran in the service, Colonel Gillmor.—THE AUTHOR.]

HALIFAX PROVISIONAL BATTALION.—Lt.-Col. J. J. Bremner, Major C. J. Macdonald, l.c., Major T. J. Walsh, Paymaster W. H. Garrison, Adjt. E. G. Kenny, capt., Qr.-mr. J. G. Corbin, Asst. Surg. D. Harrington.

No. 1 Co.: Capt. J. E. Curren, Lt. J. P. Fairbanks, 2nd Lt. A. Anderson.
No. 2 Co.: Capt. J. McCrow, Lt. W. L. Kane, 2nd Lt. R. H. Skimmings.
No. 3 Co.: Capt. B. A. Weston, Lt. A. Whitman, 2nd Lt. H. A. Hensley.
No. 4 Co.: Capt. R. H. Humphrey, Lt. B. Boggs, 2nd Lt. C. E. Cartwright.
No. 5 Co.: Capt. C. H. Mackinlay, Lt. J. A. Bremner, 2nd Lt. J. McCarthy.
No. 6 Co.: Capt. H. Hechler, Lt. H. St. C. Silver, 2nd Lt. T. C. James.
No. 7 Co.: Capt. A. G. Cunningham, Lts. J. T. Twining, C. R. Fletcher.
No. 8 Co.: Capt. J. Fortune, Lt. C. J. McKie, 2nd Lt. C. K. Fiske.

STAFF AND Co. OFFICERS 65TH BATT.—Lt.-Col. J. A. Ouimet, Major G. A. Hughes, l.c., Major C. A. Dugas, Paymaster C. L. Bossé, Ajt. J. C. Robert, Qr.-mr. A. LaRocque, Surgeon L. A. Paré, Asst. Surg. F. Simard.

No. 1 Co.: Capt. J. B. Ostell, Lt. A. C. Plinquet.
No. 2 Co.: Capt. J. P. A. des Trois-Maisons, Lt. G. Des Georges.
No. 3 Co.: Capt. E. Banset, Lieut. C. Starnes.
No. 4 Co.: Capt. A. Roy, Lieut. A. Villeneuve.
No. 5 Co.: Capt. G. Villeneuve, Lieut. B. Lafontaine.

No. 6 Co. : Capt. J. Giroux, Lieut. P. F. Robert.
No. 7 Co. : Capt. H. Prevost, Lieut. C. J. Doherty.
No. 8 Co. : Capt. L. J. Ethier, Lieut. J. E. B. Normandin.

MONTREAL BRIGADE OF GARRISON ARTILLERY.—Lt. Col. W. R. Oswald, Major W. H. Laurie, Major E. A. Baynes, Paymaster W. Macrae, Adjt. T. W. Atkinson, Qr.-mr. J. A. Finlayson, Surgeon C. E. Cameron, Asst. Surgeon . M. Elder, Chaplain Rev. J. Barclay.
No. 1 Battery : Capt. W. C. Trotter, Lieut. W. H. Lulham.
No. 2 Batt. : Capt. F. Brush, Lieut. J. D. Roche.
No. 3 Batt. : Lieut. C. Lane, Lieut. G. C. Patton.
No. 4 Batt. : Capt. F. Cole, Lieut. F. W. Chalmers.
No. 5 Batt. : Capt. D. Stevenson, Lieut. H. T. Wilgress.
No. 6 Batt. : Capt. C. H. Levin, Lieut. J. K. Bruce, B. Billings (acting).

WINNIPEG FIELD ARTILLERY.—Major E. W. Jarvis, Capt. L. W. Coutlée, Lieut. G. H. Young, 2nd Lieut. G. H. Ogilvie.

WINNIPEG TROOP CAVALRY.—Capt. C. Knight, 2nd Lieut. H. J. Shelton.

CAVALRY SCHOOL CORPS, QUEBEC.—*Commandant* : Lt.-Col. James F. Turnbull. *Lieutenants* : Lieut. E. H. T. Heward, Lieut. F. L. Lessard.

9TH BATTALION RIFLES, "VOLTIGEURS de QUEBEC."—Lt.-Col. Amyot ; Majors Roy and Evanturel ; Paymaster, Major Dugal ; Quartermaster, A. Talbot ; Adjutant, Casgrain Pelletier ; Supply Officer, M. Wolsley ; Surgeon, Dr. A. Deblois ; Asst. Surgeon, M. Waters ; Capts. L. E. Frenette, M. Chouinard, J. C. G. Drolet, E. Garneau, F. Pennee, A. O. Fages, L. F. Perrault, N. Lavasseur, — Fiset ; Lieuts. G. F. Hamel, W. D. Baillairgé, — Fiset, G. A. Labranche, J. V. Dupuis, — Casgrain, F. de St. Maurice, — Dion, — Shehy, P. Pelletier, — J. C. Routhier, C. C. Larue, and H. Beique. [It is doubtful whether the list of this regiment is either full or accurate. The Adjut.-General was unable to furnish it.]

APPENDIX.

THE TRIAL OF LOUIS RIEL.

THE drama of rebellion has been fully played, and we now come to the fitting epilogue, the trial, verdict, and sentence of its chief instigator and rash participator. With the close of the drama we have the usual war of words over the merits of the case, with an abundant crop of nicely-drawn distinctions between patriots fighting for their rights and rebels guilty of the blackest crimes. We shall anticipate much of what remains to be told, if we at once relate that, in passing sentence upon the rank and file of rebeldom, justice has been tempered with mercy; while, upon the leader of the insurrection, the death penalty has been passed, though the law has not, as yet been executed. At the present time of writing the trials have not all ended; a number of Indians who are accused of individual acts of murder, have yet to be arraigned, and the penalty exacted for wanton and unprovoked bloodshed. With Riel, the arch-conspirator, the law was first to deal; and though the defence took skilful advantage of every point in his favour, justice has doomed him to what must be deemed a merited fate. He is under sentence to be hanged on the 18th of September, 1885. As was expected, the verdict and sentence have provoked much newspaper controversy, and called forth heated arguments between the two chief racial sections of the Dominion. Both sections admit the culprit's guilt, though one side justifies, and the other condemns, him. One affirms that he has been awarded a righteous fate and must pay the wages of treason, while the other bemoans his unsuccess, and excuses the resort to arms. The East applies to him the honoured term of patriot; the West affixes on him the stigma of murderer and traitor.

A deliberate inquiry into the degree of Riel's guilt, would take us anew into the consideration of matters in the North-West—a consideration we have no intention here of entering upon. Nor is there need that we should again open up the matter, for those who are familiar with the foregoing narrative, will have seen what immediate and remote causes existed which produced disaffection and finally rebellion. These causes, we have previously said, did not warrant the half-breeds in throwing over constitutional means in seeking redress of their grievances, still less did they justify an appeal to arms. The grievances, in truth, were more imaginary than real; though the acts of the Government Half-Breed Commission, and the largess they have distributed, seem to be an admission of claims which were not sentimental but legal. But sentimental, in great measure, the claims nevertheless were.

The half-breed assumptions of proprietorship in the land were wild and extravagant; compared with the juster rights of the Indians, they were foolish and wicked. But their claims to possession of the soil were not really those of the modest and reasonable half-breeds. They were those of their ambitious and madcap representative. In Riel's ill-balanced mind they first found lodgment in 1869, when his brain was turned by his elevation to the rebel presidency. That the preposterous claims have not lost in magnitude or gained in lucidity since that period, is clear from Riel's proposed partition of the territories among the various tribes and sects with which he wished to people his kingdom. Here, if anywhere, is the proof of the man's insanity, though it is curiously mixed up with religious and patriotic fervour, and with not a little of this world's cunning.

Apart from the question of insanity, which we think the jury had little opportunity of fully weighing, there is no doubt that Riel was given a fair and impartial trial. Had the constitution of the North-West permitted it, the miscreant merited the sharp and salutary discipline of a drum-head court-martial. In some respects it is a pity that the expeditious machinery of military law was not instantly invoked. It would have consigned its victim, without circumlocution, to a well-deserved fate, and relieved the country of a disturbing political and sectional discussion. But perhaps it is well that the course which has been taken has been followed. With all the provocation that has been given, and all the loss that has been entailed, it is seemly that the nation should restrain its righteous passion, and punish crime with due deliberation, and without the suspicion of being vindictive.

Receiving a fair trial, and being condemned to pay the penalty of his crimes by forfeiting his life, why should the sentence be interfered with? Let the law take its course. In a previous rebellion Riel received the clemency of the country when that clemency was ill-deserved. For his further crime he should now most assuredly suffer, unless political offences of the gravest character are to be robbed of their heinousness and condoned at the promptings of a mistaken sentiment. The leniency of the nation has once, in his case, been foully abused: to extend leniency again is to make a travesty of justice, and to court further disaster. As a writer in *The Week* puts it: "The word 'treason' should be blotted out of the Statute Book if Riel does not pay the penalty of his offence."

The verdict of the jury carried a recommendation to mercy, but upon what grounds was not stated. It would, we imagine, be difficult to state any grounds, save those of compassion for a fanatical enthusiast, and of sympathy for a people whose simple, superstitious minds led them to see a temporal and Divine leader in a hare-brained man with a misconceived mission. But religious eccentricities are not such evidence of an unsound mind as to save a criminal from the consequences of his own acts. In Riel's case, though there is a diseased vanity, there is no proof that he is not an accountable being. That the jury found him guilty of murder shows that they considered him to be in possession of his faculties, or, as it has been observed, "of sufficient faculties to know that he was incurring a terrible responsibility when he led his dupes to take up arms against their country."

The question of the jurisdiction of the Court at Regina, and its competence to try a man for a capital offence with a jury of six instead of twelve men, are the main problems which have yet to be determined. But these objections, with the demurrer to the trial and sentence to death of the prisoner by a stipendiary magistrate, and without the preliminary investigation by a grand jury or by a coroner, will no doubt be satisfactorily met by the Manitoba Court, to which the case has been appealed, and every jot and tittle of justice will be scrupulously meted out to Riel. These matters settled, we may look for the final disposal of the Rebel Chief's case, and see the curtain fall upon the last act in the drama of North-West insurrection.

Let us now give some epitome of the legal proceedings against Riel and his fellow conspirators, with a brief chronicle of incidents connected with the trial and sentence of the incriminated Indians. The former were arraigned at Regina on a charge of treason, under the Statute of Edward III.; the latter on a charge of complicity in rebellion, under what is known to the law as treason-felony. The trials were heard before His Honour, Hugh Richardson, one of the Stipendiary Magistrates of the North-West Territories, exercising criminal jurisdiction under the provisions of the North-West Territories Act of 1880. Associated with Col. Richardson on the Bench was Mr. Henry Lejeune. For the names of the Counsel for the Crown, and those engaged for the defence, see page 382. Associated with the latter was Mr. J. N. Greenshields, of Montreal.

The first step in the trial of Riel was taken at Regina on the 6th of July, when the prisoner was produced in Court, and the indictment read to and served on him. The proceedings were taken before Col. Richardson, J.P., in the presence of the lawyers for the Crown and those for the defence. The counts in the indictment were three-fold, respectively charging Riel as a British subject, or as a resident enjoying Her Majesty's protection in the North-West Territories, with having levied war against Her Majesty, first, at Duck Lake, secondly, at Fish Creek, and thirdly, at Batoche. After the reading of the indictment, the prisoner was notified that he would be tried in open court at Regina, on the 20th of July, on the specified charges, the said Court to be constituted under sub-section 62, section 76 of the North-West Territories Act.

On the 20th of July the Court met, when Riel was formally arraigned, the clerk reading the long indictment. In reply to the interrogation whether the prisoner pled guilty to the charge of treason, his counsel rose and took exception to the jurisdiction of the Court. The plea entered by the defence was to the effect that the presiding stipendiary magistrate was incompetent to try a case involving the death penalty, and urged that Riel should be tried by one of the duly constituted courts in Ontario or in British Columbia. Mr. Christopher Robinson, Q.C., for the Crown, asked for an adjournment for eight days, to prepare a reply to the plea, which was granted. The Court then adjourned to the 28th instant.

On the re-opening of the Court, counsel expressed themselves ready to proceed. Only a few minutes were taken up in selecting a jury. Twelve persons were called, five of whom were peremptorily challenged by the defence, and one by the Crown. The remaining six were sworn in to try the prisoner at the bar. Their names are as follows:—H. J. Painter, E. Everett, E. J. Brooks, J. W. Merryfield, H. Dean, and F. Crosgrove. During the selection of the jury, it is observed by a correspondent of *The Mail*, to whom we shall be indebted for the reports of the trial, in making the present abstract, " that Riel anxiously watched the face of every man as he was selected and sworn, as though he could read their inmost thoughts as they took the oath."

After reading the indictment to the jury, Mr. B. B. Osler, Q.C., opened the case for the Crown, in which he explained the nature of the charge against the prisoner, whose career he traced through the successive steps of the rebellion, and indicated the weight and character of the evidence to be brought against its wicked instigator and chief leader. The plea of the defence of the incompetence of the Court to try the case, was first answered by the learned counsel, who remarked, that the character, and composition of the Court, as well as the provision for the trial of capital offences by a jury of six men instead of twelve, were in harmony with the Dominion Law enacted for the Government of the Territories, and that the Dominion Parliament had the right, under the British North America Act, to make that law. "The absence of the Grand Jury was explained, on the ground that such juries were essentially county organizations, and were impossible in large districts with small and scattered populations." The same reason explained the limiting of the jury to half the usual number. It was also stated that the Crown deemed it unwise, if indeed it were not impossible, to issue a Special Commission for the trial of the prisoner.

Mr. Osler proceeding said, that Riel not only aided and abetted the illegal acts of the rebels, but directed these acts.

"The testimony he claimed," says a writer in *The Illustrated War News*, "was abundantly sufficient to bring home to the prisoner his guilt in the charges against him. He (Mr. Osler) read the document in Riel's handwriting to Crozier, in which Riel threatened a war of extermination against the whites, and traced the prisoner's conduct afterwards to show that he had tried to carry out that threat. It was no constructive treason that was sought to be proved, but treason involving the shedding of brave men's blood. The accused had been led on, not by the desire to aid his friends in a lawful agitation for redress of a grievance, but by his inordinate vanity and desire for power and wealth."

"The first overt act of treason was committed," continued Mr. Osler, "when the French half-breeds were requested by Riel to bring their arms with them to a meeting to be held at Batoche on March 3rd. This indicated that the prisoner intended to resort to violence. On the 18th instant they find him (Riel) sending out armed men and taking prisoners, including Mr. Lash, the Indian agent of the St. Laurent region, and others, also looting the stores at and near Batoche, stopping freighters and appropriating their freight. A few days later the French half-breeds were under arms, and were joined by the Indians of the neighbourhood, who were incited to rise by the prisoner. On the 21st inst. Major Crozier did all he could to get the armed men to disperse, but directed by Riel, they refused to do so, and taking their orders from him, they continued in rebellion." "He held a document in his hands, in the prisoner's handwriting," added Mr. Osler, "which contained the terms on which Fort Carlton would be spared attack by the surrender and march out of Major Crozier and the mounted police. This document was never delivered, but was found with other papers in the rebel council chamber after the taking of Batoche. It was said in this notification to Crozier that the rebels would attack the police if they did not vacate Carlton, and would commence a war of extermination of the white race. This document was direct evidence of the treasonable intentions of the prisoner. Ten days previously Riel declared himself determined to rule or perish, and the declaration was followed by this demand. It would be said that, at last, when a clash of arms was imminent, Riel objected to forcible measures; but this document was a refutation of that assertion. At Duck Lake the prisoner had taken upon himself the responsibility of ordering his men to fire on the police. At Fish Creek, if Riel was not there, he directed the movement, and was therefore responsible. On the day of the fight he went back to Batoche to finish the rifle-pits. In the contest at Batoche the prisoner was seen bearing arms, and giving such directions as would show that he was the main mover. His treatment of the prisoners, his letters to Middleton, and other documents would show Riel's leadership. A letter found in Poundmaker's camp would show his deliberate intention of bringing on this country the calamity of an Indian war. All this would be proven, and it would be shown that the prisoner had not come here to aid his friends in the redress of grievances, but in order to use the half-breeds for his own selfish ends." Mr. Osler closed with a reference to the death and suffering which had been caused by the ambition of one man, and impressed upon the jury the grave responsibility they were charged with in bringing his crime home to the prisoner.

The first witness called by the Crown was DR. WILLOUGHBY, of SASKATOON. After having been sworn, witness said that the prisoner had stated to him that the Fort Garry trouble, when Scott had been shot, was nothing to what was going to take place. He said that the Indians only waited for him to strike the first blow to join him, and that he had the United States at his back. He seemed greatly excited, and said:—"It is time, doctor, that the breeds should assert their rights, and it will be well for those who have lived good lives." A party of armed men then drove up, and Riel said, pointing to them, "My people intend striking a blow for their rights. They have petitioned the Government over and over again, the only reply being an increase of the police force each time." The Indians, he said, had arranged their plans, and when the first blow was struck they would be joined by the American Indians. They would issue a proclamation, and assert that the time had arrived for him to rule the country or perish in the attempt. He promised to divide the country into seven equal portions, one of which was to be the new Ireland of the new North-West. He said the rebellion of fifteen years ago was not a patch on what this would be.

THOS. MCKAY, a loyal half-breed, was next called, who testified that he joined the Volunteer contingent from Prince Albert which formed part of Major Crozier's command at Duck Lake. Previous to that engagement he accompanied Mr. Hillyard Mitchell in his mission to Batoche, where the rebels had their headquarters. His object in going to Batoche was to point out to the French half-breeds the danger they were getting into in taking up arms. On arriving at the village he was met by an armed guard who conducted him, with Mr. Mitchell, to the rebel council room, where he was introduced to Riel "as one of Her Majesty's soldiers." We here quote part of the examination, by Mr. Christopher Robinson, of this witness.

Q.—Who introduced you to the prisoner?
A.—Mr. Mitchell introduced me to Mr. Riel as one of Her Majesty's soldiers.
Q.—That is Mr. Hillyard Mitchell?
A.—Yes. I shook hands with Mr. Riel and had a talk with him. I said, "There appears be great excitement here, Mr. Riel." He said, "No, there is no excitement at all; it was simply that the people were trying to redress their grievances, as they had asked repeatedly for their rights; that they had decided to make a demonstration." I told him it was a very dangerous thing to resort to arms. He said he had been waiting fifteen long years and that they had been imposed upon, and it was time now, after they had waited patiently that their rights should be given, as the poor half-breeds had been imposed upon. I disputed his wisdom and advised him to adopt different measures.
Q.—Did he speak of himself at all in the matter?
A.—He accused me of having neglected my people. He said if it was not for men like me their grievances would have been redressed long ago, that as no one took an interest in these people he had decided to take the lead in the matter.
Q.—Well?
A.—He accused me of neglecting them. I told him it was simply a matter of opinion, that I had certainly taken an interest in them, and my interest in the country was the same as theirs, and that I had advised them time and again, and that I had not neglected them. I also said that he had neglected them a long time if he took as deep an interest as he professed to. He became very excited, and got up and said, "You don't know what we are after—it is blood, blood; we want blood; it is a war of extermination. Everybody that is against us is to be driven out of the country. There were two curses in the country—the Government and the Hudson Bay Co. He further said the first blood they wanted was mine. There were some little dishes on the table, and he got hold of a spoon and said, "You have no blood, you are a traitor to your people, your blood is frozen, and all the little blood you have will be there in five minutes"—putting the spoon up to my face, and pointing to it. I said, "If you think you are benefiting your cause by taking my blood, you are quite welcome to it." He called his people and the committee, and wanted to put me on trial for my life, and Garnot got up and went to the table with a sheet of paper, and Gabriel Dumont took a chair on a syrup keg, and Riel called up the witnesses against me.

At this juncture Riel was called away to attend a committee meeting of the rebel government. Subsequently, by the mediation of Hillyard Mitchell, Riel's wrath at McKay was placated, and he was allowed to return to Fort Carlton with his intercessor. Before leaving, Riel apologized to McKay for what he had said to him, and asked him to join the insurgents, which witness, of course, would not do, being a loyal half-breed and a volunteer in the ranks of the Prince Albert contingent with Crozier at Fort Carlton.

McKay then detailed the incidents of the disastrous engagement with the rebels at Duck Lake, and gave strong testimony to criminate Riel, which the counsel for the defence utterly failed to shake.

The next witness was JOHN ASTLEY, surveyor of PRINCE ALBERT, who was long a prisoner of Riel's at Batoche, and the rebel chief's messenger on the day of the taking of the village by the loyal forces under Middleton. The witness gave a vivid description of his capture and imprisonment by Riel, and his subsequent release by the volunteers at Batoche. Riel acknowledged to him that he ordered his men in the name of the Almighty to fire at Duck Lake. He did not do so, however, until, as he thought, the police had fired. Riel told him he must have another fight with the soldiers to secure better terms of surrender from Gen. Middleton.

SECOND DAY OF THE TRIAL.

The second day of the Riel trial brought out sufficient evidence to incriminate the prisoner, and to lead the Crown prosecutors to waive the calling of other witnesses. During the proceedings the prisoner, it is reported, manifested more interest than he did on the first day of the trial, and his dark penetrating eye restlessly wandered from witness to counsel, and from bench to jury. "All day long a couple of medical men sat watching his actions, to discover, if possible, whether his mind was affected or not." His disagreement with his counsel towards the close of the day, caused an exciting break in the proceedings.

GEORGE KERR, of Kerr Brothers, BATOCHE, was the first witness sworn. He testified that on the 18th of March, Riel, with some fifty armed half-breeds, came to his store, and demanded, and obtained, all his guns and ammunition. His store was sacked, and later on he was himself taken prisoner, but was subsequently released. Riel, he testified, directed the rebel movements in concert with Gabriel Dumont.

HARRY WALTERS, another storekeeper at BATOCHE, was then examined, and gave similar testimony as to the sacking of his store, and of Riel's demand for arms and ammunition. On his refusing to accede to the demand of the prisoner and the breeds with him, Riel said, "You had better do it quietly. If we succeed, I will pay you; if not, the Dominion Government will." I refused, said Walters, and they forced themselves in and took the arms. I was arrested shortly after. Riel said the movement was for the freedom of the people. The country, if they succeeded, was to be divided, giving a seventh to the half-breeds, a seventh to the Indians, a seventh to church and schools, the remainder to be Crown Lands. I was kept prisoner three days, being liberated by Riel. Reil said, God was with their people, and that if the whites ever struck a blow, a thunderbolt would destroy them. They took everything out of my store before morning, the prisoner superintending the removal of the goods.

HILLYARD MITCHELL sworn, was examined by Mr. Osler. He said—I am an Indian trader, have a store at Duck Lake; heard there was an intention by rebels to take my store. I went to Fort Carlton and saw Major Crozier on the Thursday prior to the Duck Lake fight; saw prisoner on that Thursday at Batoche. Saw some people at the river armed. At the village I saw some English half-breed freighters who had been taken prisoners by Riel, and their freight also taken. Philip Garnot took me to the priest's house. I saw the prisoner there with Charles Nolin, Guardupuy and others. I think this was on the 19th of March. I told Riel that I had come to give some advice to the half-breeds. Riel said the Government had always answered their demands by sending more police. They were willing to fight 500 police. He said he had been trampled on and kept out of the country, and he would bring the Government and Sir John Macdonald to their knees.

THOMAS E. JACKSON was next examined by Mr. Osler, and deposed that he was a druggist, at Prince Albert, and a brother of Wm. Henry Jackson, an insane prisoner of Riel's. Riel, witness testified, asked him to write to the eastern papers, placing a favourable construction on his (Riel's) actions. Riel had made an application to Government for $35,000 as indemnity for loss of property; he showed the greatest hatred to the English, and his motives were those of revenge for ill-treatment at the time of the Red River rebellion. Having questioned Riel's present motives and plans, witness was taken prisoner and placed in close confinement. Riel afterwards accused me of having advised an English half-breed to desert. When Middleton was attacking Batoche, Riel came to witness and told him if Middleton killed any of their women and children he would massacre the prisoners. He wrote a message to Middleton to that effect, and I carried it to the General. (The message was produced and identified by witness). I did not return to the rebel camp. Saw the prisoner armed once after the Fish Creek fight. Riel was in command at Batoche, Dumont being in immediate command of the men. I know prisoner's handwriting. (The original summons to Major Crozier to surrender, the letter to Crozier asking him to come and take away the dead after Duck Lake fight, a letter to "dear relatives" at Fort Qu'Appelle, a letter to the half-breeds and Indians about Battleford, a letter to Poundmaker, and other documents were put in and identified by witness as being in Riel's handwriting).

Cross-examined by Mr. Fitzpatrick—The agitation was for provincial rights and their claims under the Manitoba treaty, and I was in sympathy with it. Riel was brought into the country by the French half-breeds. I attended a meeting at Prince Albert immediately after Riel's arrival in June, 1884. Riel said what they wanted was a constitutional agitation, and if they could not accomplish their ends in five years they would take ten to do it. Riel was their adviser; was not a member of the Executive Committee. Up to March last, from all I heard prisoner say or discovered otherwise, I believed Riel meant simply a constitutional agitation, as was being carried on by the other settlers. Riel had told him the priests were opposed to him, and that they were all wrong. Heard Riel talk of dividing up the country to be bestowed on the half-breeds, Poles, Hungarians, Bavarians, etc. When I was Riel's prisoner I heard him talk of this division, which I thought meant a division of the proceeds of sale of lands in a scheme of immigration. This was altogether different from what he had all along proposed at the meetings. All the documents Riel signed that I know of were signed "Exovide" (one of the flock). Riel explained that his new religion was a liberal form of Roman Catholicism, and that the Pope had no power in Canada. Think Riel wanted to exercise the power of the Pope himself. These expressions were made by Riel after the rebellious movement was begun.

GENERAL MIDDLETON was now called, and was examined by Mr. C. Robinson, Q.C. He testified that he was sent by the Minister of Militia to quell the outbreak on the Saskatchewan, and gave the well-known details of his encounter with the rebels at Fish Creek, and of his subsequent movement on Batoche. He testified to receiving two letters from Riel on the day of the capture of Batoche, in one of which Riel threatened to massacre the prisoners in his possession if he (Middleton) fired upon the half-breed women and children. The letter was produced in Court, and identified by the General.

CAPT. GEO. H. YOUNG, of the Winnipeg Field Battery, deposed that he was present at Batoche as Brigade Major under the last witness, and was in the charge at the close. Witness was first in the rebel council chamber after the capture of the village, and found and took possession of the rebel archives. A number of documents were produced, which witness recognised as those he had secured. After Riel's surrender he was given into witness's custody and taken to Regina.

MAJOR JARVIS, in command of the Winnipeg Field Battery during the campaign, and to whom the charge of the papers found at Batoche was confided, identified the papers produced in Court.

MAJOR CROZIER, of the N.-W. Mounted Police, was next sworn, and detailed the fact that he was met by an armed force of rebels at Duck Lake and fired upon, losing many of his command in killed and wounded. He testified that, subsequent to this engagement, a man named Sanderson brought him a letter from Riel asking him to come and remove his dead from the field.

CHARLES NOLIN was next called, and was examined by Mr. Casgrain in French. The deposition of this witness we take from the Toronto *Globe*. Nolin deposed that he lived in St. Laurent and formerly in Manitoba. He knew when Riel came to this country in July, 1884. And met him many times. Riel showed him a book he had written in which he said he would destroy England, and also Rome and the Pope. Riel spoke to him of his plans in December, expressing his wish for money, a sum between ten and fifteen thousand dollars. Riel had no plan to get it, but he wanted to claim an indemnity from the Dominion Government; that they owed him $100,000. Riel told him he had had an interview with Father Andre, and at that time he was at open war with the clergy, but had made peace with Father Andre in order to gain his ends. Riel went into the church with Father Andre and other priests, and promised to do nothing against them, and Father Andre had promised to use his influence with the Government to secure an indemnity of $35,000. This was in the beginning of December, 1884, the agreement being made at St. Laurent. Between December and February 14th, witness had taken part in seven meetings. Riel said if he could get the money from the

Government he would go wherever the Government would send him—to the Province of Quebec or elsewhere. Otherwise, he said, before the grass was very long, they would see foreign armies in Canada. He would begin with subduing Manitoba, and afterwards turn against the North-West. Prisoner afterwards prepared to go to the United States, and told the people it would look well if they attempted to prevent him from going. Riel never had the intention of leaving the country, but wanted witness to get the people to tell him not to go. Witness was chairman of a meeting which was held, and brought the matter up. On the 2nd March a meeting was held at the settlement between Riel and Father Andre. There were seven or eight half-breeds there. Prisoner appeared to be very excited, and told Father Andre he must give him permission to proclaim a Provisional Government before 12 o'clock. On the 3rd March a meeting was held for the English half-breeds. About forty armed French half-breeds came there. Riel spoke and said the police wanted to arrest him, but he had the real police. Witness spoke also at the meeting on the 5th of March. Riel afterwards told witness he had decided to take up arms and induce the people to take up arms for the glory of God, the good of the Church, and the saving of their souls. About twenty days before the prisoner took up arms witness broke entirely from him. On the 19th witness was made prisoner by four of Riel's men and taken to the church, where he found some half-breeds and Indians armed. That night he was taken before the council and was acquitted. Riel protested against the decision. Witness was condemned to death, and he was thus forced to join the rebels to save his life. The conditions of surrender to Crozier were put in his hands to be delivered to Crozier, but he did not deliver the letter. Riel was present at the Duck Lake fight, on the 26th March, and was one of the first to go out to meet the police, carrying a cross in his hands.

Cross examined by Mr. Lemieux.—I have taken an active part in political affairs of the country. In 1869 I was in Manitoba. In 1884 Riel was living in Montana with his wife and children. I participated in the movement to bring Riel here; believed Riel would be of advantage in obtaining redress of the grievances. The clergy had not taken part in the political movement, but had assisted them in obtaining their rights. They thought it was necessary to have Riel as a point to rally round. Delegates were sent to invite Riel to come, and he came with his wife and family. A constitutional political movement was made, in which the half-breeds of all creeds took part, and the whites, though they were not active promoters, were sympathizers. Did not believe Riel ever wanted to return to Montana, although he spoke of it. After the Government refused to grant the indemnity to Riel witness did not believe he would be useful as a constitutional leader. It was after the indemnity was refused that Riel spoke of going away. Witness denied that in 1869 he started an agitation with Riel, and then, as in the present case, abandoned him. He only went as far as was constitutional. He had heard prisoner say he considered himself a prophet, and said he had inspiration in his liver and in every other part of his body. He wrote upon a piece of paper that he was inspired. He showed witness a book written with buffalo blood, which was a plan that after Riel had taken England and Canada, Quebec was to be given to the Prussians, Ontario to the Irish, and the North-West to be divided among the various nationalities of Europe, the Jews, Hungarians, and Bavarians included. The rebel council had first condemned witness to death, and afterwards liberated him, and he accepted a position in the council in order to save his life. Witness said that whenever the word police was mentioned Riel became very excited, having heard that the Government had answered their petitions for redress by sending 500 extra police.

At this part of the cross-examination of Nolin, the proceedings were interrupted by an excited clamour of Riel, to be allowed to interrogate the prisoner, and to assist personally in the conduct of his case. This the Court could only allow with the consent of prisoner's counsel. His counsel objected, and urged that such a proceeding would prejudice their client's case; but Riel persisted, and the rest of the day was wasted in fruitless altercation, which neither the Court nor the counsel for the Crown could allay. The chief cause of Riel's excitement seemed to be the determination of his counsel to press the plea of insanity, a plea which, throughout the trial, Riel strongly objected to be urged on his behalf. The Court in the midst of the altercation, adjourned.

THIRD DAY OF THE TRIAL!*

The Riel trial was resumed at Regina, on the morning of July 30th, by MR. GREENSHIELDS' addressing the jury for the defence. The Court-room was again filled to its utmost capacity. After referring to the difficulty counsel had met, in the prisoner's endeavour to obstruct their conduct of the case, Mr. Greenshields dwelt upon the history of the Indians and half-breeds in the North-West Territories, pointing out their rights to the soil. In this Court they had a different procedure from that in other parts of the Dominion, and while not desiring to be understood that the prisoner would not receive as fair a trial as the machinery provided made possible, he questioned whether a jury of six men, nominated by the presiding magistrate, was sufficient to satisfy the demands of Magna Charta,—the great bulwark of the rights and liberties of all British subjects. He believed any of the older Provinces would rebel against such an encroachment on their rights, and he did not see why such a condition of things should obtain here. For years the half-breeds had been making futile efforts to obtain their rights. All these efforts had been met by rebuffs, or had received no attention whatever from the Federal Government, and those very rights for which the half-breeds were supplicating and petitioning were being handed over to railway corporations, colonization companies, and like concerns. He would not say that the action of the Government justified armed rebellion—the shedding of blood—but it left in these poor people those smouldering fires of discontent that were so easily fanned into rebellion by a madman such as Riel. The prisoner had been invited by the half-breeds to come among them from a foreign country to assist them in making a proper representation of their grievances to the Government. They were unlettered and required an active sympathizer, with education sufficient to properly conduct the agitation. Riel was the man they chose, and there was no evidence to show that when Riel came to this country he came with any intention of inciting the people to armed rebellion. His work was begun and carried on up till January in a perfectly constitutional manner. After that time, as the jury had seen in the cross-examination of the witnesses for the prosecution, no effort was made by the defence to deny that overt acts of treason had been committed in the presence of the prisoner; but evidence would be brought to show that at the time these acts were countenanced by the prisoner, he was of unsound mind and not responsible for what he did. The peculiar disease of the prisoner was called by men learned in diseases of the mind, "megalomania." This species of mental disease developed two delusions—one the desire for and belief that the patient could obtain great power in political matters to rule or govern, another his desire to found a great church. That the prisoner was possessed of these delusions, the evidence abundantly proved. The jury might consider, with some grounds for the belief, that the evidence of Charles Nolin, who swore that the prisoner was willing to leave the country if he obtained from the Government a gratuity of $35,000, was inconsistent with the real existence of such a monomania as the prisoner was afflicted with. But not one isolated portion, but the whole, of Nolin's evidence should be considered. Other portions of his testimony, for instance, prisoner's opinions on religious matters, and his intention to divide up the country between various foreign nationalities, were conclusive proof of the prisoner's insanity. This was a great State trial, the speaker said, and he warned the jury to throw aside the influence of heated public opinion, as it was expressed at present. There were many people executed for having taken part in the rebellion of 1837, and it was questionable if there could be found anyone now who would justify those executions. The heat of private feeling had died away, and the jury should be careful that no hasty conclusion in this case should leave posterity a chance to say that their verdict had been a wrong one. They should, if possible, look at the case with the calmness of the historian, throwing aside all preconceived notions of the case that interfered with the evidence given in the Court, and build up their

---

* In preparing this abstract of the day's proceedings, the writer acknowledges to have drawn from the reports published in the Toronto *Globe* and *Mail*, and the Montreal *Gazette* and *Star*.

verdict on the testimony brought out here. In the course of his remarks, Mr. Greenshields said, that he accused no Government in particular for neglecting the claims of the breeds ; but if the authorities had paid attention to the petitions which had been addressed to them, the rebellion would never have occurred. He paid a glowing tribute to the volunteers, who left their private occupations and came from all parts of the Dominion to suppress the outbreak.

At the conclusion of Mr. Greenshield's address,

FATHER ANDRE, Superior of the Oblat Fathers in the district of Carlton, was called for the defence. He said he had been intimately associated with the breeds for a quarter of a century. Riel had been induced to come to this country by the settlers to assist them. The witness had a thorough knowledge of what was going on amongst the settlers. He had no knowledge of petitions having been sent to the Government during the agitation ; but he had himself indirectly communicated with the Government last December, with the object of getting the prisoner out of the country. The pretensions or claims of the breeds changed frequently. After Riel's arrival the Government had been notified three or four times of what was transpiring. The Government had promised to take the matter into consideration. The Government had replied to one petition by telegram, conceding the old survey. This was an important concession. At Batoche three scrips had been issued, and at Duck Lake forty were given. The witness never liked talking with the prisoner on religion or politics. On these subjects Riel's language frightened the witness, who considered him undoubtedly crazy on these subjects, while on all other points he was sane enough. Once, at a meeting of priests, the advisability of allowing such a man to perform religious duties was discussed, and it was unanimously agreed that the man was insane. The discussion of religious or political subjects with him was like dangling a red flag in front of a bull.

PHILIP GARNEAU, of Batoche, but at present a prisoner in Regina gaol, was now sworn and deposed as follows :—I saw Riel at Batoche last fall ; had seen him several times before January. During the trouble I talked with him at my house on religious matters. He said the spirit of Elias, the prophet, was in him. He wanted the people to believe that. He often said the Spirit of God told him to do this or that. During his stay at my house Riel prayed aloud all night ; never heard such prayers before ; prisoner must have made them up. He could not stand to be contradicted, and was very irritable. Heard him declare he was representing St. Peter. Heard him talking of the country being divided into seven Provinces, and be was going to bring in seven different nationalities to occupy them. I did not believe he would succeed in that. He expected the assistance of the Jews, and other nationalities, to whom he was going to award a Province each for their aid. Riel said he was sure to succeed, it was a divine mission, and God was the chief of the movement ; only met him once before the trouble. I thought the man was crazy.

Cross-examined by Mr. Robinson—I followed Riel solely because he forced me with armed men. He had great influence over the half-breeds, who listened to and followed his advice.

FATHER FOURMAND sworn, examined by Mr. Lemieux in French—I am a priest of St. Laurent ; went there in 1875. Have had conversations with Riel since the time of the rebellion. Often conversed with him on political and religious subjects. I was present at the meeting of priests at which Riel's sanity was questioned. I knew the facts upon which the question arose. Before the rebellion Riel was a polite and pleasant man to me. When he was not contradicted about political affairs he was quiet, but when opposed he was violent. As soon as the rebellion commenced he lost all control of himself, and threatened to burn all the churches. He believed there was only one God ; that Christ the Son was not God, neither was the Holy Ghost, and in consequence the Virgin Mary was not the mother of God, but of the Son of God. He changed the song beginning " Hail Mary, mother of God," to " Hail Mary, mother of the Son of God." He denied the real presence of God in the Host, it was a man of six feet. Riel said he was going to Quebec, France and Italy, and would overthrow the Pope and choose a Pope or appoint himself. We finally concluded there was no other way of explaining his conduct than that he was insane. Noticed a great change in prisoner as the agitation progressed. When the fathers opposed him he attacked them. Witness was brought before the rebel council by the prisoner, to give an account of his conduct. He called me a little tiger, being very excited. Never showed me a book of his prophecies written in buffalo blood, although I heard of it.

Cross-examined by Mr. Casgrain—Most of the half-breeds followed Riel in his religious views; some opposed them. The prisoner was relatively sane before the rebellion. The prisoner proclaimed the rebellion on March 18th. I promised to occupy a position of neutrality towards the provisional Government. He could better explain prisoner's conduct on the ground of insanity than that of great criminality. Witness naturally had a strong friendship towards the prisoner.

The afternoon was devoted to expert testimony respecting the prisoner's sanity.

MEDICAL TESTIMONY.

Dr. Roy, of the Beauport Asylum, Quebec, said the prisoner was an inmate of that institution for nineteen months. He was discharged in January, 1878. He suffered from ambitious mania. One of the distinguishing characteristics of that form of insanity is that, so long as the particular hobby is not touched, the patient appears perfectly sane. From what he heard the witnesses say, and from the prisoner's actions yesterday, he had no hesitation in pronouncing the man insane, and he believed him not to be responsible for his acts.

Dr. Clarke, of Toronto, was the next witness. He said he was the Superintendent of the Toronto Lunatic Asylum. He has had nine or ten years' experience in treating lunatics. He examined the prisoner twice yesterday and once this morning. From what evidence he had heard and from his own examination, provided the witnesses told the truth and the prisoner was not malingering, there was no doubt of his being insane.

Cross-examined by Mr. Osler—It is impossible for any man to say that a person like Riel, who is sharp and well-educated, is either insane or sane. He (the witness) would require to have him under his notice for months to form an opinion. The man's actions are consistent with fraud. Thinks he knows the difference between right and wrong, subject to his delusion.

Dr. Wallace was next called. He said he was Superintendent of the Insane Asylum at Hamilton. He had listened to the evidence in this case. He saw the prisoner alone for half an hour. He has formed the opinion that there is no indication of insanity about him. He thinks the prisoner knows the difference between right and wrong. The person suffering from maglomania often imagines he is a king, divinely inspired, has the world at his feet—supreme egotism in fact. It is one of the complications of paralytic insanity.

Dr. Jukes, of the Mounted Police, would not say the prisoner was not insane. He had seen him daily since May, and noticed no traces of insanity.

The Court adjourned at five o'clock.

RIEL'S ADDRESS TO THE JURY.

At the outset, writes W. A. H., correspondent of the Montreal *Star*, Riel spoke in a quiet and low tone, many of his statements carrying home conviction to his hearers. " At any rate," was the subsequent comment, " Riel speaks with the belief that he is right." Gradually as he proceeded and got fairly launched into his subject, his eyes sparkled, his body swayed to and fro as if strongly agitated, and his hands accomplished a series of wonderful gestures as he warmed up and spoke with impassioned eloquence. His hearers were spell-bound, and well they might, as each concluding assertion with terrible earnestness was uttered with the effect and force of a trumpet blast. That every soul in Court was impressed is not untrue, and many ladies were moved to tears. The following is an epitome of what he said:—

" Your Honour, and gentlemen of the jury—It would be an easy matter for me to-day, to play the *role* of a lunatic, because the circumstances are such as to excite any ordinary man subject to natural excitement after what has transpired to-day. The natural excitement, or may I add anxiety, which my trial causes me is enough to justify me in acting in the manner of a demented man; but I hope, with the help of God, that I will maintain a calm exterior and act with the decorum that suits this honourable Court. You have, no doubt, seen by the papers produced by the Crown, that I was not a man disposed to think of God at the beginning. Gentlemen, I don't want to play the part of a lunatic.

"Oh, my God, help me through the grace and divine influence of Jesus. Oh, my God bless me, bless this Court, bless this jury, and bless my good lawyers, who at great sacrifice have came nearly 700 leagues to defend me. Bless the lawyers for the Crown, for they have done what they considered their duty. God grant that fairness be shown. Oh, Jesus, change the curiosity of the ladies and others here to sanctity. The day of my birth I was helpless, and my mother was helpless. Somebody helped her. I lived, and although a man I am as helpless to-day as I was a babe on my mother's breast. But the North-West is also my mother: although the North-West is sick and confined, there is some one to take care of her. I am sure that my mother will not kill me after forty-years life. My mother cannot take my life. She will be indulgent and will forget.

"When I came here from Montana, in July, 1884, I found the Indians starving. The state of affairs was terrible. The half-breeds were subsisting on the rotten pork of the Hudson Bay Company. This was the condition, this was the pride, of responsible Government! What did Louis Riel do? I did not equally forget the whites. I directed my attention to assist all classes, irrespective of creed, colour or nationality. We have made petitions to the Canadian Government, asking them to relieve the state of affairs. We took time. Those who know me, know we took time with the object of uniting all classes, even if I may speak it, all parties. Those who know me know I have suffered. I tried to come to an understanding with the authorities on different points. I believe I have done my duty. It was said that I was egotistical. A man cannot generalize himself unless he is imputed with the taint. After the Canadian Government, through the honourable under-secretary of state, replied to my letter regarding the half-breeds, then, and not till then, did I look after my private affairs. A good dealcan be said of the distribution of land. I don't know if my dignity would permit me to mention what you term my foreign policy, but if I was allowed to explain or question certain witnesses, those things would have looked different. My lawyers are good, but they don't understand the circumstances. Be it understood that I appreciate their services. Were I to go into details, I could safely say what Captain Young has told you regarding my mission, to bring about practical results. I have writings; my career, is perhaps nearly run, but after dissolution my spirit will still bring about practical results."

Striking his breast he added:

"No one need say that the North-West is not suffering. The Saskatchewan was especially afflicted, but what have I done to bring about practical results? For ten years I have been aware that I had a mission to perform ; now what encourages me is the fact that I still have a mission to perform. God is with me, He is in this dock, and God is with my lawyers, the same as he was with me in the battles of the Saskatchewan. I have not assumed my mission. In Manitoba, to-day, I have a mission to perform. To-day I am forgotten by the Manitobans as dead. Did I not obtain for that province a constitutional government notwithstanding the opposition of the Ottawa authorities? That was the cause of my banishment."

I thank the glorious General Middleton for his testimony that I possess my mental faculties. I felt that God was blessing me when those words were pronounced. I was in Beauport Asylum ; Dr. Roy over there knows it, but I thank the Crown for destroying his testimony. I was in the Lunatic Asylum at Longue Pointe, near Montreal, also ; and would like to see my old friends, Dr. Lachapelle and Dr. Howard, who treated me so charitably. Even if I am to die, I will have the satisfaction of knowing that I will not be regarded by all men as an insane person.

To THE COURT.—"Your honour and gentlemen of the jury, my reputation, my life, my liberty, are in your hands, and are at your discretion. I am so confident in your high sense of duty that I have no anxiety as to the verdict. My calmness does not arise from the presumption that you will acquit me. Although you are only half a jury, only a shred of that proud old British constitution, I respect you. I can only trust, Judge and gentlemen, that good and practical results will arise from your judgment conscientiously rendered. I would call your attention to one or two points. The first is that the House of Commons, Senate and Ministry, which make the laws, do not respect the interests of the North-West. My second point is that the North-West Council has the defect of its parent. There are practically no elections, and it is a sham legislature."

Then, as if wandering from his subject, Riel broke forth and said : " I was ready at Batoche ; I fired and wounded your soldiers. Bear in mind, is my crime, committed in self-defence, so enormous? Oh, Jesus Christ ! help me, for they are trying to tear me into pieces. Jurors, if you support the plea of insanity, otherwise acquit me all the same. Console yourselves with the reflection that you will be doing justice to one who has suffered for fifteen years, to my family, and to the North-West."

Riel concluded as follows, his language containing a strange admixture of the words applied to him by the medical experts, which he ingeniously turned against the Government :

" Your honours and gentlemen of the jury :—I am taking the circumstances of my trial as they are. The only thing to which I would respectfully call your attention before you retire to deliberate is the irresponsibility of the Government. It is a fact that the Government possesses an absolute lack of responsibility, an insanity complicated with analysis. A monster of irresponsible, insane government, and its little North-West council, had made up their minds to answer my petitions by surrounding me, and by suddenly attempting to jump at me and my people in the fertile valley of the Saskatchewan. You are perfectly justified in declaring that having my reason and sound mind, I acted reasonably and in self-defence, while the Government, my aggressor, being irresponsible, and consequently insane, cannot but have acted madly and wrong ; and if high treason there is, it must be on its side, not on my part."

At the conclusion of Riel's lengthy address,

MR. CHRISTOPHER ROBINSON, Q.C., closed the case for the Crown in a powerful speech, which went far to counteract the sympathetic effect produced by Riel's disconnected but eloquent oration. Mr. Robinson pointed out that no evidence was produced to show that the prisoner had not committed the acts he was charged with. From the evidence it was quite clear the prisoner was neither a patriot nor a lunatic. If prisoner was not responsible for the rebellion, who was? The speaker went over the evidence and showed that Riel's acts were not those of a lunatic, but well considered in all their bearings, and the deliberate acts of a particularly sound mind. The evidence as to Riel's confinement in an asylum nine years ago was not satisfactory. Why was he sent there under an assumed name? Why was the record of his case not produced along with the other papers, and a statement of his condition when leaving the asylum? Medical men were not always the best judges of insanity. Taking up the evidence against the prisoner, Mr. Robinson went over it in detail, and said no mercy should be shown one who had committed such acts. He pictured the terrible results if Riel had succeeded in his effort to rouse the Indians. The reason the prisoners Poundmaker and Big Bear had not been put in the witness box, was that they could not be asked to give evidence that would incriminate themselves.

MR. JUSTICE RICHARDSON then read over the evidence to the jury, after which the court adjourned.

THIRD DAY'S PROCEEDINGS.*

The court resumed its sittings on the morning of the 1st of August, at the usual hour, and Col. Richardson continued his charge to the jury. He read all the principal evidence, commenting thereon, and finally charged the jury to do their duty without fear or favour.

---

* This abstract of the final day's proceedings we take from the Toronto *Mail*.

THE VERDICT.

When the jury returned with the verdict at 3.15 p.m., after exactly one hour's deliberation, the prisoner, who had been on his knees in the dock praying incessantly, rose and stood facing the six men who came in bearing for him the message of life or death.

The CLERK of the Court, amid a silence so intense that, like the darkness of Egypt, it could be felt, asked if the gentlemen of the jury had agreed upon their verdict?

MR. COSGROVE, the foreman, answered in a low tone, but heard distinctly in the general hush, "We have!"

The CLERK then asked: "Is the prisoner guilty or not guilty?"

Everyone but the prisoner seemed anxious. He alone of all those present, eager to hear the message of fate, was calm.

The Foreman replied: "Guilty, with a recommendation to mercy!"

Riel smiled as if the sentence in no way affected him, and bowed gracefully to the jury.

THE PRISONER'S SPEECH.

COL. RICHARDSON asked the prisoner if he had anything to say why the sentence of the Court should not be passed upon him?

RIEL replied: Yes, your honour. Then he began, in a low, calm voice to detail the story of the half-breeds in Manitoba, and spoke at length of the rebellion of '69. He said that if he had to die for what had taken place, it would be a consolation to his wife and to his friends to know that he had not died in vain. In years to come people will look at Manitoba and say that Riel helped the dwellers of those fertile plains to obtain the benefits they now enjoy. He said it would be an easy thing for him to make an incendiary speech, but he would refrain. He said that God had given him a mission to perform, and if suffering was part of that mission, he bowed respectfully to the Divine will, and he was ready to accept the task, even if the end should be death. Like David, he had suffered, but he lacked two years of the time that David suffered. The prisoner then went into the history of the Red River rebellion at great length. He claimed that he had ruled the country for two months for the Government, and his only reward was a sentence of exile. The troubles in the Saskatchewan, he said, were but a continuation of the troubles of the Red River, and the breeds feel that they are being robbed by the Government, which has failed to carry out the treaty promises that had been made to them. The breeds sustained their rights in '69 by arms, and the people of Manitoba are enjoying the results to-day. The people of Saskatchewan only followed the same precedent, and he trusted that the same results would follow. He then spoke at great length of the part played by Sir John Macdonald, Sir George Cartier, and Bishop Taché in the Red River rebellion. The money that had been given to him and to Lépine on leaving the country had been accepted, he said, as part of what was justly their due. The whites were gradually crowding out the Indians and the Metis, and what was more natural and just than for them to take up arms in defence of their rights? He justified his claims to $35,000 by saying that it was offered to him to keep out of the country for three years. The English constitution, he said, had been perfected for the happiness of the world, and his wish to have the representatives of the different nations here was to give people from the countries of the Old World an opportunity of enjoying the blessings God had given England. God had given England great glory, but she must work for that glory or it would surely pass away. The Roman Empire was four hundred years in declining from its proud pre-eminence, and England would be in the same position; but before England faded away a grander England would be built up in this immense country. His heart, while it beat, would not abandon the idea of having a new Ireland, a new Germany, a new France here; and the people of those countries would enjoy liberties under the British constitution which they did not obtain at home. If he must die for his principles, if the brave men who were with him must die, he hoped the French-Canadians would come and help the people to get back what was being unjustly wrenched from them. Peace had always been uppermost in his thoughts, and it was to save the country from being deluged with blood later on that they strove for their rights now. He concluded by objecting to the jury and the decision of the Court, and asked that he be not tried for the alleged offences of this season, but that his whole career be put on trial, and the jury asked to give a decision as to whether his life and acts have in any way benefited the country or not.

THE SENTENCE.

Mr. CHRISTOPHER ROBINSON moved for the sentence of the Court.
Judge RICHARDSON then said : " Louis Riel, you are charged with treason. You let loose the flood gates of rapine and bloodshed, and brought ruin and death to many families, who, if let alone, were in comfort and a fair way of affluence. For what you did you have been given a fair and impartial trial. Your remarks are no excuse for your acts. You committed acts that the law demands an account for at your hands. The jury coupled with their verdict a recommendation to mercy. I can hold out no prospect for you, and I would recommend you to make your peace with God. For me, only one duty and a painful one to perform remains. It is to pass sentence upon you. If your life is spared, no one will feel more gratified than myself, but I can hold out no hope. The sentence of this Court upon you, Louis Riel, is that you be taken to the guard-room of the Mounted Police of Regina, whence you came, and kept there until September the eighteenth, and from thence to the place of execution, there to be hanged by the neck until dead, and may the Lord have mercy upon your soul !"

Riel never moved a muscle, but, bowing to the Court, said :—" Is that on Friday, your Honour ? "

He was then taken from the Court-room, and a few minutes after was driven back, under strong escort, to the guard-room.

AN APPEAL.

After sentence had been passed upon Riel, Mr. Fitzgerald, one of prisoner's counsel, gave notice of appeal for a new trial to the Court of Queen's Bench, Manitoba. The appeal case was heard at Winnipeg on the 3rd and 4th days of September before Chief Justice Wallbridge and Mr. Justice T. W. Taylor.

M. LEMIEUX, chief counsel for Riel, raised the old issue as to informality of the trial before the Stipendiary Magistrate at Regina, and contended that the magistrate was incompetent to try the case.

Mr. FITZPATRICK followed. He held that the Treason-Felony Act was one of Imperial jurisdiction, and he questioned if it had delegated any power to the colonial authorities to legislate away any rights enjoyed by the subjects of the British Empire. He dwelt strongly upon the insanity question, and said the jury were convinced of the prisoner's lunacy, hence their recommendation to mercy.

Mr. EWART also strongly questioned the jurisdiction of the Court at Regina and cited several authorities in support of his argument.

Mr. ROBINSON, on behalf of the Crown, in an able address, strongly combatted the idea that the Court at Regina was not legally constituted, and cited cases in support of his contention. He also dwelt at length on the insanity plea, showing the absurdity of the contention that Riel was insane.

Mr. Osler and Mr. Aikens followed on the same side, supplementing the arguments of the previous speaker as to the constitutionality of the Court, and cited a number of authorities adverse to the insanity plea.

NEW TRIAL REFUSED.

At Winnipeg, on the 9th September, at a sitting of the full Court of the Queen's Bench of the Province of Manitoba, judgment was delivered in the appeal for a new trial for the prisoner Riel.

His Lordship Chief Justice Wallbridge first delivered judgment. He referred briefly to the facts brought before the Court and the statutes by which the stipendiary magistrates are appointed in the North-West and to the powers given them for the trial of the cases before them alone, and to the cases, including treason, which have to be tried before a magistrate with a justice of the peace and a jury of six. His Lordship held that the constitutionality of the Court is established by the statutes passed, which he cited. If the Act passed by the Dominion Parliament was, as claimed by the defence, *ultra vires*, it was clearly confirmed by the Imperial Act subsequently passed, which made the Dominion Act equal to an Imperial Act. The objections were to his mind purely technical and therefore not valid. His opinion therefore was that a new trial should be refused, and the conviction of the Superior Court was therefore confirmed.

Mr. Justice Taylor followed, dealing fully with the arguments brought forward by the prisoner's counsel. On the question of the delegation of the power to legislate given to the Dominion Parliament, he held that the Dominion Parliament has plenary powers on all subjects committed to it. He reviewed fully all the facts relating to the admission of Rupert's Land to the Dominion, and to the statutes passed for the government of Rupert's Land and Manitoba when formed as a province. After a critical examination of the evidence in the case, he was unable to come to any other conclusion than that to which the jury had come. The evidence entirely fails to relieve the prisoner from responsibility for his acts. A new trial must be refused and the conviction must be confirmed.

Mr. Justice Killam next followed at some length, concurring in the views of his brother judges.

With these proceedings the trial of the rebel chief was concluded, though counsel for Riel has notified the Executive that they will appeal the case to the Privy Council in England. Riel will, meantime, be respited.

THE INDIAN AND HALF-BREED TRIALS.

During the month of August the participators in the rebellion among the half-breeds and Indians were brought up for trial before the Stipendiary Magistrate at Regina.

ONE ARROW'S TRIAL.

Court was held on the afternoon of the 13th of August for the trial of One Arrow, Judge Richardson presiding.

Mr. Casgrain opened the case on behalf of the Crown.

Only three witnesses were examined, viz., Ashley, Ross, and the Indian agent, Lash. Their evidence was similar to that given in the Riel trial. They proved that the prisoner was present at Batoche, although it could not be proved he actually was engaged.

Mr. Robertson addressed the jury for the defence, and was followed by Mr. Osler for the Crown.

Judge Richardson's charge only lasted a few minutes.

The jury was out only ten minutes, and returned with a verdict of "Guilty."
The prisoner was remanded for sentence.

HALF-BREEDS SENTENCED.

On the afternoon of the 14th inst., Judge Richardson held Court for the purpose of sentencing the half-breed prisoners who recently pleaded guilty and were arraigned. Mr. H. J. Clarke, of Winnipeg, addressed the Court on behalf of the poor deluded wretches who awaited sentence. It spoke volumes, he said, for the manhood of the men awaiting sentence that not a single woman was molested during the whole of the outbreak. The breeds believed they had wrongs, and like men undertook in their way to redress them by force of arms. The Court addressed the prisoners through an interpreter, expatiating on the enormity of the offence, the leniency of the Court, etc., and sentenced them as follows :—

SEVEN YEARS EACH.—Alexander Cayen, Maxime Dubois, Pierre Henry, Maxime Lepine, Albert Monkman, Pierre Paranteau, Pierre Vandelle, Philip Guardupuy, Philip Garnot, James Short, Bapti Vandalle, to seven years in the penitentiary.

THREE YEARS.—Alexander Fisher, Pierre Guardupuy, Moise Ouellette, to three years.

ONE YEAR.—Joseph Arcand, Ignace Poitras, junior, Ignace Poitras, senior, Moise Paranteau, to one year in Regina jail.

DISCHARGED.—Joseph Delorme, Alexander Labombarde, Joseph Pilon, Bapti Rocheleau, Potrie Tourand, Francis Tourand, dismissed from custody, to appear for sentence when called upon.

THREE YEARS.—The Court then adjourned formally, but re-assembled immediately to pass sentence on "One Arrow," who was convicted of treason-felony. The old Indian made an eloquent attempt to prove himself a good Indian, but was sentenced to three years in the penitentiary.

TRIAL OF POUNDMAKER.

At Regina, on the 15th inst., there was a flutter of excitement round the Court when it was learned that Pe-to-cah-hau-a-we-win (Poundmaker) would be arraigned at three o'clock in the afternoon. By half-past two, a correspondent of the Toronto *Mail* tells us, a crowd had collected outside the Court-house to catch a glimpse of the noted warrior and councillor. He is a noble looking Indian, and reminds one more of Feninore Cooper's heroes than do the great majority of North-West Indians. His eyes are black and piercing. One moment they twinkle merrily at some humorous remark, and the next they flash with fire as something is said that is not agreeable to him. His nose is long and aquiline, while his lips are thin and his mouth devoid of that sensual character so peculiar to many Indians. The scalp lock was decorated with a mink skin, while from each temple there hung one long lock of hair twisted round and round with brass wire. He wore no coat, but his vest was richly decorated with brass-headed nails in true barbaric fashion.

Mr. Scott, of Regina, opened the case for the Crown in a short speech, in which he said they would not only prove that the prisoner was associated with the rebels, but actually commanded them at Cut Knife Creek.

The proceedings were brief, the Crown relying on the evidence of Robert Jefferson, Poundmaker's son-in-law, Colonel Herchmer, of the Mounted Police, Charles and H. D. Ross, half-breed scouts, Wm. McKay, Peter Ballantine, and other residents of pillaged Battleford.

For the defence Joseph McKay, of Prince Albert; John Craig, farm instructor on Little Pine's reserve, and Grey Eyes, an Indian, were called. These testified to Poundmaker's pacific acts and intents, and his efforts to restrain his band from bloodshed and Indian excesses.

Mr. B. B. Osler, Q.C., acted for the Crown, and Mr. Beverley Robinson, of Winnipeg, represented the prisoner.

On the 18th inst. the jury returned a verdict of guilty, when Judge Richardson asked Poundmaker if he had anything to say why sentence should not be passed upon him.

POUNDMAKER TALKS.

Poundmaker drew himself up to his full height, cast a hurried glance round the room, then placing his left hand on his breast, and extending his right in a declamatory attitude, began. He spoke slowly at first, and waited for the interpreter to put his words into English. By-and-by he seemed to forget that he was not understood. His words fell without any hesitation from his lips:- "I am not guilty. Much that has been said against me is not true. I am glad of my work in the Queen's country this spring. What I have done was for the good of my people and for peace. When my brothers and the pale faces met in fight at Cut Knife I saved the Queen's soldiers, who ran away. I took the arms from my brothers and gave them up at Battleford. Everything I could do was done to stop bloodshed. Had I wanted war I should not be here now; I should be on the prairie. You did not catch me; I gave myself up. You have got me because I wanted peace."

The chief then sat down and awaited the sentence of the Court. The judge addressed him in nearly the same terms as those he used when sentencing One Arrow, and therefore it is unnecessary to repeat his words. He concluded by sentencing the prisoner to three years in Stoney Mountain penitentiary.

When Poundmaker heard the sentence he said:—"Hang me now. I can die. I would rather you kill me than lock me up for three years. But my people, the Indians, will not forget me; remember this."

THE END.

www.ingramcontent.com/pod-product-compliance
Lightning Source LLC
Chambersburg PA
CBHW020540300426
44111CB00008B/736